Alexander A Knox

The New Playground

Or, Wanderings in Algeria. Second Edition

Alexander A Knox

The New Playground
Or, Wanderings in Algeria. Second Edition

ISBN/EAN: 9783337190637

Printed in Europe, USA, Canada, Australia, Japan

Cover: Foto ©Andreas Hilbeck / pixelio.de

More available books at **www.hansebooks.com**

THE
NEW PLAYGROUND

OR

WANDERINGS IN ALGERIA

BY

ALEXANDER A. KNOX

"I speak of Africa, and golden joy"

"'Is there a felicity in the world,' said Marianne, 'equal to this? Margaret, we will walk here at least two hours.' In twenty minutes they were obliged to turn back."—*Sense and Sensibility*

SECOND EDITION

LONDON
KEGAN PAUL, TRENCH & CO., 1, PATERNOSTER SQUARE
1883

(The rights of translation and of reproduction are reserved.)

TO MY WIFE,

BUT FOR WHOSE CEASELESS CARE AND AFFECTION

THROUGHOUT A LONG ILLNESS

I SHOULD NEVER HAVE SAT HORSE OR HELD PEN AGAIN.

WE HAVE SEEN TOGETHER IN ALGERIA MANY STRANGE SIGHTS,

AND ENJOYED MANY BRIGHT DAYS.

I INSCRIBE MY LITTLE BOOK

TO THE LADY WHO TOOK ME THERE AND

HELPED ME ON MY WAY.

NOTE TO SECOND EDITION.

It seems but fair to warn travellers who may be meditating a journey to Algiers or through Algeria, that there has been a great change since the autumn of 1879, when we crossed from Marseilles to Algiers. The Transatlantic Steamship Company's services have now been organized, and I have been informed by those who have made trial of these vessels that they are a vast improvement upon the old Valery and Messageries Maritimes Lines. Not only is the passage effected far more quickly, but the steamers are much larger, and more powerful, so that the inconvenience of the sea-passage is reduced to a minimum. You may now pass from Marseilles to Algiers, to Oran, to Tunis, or from Port Vendres to Algiers by this line, or along the coast from Algiers to Bôna.

I may add that I have received a communication from Messrs. Cook's firm, by which I learn that some of the Algerine hotels of which I cannot speak from experience are really good, and deserve public favour.

The Europe, at Algiers, is described as clean and comfortable.

The Hotel d'Orient, at Blidah, is highly recommended.

The Hotel de l'Univers, at Oran, equally so; it is spoken of "as one of the best, if not the best," in the town.

The Hotel de France, at Tlemçen, is favourably mentioned.

I have given in the text the result of our personal experience, in which I see nothing to change; but it may be to the advantage of travellers to have before them the opinions of Messrs. Cook on the subject of Algerine hotels.

CONTENTS.

CHAPTER		PAGE
I.	Why we went to Algiers	1
II.	The Dangers of the Sea	12
III.	Arrival at Algiers	22
IV.	First Impressions: The Oasis of Palm	30
V.	Algiers New and Old	47
VI.	Torquay in Africa	65
VII.	Walks and Drives in and about Algiers	71
VIII.	The Irritable Town: Cap and Bells	79
IX.	The Climate of Algiers: for Invalids	95
X.	Algerine Scraps—	
	La Trappe	112
	Point de Pescade	120
	Notre Dame d'Afrique	127
	The St. Eugène Side	130
	The Jardin d'Essai	138
	The Arab Police-Court	141
	First Mornings at Algiers	155
	The Algerine Old Bailey	158
	An Algerine Library	163
	The Trans-Sahara Railroad	166

CONTENTS.

CHAPTER		PAGE
	Roman Remains in Algeria	172
	Our Fire	175
	The Mosques	177
	Algerine Piracy	179
	The Four Pretty Houses	184
XI.	The Kabyles and La Grande Kabylie	188
XII.	To Fort National and Kabylia	204
XIII.	From Pimlico to the Palms	240
XIV.	The Home Circuit	338
XV.	To Tlemçen, through Oran	386
XVI.	Algeria under the French Rule	453
XVII.	Conclusion	475

THE NEW PLAYGROUND.

CHAPTER I.

WHY WE WENT TO ALGIERS.

WE went to Algiers in search of climate and quiet;—let us say of SUN and SILENCE.

We have not been disappointed. The sun, who had been long a stranger, renewed acquaintance with us the first morning we landed in Algiers, and has been shining upon us ever since. As for silence, that is another matter. Search for her rightly, she is to be found amidst the orange trees and stone pines which surround and overlook the town. In Africa I have neither come across a barrel-organ nor a German band.

It seems but fair to tell at once what our business in Africa really is. I am recovering from severe illness. I am travelling with my wife. All we want is—to live in the open air, to feel and see the sun, and to be left alone. I do not, however, wish to write the "Diary of an Invalid," nor anything of a sentimental or lamentable nature. I might have sat down by the waters of Babylon, but I certainly should never have wept there.

If it be not sentiment, neither is it love of adventure which has driven me here. Let M. Gerard slay his lions; let M. Bombonel kill his panthers! If I heard that a lion or a panther had arrived at Algiers, and was in the habit of taking his usual "walking exercise" on the "slopes" of Mustapha Supérieur (where we are now residing), I should instantly gratify a liberal curiosity as to the site of Carthage, which has the advantage of being some way off.

Nor do I want to get at the rights of any disputed historical problem far away in the Djudjura Mountains, or to follow in the steps of Canon Tristram to the Sahara. All these achievements are very magnificent when *done*, but as to the doing of them, the matter is not so clear. I am told, and I want to test the truth of the statements, that the distances in Algeria are great; the insects, with or without wings, numerous; the victuals, in themselves rather a remedy against obesity than a support or a comfort to the indignant inside. Besides, beyond a certain point (so they say), roads there are none. The leathern conveniences, such as they are, which you can see in the Place du Gouvernement, urged to mad speed by a Hebrew gentleman who tries to give himself the airs of an Arab, are not to be thought of. A camel may be one's best chance, and that is a poor one.

Eheu! I am no longer young, I am no longer strong; but I can get about and simmer away on the hob comfortably enough. The question is, Where could one do so to the greatest advantage? There must be many thousands of people in England who are interested in the solution of this problem. Some say that it is a wise and prudent course to buy or hire a pretty villa near London, or a country house in a pretty neighbourhood, with a pretty garden, and to give yourself up to the cultivation of pretty roses, after the fashion of Canon Hole. Well, I have tried it in a way, and I don't like it. After thirty years or more of London, it is difficult to acquiesce in the mild monotony of country life in England. Well enough for the rector of the parish, who has his occupation, and who can at any moment engage in a vigorous controversy with his bishop, on the subject of candlesticks. Why should time ever hang heavy on the hands of so fortunate a man? But then there is your library. Spread a report that you are engaged in writing a history of the Byzantine Empire, but never "publish." So you will acquire much dignity. Alas! again, there is one person on whom you cannot impose, and that is —yourself. Besides, there are the daily newspapers; the irritation about politics. There is sure to be, in a country place, a retired despot within reach, who will trample on your dearest convictions, and keep you in a state of hot water on the subject of Mr. Gladstone. Above all, there is the CLIMATE.

Were I well and strong, no power on earth should force me to fix my home away from England. Without the faintest pretension to be a traveller, in these days when people go round the world in very wantonness, I know Europe well, have lived in most of the great towns, and have spent more summers and winters than I care to think of between Norway and Naples—both inclusive. You will not find Swiss, or Norwegian, or

Pyrenean, or Tyrolese scenery in the British Isles, but nowhere more beautiful places in which it is delightful to dwell, and all endeared to one by the recollection of what has been.

A man must be hard to please who could not live contentedly amidst the Surrey downs, the Sussex woods, the Derbyshire valleys, the Devonshire streams, or the sea-beaten crags of Cornwall. When I think of the elms, and beeches, and of

> "The oak, the ash, and the bonny ivy tree,
> Which grow so well in the north country,"

I can scarce say that the palms and cypresses which are now flaunting before my window have the best of it. Can all Africa beat a buttercup meadow? I am inclined to deny that an Algerine spring can show anything lovelier than our own lilacs and laburnums and many-coloured thorns, or than the myriads of delicate yellow primroses which harmonize so well with the red soil of the Devonshire lanes. And then—how of the past life? how of all those with whom you have lived and jested and wept? As Tennyson writes in those two lines which go as straight to an old man's heart as a rifle bullet, aimed by Captain Ross, to the bull's-eye—

> "O for the touch of a vanish'd hand,
> And the sound of a voice that is still!"

One leaves a good deal behind in England.

But, as against all this, if you cannot live in this beloved country without grievous physical discomfort for many months of the year,—what then? Your heart may beat well and truly, as an honest heart should;

but how if the mucous membrane which lines the nose and throat be weak? Had Romeo and Juliet been suffering from severe colds in the head (as they might well have been, considering the time and place they chose for exchanging their amorous ecstasies), how about the immortal verse? I could not live in decent comfort in England for six months of the year, i.e. from November to April, both inclusive (one may almost add May), so I suppose one must leave it. Some people say, "Remain in London, but shut yourself up." Last year I did so for six terrible months, and I found that imprisonment without hard labour is a very serious matter; not even the snug little dinners, not even the quiet rubbers will carry you through. You are not ill enough to make a magnificent resistance, and to call your friends in to enjoy the spectacle of Prometheus Bound. Your liver may be causing you serious discomfort, but there is no visible vulture to arouse the sympathy of the bystanders. No; come what may, I will not shut myself up for another winter in London. Troops of friends there may be there, but if all you can do is to sneeze in their beloved faces, I think it is time to move off elsewhere.

Well, I have made proof of that also. Let me see; in England I have tried as health resorts—Penzance, Falmouth, Torquay, Sidmouth, Bournemouth, Hastings, The Undercliff (Isle of Wight), Broadstairs, besides Malvern in the summer and autumn. Each of these places has advantages and disadvantages, but everywhere there was damp, and (if I may use the phrase) absence of sun, not to say severe frost and cold in many instances. We liked Penzance best of them all. Were I compelled to remain a winter in England, it is there I should again fix my gloomy tent from November to March. The scenery and drives are magnificent, and words would fail me to express the gratitude I feel for the kindness we received from the inhabitants of West Barbary. Still, if one must move away from one's own set; if one must be wrenched from one's pet seat at the club, and be forbidden to wait upon Mrs. Kendal when she plays her best parts;—it is but fair to look for a little sunshine in return.

Where shall we go? Biarritz? The very name chills me to the marrow. At Pau it has rained for three years. The Riviera is doubtful. I have tried a winter at Florence, and know how cold it can be there, genial and sympathetic as the city undoubtedly is. I only know Rome in the spring and autumn, but many friends who have spent the winter there speak of the terrible amount of rain which had fallen upon them. One is frightened away from Naples by dismal stories about the fever, and tales equally ghastly, but under the head of brigandage, reach one from Sicily. We spent a November at Palermo, and it was delightful; but as good luck would have it, neither my wife nor I were carried off to the mountains. As a consequence, we retain (between us, of course) two noses and four ears, and our bodies have not been found in the caves of Mount Pellegrino.

After forty years of age,—have done with romance and adventure. Even if the safety of those "dearer to you than life" (I believe that is the correct phrase) be secured, you cannot hope to run away yourself with any prospect of success. Although I know Seville pretty well, I have never tried a winter there; but, if not too rainy, it might do, with Granada for a *bonne-bouche* in the spring; but I am afraid it would rain. Had I to choose between death and a month at Malaga, I think I should prefer the first alternative. You might pass a not unpleasant month between Gibraltar, Algeciras, and Tangiers, but I doubt if patience would hold out longer. At Malta you do, beyond question, meet with the sun; but the sirocco and the greasy streets, and the white walls,—it is a wearisome place after three days. There is the resource of Madeira—I have never been there—but it seems like a long run from Dartmouth to Funchal, and it is said that the climate, if warm, is damp. Besides, if one does not happen to be one's self on the black list, I should think the sight of the poor invalids must be most depressing. Teneriffe might do better, but it is a very small island. The thought of Mr. Jones at Teneriffe, or of Napoleon at St. Helena, appears almost equally dreadful.

The mention of Napoleon reminds me of Corsica and Ajaccio. We spent a delightful November there a few years ago, but even then I could scramble up and down the mountain paths in a way which—well! I would give a good deal could I do as much now. Corsica is queer and delightful. Napoleon used always to say that there was a fragrance about the *maqui* of his native island which he had never smelt elsewhere. This is true. In and about Europe there is nothing to surpass Corsica when you can scramble about amongst the big trees, and amuse yourself with the sight of the strange people. Read Alexander Dumas's "Corsican Brothers"—it is far better than the play—and that is what you will see in Corsica even now. But Ajaccio is the smallest of small towns; gossip and squabbling are the order of the day; you would go melancholy mad if you tried to spend a winter there,—at least so I should suppose. Besides, I am by no means clear, as far as cold goes, that during the winters of 1878–79 and 1879–80, you would not have been as well off in Upper Baker Street. All these places, bar Madeira and Sicily (but for the brigands), are but half measures. It is not worth while to leave England for the winter months in order to be uncomfortable elsewhere.

The Nile and a winter in Nubia might be tried—I cannot speak from experience; but failing the Nile, I can tell my brothers and sisters, the semi-invalids, that there is no mistake at all about the *climate* of Algiers. I am writing on the first half of December, with the window open; violets and roses, just plucked from the garden, on the table; and the thermometer in the room at 70°. We have had a very hot summer during November and thus much of December.

To sum up this chapter in a word—I am considering Algiers from the Brighton or Torquay point of view; I am looking for comfort, i.e. clean beds and good food indoors; and am quite willing to penetrate into the interior of Africa, if it can be managed in a carriage and pair. A walk of two or three miles under favourable circumstances of sun and temperature is quite enough for me. If all this be egotism, it is egotism for the sake of others. On the whole, does Algiers offer the best quarters on the shores of the Mediterranean for elderly people, for semi-invalids, for those who have done with political ambition, business flurry, and social fuss,—for all who would spend pleasant warm hours in the open air, which would otherwise be cold and unpleasant hours indoors? If any such there be, let them come and gossip with me for half an hour. I am not writing a guide-book.

Before we stretch out our limbs under the somewhat dusty oasis in the Place du Gouvernement at Algiers, it is necessary to get there. Now, as I wish this disjointed chat to be of use to the "outward bound," I would venture to offer a hint or two about the journey, on an honourable understanding that nothing from "FRANCE, John Murray," shall be imported into these pages by way of "padding." Take "through tickets" from London to Marseilles—it saves trouble. Sleep at Dover—it is a long day from Victoria to the Gare du Nord for a weakly traveller. Next day the train which leaves Paris about 11 a.m. reaches Lyons about 10 p.m. There is a new and comfortable hotel—the Hôtel de l'Univers—close to the railway station, where the traveller will find good bed and board for the night, and will avoid the necessity of a long cruise in an omnibus to and from the hotels in the centre of the town. The train leaves for Marseilles about 11 a.m. next day, so there is plenty of time for a cup of tea at night, eight hours of bed,—toilette-comforts, and an unhurried breakfast. You would reach Marseilles about 8.30 p.m. the following day. It may interest those who have visited Marseilles in former days to know that the

Hôtel du Louvre is passing this year into other hands, which may or may not manage it discreetly; but at any rate it will not be the same thing as of old. The Grand Hôtel de Marseilles is well spoken of, but I have no personal knowledge of it. I should recommend a day or two of rest for invalids at Marseilles. They might even call a halt at Hyères for a week.

At this point of the journey a little dilemma arises. Is it wisest, on the whole, to telegraph from London or Paris, and to secure your berths in the Algerine steamers beforehand? If you do, you are bound to the day. If not, you may find all the places engaged over your head. The pleasant method pursued at Marseilles is to inform you that all places are engaged for the next departure, and for weeks to come; and that nothing remains but a four-berth cabin, which you may have on paying for the four places, or leave, at your pleasure. I should distinctly recommend the traveller to transact his own business at the Steam-Packet Bureau; the employment of a *commissionaire* is a costly luxury. In our case, I was travelling with my wife, and was far from strong. We acquiesced in our manifest destiny, and engaged the apartment with four beds, or four-berthed cabin, simply because we could not help ourselves. The price was 300 francs, or £12 English.

I am speaking of the Messageries boat, which all travellers not being "sea dogs" would do well to use in place of the rival line, the *Valery*, which carries the mails, and which is said to have a trifle the advantage in point of speed. The *Valery* is accused of rolling in a very terrible way, whilst we, by reason of our being "broader in the beam," and possibly of our carrying more ballast or weight, only rolled in a half-hearted but quite sufficient sort of a way. I may here incidentally mention (and I do so with a glow of internal satisfaction) that in our run we left the *Valery* moving like a fly through a glue-pot amongst the Balearic Isles. Could this in any way be connected with our presence on board? Were there in us potentialities of seamanship as yet undeveloped, but which told in the long run? Be this as it may, we got in first, reaching Algiers between 2 and 3 a.m. on Monday morning. We had "let go"—I like the marine smack of the phrase—at Marseilles at 5 p.m. on Saturday evening, October 18. It was a run of about thirty-four hours.

At this point I pause. I have tried to tell why we went to Algiers, and why we did not go to other health resorts; and we have arrived at Marseilles, with a suggestion that we subsequently reached Algiers in safety. But as I have told my fellow-sufferers or fellow-travellers how they may perform thus much of the journey in the greatest comfort, I should like to say a few words about our passage, as I suppose what has been will be. So many people have asked me questions about this terrible run that I desire to state our own small experience. Members of the Geographical Society, and all persons interested in Arctic or Antarctic discovery are requested to skip the next few pages.

CHAPTER II.

THE DANGERS OF THE SEA.

For some days before our arrival at Marseilles, the terrible mistral had been blowing over this part of Provence. On the Thursday that we had passed down from Lyons to Marseilles it was at its worst, and we were welcomed with the intelligence that so great had been the force of the gale, that trees had been torn up by their roots and sent spinning through the air. That venerable nuisance, "the oldest inhabitant," had not remembered such a gale in his lifetime. "*Monsieur, c'est la fin du monde*" was the phrase in which he summed up the situation. This being so, it seemed as wise to go on as to stay where we were, for, on the presumption that the end of all things had arrived, whether a man was caught afloat or ashore did not seem to be a matter of much consequence. Besides, there was a theory at Marseilles that the fury of the mistral only lasted three days. On Thursday evening the three days had expired, and the steamer did not start till Saturday at 5 p.m. So we determined to go on, and on Friday morning (by the agency of a *commissionaire*) engaged the four-berthed cabin spoken of above, on board of the good ship *Saïd.* It was quite the right thing to do at the time, but when one looks back upon it, what a cruel mockery was the attempt to persuade each other that after such a storm the sea would be "like glass" or "the Thames at Richmond"! Just when you were launching these illustrations, you would see a poor fellow fastened on to an advertisement board, carried along at no mean rate in the direction of the port, or a *bonne* in difficulties —the central figure of a dust-storm, trying to make her way against the wind in the opposite direction. There was, however, one real and reasonable source of consolation: let the storm do its worst, it was a fair storm for Algiers.

On Saturday morning the genial little head waiter announced the fact, "*Qu'il faisait un temps magnifique.*" So it did in front of the house, but as for the side street—oh, dear! The last luncheon was taken at 3 p.m.; the time had been carefully considered, also the *menu*—anything nutritious, but not too rich; and so we prepared ourselves for the misery, as we supposed, of two nights and a day. How the wind did whistle through the cordage when we got down to the port! How cold and steely the sky looked overhead! And how I dismissed from my mind all idea of being put up for the R.Y.S. at Cowes! On board we got, however; dealt successfully with the small parcel difficulty; and saw that the greater *impedimenta* were lowered down into the hold. As we passed the *salle à manger* or whatever the marine name of the department might be, I noticed with a shudder that "the fiddles were on." Landsmen may not appreciate the full significance of the phrase, but it means that experienced men had taken care that every plate, and dish, and bottle, and salt cellar had been made fast, so that they should not act as spontaneous missiles, and hurl themselves at the heads of the guests who were enjoying the nautical banquet. As you looked round, your mouth filled with water, but not from the usual cause about dinner-time. Slipshod *garçons-de-café*-looking men moved about amidst these terrible preparations. There was something sarcastic in their manner; no, it was not sarcasm—it was compassion. They had human hearts after all, and the wind was still moaning on, like a "Dead March" played over you before you had given your last groan.

On the deck I found that Monsieur le Capitaine, the leader who was to conduct this orchestra of misery, had just come on board, and was expending blandishments innumerable on a lady who was attended by two *bonnes*, one of whom carried a yelling babe, and the other holding a sticky Russian child, who was sucking at some sweetstuff, which I doubted not would soon bring affairs to a crisis with him. Oh, that child! worse to us than the mistral; worse than the Gulf of Lyons;—he was standing at this moment near the hatchway, and had I been a prophet, I think it not impossible that an accident might have happened. But madame and Monsieur le Capitaine all this time continued their compliments all about "*cet excellent Jules*," and how Madame Somebody at Arles was getting on. Bah! who cares? She may be as *aimable* as ever she likes, but she is not going to face the Gulf of Lyons, with the tail of a mistral wagging in her delightful old face. Would a man, to say nothing of a captain, of any sensibility, choose such a time for descanting upon the amiability of an old French lady who was at this moment a hundred miles out of the way of all danger?

As I knew the number of our own cabin, I heard with great pleasure Monsieur le Capitaine at last telling the stewardess to conduct madame to another little black-hole which I knew to be well at the stern, where the dear little children would be softly rocked to their sweet slumbers, and where madame herself would be enabled to enjoy the music of the screw to its fullest extent;—she would not miss a single revolution. Alas! alas! Nemesis stands close to your elbow if you indulge an unkind thought. If instrumental music was furnished by the Messageries Maritimes for the use of that lady and her amiable family, she in her turn had provided for all the ship's company a vocal entertainment which they were not likely to forget the longest day they had to live. But of all this anon.

We descended to our cabin, determined to turn in to our berths. Our one idea of how best to escape from the wrath to come was to lie down before they had untied the ropes which bound the ship to the quay, to remain flat upon our poor backs, not to open our eyes, not to wag a little finger, and to leave the result in the hands of a Higher Power. The watches had been carefully wound up, for we knew how futile would be the attempt to regulate them when the storm was at its height; and these had been duly hung up on the pegs, when the idea occurred to us that they would dash themselves to pieces against the sides of the berths.

This also had to be looked to, and just in time, for at this moment there was a grating sound as of a gangway withdrawn—improper language in French—and the first horrible turn of the screw. Now we are in for it. The right thing is mentally to count a million, or to conjure up the names of the old French worthies connected by blood or marriage with the family of Clovis. But what is the meaning of all this? We are moving on slowly, surely, smoothly. Bother the mistral! Would it not be wiser to slip on one's things, and to partake of a slight refection amidst the "fiddles" up above?

"I say we're a great nation. How people can be such idiots as to fear a sea passage——it is much nicer than ashore. Don't you think that, after all, a trim little yacht would be the thing?—a small floating hotel, and just to look in at all the ports in the Levant? Observe how smoothly we glide through the water. I did not like to say anything at the time for fear of alarming you, but it did blow a trifle at Marseilles this morning. So this is the worst of it? I always said that as sailors we were somewhat above the average. It was all nonsense! Thirty-six hours of calm and quiet, rather pleasant than otherwise after that tiresome railway journey across France. Yes, this is——". At this moment the *Saïd* took a five-barred gate—in fact, there might have been six bars—and then playfully threw herself on one side. Away flew the tooth-brushes and nail-brushes, and a bottle of glycerine. The nice little heaps of wearing apparel scattered themselves into the middle of the floor. The good ship righted herself, made a pause as if she were out of breath, took another five-barred gate, lay down again on one side, and then turned on the other. For our sins our berths were across ship (I do not know if that be the nautical term, "athwart" sounds more in the style of the late Captain Marryat), and all I know is that for about twelve hours we were at one moment standing on our heads, and were then replaced upon our heels; but oh, the awful moment between the two processes! The fact was that we had just shot out of the harbour into the open sea. It was idle to say, "this was the worst of it," as if that were any comfort when the worst was so very disagreeable. There was a sound of crockery, and of people running. Alas! that was no banquet, no scene of genial hospitality, for which they were making preparation. Will it be believed that this moment was chosen by a monster in human form as an appropriate one for silly jocularity? Yes, I heard a strong English voice uttering words which seemed throughout the night to be seared as with marking-ink upon my brain. "My dear Jones," said the speaker, "a nice bit of crackling, eh? Let me recommend a little more stuffing, and a spoonful of gravy." I felt he meant roast pork—but at such a moment! Then shrill above the other terrible noises was heard the tinkle of a small bell. "Jones," continued the fiend outside, "there is the dinner-bell. Let us go up and stoke"—yes, that was his expression—"and stoke a bit." I believe in a state of future retribution. May that man be condemned to eat roast pork throughout eternity, and may it disagree with him!

Well, well, on we rolled. I tried to think of the French words for pitching and tossing. Alas! one of us was on the floor; the mattress had glided away from under the poor lady, who was lying in her misery on the other side of that temple of little ease. Talk of the primitive martyrs! There was nothing for it but to yell for the stewardess, who came at last, and made the rack comfortable as before. The only solace left to us was a candle-end stuck in a lantern. There was a feeling of not being in the dark; we were not quite at the bottom of the sea. Mermaids were not, as yet, ringing our knell—Ding-dong, you know, and that sort of thing.

In the middle of the night, as I believed (I knew afterwards that it was 10 p.m.), a hairy monster (next day I ascertained that it was the under-steward) opened the door, and without ceremony puffed out our candle-end—I smelt the smell!—and left us in darkness. For the rest of the night I remember little but the wails of exhausted men and women, who had lost the power of groaning; the long-drawn swish of the seas which we had shipped along the deck; the absurd jingle of the bell above, as the poor ignorant sailors made it out to be two bells, or six bells, or as it might happen. What have bells got to do with it? Say it is a hundred bells at once, and have done with it, if you can't tell us what o'clock it is in a rational way. I got to look for and to hate the bells. There was a French gentleman in the next cabin to us, who kept wailing throughout the night, "*Ah! mon pauvre ami! ai-yai! est-ce que je souffre?*" He was himself the friend; but what does it matter? what does anything matter now?

So the rolling and the pitching went on. Nature was

exhausted, and one fell at last into an uneasy slumber. There were two or three wakings, two or three sleepings again. I suppose it must have been 4 a.m. or thereabouts, when—is it possible?—she doesn't seem to roll so much. There was a kind of dim religious light in the chamber of torture. About an hour passed away, illustrated mainly by the yelling of a child in the after part of the vessel. It was that sticky Russian boy I had seen over-night, and who, during the storm, had been overpowered by the noise of the wind and sea and by the gigantic screw; but now he was master of the situation. "*Faites donc taire cet enfant!*" shouted the Frenchman next door. "D—n that child!" rumbled out an Englishman from the other side. I hope it was the roast pork man. Nothing, however, availed; the child yelled on, and aroused the whole after part of the ship to a sense of sea-sickness and misery. If we could but have got at him! Presently came in to us the stewardess. "*Est-ce que madame a bien dormi? Oui, la mer a été un peu rude mais maintenant ça va mieux.*" We entered upon the subject of the child. "*Oui, madame, ce petit malheureux vient de crier toute la nuit, et madame sa mère le laisse faire.*" There was no help for it. Could we have a little hot coffee? By a miracle neither of us had been—you know what I mean—and we thought we could enjoy something warm. "O woman, in our hours of ease!" That ministering angel departed, and presently brought us back two bowls of steaming hot coffee. Who cares whether it was chicory or right Mocha? Fragrant saloop, such as the little chimney sweeps love it in London, would have done as well as anything else. So we nodded at each other in a friendly way from our respective berths, and had it not been for that horrible child, we should have been lapped in Elysium as we were lapping our coffee. But things were not so bad but they could be made worse. An irritable gentleman, some cabins off, who had used improper expressions in various languages, was at last driven quite beside himself by the hideous monotone, and took to imitating the child's cries. Henceforward we had not one child, but two children. I could not help thinking at the time that his system was logically wrong; he should have imitated the sound of slapping, after throwing in a yell or two. So, as the old Greek philosopher has it, he might have purged the passions of the child through terror; but it was not to be. The noise went on till one was driven in despair to clothe one's self somehow or other, and to get on deck. Oh, joy! the sea was remarkably quiet. It was now about 6 a.m. There was a blue arch overhead; sunrise was imminent.

I am glad to write, as I certainly was at the time to feel, that the storm was over. We were out of the Gulf of Lyons, and should soon see the Balearic Isles. This we soon did. The sea grew calmer and bluer, and at last the breakfast bell rang. Who could have thought last night that we should ever again have breakfasted with anything like zest? Yes, that is Minorca, that is Majorca (we were always making mistakes between the two islands), and that clumsy craft you see lagging astern is the *Valery*. She left Marseilles some minutes before us, but we walked away from her in the night. It is idle to dwell upon the next twenty-four hours; they really were hours of calm enjoyment. The blue arch overhead, the blue sea below, the warmth throughout the day, the blessed feeling that one had been sentenced to death and that the hanging was over, the gradual fading of day into short twilight, the big stars overhead (I was always "worriting" myself to fix the poor old north star, for that was the direction in which there were so many good people I loved); and then there was the moon, of course. And so we "turned in," not in a fright, but as seasoned sailors should. In the joy of my heart I could have called out " Luff," but for that hideous child. Why should not a child have six dozen slaps at the gangway? We fell asleep, and between 3 and 4 a.m. the stewardess put her head in, and told us we were at Algiers. The screw stopped. There was nothing for it but to go on deck, and to swagger over our achievements.

CHAPTER III.

ARRIVAL AT ALGIERS.

THE *Valery* was nowhere—a fact upon which we early pirates interchanged remarks not altogether free from sarcasm, as we sipped our coffee, and smoked our cigars in the half darkness, and considered where we should "berth our vessel." Were I writing a regular work upon Algiers, now would be the time for a little appropriate "gush." At first it was darkness, then it became darkness visible, and where the town was supposed to be there was a sort of white blotch, but above us were "the eternal stars of Africa, and, oh heavens! the moon!" As time wore on, there was a long red line in the east, over Cape Matifou, and—dare I write it?—mountains, probably the Atlas range, loomed dimly in the background. The eternal stars, as above, gradually paled their ineffectual fires; the white blotch became a Moorish town, surrounded by "darkest green" (this is the "diamond set in emeralds," when the subject is handled by competent writers). Yes, that is "The Pirates' Lair;" we have got home at last. We can proceed to make ourselves comfortable with sweethearts and wives—that is, with the wives and sweethearts of other people. We can divide the spoil; not only the heavy luggage down below, but all the small parcels which are littered about the cabin. "Oh, Fatima! oh, my soul!" But just then a tall, severe-looking lady, distinctly the worse for wear, with her front a little awry, sharply asked me, and with a strong Scotch accent, "Wad this be Awlgiers?" Is the Dey's humour good? I have still so much of humanity about me that I can be sorry for his Highness if this fair being should fall to his share. "Yes, madam, and this is the Mole, where, as you will remember, in the year 1816, Lord Exmouth," etc., etc. (at least three pages of padding). "Yonder is the Kasbah, where the unutterable Turk, who respected nothing, not even the down upon the peach, not the faint odour of the violet, not the most delicate feelings of the most evanescent and loveliest portion of the human race—that is the place, I say, to which, in old days, and amidst the curses of assembled thousands, the fair creatures who soothe human existence were dragged up to the tyrant's footstool by the hair of their heads."

"I'm thinking," broke in my Scotch friend, "nowadays it would just come off in their hands. But could you tell me, sir, where might the hottel be?—the Regency Hottel, I think they call it."

So there was an end of that. I turned away in disgust to contemplate the "amethystine vault," and the gradual conversion of the white houses to a "glare and glory of most yellow gold" (gushing books of travel help me with the style). In fact, what I did see was a jumble of white houses built on the slope of a hill—an amphitheatre, on which were dotted about villas innumerable, very much like Torquay, lit up by the slanting beams of the sun which had just risen. It was really very nice, and when I turned back my thoughts to the Victoria Station, which I had quitted that day se'nnight; the fog; and the damp platform ; and the hoarse newspaper boys, with red comforters, and severe catarrhs in their poor little noses ;—I could not but hope we had done a wise thing in coming to "Awlgiers," as my Scotch friend called it.

But my thoughts were heavy. I have arrived at that period of life when it is difficult, as the proverb says, to catch a bird or man with mere chaff. That Ethiopian Emperor—Seged by name?—was a terribly wise old fellow: "Who shall say that this shall be a day of happiness?" Accordingly, leaving my Scotch friend to her grovelling meditations about her "hottel," I turned to the taffrail, and folding my arms under my plaid (it was a real homespun ; I bought it in the mills near pleasant Inverness one afternoon when it had left off raining), and scowling at things in general (I did nothing of the sort), I proceeded to apostrophize the Pirates' Lair, or rather I thought these things, but did not say them.

"Here in this blood-bespattered health resort I must pass the next five or six months of my chequered existence. Is the place comfortable? As King Joram in the olden days said to Jehu, 'Is it peace?' or as King Joram did not say, Is it mosquitoes? Shall we find the cookery tolerable? Was there anything in what that genial medical man said to me yesterday off Minorca about the sewage, whilst we were discussing our savoury omelette? Bah! the good fellow had typhoid on the brain. He could not have been right concerning the 150,000 infuriated dogs, who roam about the streets of Algiers at night in search of victuals. I am very sure my French friends would have clapped 150,000 baskets upon their hungry jowls, and so have left them to the chances of a precarious existence. How about the hotels? A lady of rank and fashion has been good enough to make a pause in her majestic career, and to warn me that one hotel in particular (which shall be nameless, as I am not well posted in the French law of libel) is a mere 'den of fever,'—such was her ladyship's expression. Avaunt, ye whited sepulchres! It turns me sick as I gaze on your flaunting titles and inscriptions. The mottoes should run 'Hôtel de la Mort,' 'Hôtel des Fièvres Réunies.' Those are the places from which the bodies of the young ladies, upon whose education a mint of money has been spent, are removed at night in sacks by swarthy Moorish waiters, lest the credit of the hotel should be shaken in public opinion. Alack! alack! would not bronchitis in London have been better than fever in Algiers? Or, shall we choose a villa? There seem plenty to choose from. Some of them are new, mere lath and plaster, I doubt not, with sticky Utrecht velvet chairs, and ormolu clocks, surmounted by warlike female figures, naked and not ashamed. There must be landladies just like the Brighton landladies, only of a far sharper and more pungent humour, as they are of French origin. Were not the last words of that kind and great physician, Sir William Gull, 'Avoid emotion at any cost'? How if I should be drawn into a discussion with a French landlady? Or there may be Moorish villas, Arab houses, and so on, which look so well on the pages of your great work on Algiers. I know the trick of it, and how the flies are caught. But Moorish villas—I was warned of the fact in London—contain ants innumerable, and these creatures have the pleasant habit of moving about in long triumphant processions, and of scaling your bed, or chair, or wherever you may happen to be. To Sir John Lubbock this might afford an additional inducement for taking a Moorish villa, but I feel no curiosity on the subject of ants. Well, well, it must be as it must; for here come the boats with the descendants of the pirates aboard, and it now becomes my duty to protect my wife and the small parcels. I cannot hope to do much in the way of serious fighting, but perchance a stern glance and the majesty of the human eye may avail something. It is but a skirmish after all. Once ashore and past the Custom-house, we shall find nothing but 'Peace on earth, and good will towards men.'"

I had heard terrible stories of these Moorish boatmen, and having in my own proper person and in former days seen the manner in which the intelligent foreigner was handled just below London Bridge, on his first landing on British soil, I could not but fear it might be still worse at Algiers. The Thames waterman had had the advantage of the Sunday school, and had been taught his duty to his neighbour. But these poor infidels, the descendants of the pirates who had fought under the red flag in the days of Admiral

Barbarossa, what mercy could we look for at their hands? In my agitation I had completely forgotten the Mohammedan *formulæ*, which I had carefully studied in London with an eye to business, lest I should at any time get into trouble with the children of the Crescent. Of course it was far from my wish to hold out any hope that my conversion was imminent, but I should have liked these black fellows to feel that I was open to fair argument on the subject of Mecca, if they would only leave the umbrellas alone.

There they are, black, brown, and olive-coloured, bobbing about in their little floating pannikins, and suggesting by their uncouth gestures that they were willing to convey us to the shore. The moment had arrived. But what was my delight and astonishment when I saw that two guardian angels—I presume two gentlemen attached to the French police service—had taken possession of the gangway, and were handling the pirates pretty much as their French colleagues manage the *queue* at a Boulevard Theatre on the occasion of a first night. There was the polite French captain, the pilot who had weathered the storm on Saturday night in the Gulf of Lyons, bowing gracefully to the departing passengers; there was the cross steward, now all honey, and waiting for his tip; there was the good-humoured stewardess, equally waiting with the same object, but she deserved it, as she had brought us hot coffee in the hour of our extreme need, when the tempest was at its height. There were the band-boxes and things carefully handed down, and there was the Scotch lady going over the side. For the honour of humanity

I am proud to record the fact that Abdallah, or Osman, or whatever his name might be, so far from displaying by his actions any wish to bear this fair creature off to his black tent or his horrible harem, was, on the contrary, doing his best so to manage her chaste draperies, that not even the temptation of an ankle might affect the minds of his swarthy shipmates below.

Well, here we are in the boat at last. "Give way, men; yonder is Algiers!" A few strokes, and the water hissed around us, when the Scotch lady remembered that she had left a small parcel "just by the big black chimley," and this she must have at any cost. Imagine a boarding party checked in their decisive rush because one of them wanted to tie his shoe! Resistance was impossible, for the loud Caledonian shriek had completely mastered that living mass of fiery valour. Back we went, and the meaning of our return was translated to the astonished Gaul from Aberdonian into French, and after brief delay the property was recovered. The precious box was of cardboard; it was round, and not large. In former days I had seen such boxes on the counters of hairdressers. That box, I say, did not hold any family relics (connected, perchance, with the fallen House of Stuart); it contained a "front." This only will account for the strong feeling displayed upon the occasion.

We were soon ashore, the distance to be traversed being but small, and were received in the most courteous manner by a knot of custom-house officers, who in the most chivalric manner assisted us to land. They never insulted us with even a formal inquiry as to "whether we had anything to declare." There was not even a lurking suspicion in the eye of any one as to brandy or tobacco. Their confidence in human nature was unlimited. They helped us into a nice little open carriage, and handed in the minor parcels without any offensive innuendo. A small excited Arab asked us, in his poor broken French, if he should pass our heavier things through the Custom-house, when they were landed from the steamer? Certainly; but we felt it would be better if we attended ourselves on so momentous an occasion, my wife fearing that certain objects dear to her heart might be "tumbled;" I (to my shame be it written) not without some lurking doubt as to the thorough integrity of the little jumping Arab. No; monsieur was to give the number and description of the trunks, and to say to what hotel they should be conveyed. Keys? No keys. The Algerine *douaniers* were utterly incapable of meddling with a lady's trunks. *Inshallah!* So off we drove to the Hôtel de la Régence, in the Place du Gouvernement, amongst the palm-trees and bamboos.

CHAPTER IV.

FIRST IMPRESSIONS: THE OASIS OF PALMS.

I HAD been told that the Hôtel de la Régence was the best in Algiers, and after some months' experience of the town I think I may say that the impression was correct. The Hôtel d'Orient is the most "fashionable;" but I had been warned against it on account of certain drawbacks. The warnings given in London were confirmed here by the reports of persons who had remained for a while in this hotel on their first arrival at Algiers. It stands in a noble situation, overlooking the harbour, but has not a southern aspect like the Régence.

The other hotels in the town to which English travellers might resort are—first, the Hôtel de l'Oasis, equally overlooking the harbour; secondly, the Hôtel de Genève, on the Place Bresson, but it stands a little back from the sea,—it is said that the restaurant is good; finally, there is the Hôtel de l'Europe, also at a distance from the sea. I have heard it both well and not well spoken of; but I dare say that late arrivals are glad enough to be taken in there. The three last in Algiers would be reckoned second-rate hotels; and I suppose that, out of Algiers, the two first would not be rated as of the first rank. In truth, the hotel accommodation of this new health resort is defective even in the town. We will at the proper time speak of "harbours of refuge" outside, and on the slopes of Mustapha.

In old days, as I have been informed by persons whom Macaulay would have described as "ancient men," the Orient and the Régence stood alone, though the Europe in point of age might have competed with them. It was at Algiers as at Scarborough. The Orient people flouted at the Régence folk as being—well, "not in good society." The Régences retorted that, "true it might be that they were not exactly the cream of the cream; but, at least, they had plenty to eat; and, when they rang their bells, it was fairly on the cards that a servant would answer them. How was it that hungry, worn-out Orient people came to dine at the Régence? but in the memory of man there was no record of a Régence family which had dined at the Orient. The upper ten thousand might be very well in their way, but if they were half-starved, and could never get hot water, better be vulgar and comfortable." Besides, the Régence people were not quite without resource. If they suffered from the disdain of the Orient, they in our time could handle the low people at the Genève and Europe in a manner not calculated to flatter their self-love. Finally, there was one overwhelming fact in favour of the Régence. Middle-aged Frenchmen, more especially the gallant members of the military profession, know a good dinner when they see it. To a man they dined at the Régence.

The hotel does not look directly over the harbour,

but faces south. It stands on one side of the Place du Gouvernement, where the band plays twice or thrice a week, and where live Arabs and Moors and Kabyles, and Jews are to be seen walking about all day long. In front of it is a considerable group of date palms and bamboos, which gives quite an Eastern tone to the place. You feel that you are no longer loitering out your commonplace life at the Duke's Head or the Royal, but have really taken your first serious step towards Mecca. In place of calling out for the *garçon*, your first exclamation would naturally be *Inshallah!* or *Mashallah!* (I am not sure which). "In the name of Allah! the All-Wise, the All-Merciful!" but a "*Voilà, monsieur!*" soon informs you that you are just in a French hotel after all. You enter a court-yard, glazed over at the top, ascend certain flights of stairs, and on the first floor, behold, you are in the hotel. We had yet another flight before us, for in all Continental hotels I am careful to get as high up as I can, for reasons connected with my hopes of longevity, as well as of personal comfort during my earthly pilgrimage. On the second floor we were met by an old man in his shirt sleeves, who was busy, with a long broom of feathers, dusting away, or making believe to dust away, at the rooms.

Brave old Dominique! I learnt to know him well afterwards. He was our housemaid, our lady's-maid, our valet, our shoe-black, our groom of the chambers, our butler or waiter at the *table d'hôte*, our guide, philosopher, and friend. Who would have thought that that small white-haired old man had been at the storming of El-Aghouat, and had been through the Crimea? Bad jokers tried to make out that this was merely in the capacity of sutler, but this was an infamous calumny. Dominique had fought his way as a soldier should. By him we were introduced to two small rooms opening out of each other, and our first rush was to the window. What a sight of the bay and of the distant mountains! For a moment I envy the professors of gush. It was the 20th of October, about 6.30 a.m., and the sun was hotter than it is in August in England. My first impression was, "How luminous it all is!" and this impression I have never lost during the months I have since spent in Algiers. Poor Sydney Smith, at Combe Florey, when he came down to breakfast, used to say, "Draw up curtains and blinds; let us *glorify* the room!" This was exactly Algiers—the room had been "*glorified*." We had left night and darkness behind us in the North; here were light and day. What Naples is to London, that is Algiers to Naples. A few strange figures, draped majestically in rags, on whom I should scarcely deign now to throw a glance, were stalking about in the sunshine, just as we should on the sweet shady side of Pall Mall, and apparently enjoying it. "Oh! give me but my Arab steed!" This is something like a watering-place. Eastbourne may do well enough for cockneys, but Algiers for me!

Let us be quick, or perhaps the Arabs may walk off for the day. Dominique did not appear to think there was any cause for hurry; so to unpack. Yes, the rooms were very small; but they had this advantage, that we had a clear prospect over the palm trees. By George! those are dates actually growing. The rooms *were* small; but they were state apartments at Windsor as compared with that desirable marine residence from which we had just escaped, and where we had spent two nights and a day. All things are relative, and here at least (*bar* earthquakes) there is an end of pitching and tossing.

We proceeded to unpack, when, of course, we found that *the* parcel was missing. Had it been any other but that one, the loss might have been endured; but, oh, *Ciel!* the mackintoshes and overalls and cunningly devised garments, which were to be our protection against the tropical or Southern rains. If the cross steward now should find the property, what easier than a flat denial? Were it the stewardess (she of the coffee in the storm), we had given her a good baksheesh, and she seemed not altogether devoid of human feeling. To Dominique we explained our loss; but that callous old man must be accustomed to "forgotten parcels" and the despair of travellers. There was no sympathy; he did not drop a tear; nay, rather grinned a grin, and disappeared.

What a delight to get rid of the clothes in which we had faced the fury of the elements! Nothing on us but had suffered a sea-change into something which might be "strange," but was certainly not "rich." Oh, the delight of the ample bath and the abundant linen!—not that mugful of water which you extorted from the pity of the stewardess; not that tumbled shirt which you had rolled up into a tight bundle, on the chance of being able to put it on.

Here comes the jumping Arab with the trunks. They are all right, so we offer him a fee rather calculated on the scale of London than of Algiers. It was about five times what he was entitled to. With what calm disdain he placed our humble offering on the table, and gave us one pitying glance, more in sorrow than in anger! We feared that, without knowing it, we might have wounded the poor fellow's religious susceptibilities, and that it was in his mind rather a question of the Crescent and the Cross. What were we to do with the infidel, who soon abandoned his attitude of tranquillity, and was now executing a sort of hornpipe to the music of his own gutturals? Was he saying anything disrespectful about our grandmothers, or announcing his intention of acting disagreeably on the tombs of our ancestors, just as they do in Hadji Baba? "I say, halloa! Dominique. What's this fellow going on about? There is what we gave him for bringing up our boxes; he does not seem quite happy. We'll pay anything to get rid of the Arab." The chivalry of France was with us at once. After one glance at the table and our humble offering, the dear little old fellow seemed converted into a perfect fury, and brandished his *plumeau* about like a weapon of war. "*Comment, canaille, est-ce que c'est ainsi qu'on se moque des voyageurs? Prends, et à la porte!*" taking up some of the coins. The Berserker fury of the dark Arab had subsided; he was now all humility and politeness. We told him, despite of Dominique's energetic remonstrances, that it was still open to him to accept the sum in its entirety, which he did with apparent thankfulness, and departed.

This was our first encounter with the Arabs, and we might give a thought to breakfast. Had it not been for the mackintoshes, we should have been perfectly happy; for it was no slight matter to have travelled from London to Algiers, to have defied the cold of France, the mistral of Marseilles, the storm in the Gulf of Lyons, without so much as the loss of an umbrella, until this late unhappy occurrence. Well, it was written, we are in the Land of Kismet, we are bound to put on an appearance of Oriental indifference and resignation, though the worm may be gnawing at our hearts. Let us go down to breakfast in the name of Allah! and be cheerful before the waiters.

At this moment Dominique entered with a "*Voilà, monsieur!*" and deposited the parcel with the mackintoshes on the table. On hearing of our loss, he at once despatched a high-spirited and cunning *commissionaire* in a swift boat to the *Saïd*, which was still lying in the harbour. Without asking any questions, that "able" man had got on board, had passed down to our cabin, and there, under the very berth, he found the lost ones. With what joy we received them it would be idle to say. There was no longer occasion for any feigned tranquillity. Between Algiers and London we had not lost a pin. The *salle-à-manger* in the Régence is on the first floor, and a nice cool room it is, paved with marble, and with blinds drawn to keep out the strong sunlight. The breakfast of prawns, and sardines, and (for a wonder in the South) of good fish, and an omelette, with figs, bananas, grapes for dessert, was really good; and I think travellers must be hard to please if they do not find the "eating" arrangements of the Régence sufficiently good. Breakfast finished, it was time to go down below, to find seats under the palm trees in front of the house, and to watch the queer people.

I doubt if a chance traveller who had but a few days to spare for Algiers, could do better than to take his seat in this place, and simply to keep his eyes open. Imagine a masked ball, or the behind scenes of the opera when they are giving the "Italiani in Algieri," the mummers being multiplied by scores and by hundreds. What fine stately figures are the Arabs, though they are in rags! and the Kabyles, with their ruddier and somewhat more European faces; and the Moors, and Jews, and the negroes, some of whom are black, and the others not so black; and the trim little French soldiers, and the gay *Chasseurs d'Afrique*, and Zouave officers; and then those strange-looking women all in white, their legs—saving your presence—like two moving bolsters, and the face-cloth drawn so deftly across their features, that the slit left for the eyes gave the effect of a long mouth! I would not believe a man on his word who told me that this concealment of the face did not excite curiosity. An archdeacon not actually engaged in the exercise of his archidiaconal functions, would have peeped, or tried to peep, just like the famous Thomas of Coventry.

As matter of fact, I have little doubt that if all their head coverings had been torn off them, a man would have gazed with apathy, if not with horror, at the grim spectacle; but the veils and shrouds made a difference. As little did I doubt that if one could have got into the very heads and hearts of those majestic-looking creatures, who were stalking about in their rags with a dignity which Mr. Irving might have envied, they would have turned out to be—dare I write it?—a pack of preposterous humbugs. Belisarius would have picked your pockets. That venerable Arab, whom you would have credited at the first glance with deep thoughts as to the fallen condition of his people and his faith, was simply reflecting how he could best impose upon the infidel with some twenty-times-told tale. All this might be right enough if your object was to get at the truth about these majestic creatures; they were probably neither worse nor better than a crowd of free-born Britons at Charing Cross.

But if the "picturesque," not the "truth," was your object, the sight was perfect of its kind. I doubt if there be anything better worth seeing within four days' post off the Royal Academy, than is the Place du Gouvernement at Algiers. With what lofty courtesy the Arabs exchanged salutations, and, if of equal degree, straightway took short turns with each other, as though they had to exchange confidences of the most vital importance! On the meeting of "unequals," the humbler creature would make a dive to secure the hand of the loftier individual, and straightway kiss, not the loftier hand, but his own humbler fingers, which had been sanctified by contact with those of the superior being, who just let him kiss away, and stalked on in search of somebody whom he might know without loss of self-respect. It was very like London society in rags, only that the Arabs had immeasurably the advantage in dignity and high demeanour. Then there were heaps of Kabyles. I vehemently desired to know how I could recognize at a glance the difference between a Kabyle and an Arab. An acquaintance on board the steamer had informed me that the Kabyle was in the habit of twisting a camel's hair rope round his head-gear.

This theory turned out to be the reverse of fact. After the experience of a few days, and having been once set on the right track, you might distinguish between the Arab and the Kabyle, by the general cut of the features, by the depth of the complexion, and by the bearing of the men. It was the difference between Norman and Saxon, between Cavalier and Roundhead. The short, yeomen-looking fellows are the Kabyles; the thin-featured, slighter-built, idler, and more aristocratic-looking creatures are Arabs. I have observed that many of my predecessors in the matter of the Algerine travel have at this point hit upon a very notable plan. As they jot down their recollections of this motley crowd, they say, "Oh! joy; oh! ecstasy. The little boy in the fez cap, now 'overing' the posts and breaking his mother's heart, might be that naughty Aladdin. The female figure in the baggy unmentionables is Morgiana beyond doubt. That rough-looking fellow might be Sinbad ashore after his third cruise;" and so on. Now, as there are a "Thousand and One Nights," and as there is a constant crowd of what our French neighbours call *indigènes* at the Place du Gouvernement, it is clear that, on this system, one may produce "copy" at a great rate. The idea is good enough once in a way, but it has been thoroughly worked out. Here come Jews, some of them in dark costumes, others very splendidly dressed. If ever I saw Shylock—— But I must hold my hand, as not being unmindful of my own remarks. Some of the younger Jewish women (all wore black skull-caps with veils) looked well enough, but as they grow older and are more inclined to *embonpoint* (that last phrase, I hope, is strictly correct), they are certainly less attractive, and very heavy in the jowl. There would be no end were I to speak of the good-humoured negroes, with their eternal grin ; of the water-carriers, or Biskras, and so on.

It is well worth a journey from London to Algiers to enjoy a couple of hours' lounge in the Oasis. I speak merely of a first glance, for as you come to understand the meaning of the sight, the interest changes in kind. But what is the meaning of this ? A file of majestic creatures is passing ; their step is grand, as always ; but there is something uncomfortable about the arms and hands. I regret to say they are handcuffed. They are under the escort of four little *sergens-de-ville*—trim, tight, and fussy, as a Frenchman is when engaged upon the service of the State. They are coming from the direction of the Mole, where the poor Christian slaves were used as navvies in the old piratical time, under the lash of their pitiless masters. They disappear in that little narrow street which leads up to the cathedral, and where a slave bagnio, they tell me, was in those wicked old days. Well, if this be not turning the tables with a vengeance. Bravo ! Jean Pierre ; well done ! Athanase. Run them in by all means. Were not our fathers " run in " here of old, and their feet beaten to a jelly because they had fainted at last under their too heavy burdens and the broiling sun? The noticeable point was that, as they ran them in, they passed along the very Via Dolorosa which had been so often trodden by the Christian captives in their despair. This was turning the tables with a witness, and I could have shouted out my sympathy with the proceeding and with French grandeur in a way that might have won for me the approbation of M. Victor Hugo when descanting in a calm and philosophic spirit on the virtues of his countrymen, and the brilliant superiority of Paris—that eye of the universe—over all other towns past or present. Whether or no the wretched Arabs had been caught picking pockets or offending against some of the clauses of the French Vagrant Act, I know not; and I trust they got justice when brought up. It was clear at least that here was an end of Algerine piracy, and one might smoke one's cigar in peace under the Oasis without fear of being set to work upon the Mole.

But as we have done with the pirates, I should be a very insufficient historian of this agreeable spot if I failed to introduce my readers to pleasant Mme. Cornuz, the *fleuriste*, who is the presiding genius of the place.

The paradise where she cultivates her flowers is in the "Vallée de la Femme Sauvage," some three or four miles away to the eastward; but I understand that she has some agreement with the municipal authorities of Algiers, which gives her the floral monopoly of the Oasis. Mme. Cornuz, on the one part, decorates the Oasis with flower-pots; and the municipality, on the other, leave her alone, and agree to drive away all rivals and intruders. Madame has set up her table in the very middle of the palm trees, and here from morning till night you may see her deft fingers at work weaving flowers—and such flowers!—into bouquets. She stands behind her table, which is covered with basins containing flowers in water, and, snatching up now one, now another, as her taste may direct, throws off bouquets with the regularity of a steam-engine. But what a gracious smile for all who come within reach of her table, or who may drive or walk past! She has the true royal gift of "seeing" everybody, and each one gets a smile, and, if it be an acquaintance, a good-humoured nod. The *fleuriste* has the bearing of a duchess; you never see an awkward movement whilst she goes on throughout the day, smiling, nodding, chattering, and weaving flowers. Now a shade passes over her face,—she is being told of illness or death; now a bright smile,—mademoiselle is going to the ball; now a look of deep meaning,—a lady is telling her something, but Mme. Cornuz had long foreseen how it would be. Then her husband, a short, good-humoured-looking fellow, will appear upon the scene. He has "made a long illness," and it is clear enough that for a while the stability of the family rests upon the very competent shoulders of madame. He is welcomed as "*Mon gros*," "*Vilain garçon*," "*Gros paresseux*," and so on. Was it not his evident duty to fill up the basins? Was she not in want of jasmine or roses; and had she not had a presentiment of the moment when she would be reduced to chrysanthemums? and all because monsieur chose to idle away his time at the *café*. She had, however, handled the fat man better than he deserved. She had put off her own coffee till such time as he might show his ungrateful face.

"*Tiens, Beschir, le café.*" This to a one-eyed Arabian youth, formerly a shoe-black, but actually engaged in collecting the chair-money (ten centimes for each chair) under the Oasis. There was, if I remember right, an Emir Beschir, who played rather a distinguished part in Syria, in the old Druse and Maronite squabbles; but I do not suppose that our Beschir was in any way connected with him; if so, the family had certainly suffered reverses. He turned out to be a very good lad, but at first I was not prepossessed in his favour. He had a way of piercing a stranger as with a gimlet with his one eye, as much as to imply that (had he not been too sharp for you) you would have taken advantage of him in the matter of chairs. There was something ironical, not to say sarcastic, in his glance; it said quite plainly, "Beschir never gives credit." This was felt as an affront, as at the moment you have or had no intention of asking for any accommodation of the kind, but were perfectly prepared to complete the transaction on the basis of "cash payments, and no discount." Beschir, however, grew on you upon better acquaintance; he got at last not to pounce upon us the moment we had taken our seats, and conducted the business upon a principle of honourable confidence equally creditable to both parties.

Another worthy of the Oasis was poor little Mohammed, the shoe-black, a bright, dirty little Puck of an Arab, with a fez cap a world too big for him, ornamented with a long blue tassel, which was the pride of his heart, but which was always getting into his eyes. We won his confidence at last by timely jocularity and the administration of certain sous. It was some time before he could comprehend that the sous were of the nature of unearned baksheesh, and did not imply the necessity of shoe-blacking in return. But when it became clear to his mind that all that was expected of him was that he should flit about amongst the palms, and "over the posts," in a picturesque fashion, I am bound to say that he was not slow to perform his share of the implied contract. The posts had a nasty sharp iron spike at the top, which the youth of the Dials at home would have looked upon as an outcome of the permanent malignity of the police (or the "coppers," as they describe them), and an evidence of a conspiracy against their peace and happiness. This was not Mohammed's view; on the contrary, he liked these excrescences. By a half leap-frog or fly-the-garter kind of effort, he would land himself safely on the top, either falling short of or clearing the difficulty, and then, in some inconceivable way, wriggle himself into a standing position, blacking-box and all. In this attitude he would actually avail himself of the spike as a help or security, by holding it between his little black feet, whilst he chirruped out his small guttural defiance to the *sergens-de-ville*, with the blue tassel covering his eyes. He was a good child, though, and a grateful one, though his gratitude took a somewhat inconvenient form—that of perpetually blacking your shoes.

As the afternoon wore on, and we came to know the place better, we found that the *habitués* of the Oasis would drop in. It was like a London Club. One must not, in a few pages of idle gossip such as this is, mention names; but what was my surprise and delight to find in this place an English gentleman, long a resident in Algiers, of such quaint humour, and with so marked a gift for telling stories, that he would have kept a Pall Mall Club in a roar from 4 to 6 p.m., when the weaker brethren drop off for a quiet pool before their modest evening repast. What an Asmodeus it was! How he took the roofs off all the houses in Algiers, and taught me to distinguish between the true and the false! Humbug and pretence had not a chance before this quiet but terrible joker. He had a way of throwing into his features such a look of deep veneration and respect when he wanted to get rid of a vulgar fellow or a bore (for, alas! such people exist in Algiers as in London), that even such a one seemed to lose his powers of offence, or to be converted into a comic character for your amusement. All this, of course, I came to know afterwards. On this, my first day under the Oasis, I just remember him as the quiet, courteous gentleman, who would have been a general favourite in London; the only taste he gave me of his quality at that time (after a long preamble about Algiers and the curious people who dwelt therein) was an inquiry as to whether I should like to be introduced to the coroner? No? Well, we could put off the introduction to another day. The learned functionary was at that moment flirting with Mme. Cornuz, and must have said something more agreeable than usual; I suppose so, from the fact that madame rapped him over the knuckles with a bunch of carnations, in a "Go-along-now-do" sort of way. Even coroners can unbend, and are no more free than ordinary mortals from the chances of "accidental death" in the presence of agreeable *fleuristes*.

I could ramble on for many a page about the Oasis of Palms as I saw it that afternoon; but, however much such a proceeding might amuse me, it might have a reverse effect upon my readers. I have already succeeded if I have given an idea of what we actually saw, and how we were handled on our first arrival in Algiers. Not that I think myself that I have anything very valuable to tell; but it struck me when I was still in London that I should have been glad to read any account of the place which would bring it, as it were, before my eyes and prepare me for what I should see when I got there. We will let Syphax and Masinissa, and the question of the Roman remains in Africa, and the Arabian conquest, etc., etc., stand over till further notice. This is all "paste and scissors," or at least "gum arabic" work, to be done out of books. It bores me to read it; how much worse would it be to write it! Just now, all I can recall is a vague vision of Sallust and his more difficult passages, during such times as I stood on the thrashing-floors of various learned men, in those happy, happy days, when a poor fellow was caned by an M.A. and flogged by a D.D., if he fell into any error about Juba or those confounded Numidians.

Let us call a carriage, and have a nice little drive.

CHAPTER V.

ALGIERS NEW AND OLD.

THE preceding chapter may be flimsy enough, but it is an attempt to let the reader know what he would certainly see on the morning of his arrival at Algiers. The Place du Gouvernement is the first object which attracts, and for a time retains, curiosity. The strange dresses, the strange aspect of the wearers of those dresses, the wonderful sky above, the great glare and heat (we found them, on the 20th of October), the feeling that you are in Algiers at last, are quite enough for one morning. The historical associations, the dreadful traditions of the pirates, certainly passed into my mind as an after-thought. As I have endeavoured to explain, I was not disappointed with what I saw; but I saw what I did not expect to see, and the reverse. There is an "Arab fever" for new arrivals at Algiers, just as there is a "Gallery fever" at Florence, or a "Ruin fever" at Rome. The attack is longer or shorter, according to the constitution of the patient, but to us all there comes a moment when we feel that we have had enough of the Arabs for a time, and had rather look about us.

Now, I think that at the bottom, not of the disappointment, but of the unsatisfied expectation, is this, that you find yourself not in a pirates' lair at all, but rather in a bustling French town of the third or fourth order, in which the stately creatures in rags are mere accessories. What you see might be a bit of Marseilles; you are obliged to go a-hunting after the Arab town. When you have found it, take my word for it you have a nice morning's work before you if you wish to explore it properly; but you must go in search of it—it will not force itself upon your notice. The Algiers of the Turks and Arabs, then, is one thing, the Algiers of the French quite another.

First, of the new or French town. Imagine a long line of quays something under a mile in length, backed by rows of houses such as are dear to a Frenchman's heart, "*les quais sont dominés par un boulevard qui présente l'un des plus beaux fronts de mer du monde.*" The quays are down below, the boulevard at the top, and you walk or drive from the one to the other by a set of zigzags on an easy gradient. Rather think of the Rue Rivoli than of anything romantic, and you will be much nearer the truth as far as the seaward aspect of modern Algiers is concerned. Strangely enough, the row of tall white houses is not the work of Baron Hausmann, but of our countryman, Sir Morton Peto, who was of course bound to give effect to the wishes of his employers. In front of you is the harbour, which is almost entirely of modern construction; it is mainly enclosed between two moles, or breakwaters. The old Mole (Lord Exmouth's Mole), the Mole of the Christian slaves, with the lighthouse, is there still, but forms, comparatively, a small portion of the works. The raised ground between the quays and the boulevards has been utilized in the form of vaults for warehouses, and other similar purposes. The whole forms an undoubtedly fine and convenient line of quays and white houses; but you would rather expect to find them at Nantes or Marseilles than at Algiers. The idea of the French seems to be that they will leave old Algiers to its fate, and, moving on to the southward and eastward, construct a new Algiers of their own. On the hill landward, the builders and masons are at work; there is to be a grand new church, a grand new Palais de Justice, and everything grand and new. Two large open spaces—call them squares, "places," or what you will—occur on this long line of boulevard.

The one at the northern end is the Place du Gouvernement, to which we have so often referred; the other is the Place Bresson, at one end of which stands the theatre. This place is worthy of remark, because it was, as far as I have been able to make out, the end of old Algiers in this direction. You will see a number of omnibuses at all hours of the day standing nearly opposite the theatre. Just about here was the site of the old Bab-Azzoun, and if you ascend a flight of steps close to the theatre and work your way upwards, you will come across traces of the wall which enclosed the town in the old days of Algiers.

The idea of Turkish Algiers would be a walled and fortified town, covering an irregular triangle, the base being the seashore, or as much of it as would be enclosed between the Bab-Azzoun just spoken of and

E

the old Bab-el-Ouad (not the modern gate to the northward). The apex would be the Kasbah, or old fortress residence of the Deys. You may place the old Bab-el-Ouad (or water-gate) near to the Lycée and Fort Neuf. From Bab-Azzoun, then, and Bab-el-Ouad, the two old gates, draw two lines to the Kasbah, respectively; the enclosure would be old Algiers, if you add on to it, as a sort of excrescence, the Mole, on which the Admiralty now stands, and the little island (Peñon) on which is the lighthouse. But you must not imagine you see the shore as the pirates saw it, for to realize this you must begin by obliterating all that is French. Under and near the Grand Mosque you may catch just a notion of the shore as it was. By doing away in your own mind with the steps which lead down to the fish market at the corner of the Place du Gouvernement, and with the fish market itself, and by substituting a short, steep descent of rough earth, and a bit of sea-beach at the bottom, with, I believe, an old gate, you can in a way reconstruct the scene.

During our stay at Algiers, an English gentleman, an artist, Mr. Pileau, came amongst us, and made some very pleasant sketches of the place. Amongst other things he took this bit of shore, carried the white walls of the mosques down to the beach, wiped away every trace of modern work, and threw in a few Turks, Arabs, and camels. The result was that he brought before the eye a very striking and, I doubt not, a very correct notion of Algiers as it was.

But, again, take your station at the southern end of the islet (Peñon), looking across to the modern Health

Office, and you will have before you the old harbour to which the cruisers returned after their expeditions. It is small enough, but the shore for a considerable length was defended by batteries even down to Lord Exmouth's time, and there was another small islet also available for purposes of defence. To reconstitute old Algiers in your mind from this point, sweep away the jetties, northern and southern, which, however useful, are French and modern. The two mosques, De la Pêcherie and the Grand Mosque, are, of course, relics of the past. Close to them, on the Place Mahon, was the Babestan, or place where the captives were sold, and near to which you are shown some horrid holes—one of them is now used as a *café maure*—into which the poor creatures were driven when not at work.

I have seen many dungeons and *oubliettes* constructed by the forefathers of our philosophical friends in Germany—the Pozzi and Piombi, in the Doge's Palace at Venice, are not precisely nice places—but none of them ever inspired me with more horror than I felt when looking into these filthy holes. What must the feelings of a poor creature have been when thrust and kicked into one of them? It was all over; the hurried and useless flight; the short and equally unavailing struggle; the run into port; the exposure on the slave market. When no private bidder was found, the new slave was to toil on the Mole yonder as long as he could drag himself to his work under the burning sun. When he sank down exhausted, and could not be revived by the bastinado, or at night, he was to be thrust into such a place as this, amidst a number of starving, shivering, worn-out wretches like himself. Henceforward no home, no hope, wife, children, friends; his own pleasant native land he must not look to see again. Life for him was henceforward to be merely lashes and starvation; to suffer the extremes of cold and hunger, to work in chains, to be blotted out of the book of humanity, and perhaps not to die for many long years. When I came to know Algiers better, the thought has often come across me that it was unnatural to enjoy the beauty of the place when one reflected how often the poor Christian slaves must have cursed this blue sea and sky; that distant view of the snow-covered Djudjura Mountains; those beautiful slopes of the Sahel, now dotted over with the white villas of idle, chattering tourists (I am one of them), who have come to Algiers because England was not good enough for them. Algiers a health resort! What would the poor fellow not have given to be back at Wapping or Rotherhithe in the thick of the yellowest fog which ever adorned the eastern quarter of his native London?

I have given the old Bab-Azzoun and Bab-el-Ouad as the limits of the former town. To complete the picture, sweep away from the prospect all those tall modern houses. I fancy that, where the Place du Gouvernement now is, there were native bazaars, with the town house of the Dey where the telegraph establishment now stands. There would be Arab houses, with flat roofs, scattered along the shore, and, of course, the streets Bab-Azzoun and Bab-el-Ouad, with their rows of arcades in their present form, had no existence, nor the Place du Chartres, nor the Rue du Chartres, nor anything of the

French town in this quarter as we see it now. Ascend to the Kasbah, through the old Arab town, which lies behind the cathedral—then a mosque—and the synagogue still higher up. Grope your way and stumble along the dirty streets or lanes, and when you have reached the top, at the Kasbah, you will have a notion of at least part of the old pirates' town. Even here the French have been busy, and have done their best to destroy the characteristics of the place. It is not the snarl of a passing stranger when I write that they have done their work of destruction only too well. I could, were it worth while, copy in pages of lamentations, written by Frenchmen themselves, over the sweeping ruin worked by their countrymen. Their motto would seem to be "'*Delenda est Algiers.*' Let us do away with all relics of the past, sweep away all that is old, and sip our absinthe in peace in a commodious new French town, well supplied with *cafés* and drummers. So shall it be well with us!"

The Bab-Azzoun was the place where death-sentences were carried out, though I have been told that executions took place at either gate. Any way, the front of this gate was bristling with huge hooks, and the custom was to take the patient to the top, and hurl him down. The body would be arrested in its fall by one or other of the hooks, and there the poor wretch was left suspended till death put an end to his sufferings.

To sum up, run a white wall, not very high, which shall contain the triangle so often indicated; add the gates; and I suppose you will have old Algiers. I should presume the sort of barrack-looking place just outside the Porte d'Isly was an outlying fort. Otherwise the scrub, or undergrowth, would come up to the walls of the town, spotted here and there with country houses and little Arab villages, or collections of huts such as those which can still be seen at Tixeraïn or Bou-Zarea. On the side of the slope of Mustapha there were a few houses of superior pretensions, besides smaller ones, of which samples still remain. I can see them from the window at which I am writing; but one must in imagination make a tolerably clean sweep of all the modern white villas in the sort of kettle between this spot and the cemetery, or even the Koubba, and away to the Maison Carrée. It was all wild hill—I must not write *bleak*, for that word gives one rather the idea of a Cumberland fell—here, at least, was sunshine. On the other, or Bab-el-Ouad or St. Eugène side, there would be equal desolation, save a small fort or two and a few Arab houses, the country house of the last Dey (now the military hospital), and so away to the Valley of the Consuls, which it is not very easy to reach. You must drive up to the Church of Nôtre Dame d'Afrique, which is of course of modern construction, but where you will certainly stop to admire the splendid view. Beyond this the road becomes narrower and narrower; but, if you persevere, you will reach a point close to a modern fortification, further than which you cannot drive. The village of St. Eugène lies below. The furthest house from the town on the hill to the left was the house of the British Consul, Mr. Blanckley, the father of Mrs. Broughton, who has given us so interesting a book about the last days of Turkish Algiers. The really valuable part of this work is the diary of her mother, Mrs. Blanckley, who is quite an Algerine Boswell, and who, in a simple, unpretending way, paints a picture of Turkish Algiers as it was, which has not been equalled by any professed writer. I say it with regret, but I hope without discourtesy, that, judging from her own half of the book, Mrs. Broughton does not seem to have inherited her mother's literary gift of recording her impressions of the day as she felt them, and the facts of the day as she saw them. A certain interest will always hang about the old Consulate for the kind, shrewd old lady's sake.

Return somehow to the road, which runs by the seashore, and about a couple of miles from Algiers you would reach the modern village of St. Eugène, and about as much further the Pointe Pescade, on which there was an old fort, a relic of Turkish days, and beyond this yet another. The two forts (or what remains of them) belong to the past, as far as old Algiers is concerned; you may pretty well sweep away all the rest. You may easily reconstitute this northern side of Algiers in your own mind. Little need be done save to watch the sea breaking on the rocks in a way which would be creditable to the Cornish coast, and to glance upwards at Bou-Zarea, some 1200 or 1300 feet above you. This, and the forts, and the sparse villas in the Consular Valley, and the Dey's country house near to Algiers, and a few Arab or Turkish houses, would be what the pirates used to see. (I will speak in proper place of the winding road up to Bou-Zarea, of the Frais Vallon, etc.) This side of the town has only what may be called a tourist's interest for the visitors to Algiers, as no one seems desirous of fixing his residence here. People say it is very cold, and at any rate, as we drove along, and I asked the driver who lived in the various modern villas, his invariable answer was, "An enormously rich Jew."

I cannot say whether or no, as the town is in progress of development as a place of winter resort, builders and speculators may not turn their attention to this side, from over-populated, over-priced Mustapha; but certainly this has not been done yet. The Jews ought to know what they are about, as witness the West Cliff and King's Parade at Brighton; and, I suppose, if they see their way to making money, they will let their villas or build new ones; as yet no one seems to think of it. At Brighton it is West and East Cliff; at Algiers (speaking in a very rough way) it would be South and North Cliff; for the time visitors only affect the South Cliff. What will come of it I cannot say.

Returning to Algiers. I would recommend the visitor to pass through the modern Bab-el-Ouad, and not to waste too much time on the Jardin Marengo, which is only so far interesting inasmuch as it leads to the *Zaouia* of Sidi Abd-er-Rahman, an undoubted relic of the past. It is, I believe, about three hundred years old. The visitor must make his way through the usual knots of beggars affected with blindness and many forms of human infirmity, and, descending some flights of steps, he will reach the room which contains the tomb of this famous saint. I cannot say it affected me with much religious or solemn feeling. The room was covered with a collection of trumpery hangings and shawls and flags, with the invariable ostriches' eggs, and had much the look of the small show-room of a Turkish bazaar in our unbelieving land. We have all visited the sort of place, where you are made faint with the smell of pastilles, and where you make haste to buy a pair of slippers or a brass tray (probably made at Birmingham), and to effect your escape. Learned people who can decipher the inscriptions may think well of this holy place, but to me it seemed very like a doll's house. I have no doubt it is of considerable historical interest, as the slip-shod lad who served us as guide pointed out the graves of various worthies who were great men in the old Turkish days. See it by all means, and I trust the visitor may be inspired with thoughts more magnificent than any I was conscious of during my peep at the tomb of this famous saint. I did not see any of the cats which seem to have attracted the attention of Dean Blakesley when he visited the tomb in 1857. Perhaps they were asleep, as it was a hot afternoon when I was there.

I would parenthetically write a sentence or two about another monument which I found in the Jardin Marengo. I should no doubt have come across it myself, but—let the truth be told—Dean Blakesley set me a-looking for it. Here is the dean's description of it. " In the Jardin Marengo is a colossal bust of the first Emperor Napoleon . . . and near it another monument. On the top of a column is a half-globe, on the top of which is stuck an iron spear. On the east and west sides of the column are the names of the victories won by the great commander; on the north, those of the capitals which he had occupied by a victorious army; while, on the south, an eagle, all beak and claws, hovers over a hat of the peculiar kind which the emperor used to wear, from which are suspended the insignia of the Legion of Honour. Under this delicate symbolism, which, as far as its execution is concerned, might have been carved by a stone-cutter's apprentice, are the words, '*Il avait rêvé cette conquete,*'"—meaning, no doubt, of Africa. His African conquest certainly remains a dream. Even in Egypt, where the centuries contemplated the French troops from the top of the pyramids, not much came of the actual attempt. But here in Algiers! Have Frenchmen any sense of the ludicrous? The Boulogne monument at one end of the territory, and its Algerine fellow at the other, are, to say the least, remarkable works of imagination.

The emperor's cocked hat and his dreams have, however, not much to do with my present theme, so let us get back to Algiers, Turkish Algiers, for the moment. No doubt there would have been seen streets to the right and left like the modern Bab-Azzoun, and Bab-el-Ouad, and others winding up to the Kasbah; many of these last still remain. Perhaps the best way to obtain an idea of them is to ascend from the Place du Gouvernement to the synagogue, and, taking for your motto "Excelsior!" to stumble upwards as best you may through the narrow tortuous streets or alleys. As the walls of the houses in great measure bulge outwards, reckoning from the first floor, you will not be troubled with too much sunshine. You would scarcely suppose, as you pass the dirty, blank walls, with their mean-looking wooden doors, how very pretty the interiors often are, even in houses of small pretensions.

Here is an idea of an Algerine house. Push wide the half-opened door, and you will find yourself in what would be the hall in an English house. The hall varies in length as the depth of the house, and is narrow in proportion to its length. Little seats are constructed in spaces hollowed out in the wall, for it was here strangers had interviews with the owner of the house. At the end of what I have named the hall, you will find an opening, and an irregular, steep flight of steps, by which you ascend to what we should call the first floor, but here to a gallery, which goes round the interior court of the house. The gallery rests upon arches of the usual Arabic form, and upon pillars which are generally graceful and elegant. There may, though scarcely in this dirty quarter, be a second and upper gallery according to the size of the house. The rooms open on these galleries; those which I have seen are narrow, dark, and generally lofty. At the angles you will often find quaint little domes or *marabouts*. The walls of the rooms to a certain height are decorated with tiles, and there are narrow openings (in place of windows), frequently ornamented with stained glass, which let in a parti-coloured daylight.

In the older houses you will meet with very delicate woodwork, and work in plaster of a very exquisite kind, especially on the ceiling. I asked an Italian gentleman, a painter, who was kind enough to take me over his house near the port (it is one of the most beautiful in Algiers), what was the meaning of this profuse ornament in the upper portion of the room. His answer was that in the old days the Turkish or Arab owners used to make some sort of shake-down on the floor, and lie there for hours, smoking their pipes and delighting themselves with the ornaments above their heads. "*If not true*," etc. The invariable white terrace "crowned the edifice." The servants or slaves were huddled into dark holes on the ground floor, and round the walls of the gallery you will see recesses made for sofas and couches, deep cupboards, closets, etc. The fireplaces I saw at various times I set down in my own mind as a modern innovation.

One house seemed very much like another, distinguishable as larger or smaller, or as the property of a richer or a poorer owner, with the natural consequence of beautiful marble pillars or cheap white-washed pillars, as the case might be. All would be white, and, seen from the sea, would have much the appearance of a flight of white steps ascending from the port to the Kasbah.

The dirty lanes are pretty much as they were, save in so far as the French element has intruded itself. I reserve for separate mention the half-dozen really fine houses which have been spared by the French—such as the Governor's and Archbishop's palace, the Museum, the Cour d'Assises, and so on. Externally they could not have produced much effect. In the old Turkish times there were seventeen mosques, four are left—the Grand Mosque and the Mosque de la Pêcherie being the chief in importance.

At the beginning there was but one bagnio, or slave depôt, but afterwards, as the slaves increased in numbers, others were built. As old writers tell us, the bagnio was a large edifice, divided into cells capable of holding fifteen or sixteen wretches. Some few had the privilege of using a filthy mat, but the bulk lay upon the ground, which swarmed with vermin, insects, scorpions, etc. Five or six hundred slaves would be about the complement of a bagnio. There were many bagnios—one, I am told, near the Admiralty, another near the Bab-Azzoun gate, and I suppose some more. I have seen a good many pictures and read a good many books about old Algiers, which inspired me with much respect for the imaginative powers of the artists and writers; but really there is little more to be done than to sweep away every trace of everything French, reconstitute the triangle so often described, run a Turkish wall round it, and fill in the contained space with the mosques, the Dey's town palace, the bagnios, and a certain number of Moorish or Turkish houses; put in the gates, not forgetting the new gate (at the Boulevard Central) now destroyed, and the Mole gate, as well as the Fisher's gate; and the result would be Turkish or Piratical Algiers, with the sea at the base, and the Kasbah at the top. Old Dr. Shaw was chaplain to the British factory here about the beginning of the eighteenth century. He, of course, saw the place as it was, and he writes—

"This place, which for several ages has braved the

greatest Powers of Christendom, is not above a mile and a half in circuit, though it is computed to contain about 2000 Christian slaves, 15,000 Jews, and 100,000 Mahometans, of which thirty at most may be renegadoes. It is situated upon the declivity of a hill that faces the north and north-east, whereby the houses rise so gradually above each other, that there is scarce one but what, in one or other of these directions, has a full prospect of the sea. The walls are weak, and of little defence, unless they are further secured, which is chiefly at the gates, by some additional fortification. The Casaubah, or Citadel, built upon the highest part of the city, towards the south-west, is of an octagonal figure, each of the sides in view having port-holes or embrasures defended with cannon. A ditch formerly surrounded the whole city to the landward, which is at present almost entirely filled up, except at the west and south gates, called Bab-el-Ouad, the gate of the river, and Bab-Azoona, where it is still of little consequence or defence. But towards the sea it is better fortified, and capable of making a more strenuous defence. For the embrasures in this direction are all employed; the guns are of brass, and their carriages and other utensils in good order. The battery of the Mole gate upon the east angle of the city is mounted with several long pieces of ordnance, one of which has seven cylinders, each of them three inches in diameter. Half a furlong to the west-south-west of the harbour is the battery of Fisher's gate, or the gate of the sea, which, consisting of a double row of cannon, commands the entrance to the port and the road before it.

"The port itself is of an oblong figure, a hundred and thirty fathoms long, and eighty broad. The eastern mound of it, which was formerly the island which gave name to the city, is well secured by several fortifications. The Round Castle, built by the Spaniards whilst they were masters of the island, and the two remote batteries erected within this century, are said to be bomb-proof, and have each of them their lower embrasures mounted with thirty-six pounders. But the middle battery, which appears to be the oldest, is of the least defence. Yet none of these fortifications are assisted either with mines or advanced works; and, as the soldiers who are to guard and defend them cannot be kept to any regular course of duty and attendance, a few resolute battalions, protected by a small squadron of ships, would find little difficulty to take them.

"*There is very little within the city that merits the attention of the curious.*

* * * * *

"The hills and valleys round about Algiers are all over beautified with gardens and country seats, whither the inhabitants of better fashion retire during the heats of the summer season. They are little white houses, shaded with a variety of fruit trees and evergreens, which, besides the shade and retirement, afford a gay and delightful prospect towards the sea. The gardens are all of them well stocked with melons, fruits, and pot-herbs of all kinds, and what is chiefly regarded in these hot climates, each of them enjoys a great command of water, from the many rivulets and fountains which everywhere abound in this situation. The fountain water made use of at Algiers, universally esteemed for its excellency, is likewise brought through a long course of pipes and conduits from the same sources."

So far Dr. Shaw, who is a direct witness of what he saw with his own eyes, so his description is of value.

CHAPTER VI.

TORQUAY IN AFRICA.

I HAVE now come to that point in my poor attempt at description which most closely concerns my countrymen, or at least as many of them as are in the habit of going far a-field to seek for warmth and blue skies during the *nivoses, pluvioses,* and *ventoses* of Northern Europe.

"Mustapha Supérieur," say the enthusiasts, "is the Torquay of the future." Let us have done with all half measures. If we are driven from our pleasant firesides and our pleasant friends, at least let us get something real in return. I, for one, do not think that Torquay is in any immediate danger. The change will not come suddenly. Many people will shrink from a sea voyage of five hundred miles. The accommodation on the European side is vastly superior to anything which can yet be found at Algiers. In time, supply will of course follow demand, if demand there should be. As it is made clear to speculators that money is to be made by building villas and hotels here on the slopes of the Sahel, the villas and hotels will no doubt be built. At present let English families, *especially if they count invalids amongst their members,* think well of it before they allow themselves to be cast ashore at Algiers. There are very few good villas in the market, and these probably will have been snapped up by people who know the truth of things; or by those who have friends on the spot who know Algiers well; or, in the last resort, by the early comers. During the winter, family after family have been compelled to return to France, or to go on to Spain (through Oran), or to content themselves with very insufficient accommodation.

A friend in England, exhilarated, no doubt, by my rejoicings over the warmth I had found at last, wrote me word to secure for him at once a little "box" on Mustapha—"A sort of 'sun-trap,' don't you know? that kind of thing." I did know, too well, but, alas! you don't stumble upon sun-traps in the country at every step. In the first place, the villas are built with an eye to the prospect rather than to the sun; and, in the next, they are constructed rather as refuges against the sun in the summer than as hot-houses in which to enjoy the sun during the winter. Then there was the question of price to be considered. However much a man may desire sunshine, it is not every one who has so much of it in his pocket that he can cheerfully engage himself to pay £300 or £400 for a sun-trap during the winter months, being conscious that he must at the same time keep up the establishment in Ennismore Gardens, or that semi-feudal arrangement at Squattlesea-cum-Slush, with the various retainers of stables, kennels, and farm-yard. A man will dribble out a sharp rent at Torquay or Bournemouth, month after month, but he does not like to look the truth boldly in the face, and write off the £400 or

£500 for winter rent at one stroke of his pen. No! the comfortable hotel, such as you find it on the Riviera or on the Italian lakes (where you get taken in, and lodged, fed, and so on, at a reasonable rate per week or per month), simply does not exist on Mustapha, nor will you readily find a small villa adapted to small pockets; nor even a large villa where money is no consideration. As for the few places which are described as *Pensions*, as I have said elsewhere, the best advice I can give to any one who might be driven in a moment of despondency to make trial of them, would be contained in the simple monosyllable, "Don't." Either under the head of hotels, villas, or pensions, Mustapha at present is sadly wanting in resource.

Mustapha is on a long range of hills, or on a basin of hills, if you like, called the Sahel. Although not of uniform level, it may be taken as being six hundred feet above the bay; but the villas which, even now, are dotted about it, stand at all heights, from six hundred to two hundred feet above the sea-level; and, under the name of Mustapha Inférieur, even go down to the sea. The views from most parts of it are most lovely. It would be difficult to exaggerate the beauty of the place. All round the semicircle, from the gate of Algiers to the Koubba, it is all Mustapha. Call it the Village d'Isly, the Chemin de l'Aqueduc, the El-Biar road at the top, the Telegraph Hill, and round to the cemetery—I repeat—it is all Mustapha. With the range of distant mountains in view (even with the snow-covered tops of the Djudjura at times), with the cloudless African sky above, and the blue sea below, it is indeed a good place of refuge from snow, fog, and semi-darkness.

But we cannot always live amongst the sublimities. Human life largely consists of eating and drinking, and of going to bed, and of being comfortable. What is wanted at Algiers is a good hotel, or, indeed, half a dozen good hotels on Mustapha, such as there are at Cannes and elsewhere, and, until this be done, Algiers will prove a disappointment to most people. The heads of the good people here seem all turned upon the subject of villa building. Last year there was a bad season. This year, 1879–80, the number of visitors has been far in excess of the accommodation. The cry has followed, "Let us build, and be rich." The land on Mustapha is limited in quantity, and is for the most part bought up. The happy owners think they have got hold of a mine of wealth. I strongly recommend caution. Fashion has accommodated itself to the southern shore of Europe; the sea voyage to many is a great drawback; the disappointed visitors of the season have all gone home in a state of exasperation, and that "Den of Fever, Algiers!" will be the cry of too many of them. Besides, political uncertainties must be taken into account. I see by the *Akhbar* of this morning (March 5) that the Algerines are beginning to look askance at the numerous Germans who are coming over, and have already raised the cry of "Prussian spies." They are persuaded that Germany is undermining the ground under their feet, in Morocco on one side, and the Italians at Tunis on the other. All this may be midsummer madness, but there it is. As long as they are left in peace, the hold of the French on the country is firm enough; but I would not answer for results in case of conflict with any European Power. The natives, thoroughly crushed and beaten, will not stir by themselves; but, if they found serious European backers, I should be sorry to deliver policies of insurance upon their lives to French residents in Algiers. One of the consequences of their conquest, and, far more, of their administration of half a century, has been that the French have concentrated on themselves all the hatred of race and religion which this country can provide. I admit the political danger to be a remote contingency; but still people who were thinking of building or buying land here should certainly take it into account. The more present and obvious objections are many. Here, if anywhere, act upon the old saying, "Let fools build houses for wise men to live in." Should excited capitalists operate freely in villa building at this place, I, for one, should be well content to wait and see what the price of a villa would be a few years hence.

But about the hotel or hotels. If a company with sufficient capital could be found to take the matter up, I think there could be little doubt of a favourable result. People don't want to be tied for years, or even for a season. They desire to come and go at their pleasure, and I am very sure that sufficient enthusiasm already exists about Algiers to send people here in shoals if they could find easy accommodation. Both in town and country it is sadly deficient as yet. That is my cuckoo cry. Until the public know that Algiers and Mustapha are thoroughly well drained, and until we have good hotels, the Riviera is safe enough from serious rivalry on this side. The place is most beautiful;

the delight of spending so many hours in the open air daily is great; but the disadvantages are numerous at present. It is a shame to send invalids to Algiers until you have made sure that they can be housed or lodged in a comfortable and sufficient way.

CHAPTER VII.

WALKS AND DRIVES IN AND ABOUT ALGIERS.

ALGIERS is the great sight of Algiers, though not of Algeria.

Could a curtain be drawn up in November in poor old foggy London, and could the benighted inhabitants catch but a glimpse of what we Algerines behold every day of our lives, there would be such an exodus southwards as would soon clear the banks of the Thames. It is the sky, the sun, the sea, which to me make up Algiers, and it is impossible to exaggerate the beauty of the scene. I have had to speak, and I shall have still further to speak, of various drawbacks on the place, but *Algiers is very beautiful*. To use the common phrase: "One's breath is quite taken away" at first. "Gush" would appear to be the natural language of mankind. But when one gets down from these transcendentalisms and looks about him a little, it is only right to describe mere fact. Ingenious guide-book writers have taught us how to see Venice in eight days—a task which, when I was younger and stronger, I could never accomplish; I really think, if your strength held out, that you could see Algiers in eight hours. Use one of the little open carriages, which you will always find ready on the Place du Gouvernement, to supplement your bodily powers and save your legs, and to carry you about from point to point.

I suppose a visitor would walk out to the lighthouse, and have a peep at the old piratical harbour; he might spend half an hour poking about in the immediate neighbourhood. He would enter the two mosques, which are taken in almost at a glance, and, if the kadi were actually sitting, he would spend a few minutes over an Arabic divorce case; and visit the fish market. He would come back to the Place, and would ascend by the cathedral (a very few minutes would suffice for this), and give a couple of hours to the old Arab town. The Kasbah and the little mosque with the long name, overlooking the Jardin Marengo, would require but a very short time. With the help of the carriage, you would soon see what little there is to be seen of the old walls. The town palace of the Governor, the Archbishop's palace, the Cour d'Assises, and the Museum, are the four old houses most worthy of notice, and having been to these you would have seen houses enough. In an hour's drive you would easily have run through the various boulevards, places, and streets, as a mere sight. If this should be thought too heavy a programme for a single day, in two days it might be lounged through, and you have seen Algiers—the town.

Those who are strong afoot would find half a dozen good "long walks" in the neighbourhood; but as I am, unfortunately, compelled to undertake such adventures in a light carriage, I prefer to speak of them as "short drives." Were I asked for a suggestion or two by any one whose time was short, I should say there are six drives, which would include many smaller ones. One of them is a real drive—and you must give the best part of a day to it—I mean that to the Trappists' Convent. You leave Algiers by St. Eugène, and so pass round by Guyotville, Staoueli, Cheragas, and home by El-Biar. There is a much shorter but a very pleasant drive on the other side to Birmandreis and the Valley of the Femme Sauvage. This can be enlarged by a turn to Birkhadem, and the little Arab village of Tixeraïn, about which, under favour, the guide-books have been far too magnificent.

The best of all the Algerine drives is that to the hill of Bou-Zarea. Leave Algiers by the Porte du Sahel, pass through El-Biar, and, turning to the right, you will soon reach the few houses which constitute the village. Pass on, however, from a quarter to a third of a mile further, to the little Arab cemetery (by no means omit to do this), and you will have a view which is unequalled even in this place of beautiful views. Nor should you forget to visit the Arab huts, in the midst of a labyrinth of prickly pear on the other side of the road, which are better worth seeing than those of Tixeraïn. Return home by the valley of Bou-Zarea, a most beautiful road, and you will find yourself again at the Bab-el-Ouad. This was our favourite drive during our stay at Algiers.

Another and a shorter one, but easily within the competence of a man of moderate walking powers, as a walk, is the drive to the Frais Vallon. You leave Algiers by the Bab-el-Ouad; instead of keeping the

Bou-Zarea Valley road, hold more to the left, and in a short time the carriage will deposit you at a little *café*. The rest must be done on foot, and you will make the walk longer or shorter according to your powers. We used to get as far as the house of the Arab doctor. Another short drive is to Nôtre Dame d'Afrique; after enjoying the view, out of respect for the memory of kind old Mrs. Blanckley, in place of returning to Algiers, continue on past the seminary—in fact, till you can go no further, and see the surf and the village of St. Eugène below. If you want to get absolutely to the old British Consulate, you must turn to the left before reaching this point. It is pleasant enough to drive to the Jardin d'Essai after lunch, and to wander about for a while under the stately avenues of palms. If time serves, you can afterwards continue the drive by the Ruisseau and the Koubba, and reach Algiers by Birmandreis and the Colonne Voirol; this is a very pretty route. I think these are the chief drives about Algiers which we were in the habit of taking (with the exception of La Trappe, which is distant some ten miles). Of course they may be considerably diversified by different turnings here and there; but these make up substantially the domestic drives from Algiers. The habit of disseminating cards, which exists in full virulence at this place, will take you into many an odd lane and turning; but these are the drives. We lived on the top of Mustapha, and a very constant drive with us (I do not include it in my list) was to the Colonne Voirol, by the El-Biar road, and the Cheragas road, nearly to Cheragas, but this was repeated for the sake of the view, and mainly of the fresh air. Much will depend on the starting-point.

There are many pretty walks about Mustapha. I think our favourite one was to a quaint little Moorish *café*, called the Café Hydra. You reach it from the El-Biar road by turning off through the grounds of "The Sisters." Here are to be seen the remains of an old Roman aqueduct, picturesque enough. There are pleasant walks about the Telegraph Hill, with fine views both of old Algiers, and of the Atlas range across the Metidja. The English cemetery is a picturesque, if a sad sight, and the walk there from the Telegraph Hill is delightful. One of the great charms of this stroll will be found in the back views on Algiers. You see the town face to face—Arab town, Kasbah and all, and the geometrical-looking harbour so full of steamers and shipping and yachts. (Egad! I wonder if there are any letters for us to-day.)

There is one ravine in particular which would make a perfect picture, with its African scrub, and the blue sea down at the bottom. At length we reach the cemetery, and I begin to feel something pinching at my heart, for I am here to look for the grave of a dear friend who went to his rest at Algiers many years ago. The English cemetery is apart from the Roman Catholic division, and is very tidily kept. Alas! for that fresh grave; in it there lies a poor young fellow with whom we had laughed and jested not so many weeks ago, under the Oasis. Some pious hand has laid a garland on his grave. There lies a young lady whose relations at least were well known to us. But it will not do to give way to this sort of thing; I myself may be here before the winter is out. What is the use of making a disturbance? No! the grave of which I am in search is some way off, in a corner, and there lies poor

AUGUSTUS EGG, R.A.,

dear to many, distasteful I should think to none. What bright evenings we have seen with him at Little Camden House, where he had fixed his abode, and where we used to play bowls with lanterns on the ground, when it grew dark! What a society, and well-nigh all gone of those bright spirits, save Wilkie Collins! Of the others, Charles Dickens, John Leech, and many who have not left their like amongst living men—*gone*. How it comes before me, the bright room ringing with laughter, with the laughter of the immortals—for such they are now! I cannot, however, say fine things to make me content. They stick in my throat. Why should such men be swept prematurely away, whilst others———? A fig for your stale commonplaces, and pills of consolation. God bless you, dear old friend! I can't do you any good by loitering here with wet eyes; so, farewell, since it must be so.

There are plenty of lanes, and plenty of paths by which you may diverge from the main roads, so that Algiers cannot be said to be without walks; it is, in fact, rather above than below the average of Southern watering-places. There is one point emphatically in its favour. You are not wearied here with the eternal white walls which render the neighbourhood of most

Italian towns a mere tiresome monotony to the visitor. I would only add that the country walks about Algiers are rather far from the town, certainly those on the Mustapha side. A man stopping at the Orient or the Régence, who wished to take his pastime in our lanes, has a good way to walk on what we should call in England the turnpike road, or in other words, along the dusty suburbs of a French town, before he reaches our Mustapha lanes. The best plan is to take one or other of the omnibuses which constantly ply between Algiers and Mustapha Supérieur (twice in the day between Algiers and the Colonne Voirol, distance about three miles); he can then begin his walk. A visitor must find out most of these for himself, but let him remember that after rain that nuisance, an "Arab lane," is more of a nuisance than ever; let him prefer bye-paths after a couple of days of dry weather. As I am writing in the hope that my suggestions may prove of use to visitors, I will here recapitulate the six drives I recommend.

1. Trappist Convent at Staoueli. Go by the coast, return by Cheragas and El-Biar.

2. To Femme Sauvage Valley by lower road; Birmandreis, Birkhadem, Tixeraïn; home by Colonne Voirol.

3. Bou-Zarea. Go by the Porte du Sahel and El-Biar; return by Bou-Zarea ravine, and the Bab-el-Ouad.

4. Frais Vallon; partly walk.

5. Nôtre Dame d'Afrique; old English Consulate.

6. Jardin d'Essai—home by Ruisseau, Koubba, Birmandreis, Colonne Voirol.

The Jardin d'Essai and back would be a pleasant little drive by itself, allowing time to see the garden. I say nothing more in my list of the drive on the Cheragas road, which simply means carriage exercise for residents on Mustapha or El-Biar.

CHAPTER VIII.

THE IRRITABLE TOWN: CAP AND BELLS.

"'AGATHA, shut the door,' but Agatha stirred not." Such is the opening of Mrs. Opie's notable work on "Temper." Well, I recommend all persons who are meditating a sojourn at Algiers to read that little book before they do anything decisive. Charles Lamb's hints as to the best way of nursing a grievance against your nearest and dearest might also be profitably considered. The fact seems to be—account for it as you may—that the temper does become wonderfully "short" at Algiers.

Dr. Bodichon tells us, "Algiers possesses a climate favourable for lymphatic temperaments. The excess of heat and light is favourable to them, giving them the tone they require. . . . It is prejudicial to persons suffering from any malady of the nerves, since the climate increases nervous irritability; also to drunkards, who will pay their penalty in sanguineous congestion and fevers; and for all subject to derangement of their mental faculties."

That last clause is a large drag-net. Take the bulk of pilgrims from London or Paris, who have been passing their existence under high pressure, and I fear they are all slightly cracked, or, as our French friends would say, *surexcités*. It would scarcely be civil to dear Mrs. Jones to hint to her that her numerous admirers had become painfully aware of the fact that a large bee was always buzzing about under her graceful little bonnet; but such is the case. She would no doubt have a good deal to say for herself by way of confession and avoidance. "Six girls, my dear, to bring out, and marry off; hypertrophy in the red books every Monday morning; the necessity of keeping up our entertainments upon a falling budget; and then dear Mr. Jones's little peculiarities whilst my poor head is too often distracted. My dear, I often wonder that I am still alive." Let Mrs. Jones avoid Algiers, and try Holland, the Hague, Scheveningen, and cold bathing. Nor should I advise dear old Lady de Chignon to pass the winter on the Sahel without a little preliminary talk with her ladyship's maid and her long-suffering companion.

"The climate of Algiers," writes that terrible Dr. Bodichon, "produces selfishness by augmenting the personality." I can scarcely think that, medically speaking, it would be politic to augment her ladyship's personality or her selfishness, for, were this done, a catastrophe might occur at the Moorish villa on Mustapha; and the maid and the companion might be found some morning only too fast asleep.

"The climatic action," Bodichon again, "results from an over-excitement of the nervous system, and an increase of sensibility to the detriment of reason." I should suppose that a course of mud-baths somewhere or another in Germany might meet the exigencies of her ladyship's case; or still better, let her remain in England, and take her usual carriage exercise, attended by the poodle in a yellow vehicle hermetically sealed so as to exclude the outer fog. Great advantage might also result from the constant society of experienced ladies who could reckon by springs equal in number to her own, and who were not wholly unaware of the secret workings of English society. To speak plainly, let the lady stop at home in her own set. Young gentlemen who have indulged too freely in what they call B S—whatever they may be—and interminable "pegs"—the word has a meaning—had better keep away from Algiers, or they will pay the penalty in "sanguineous congestion." *A fortiori*, the red-faced old Pickwicks of the Pall Mall Clubs, who have fared sumptuously every day for three score years and ten, would do well to avoid our African health resort. As you value your safety—*Boodlers, Beware!* Chance bronchitis in England; but do not rush on grim certainties in Algiers.

Now for a word of comfort. The doctor is of opinion that Calvinists and Puritans will "be able to resist the baleful effects of the sirocco better than other people." If they be of lymphatic temperament, all the better. But if too fat—lymph and Calvinism to the contrary notwithstanding—let them stay away.

"The diet of the European in Algiers," writes Dr. Bodichon, "should be tonic; use meat, fish, oysters, lobsters, and other substances containing iodine. Use port or claret as a beverage; avoid tea, since it increases perspiration." All this reads strangely like a page from Tristram Shandy, but I suppose the doctor knows what he is talking about. So, if you are of a lymphatic temperament, of Puritanic or Calvinistic tendencies, but not too fat, come to Algiers and crunch your lobsters in peace. Nor will an oyster or two thrown in from time to time cause you prejudice.

An English gentleman, a traveller, who seemed to have given great attention to this subject, was good enough to tell me the other day that, hygienically speaking, we are all in zones. Whether the zone be atmospheric or terrene I cannot say. Now, Algiers, according to him, was in the plague and fever zone. Let us put up our boots and brushes, and be off at once. But stay, not so fast. Plague and fever are not instant and constant, there is only a remote liability; but human infirmities take this direction. In this present winter of 1880 you are not likely to gain the plague; but you will, pretty surely, lose your temper. That is a very different matter, so I will go out for a little walk, and think it over.

I know not how it may be with others, but my poor attempts to think a matter over generally result in my thinking of what I shall have for dinner, or something equally frivolous and nugatory. But who comes here, flying rather than walking up the Arab path? An Arab path is merely a stiff, dirty lane, full of stones and disagreeables of all kind. It is my dear little friend, Violet Dash. I have known her since she was a child—in fact as well as in name; and a brighter, more reasonable, a more truthful and straightforward girl I have never known.

"Well, Violet, how are you getting on this morning? How are you?"

"Cross, decidedly cross. Don't speak to me."

"But, Violet, I have not done you any harm."

"No, but I dare say you will—everybody is so spiteful at Algiers."

"I hope there are exceptions, Miss Violet; but where are you bound?"

"I am going up to the Joneses, to have it out with Sybilla; she was quite too nasty at lawn tennis yesterday."

"I say, Miss Violet, keep your temper."

"My what?" screamed the young angel. "I am the only girl in Algiers who does keep her temper. However, I will tell Sybilla my mind 'in plain English.'"

"That I am sure you will, Violet."

"What's that? You do not mean to hint that I have lost my temper? But goodness gracious! what's all this noise about?"

The noise proceeded from five Kabyle dogs, clearly out of temper, who were chained up all in a row, straining at five chains, and barking and yelling like five fiends. Above each of their heads was a board inscribed with the words, "*Passage interdit, chasse reservée;*" this being the amiable way in which kind people guard from intrusion their residence, in Mustapha Supérieur, and protect their game, which may or may not consist of an over-excited sparrow. It was with considerable pains I could induce the young lady, who is as brave as a young lioness, not to go up, and what she called "thump" the dogs with her parasol, for I feared one of the animals might break his chain; so Violet contented herself with pronouncing an allocution over them upon the advantages of never getting out of temper.

The whole concluded with a laugh like the old times, and a—

"Well, I suppose I'm out of temper myself, and as ridiculous as any one of you brutes. I never used to be so till I came to Algiers—not what you'd call really out of temper; just put out, or 'tiffy,' for a moment; but that doesn't count. I don't think I will go up to the Joneses this morning."

"Bravo, Violet; and give Miss Sybilla a wide berth for the next week."

"I am not sure, but I am cross. I suppose it is something in the air."

I thought so too, and I want to preach for a page or two with my dear little friend Violet for a text. I elicited from her on other occasions that all the other girls at Algiers (I should say young ladies, Violet), were just as bad, nay, worse, as she called it, than herself. Now, here was a young girl, with all on her side—youth, strength, happy disposition, all the world could give her; and, there was no doubt about it, "Violet's temper was gone."

What, then, was to become of the old people who had gone through the various troubles of life; who had been condemned to the perusal of Parliament out of session, and such like; who had been privileged by the kindness of friends to take shares in various industrial projects of great promise; who had dined out too constantly in London; who had had their young hopes blighted by sylphs of all sizes and complexions; and finally, all the tops of whose heads wore that shining and "polishy" appearance which induces gifted hairdressers to recommend the use of various valuable nostrums?

If my bright young friend Violet could not keep her temper in check at Algiers, how about the poor fellows who placed their hopes on dinner pills? However, "elegant females," as Mr. Norris calls them, are mere bundles of nerves. It might be better with males of more robust texture; so I thought I would prosecute inquiries in this direction. Now, I know at Algiers, a gentleman in middle life, apparently calm, *debonnaire*, and self-controlled, to all outward seeming the most courteous of human beings. He hails from South Devon, and has been nourished for years on clotted cream, and the damp and somewhat "muggy" air of delightful Devonshire. Surely here was a crucial case. I met him by chance, and stated my difficulty.

"I say, Brown, do you think there is anything in the air of this place which makes a man, say, a little touchy?"

A shade passed over Brown's face, and he cast at me a somewhat inquiring glance. "Have you heard anything about it?"

"No. What do you mean?"

"I mean my adventure with the cabman the other day, and my little passage of arms with the clerk at the telegraph office. They were very irritating; but I am thoroughly ashamed of myself—in fact, I lost my temper. The truth was I hired a cabman the other day to take my wife and myself from the Place to Mustapha and back again, and he had the face to ask me 12fr. 50c. I couldn't make him hear reason; one word brought up another, and the end of it was I seized him by the cravat, and gave him a good shaking. Two of their policemen, with swords, came up and pulled me off, saying, '*Soyez calme, monsieur! soyez calme!*' but they got just as bad as the cabman or myself. I had to pay the 12fr. 50c., and something besides, to save myself from being dragged off to the station, and finally the man who had foamed at the mouth himself, let me go, saying, '*Dorénavant, monsieur, soyez calme! à Alger il faut du calme, beaucoup de calme!*' As for the telegraph office, I was there trying to make the fellow understand what I wanted. It was only to send a telegram to Bovey Tracey, written in a fair clear hand, and you know I speak their language pretty well. But the man couldn't or wouldn't understand; so at last, in a moment of excitement, which nobody can regret more than myself, I flung the pen—it was full of ink—in his face, saying, '*Prenez ça!*' But I was myself in a moment again, and made a handsome apology, which stuck a good bit in my throat, but I got through it somehow. I was never so before. Yes, there must be something in the climate which makes a man *lose his temper*."

I thought so too, and, strangely enough, that very day I met a lady, a very valued friend, who had also had an altercation with a cabman; needless to say, she had not shaken the man, but declined to pay him, and allowed herself to be called to the police-court.

Her case was that, according to the tariff, she should have paid five francs (any arbitrary sum you please) from the Place to any part of the Commune, in which she resides, emphatically to the church. Now, her house lay a little off the road—in the Commune, but not as far as the church. At the hearing—I was not present—everybody seems to have got *surexcité*: the cabman was desired to *rester calme;* my friend is cursed with a sense of justice and an indiscreet zeal for fair play; the presiding magistrate's cry was, "*Soyons calmes!*" the usher roared out, "*Soyez calmes!*" and a nice time they must have had of it. Of course, the case was decided against the lady on the first attempt at a calm and friendly settlement; so it was resolved they should have a regular summons, and proceed *secundum artem*. The clerk of the court recommended calmness, but as his worship had merely to grind his teeth and repronounce his interlocutory judgment, you may be sure he did so. My friend sarcastically observed that her sole desire was to ascertain whether or no the tariff made and promulgated by the police was or was not a valid document? (*Soyez calme!*) She was now satisfied that it was merely frivolous and vexatious (*vive sensation*), and would know what to do for the future (*du calme, madame!*); meanwhile she would try the prefecture. The court proceeded to grind its teeth over a fresh case. The poor lady had certainly been mistaken in her choice of a domicile, for she was afflicted with a sense of justice, and a more terrible affliction could scarcely be conceived at Algiers.

As I cast my eyes round Mustapha, now that I

know something of the people and their lives, I have learnt that each villa has a *procès*—some of them two or three—with its neighbour. "The right of way" is the direful spring of woes unnumbered upon Upper Mustapha.

A Hebrew solicitor in London, when handling a party wall, would, however, have a good deal to learn from an Algerine colleague who had got hold of a "right of way" case.

Judging from the experience of all persons I have consulted, from the endless squabbles of the place, from the multitude of cases in which the intervention of the authorities has been invoked, and from the entirely trumpery nature of the matters in issue, I can with difficulty avoid Dr. Bodichon's conclusion, that "the climate of Algiers increases nervous irritability."

A word, then, to the wise. If you are conscious of this tendency in your constitution, keep to a milder and less exciting climate. *Algiers is scarcely the place for Sir Anthony Absolute.* The fact must have a distinct medical significance, although I am too ignorant of such matters to give it fair discussion.

Closely connected with this question of nervous irritation is the all-important one of sleep. My own experience is merely that of an individual, and each case should be judged on its own grounds. Although throughout the day I may, like my neighbours, have felt the climate to be an exciting one, I have never slept better than at Algiers. It is a blessed conclusion, indeed, that you can lay your head on your pillow at 9 or 10 p.m., and be sure of seven or eight hours of refreshing and continuous sleep. No more of those terrible watches of the night, when you awake between 2 and 3 a.m. after the first false start, and lie awake till daylight, quietly thinking over every disagreeable event of your life, and none of the pleasant ones; when the thought of the two or three persons who have done you wrong makes itself felt with such terrible effect, and you lose sight altogether of the scores of pleasant women and good fellows with whom you have passed many agreeable days. No more of those unsatisfactory uprisings when you enter upon the duties of the day, with your eyes scorched and your temples throbbing. You really have had a good night's sleep. I am told this is the crucial test, if you would know whether the place suits you or not. Do you sleep well at night? If you do, stay; if you do not, go.

But again, in discussing the matter with many of my fellow-sufferers, it was a very common case to find that a patient slept well on his first arrival in Algiers, and for some weeks afterwards, but then not so well—in fact, very badly. In such cases I suppose that two or three weeks at Algiers may give the constitution just the fillip it requires, but when sleep seems about to fail, I should be off to Cannes or the Riviera, which are the handiest places for an Algerine fugitive.

It would seem as though the irritating qualities of the air affect the French much in the same way as the English residents, and sometimes with tragical results. Within a few days of our arrival a duel was fought between two French gentlemen, a military officer and a civilian. The civilian was shot, and I was informed that the quarrel was the result of a discussion about the old, old story. I was also told that duels were frequent, but as the custom has almost passed out of the habits of English life, it would be idle to waste much ink upon the subject.

It is pretty clear that if the same state of feeling existed at modern Algiers as prevailed in Dublin in Sir Jonas Barrington's time, we should hear the crack of the pistol over Mustapha throughout the day. It certainly astonishes any one who is not accustomed to the ways and manners of the place to remark the lively fashion in which two of the old hands will flatly contradict each other upon the most trivial point, and how hot the discussion will wax. If I remember right the formula used by the great tragic actor in Charles Dickens's tale was as follows :—" Object of my scorn and hatred, I regard ye with contempt." Well, they don't say that; but the discussion would run : "Sirocco again to-day." "Nothing of the sort." "I know better." "You are quite wrong; nothing of the kind." "Pooh!" "Pish!"

I cannot help thinking there is a good deal of sirocco about, and that such an interchange of amenities is the proof of the fact. To a casual visitor, however, all this signifies but little. His business is clearly not to contradict anybody, and to possess his soul in peace. As accommodation increases, and as people become less dependent upon each other, there will be less and less of these absurdities. Of course, there are bores and positive ladies and gentlemen at Torquay or at Nice, but they are lost in the general crowd. If the society of a particular person is distasteful to you, you simply avoid him; but here at Algiers he is your fellow-yachtsman, your fellow-traveller, your fellow-guest in a country house. You must live with your bore as you would with a bodily ailment, and look to palliatives.

The great remedy—and I cannot insist on the point too often—is the creation of an hotel or hotels in sufficient quantity upon Mustapha; just as you find them at Cannes, on the Riviera, on the Italian lakes. You should be able to come when you like, go when you like, have the quiet of your own apartment when you like, or the mad excitement of the *table d'hôte* to raise your spirits as you may please. If anything or any person be disagreeable to you, you should have the same facilities for shifting your quarters that you have in Europe; and then pretentious bores and tiresome people would shake into their proper places. This is in the common interest of us all; but I am sorry to say the dog-in-the-manger feeling appears to prevail amongst the residents. "What! bring an annual crowd of visitors in on us from Europe, and vulgarize the place? Rather let typhoid and phylloxera and the Gulf of Lyons do their worst than that we should see rows of villas and invalid crescents on sacred Mustapha. Who can bear this intolerable wrong? Let us retire to Timbuctoo, and the sublimity of genteel solitude." Try Timbuctoo by all means, and when the world may require Timbuctoo, try further off.

There is, however, no mistake at all about the climate of this place, though it has proved very different from what I supposed it would be last October when we landed here. The climate has been delicious, though we have had a good deal of rain (there had been three dry seasons). On many days we have found it fresh enough when out for our afternoon drive on the Bou-Zarea heights or on the Cheragas road. Bring with you the same clothing that you would provide for autumn and winter use in England; you will not want it every day, but days will come when you will want it. But the climate *for those it suits* is delicious; I do not believe there is anything like it within four days or seven days of London.

The accommodation, both in the town and in the country, is sadly deficient.

The French, by universal consent, appear to avoid the place; it clearly does not suit *them*. People tell me that in the days of General Chanzy, the late governor, there was some little life and stir at Algiers; but M. Grévy, his successor, does not appear to consider it any part of his duty to exercise hospitality or to "receive." This, I suppose, accounts for the fact that the French people stop away. No doubt amongst the married officers of the higher grades, and the upper civil *employés*, there must be esoteric society of a certain kind, but foreigners will not see much of this. The English residents appear to give occasional luncheons to each other and to their intimates, and lawn-tennis to the young folks. I should say, despite of these praiseworthy efforts, that Algiers for young people is a dreary place. There is a theatre which may be visited by those stopping at the hotels in the town, but it is beyond the reach of those living on Mustapha. A casino, with its balls and its music, does not exist. Although the subject possesses no personal interest for myself, I should think that young ladies and gentlemen who want amusement would do well to avoid Algiers as I would a London fog in November. Nor, indeed, will older persons find much of the pleasant little sociabilities to which they have been accustomed at home. If you want to be comfortable here set about the business as Robinson Crusoe would have done in his island.

I have had the pleasure of being on terms of cordial friendship with Robinson Crusoe, and were it permitted me to mention his name, I should be glad to acknowledge publicly, as I have often done privately, our grateful sense of the kindness we (in common with scores of others) received during the winter from his lady and himself. My friend, Mr. Crusoe, is a man of large fortune, so he can do what he likes. Now, he has liked to take one of the few good villas in Algiers, well up on Mustapha, handy to the high road but not too near it. He has good stables, good carriages and horses; he has brought over from England everything his heart can desire, and his own servants. Even so, as he told me, it took him two or three years to make himself comfortable. As it is, he spends his winters in a pleasant, sunny house on Mustapha. As expenses, *aliunde* (as of provisions and such like), are the same at Algiers as in England, it comes to this, that the cost of these winter quarters is just the rent of the villa and the travelling fares.

Yes, there is the plain truth. With a villa on Mustapha—if you can get one; with a carriage and horses, which you can hire here, if you can't do better; with a spare bedroom or two, which you can fill with friends from England, who will be only too thankful for the chance of "a month at Algiers,"—you may get on comfortably enough, and enjoy the **climate.** Algiers will give you sunshine—it will give you little else.

I hope this little dissertation about Mr. Crusoe will not sound like "tall talk." Take a villa on a more **moderate scale, if it suits you.** I repeat it, other things being equal in either country, the difference of cost between spending your **winter** in Algiers **or** at home is just the **rent of the** villa and the travelling expenses.

CHAPTER IX.

THE CLIMATE OF ALGIERS: FOR INVALIDS.

I WRITE this chapter under a sense of serious responsibility. These words of mine can never rise to the dignity of a well-weighed conclusion thought out by a competent person. They may, however, fall into the hands of some poor invalids who may be tempted into a trap which I have unwittingly baited with sunshine, and the sun-trap may be just the wrong place. It is a shameful thing to write careless words which may do harm to others; so here is my preliminary caution, and let it be seriously taken to heart. The climate of Algiers, for good or for evil, must be a potent agency, therefore, "Do not let any real invalid come to this place save under medical advice." I would not only take counsel in such a case with European doctors, but I would, on arrival at Algiers, place the patient under the immediate eye of one or other of the very competent medical gentlemen here, who know the climate and its effects.

A word or two about the climate generally *as we have found it*, but they tell us here that no one season is like another at Algiers. One can scarcely go so far as that, or it would not be worth while to record the impressions of any particular season. There are, I suppose, at Algiers, as elsewhere, wetter and drier winters, warmer and colder seasons, but there must be an average. I copy in here from Colonel Playfair's "Guide," page 5, an official table of the vagaries of the thermometer at this place. It is drawn up at the Hôpital du Dey, the military hospital, under the direction of the Government, and being a public document, it is, I suppose, *publici juris*, and I may use it without indiscretion.

Thermometers, 300 yards from sea-beach, 50 feet above sea-level, 6 feet from ground.	Hottest day. Highest maximum in 13 years.	Coldest night. Minimum in 13 years.	Coldest day. Lowest maximum in 13 years.	Warmest night. Highest maximum in 13 years.	Average maximum in 13 years.	Average minimum in 13 years.	Average mean temperature in 13 years.
January ...	77	32	48	62	60½	48	54
February ...	75	32½	48	63	62	48½	55½
March	82½	34	51	66	64	50	57
April	95½	37	50	70	68½	53½	61
May	89½	45½	57	72½	73½	58½	66
June	101	53	66	75	78½	63½	71
July	102	57½	75½	77	84½	69	76½
August... ...	111	56½	75	82½	86½	70	78
September ...	109	53½	68½	79	83	68	75½
October ...	97	44	61½	79	75½	61	68½
November ...	84½	40	53½	68½	66½	54	60½
December ...	77½	34	50	66	61½	48½	55

We have had a late season, but, as I have before said, wetter and colder than is usual; but, speaking in a general way, I should say that few indeed have been the days in which we have not spent five or six hours daily in the open air. We have almost invariably kept our window open during the day, when reading or writing at home. We have always had upon the table great bouquets of roses, geraniums, heliotrope, mignonette, jasmine, stocks, and wallflowers from the garden, and, of course, grown in the open air. We have been living in a villa six hundred feet above the sea—in fact, pretty well as high as a place can be on Mustapha; so that there can scarcely be any peculiarity of warmth about the situation. We look east-south-east, one side of the house facing south-west. But a good deal of rain has fallen, though not so as to interfere much with our movements. We have not seen snow, save on the tops of the distant hills, notably on the Djudjura, which, from our windows, has looked very much like a bit of the Oberland, or Monte Rosa group, moved across to Africa. We have heard hail striking against our bedroom windows once or twice in the early morning. There was one real hailstorm. We have heard thunder, and seen lightning also, once or twice. We have not seen ice, though a terrible rumour ran through the English colony that an elderly lady, a valued member of our little community, had on one occasion come across it at some high point of sacred Mustapha. We have had one terrible day of duststorm, but only one. I think, however, that you feel what there is of cold more than you would feel corresponding, or even far greater cold in England; and I am reasonably confident that the combination of hot sun and cold or cold wind laden with dust, which I have constantly met with here, must be trying to invalids with weak chests. We have had—oh, joy!—one fog, which, from patriotic motives, we welcomed with delight. This blessed occurrence took place on Friday,

February 27. On going to the bedroom window in the morning, you could not see five yards in front of you. The orange trees and Moorish villas were all hidden under a veil of mist, and there was that peculiar sough in the air which you hear upon such occasions in our own dear native land. "Why, this is a fine day for Devonshire!" was our exclamation, whilst fascinated by the pleasing sight. Alas! this was our only chance, though I am told that fogs are of very common occurrence in Algiers during the summer months; but, then, only a few lunatics remain to enjoy them. Finally, I would emphatically record again that Algiers will always remain fixed in my memory as the "luminous town." So it was with me in October on landing, so it is now on the 1st of March. I fear that, wherever I go hereafter, I shall feel that some ill-disposed person has turned off the gas and snuffed out the candles.

Invalids come to such a place as this for various reasons; but I suppose that consumption, that terrible scourge of Northern Europe, is the chief amongst these. Whilst casting about for something like a trustworthy statement upon this matter, I have come across an essay contributed to the *Journal de Thérapeutique*, written by a Dr. Edward Landowski, who is Director of an *Institut Sanitaire* at Algiers. He takes in patients as boarders at, I believe, not unreasonable rates, so that he has a certain interest in the matter; but I can scarcely think that this would affect his statement of facts. The situation of his house and grounds is certainly good—on Mustapha, with an eastern and south-eastern aspect, high enough up, yet not too far from the town. The first intention seems to have been the creation of a regular establishment, to be called a "Health-City," at Tipaza, a little way to the westward, and I think there was a company; but somehow or another the scheme has fallen through. Of the arrangements and how the thing answers, I cannot speak, not having any personal knowledge of the patients. The situation, I repeat it, is a good one, and that is all I can say.

Dr. Landowski appears to be an authority upon the treatment of consumptive cases at Algiers, and he handles the subject with caution. His theory is that all you can expect of climate as a winter refuge for a consumptive patient is that it should be a continuation of the climate in which the summer has been spent. It should be dry, without sudden changes of temperature, and this temperature should not be under 8° Centigrade, so that the patient shall be able to pass the day without fire, and with the windows open. Here are his words, and his suggestion of the curative or remedial system which has found favour in his eyes: "La condition unique est que le malade puisse rester en plein air 8 ou 10 heures dans la journée, jouir le plus long temps possible des rayons du soleil, et brûler, comme dit Pidoux, avec plus d'énergie les matériaux réparateurs qu'il prend chaque jour, sans courir le risque de contracter des phlegmasies brencho-pulmonaires."

This is just the open-air cure, a system which recommends itself to a layman's common sense; the only question is—Is Algiers the right place? Dr. Landowski backs up his own opinion of the climate by a quotation from the "Clinique Médicale" of M. Noël-Guéneau de

Mussy, who seems to be considered a great authority on the question at issue. "The climate of Algiers," writes M. de Mussy, "is warmer and more tonic than that of Pau or Pisa, and less exciting than that of Nice or Cannes; that is to say, the climate of Algiers is intermediate between a dry and exciting climate and a humid one; in a word, it is neither too wet nor too dry. Its value consists in *the purity of the atmosphere, the splendour of the light, the permanence of fine days.*" Dr. Landowski resumes by insisting on the fact that there are no sudden changes of temperature, no surprises.

During the *seven* months of the winter of 1878–79 there were only twenty-nine days on which rain fell or wind blew, against twenty-three days of rain in Paris in the month of June (1879). The climate offers a combination of sea air with a warm temperature. The advantage of it is that it permits invalids to live out of doors; but it possesses no other special quality, "*ni spécifique, ni thérapeutique, il ne peut être contreindiqué dans aucune forme de phthisie.*" Dr. Landowski remarks on the rare occurrence of phthisical cases amongst the population of Algeria, putting it as one-half of those found at the most favoured points on the surface of the globe, and at one-fifth of the general average of Europe. On one hundred deaths from all causes in the four following countries, there were from pulmonary consumption:—

In the United States	15
In England (? the British Isles)	18
France	20
Algiers	4

The doctor gives as the outcome of his own experience with his patients during the last winter, 1878-79: "During seven months they enjoyed 138 days spent entirely in the open air. Of the twenty-nine days marked as bad, one only was absolutely lost; for eight days they were able to get out only two hours daily during the intervals between fair and foul; for twenty other days they were able to enjoy from four to six hours daily of open air and sunshine." He adds, and the fact, if strictly correct, is significant, that several French doctors who were themselves suffering in France from tubercular consumption, have settled in Algiers, and are doing well. His treatment is to turn his patients out of doors at 9 a.m. into the gardens, to make them take their midday repast in the open air, and to admit them indoors only at dinner-time. They remain in till 7 p.m., when they can go out of doors for two other hours, that is to say, till 9 p.m. The clothing must be the same as in Europe, a light merino guernsey (*tricot de laine*) next the skin, and over this a thin waistcoat of flannel; after 4 p.m. a light overcoat. No respirators, no shawls or plaids.

The doctor extols the climate of Mustapha Supérieur at a great rate, and I recognize the value of many of his remarks. Avoid Moorish houses, and all that sentimental rubbish. They always strike cold; the windows are too small, and the rooms are aired and lighted from the central court. They are built to keep out the sun, not to keep the inmates warm in winter. No; *if you can*, get a good vulgar modern house, with high, wide windows; let the rooms be large and lofty, let in a deluge of air and sunshine, and face east, south-east, or south. The doctor adds, "Don't fix yourself *too near the sea.*" The St. Eugène side of Algiers is not well protected from the strength of the winds, so that will not do; he does not like the town; it is Mustapha or nothing. The doctor considers that the absence at Algiers of what the French call *distractions* is a positive advantage to his invalids. He does not wish them to sit up late; he does not approve, for them, of balls, concerts, theatres, nor the emotions of the gaming-table, but he has provided them with a series of occupations and amusements within the walls of the Institut Sanitaire, which guards them against *ennui*, or what we should call boredom. The patient walks for an hour; then has an hour of music; an hour for being rubbed (*massage*); an hour for gardening, for painting, for lung gymnastics, and so on. All this sounds whimsical enough, but I dare say, if cleverly contrived, the system is not without its advantages.

Dr. Landowski believes in the milk cure. This gentleman is of opinion that his method of treatment has been attended with the happiest results. I can only give the information, and say where I found it, and who is responsible for it. A layman's opinion on such a point must be as absolutely without value as I feel my own to be. Here we find gentlemen who ought to know something about the matter recommending Algiers, with its warm luminous climate, as favourable to consumptive patients. Whilst I am reading their recommendations the post brings me letters from Platz Davost in the Engadine, where a friend tells me he is trying the cold cure with great advantage, and that other poor fellows around him are reaping similar benefits from the ice and snow. Each person must decide for himself. I was talking the matter over with a friend who has come here to Algiers under more than the menace of the first symptoms of tubercular consumption. He has tried I know not how many doctors, and how many health resorts, from Madeira to Algiers. He tells me his idea is that Algiers is of great advantage to consumptive patients in certain stages of the disease—emphatically at its commencement. Algiers, according to him, will arrest the progress of a case just at the outset, but it will do something more. When it is certain that the case can have but one end, it will wonderfully alleviate the sufferings of the patient at the last fatal stage, and make easy the transition from life to death. Even this is an advantage, but much must depend on the patient's own feeling. I think I had rather turn my face to the wall in the old place, and pass away amidst my old surroundings, even at the cost of a little extra suffering; but this may not be the opinion of all.

The outcome of all this is—and I am about to repeat myself—were there any friend or relation of my own in England who, being afflicted or threatened in this way, wrote to me for an opinion about the propriety of coming to Algiers, I should say, "Only do so under the direction of one or other of the great London physicians." If he signed the passport, immediately on arrival in Algiers I would put myself under the eye of one or other of the local doctors. We have here an English gentleman of good repute, Dr. Thompson, who is well spoken of both for his skill and kindness. We have Dr. Bruch (an

Alsatian), one of those remarkable men whom we occasionally find relegated to the comparative obscurity of a provincial town, but who **could** hold his own with the best men of London or Paris. These gentlemen know the climate, and can forecast its probable effects upon the patient.

So far of consumption. Of asthma I can speak with more confidence, as having conversed with several persons whose lives, as they told me, were a mere burden to them elsewhere, but who have found almost absolute **relief at this place.** *Algiers is good for asthma.* I am **not** so sure as to **what one** should write about bronchitis. It is something, however, that in **three or** four months, I have not heard **of** one fatal case (amongst the English colonists) from this cause. An English medical gentleman who knows the place well told me that "the chances of your getting bronchitis (so you use reasonable precaution) are not great, but **if it does** get hold of you, it will **make short** work of you here." When one compares this result with the terrible records of the obituary in the papers we receive from London during the autumn and winter, it seems scarcely unreasonable to say that a person apprehensive of bronchitis puts himself under favourable conditions by coming to Algiers. Absolutely to avoid this **fearful** disease in this place seems to me **merely** a question of wearing proper clothing; of remaining indoors for the two hours about sunset; of not sitting down to rest in the shade when heated with exercise in the sun; in a word, *of avoiding chills in any form.* I have not **had a cold** since I have been at Algiers, and, with the exception of half a dozen days when it was raining, or the air was impregnated with moisture, I have spent at the very least four or five hours of every day walking, sitting in the garden, or driving in an open carriage. Think what that is—when you set against it the long confinement to London rooms—the way you get your death-blow by merely waiting for your carriage at the theatre, or by stepping from the well-warmed drawing or dining-room into the cold fog of Northern climates! Five or six hours of open air and sunshine daily! Londoners, think of that from November to April!

In cases of rheumatism and rheumatic affections of all kinds, I have heard what the French call "mountains and marvels" of the effect produced by the hot mineral baths of Hammam R'Irha (the *aquæ calidæ* of the old Roman world). They are only four hours from Algiers by rail, and there is to be found there a comfortable hotel, etc. The baths are seven miles from the station. The price per head for board and lodging, coffee, afternoon tea, etc., is only thirteen francs a day. There are hot baths for external treatment, and there are springs of cold iron water for drink. The scenery around is said to be very beautiful. When I have seen the place—which I have not yet done—I will add a few words about it. Patients troubled with gout, rheumatism, neuralgia, and eczema, might find their account in asking a few questions about Hammam R'Irha.

I think I can scarcely conclude this little account of Algiers for invalids better than by giving a copy of what may be called the Registrar's report of Death's doings at Algiers, during the last quarter of a year. I take it from the *Akhbar* (a local newspaper), for the 4th February, 1880. It is headed—

NECROLOGY FOR ALGIERS FOR THE FOURTH QUARTER OF 1879.

Diseases.	Oct.	Nov.	Dec.	Total.
Fevers, intermittent or remittent	14	6	2	22
,, pernicious	—	4	—	4
,, typhoid	9	21	14	44
Measles	—	1	—	1
Scarlatina	—	—	—	—
Small-pox	—	—	1	1
Teething	9	4	6	19
Thrush	2	—	—	2
Gastritis (gastro-enteritis)	11	6	3	20
Diarrhœa (dysentery)	15	10	8	33
Diseases of the liver	6	3	6	15
Erysipelas	1	—	—	1
Metro-peritonitis after childbirth	3	—	2	5
Peritonitis	3	1	2	6
Urinary disease	3	4	1	8
Ascite-Anasarque	1	1	1	3
Croup	5	8	9	22
Bronchitis, pleuro-pneumonia	28	45	55	128
Pulmonary consumption	30	44	40	114
Asthma	1	1	1	3
Heart-disease	7	6	4	17
Hemorrhage	—	3	1	4
Encephalopathy	12	6	18	36
Meningitis	11	10	10	31
Epilepsy	1	—	—	1
Trismus convulsions	3	3	1	7
Mental aberration	—	—	1	1
Hydrophobia	1	—	—	1
Scrofula, rachitisme	2	1	—	3
Syphilis	2	1	—	3
Cancer	4	1	2	7
Anæmia	—	3	2	5
Marasme	3	—	—	3
Still-born	22	18	19	59
Old age	8	11	19	38
Wounds	8	7	6	21
Violent death	2	1	—	3
Sundries (unclassed)	5	11	7	23
	233	241	242	716

		Oct.	Nov.	Dec.	Total.
Age	1 day to 12 years	103	90	80	273
	12 years to 20 years	9	10	9	28
	20 years to 50 years	72	85	78	235
	All above 50 years	49	56	75	180
Sex	Male	146	134	153	433
	Female	87	107	89	283
Nationality	Europeans	169	165	178	512
	Mussulmen	45	58	51	154
	Jews	19	18	13	50

Bronchitis figures for a good total, but, I repeat it, I have not heard of a single death amongst the English residents or visitors (for whom I am now writing) from this cause. Mine, however, is only the experience of an individual; such a thing may have happened without my hearing of it. Consumption stands at 114; but it must not be forgotten, that patients from every country, and at every stage of the disease, are brought here in hopes of a remedy which all cannot find. Typhoid fever stands for forty-four in the quarter, twenty-one deaths being registered for November. But November this year was a very abnormal month; the heat was excessive; the rain, which was overdue, never fell till December 12.

Here, on Mustapha, I have heard of the following cases during the winter. An English family was residing in a comfortable villa—a villa which any one would have engaged without hesitation. The lady and her daughter were both attacked with typhoid; the mother recovered, the daughter died. It is only fair to add that the young lady was a consumptive patient—but the typhoid killed her. As a third case, a young lady, the daughter of rich parents, living in, perhaps, the best villa on the heights, was attacked with this horrible disease, and fortunately recovered, but after a long and desperate struggle for life. The coachman of a lady of rank, residing in one of the best villas on Mustapha, also succumbed, after a most painful illness; but it is also fair to add that common report said that he had been occupied in cleaning out an old drain, and so caught the disease. Besides these, I have heard of the case of a young gentleman; he had a severe attack, but he recovered. This is the story of four months on the heights of Mustapha, as far as I know it. There may have been other cases.

I will conclude this chapter by remarking on two points to which I think all visitors, emphatically all patients, should give their earnest attention before making up their minds to try a winter in Algiers. 1st. The accommodation for visitors is sadly deficient. 2nd. Although a "scare" upon the point would be an absurdity, I do not think that the town of Algiers or the villas on Mustapha are properly drained.

The best villas are occupied by permanent residents; at least, by residents who come back here for the season year after year. There are a few of what one may call first-class villas in the market; but they are soon snapped up. These would let for, say, £500 or £400 for the season. There are more of a second class, which would let for about £250 or £200, but not very many of these. Some of these are picturesque old Arab houses or villas built in the Arab fashion. I should entertain the gravest doubts as to the propriety of hiring any of these, not only on account of the drainage, but because they are chill and cold. When you get below these, it is a very happy-go-lucky business indeed. A few succeed, most fail, in getting what they want; but you could almost count on your fingers the few who are able to establish themselves in real comfort. My earnest advice to my countrymen would be to look well before they leap, if they are thinking of a *pension*. Take counsel, not from one, but from many persons, especially from those who have actually resided at the house of which you may be thinking. Of course, I am not speaking of such establishments as the one kept by Dr. Thompson, or the Institut Sanitaire, which seems right enough, but of the ordinary *pension*. There is the alternative of remaining in the town.

There are a few, a very few lodgings, high up, and with a southern or south-eastern aspect, which might be tried; but the trouble would be infinite with landlords and servants. You might stop at one or other of the hotels during the winter; but my own feeling is that the town of Algiers is a better place to pass through than to stop at. You might get on at a hotel for a month, not for the season of four or five months. Whenever any occasions during the past winter have taken me down to Algiers, I have always felt, in the town, a sense of "stuffiness," and sometimes odours the reverse of satisfactory; and a great relief whenever I reached a certain height on the Mustapha slope.

After the question of insufficient accommodation follows the vital one of drainage, both in the town of Algiers and on the heights of Mustapha. He would be no true friend to this place who shrank from speaking out the plain truth about it. Any mere "scare" about typhoid, diphtheria, and such like would be unreasonable; yet much remains to be done by those whose interests are primarily concerned in establishing Algiers as a real health resort. The town of Algiers is drained, in a way—but in a very insufficient way. When rain comes, or, as here, drought followed by rain, the odours, both inside and outside the houses, indicate the presence of great pollution below. You find this sort of thing both in French and Italian towns, and people come and go as though it existed not, until Death steps in and calls attention to the question by snatching away some notable personage. The French seem to regard the matter with calm indifference, and pass their lives in apparent security amidst bad odours which would drive an English family away from any place. Nay, in England itself, in our old country inns, our country houses, our sea-side lodgings, are we altogether immaculate? Under the head of "bad smells," Algiers out of doors is just about the same thing as any ordinary French provincial town. In many of the houses the nuisance is marked and most disagreeable. In one of the local papers to-day (March 3) there is a vehement attack upon the municipality, written by a French journalist, in terms stronger than any I should care to use, about the drainage of the town. Until the nuisance has been remedied, I would not advise any invalid to select the town of Algiers as a winter residence, despite the beauty and exhilarating influence of the climate. We English are more practically concerned with

Mustapha. The owners should be told that until their villas are better looked after in this matter of drainage, they need not expect that any conscientious man would undertake to write up the place.

Despite the climate, if the night undoes all the good which has been done during the day, why come to Algiers? From obvious motives I do not care to select particular houses for animadversion; there are too many of them; but let the friends and advisers be careful in their selection of a villa upon Mustapha for an invalid. Again, I say, let there be no "scare" about the matter. Rome, Naples, Venice are, I dare say, worse than Mustapha or Algiers; but people go continuously to Venice, Rome, and Naples. I write not in hostility, but as a friend to Algiers, and with the full consciousness of the advantage which invalids may derive from the splendid climate.

The French scientific men have made a remarkable discovery on the subject of the Algerine climate, which I will venture to add to my remarks upon the general subject. According to Dr. Ricoux, the climate is prejudicial, if not fatal to *Germans*. The Spaniard, the Italian, the Southern Frenchman, can live and flourish in Algeria; a delicate German will pine and die there. Brandenburgers, beware!

CHAPTER X.

ALGERINE SCRAPS.

LA TRAPPE.

ONE of our earliest drives from Algiers was to the monastery of La Trappe, distant some ten miles. You drive out by the Bab-el-Ouad gate, in the Sidi-Ferruch direction, through St. Eugène, and past the Point de Pescade. As you drive along the road, which skirts the sea, you are reminded of the Cornish coast, for the waves break with such violence on the shore. On subsequent occasions I always found the sea very lively here, so I suppose there is something in the set of the tide or the configuration of the coast to account for it. Nothing can be wilder than the scene: the tumbling sea, the ruined forts, on your right hand; on the left are the Bou-Zarea heights, and a succession of hills covered with African scrub. It is a long and a fresh drive to Staoueli, and at length you get a good sight of the little peninsula of Sidi-Ferruch, where the French landed on the 14th of June, 1830. The idea was to keep possession of this peninsula as a basis of operations, for it was not anticipated that the opposition of the Dey's troops would be so feeble as it turned out to be.

I will venture to interrupt my story for a few lines, that I may tell the legend of a Mohammedan saint, which I found in M. Piesse's pages. Sidi-Ferruch was a great saint in Algiers, but, despite of his sanctity, a Spanish sailor resolved to kidnap him. He got the saint on board somehow, set sail, as he thought, and away they went, or rather did not go. In the morning the Spaniards found that they had not made a knot; where the vessel lay when they shipped the saint, there she was still. This was past a joke, for as soon as the rumour of the saint's abduction got about at Algiers, they were sure to have a swarm of cruisers after them, and it was probable that the Spaniards would take a graceful farewell of the world at the Bab-Azzoun. There was nothing for it but to conciliate the holy man. "No one could regret more deeply than the Spaniards did the unfortunate occurrence, which was purely an oversight. At what point was it his reverence's pleasure to be put ashore?" So said, and so done; but still the wretched ship stuck fast. Studding-sails and sky-scrapers did not produce the smallest effect. What could it mean? The saint had forgotten his slippers, and they were despatched on shore, when the ship at once began to make way and answer her helm. The Spanish sailor, the original wrong-doer, was so much struck with the miracle, that he turned Mohammedan at once, and craved the privilege of entering the saint's service at nominal wages. He died in the odour of sanctity.

Meanwhile we are approaching the monastery, and it is a striking thing to see how much of the land has been devoted to vine culture. The minds of men in Algiers are in great excitement upon the subject of wine-making. The difficulty of France is the opportunity of Algiers. The fortunes of the colony may hinge on the phylloxera. There could be no doubt as to the culture of the vine in the neighbourhood of La Trappe. It was pleasant to see how much ground has been redeemed from mere waste.

The little carriage drove on through fields where labourers in numbers were at work, carts drawn by oxen or horses were passing to and fro; you were on a large and flourishing farm. We drove up to the gate, and were shown into a long room, where we were received by the father who had been told off for the day to attend visitors, and who turned out to be a very courteous and pleasant host. The foot of woman must not pass further than this ante-room to the monastery. From what I heard afterwards at Algiers, the ladies, so far from being affronted by the exclusion, seemed rather to take it as a tribute to their powers. There are, I believe, convents of female Trappists from which men are religiously shut out. Perpetual silence is the rule of the order.

We looked about in search of something we might purchase in return for the hospitality we received. There was a glass case full of *objets*, so we settled for a fair-sized flask of essence of geranium (they manufacture perfumes at La Trappe), a few photographs, and ultimately for a bottle of a very pleasant liqueur.

Lunch was served, which consisted of some soup not worthy of commendation, a very good omelette, and some excellent potatoes. What was the wine like? There was a strong, rough, red wine, which did not, even when heavily dashed with water, commend itself much to our palates. There was a better red wine, which might be classed as a very fair *ordinaire*. There was a very pleasant white wine, like *chablis*, which may have a commercial future before it; and above all, there was the liqueur. When I think of "La Grande Chartreuse," I will not forget Staoueli.

A very agreeable gentleman, with a distinct tendency to jocularity, and who I fancy must have been the cellarer, unearthed these treasures for us from a cupboard in the corner of the room. It was explained to the lady that she must remain where she was whilst I was conducted round the building—an arrangement in which she acquiesced with a smile. "Time would not hang heavily on her hands." What could she mean? The monks are not allowed to speak.

I was led into a court, in the middle of which stood the group of palms so famous in Algerine story. We are standing in the battle-field of Staoueli, and I think I have read somewhere that the Turkish general's tent was pitched just under these palms. We met here the father superior, who was passing accidentally this way, and I had the honour of being presented to a general of Trappists. There was nothing very tremendous about him at all—I should say a chatty, agreeable man; I wish to speak of him with all respect —but what an overthrow of all my preconceived ideas of

Trappists! I had thought of them as of a set of hollow-cheeked, grey-bearded men, always digging graves, and who would never have left off groaning had not silence been imperative.

Is it not the rule in French novels, that the heroes, when they have committed as many crimes as the ingenuity of the author can devise, finally retire to La Trappe? Raoul, who has seriously compromised the duchess—now a lunatic—and shot the duke off-hand for daring to interfere with him, is thus enabled to pass his declining years in peace. If he be slightly bored, and looks back with occasional regret to his pleasant boulevard days, he can comfort himself with the inscription which meets his eye at every turn—"*S'il est triste de vivre à La Trappe, qu'il est doux d'y mourir!*"

We continued our round. My guide laid his hand upon my arm, and put his finger to his lips. A brother was working in the garden, and his ears must not be profaned by the sound of talk. I could not help thinking with myself that here was a "brother" stationed for the purpose of impressing visitors; but it was best to acquiesce in the spirit of the place. So I tightened up my lips, threw a look of deep sympathy on my guide, and crept on silently by his side, just as though we were going to rob a till and were afraid of being caught. Through dormitory and refection hall, through chapel and galleries, I was conducted; everything was very plain, but very clean. Then I was taken through endless stables, farmyards, and many workshops. It was clear here that work was done in earnest, and my soul was filled with reverence for the monks of La Trappe. My guide had been, of course, relieved from the obligation of silence, for it was his duty to explain to visitors the meaning of what they saw.

The brothers all worked hard in the fields. They had (I think he said) hired labour besides; but in addition the assistance of the military prisoners who were assigned to them by the Government. They had reclaimed a very large extent of ground round the monastery. They exported and sold their wines, perfumes, etc. Many youths entered the order quite young, and never sought to escape from it. For himself, he was well content. If the world had its pleasures, it had its drawbacks; and here was freedom from care and anxiety. He did not mind the silence; it became a habit. He had almost forgotten the *patois* of the place in France from which he came—I think it was Nismes. He should say they were all reasonably happy—as happy as an industrious and peaceful life could make them. He desired no change.

Now, were these words of course for a stranger? or was this very truth? What becomes of the theory of persons who have committed horrid crimes—of endless remorse, of silent agony? La Trappe would just seem to offer a career to a lad of quiet and methodical habits. There is a good deal to be said in favour of the quiet and silence. No more brass bands; no more jingling pianos; no more horrid newspaper boys, with their eighteenth editions; any brother who sneezed or coughed to be shut up summarily in his cell, till he became less unpleasant, and fit to take his place again in that silent society. The guide, however, turned upon me with a remark that I was English, to which I bowed assent, and then, *de but en blanc*, he asked me why the Prince of Wales did not come and see them. It was not for me to enter into the question of his Royal Highness's engagements; but I was struck with the fact that our prince's popularity had been felt even in this out-of-the-way place and amongst these silent people.

We had at last accomplished our round, and found the lady in the full swing of conversation with a brother, and surrounded by people who seemed to have afforded her good entertainment. She explained to me that in that arcade opposite a brother had been serving out soup and doles of one kind or another to the Arabs. They came up by twos to a little door, where a bowl of soup was handed out to the pair. Of this they partook, each armed with a wooden spoon. The difficulty was to make them sup fair, which could only be done by depriving them of the soup, as a warning, and then handing it back. Another trick of the Arabs was, after soup, to retire to the back, change *bernouses* with a friend, and boldly step forward for another supply. Sometimes they were caught out, and then they were experimented upon with a wooden spoon. "*Ils sont tellement roués, madame, que le bon Dieu s'y tromperait parfois.*"

It was not, however, always the Arabs who were in trouble. A Frenchman had received a bowl of soup, and whether it was short measure or not flavoured to his taste, he was not pleased. Thinking the almoner's eye was off him, he hung out his tongue over the soup at great length, as only Frenchmen can do it; but he was in error for once. The almoner had seen him. He rushed out, seized the soup, and poured upon him a volley of abuse which must have been collecting in his breast during months of silence. At this moment a brother, who had been handling a broom to give himself the appearance of occupation, but was constantly edging up for a gossip, was asked by the lady if the system of silence worked well? if evil thoughts, so forcibly kept down, did not get the mastery at times? in short, might you not arrive at one great sin, as you were not allowed to take it out in the small change of peccadilloes? " No, madame; it is evident that, as we are not allowed to speak, we cannot indulge in *diffamation*, nor quarrel, *nor use angry words*. But, Monsieur l'Aumônier over the way—— *Ah! madame, ce coquin vient de tirer la langue d'une manière inouïe!*"

Perhaps so; but I am half ashamed of recording these absurdities; my only excuse must be that this is really what happened to us in this romantic place. We shook hands with the brother at parting with great cordiality, but it was only after *des façons* that he gave his left hand to the lady. It was a morganatic adieu.

There were signs on every side of great and successful industry. There was cleanliness and fair accommodation for all. Where all around was waste, La Trappe was a model farm in full operation. Personally I would add that nothing could exceed the courtesy we received from all with whom we came in contact. I shall always think of the monks of La Trappe at Staoueli as of men usefully and honourably employed. One can only wish, for their own sakes, they would do away with their absurd regulation about silence, which I doubt not is evaded in a thousand ways. Their remorse is all nonsense. After all, it is their affair.

We drove home by an inland road, not so interesting as our sea-coast drive of the morning, through Cheragas and El-Biar, back to Algiers and the hotel in time for dinner. If there is some absurdity, there is much good about these Trappists.

Point de Pescade.

Greenwich in Algiers, with a Dish of Chicken.

I had been told that at Algiers we were not wholly without resource in the matter of fish dinners, or rather fish luncheons. At Algiers luncheon takes the place of dinner. A resident who wishes to do you a good turn asks you to lunch just as he would in England woo you to partake under his auspices of the nobler meal. Such is the custom of the place, and I have nothing to say against it. I doubt not that it is kindly intended; it certainly saves ladies the trouble of elaborate dressing—if that be a trouble—and spares you all the annoyance of turning out of an evening, when, probably, you are reluctant to be disturbed. On the other hand, when you are bidden out to a luncheon, it is a day gone. It is like a wedding breakfast—it causes you to fritter away your morning, and to regard your evening with contempt. It causes you to drink wine in the middle of the day, when you are in the habit of drinking water; it gives you satiety at midday; it deranges your habits;

but for all this I would not look a gift horse in the mouth, nor speak with unkindliness of what may be kindly meant. Be all this as it may, we were perfectly willing to sacrifice a day in order to visit the Trafalgar near Algiers, and the more so as we were told that on our way we should have a peep at one of those strange old-world rites, in which negresses are the sacrificing priestesses, fowls the victims, and languishing Moorish ladies the devotees. It shall be spoken of in its proper place.

One fine morning we drove down Mustapha to meet, on the Place du Gouvernement, our friends who were, like ourselves, desirous of seeing what a fish banquet at Algiers might mean.

We had during our stay at Mustapha secured the attendance of an old ram-shackle waggonnette drawn by two mules, whose hair had been clipped into strange patterns and devices. The custom was to stick flowers into their ears, and they bore about them a perfect *carillon* of bells. It was just the sort of vehicle in which a heavy Spanish family would take a respectable airing at Murcia or Toledo. At Barcelona or at Seville the people would have been finer, and had you been seen in such an equipage at Madrid you would have faded somehow from the ranks of good society. Such as it was, we delighted in our mule-carriage; if the springs did not spring very much, at any rate the mules were never tired. It took you back to the days of Gil Blas, and, by "making believe" a good deal, even to the stately times of Don Quixote.

Such as it was, in it we jingled along through the

Bab-el-Ouad gate, and in the St. Eugène direction. I hope, nay, I think, the wayfarers regarded us with a kind of tender awe, so musical were the bells, so perfectly appointed the equipage, if the coachman would have refrained from driving in his shirt sleeves. This did not look well in the eyes of the society people, but it brought us within the range of human sympathy. There was a stream of people all bound in the same direction, and the point was the "Seven Fountains," you know, just above the Koubba of Sidi-Yacoub. There were Moorish ladies in good store, on mule-back and donkey-back. It was, however, a question of concealed loveliness; they were all veiled and swathed, and as they jogged along they might have been—I ask pardon for the vulgar expression—mummies "on the burst." Attendants were carrying fowls. Were we all coming back from market? No; we were going to the sacrifice.

It seems that at the Seven Fountains the genii (the djinns) are all-powerful, and, if properly propitiated with chickens, will give you not a few useful hints as to the future. I did not know it at the time, but I found it out afterwards in the pages of my good friend, M. Piesse, that the good djinns are green, white, blue, and *fleur-de-pois* colour; the red, black, and brown genii can make themselves disagreeable.

Now, after passing through a not very savoury French drinking-house, and on to a ricketty balcony, this is what we saw.

There was a lighted brazier on the seashore, round which two or three decrepit old negresses were standing.

A Moorish lady, all bags and veils, would join them, and say a few words, whereupon one of these grinning hags would scatter something on the brazier, which caused a little smoke to arise. An attendant would hand a fowl to the hag. The hag would pull out a long, thin knife, half cut the poor creature's throat, and fling it on the sand. It seems that if the wretched bird, in its agonies, flutters towards the sea, the sacrifice has been accepted. The "Ayes have it," *i.e.* the white, blue, and green genii. If otherwise, the red, black, and brown gain their point, and the words "Bad luck" remain in the answer to the petitioner. It was a disgusting sight, and to enjoy it a man must take pleasure in the slaughter of poultry. All I can say in excuse for being present at all is that we were told it was a weird sight, that it was a touching relic of the old superstitions, and so on. It was nothing of the sort; it was mere dirty, vulgar cruelty, and every person present, emphatically including ourselves, should have been soundly fined, and still worse, "admonished," by some worthy magistrate or other, be he kadi or *juge de paix*. I wish the S.P.C.A. could have handled the case. Faugh! Let us get into the mule-cart again, and jingle off to the Point de Pescade, and to luncheon.

It is a fresh, breezy drive, and the restless waves break merrily on the shore and make curling white arches just like off the Logan Stone. No doubt we are at Greenwich at last, for we pass certain establishments which announce that they are always ready to set forth military banquets, *repas de noces*, and others; but we resisted the blandishments; we were bound for the most distant one, near the Point. Aha! we knew better. So we reached the Trafalgar, and got hold of a waiter with that weary, cloth-laying, half-washed, been-up-all-night look, which distinguishes the class all over the world.

Now about the whitebait. We would not order too many kinds of fish, for it might lead to delay. What could we have? Everything. What did we get? Little or nothing. It seems we should have ordered the lunch beforehand. Well, we did so upon another occasion; but it came to much the same thing, save that we got more *filet-de-bœuf* and omelette. There was not much fish; but we might go and see the tank in which they were kept when there were any. We went to see that tank; but by this time it was blowing fresh, so it was not very easy to get there. Oysters? There were no oysters to-day; but we might have any amount of delicious cockles, and so we had.

Our lunch was set forth in a *cabinet particulier*, for we were not numerous enough to be entitled to the honours of the grand *salon*. I sat at meat, or at fish, in that gorgeous apartment upon a subsequent occasion; but we had, unluckily, a gentleman in the party who could not conceive existence to be tolerable out of a thorough draught. Every window was thrown open, and the elements had it all their own way. The wind was always getting under the table-cloth, causing it to rise into uneasy bulges. So we coughed, and used our handkerchiefs, and ate our cockles, and caught stiff necks. I preferred the comfort of the *cabinet particulier* to the gusty dignity of the *salon*.

How about wine? Cockles and oysters are, presumably, much the same thing, so let us have *chablis;* and, as we are making a day of it, a luncheon.

Presently the worn-out waiter brought us in our huge dishes of cockles or whatever they might be—little bits of hard fish gristle, sticking to flat shells. They could scarcely be cockles; but what does it matter? Tear away at the molluscs, as little comes away; you cannot hurt yourself. And, *garçon,* another bottle of that rare old *chablis* (it was sour, and a country wine, I believe). Poor is the heart which never rejoices. Let me fill you up, for to-day we'll merry be! Another cockle?

All this time the worn-out waiter remained in the corner, and kept on giving himself back-handers of *chablis.* The offence carried its own punishment. I understand the man's depressed look. He is another victim to Algerine *chablis,* just on the verge of shivering delirium.

As I live, these scanty, horny molluscs *were* the fish. All one's dreams of lobster *rissoles,* whiting pudding, water *sootje* distinguished by fairy flounders suggestive of violet odours, salmon *à l'Indienne;* above all, whitebait, attended by piles of brown bread and butter, such as one nowhere else sees;—all these good things, I say, were but the baseless fabric of a vision. No bacon and infant beans to follow; no duck and green peas; no iced pudding, built up by an able man. A tough *filet,* an omelette, and a lot of potatoes supplied their place.

Well, well, go out to the Point de Pescade, and lunch there by all means; but do not look for what you certainly will not find there. I have great doubts if any length of notice would have secured fish worthy of regard at Algiers. All the fish of the Mediterranean, so far as I know it, along the French, Spanish, and Italian coasts, and on the islands, is very poor and tasteless as compared with the Atlantic and Channel fish; nay, even as the Baltic. Did I not linger over a mackerel at the Phœnix, at Copenhagen, the recollection of which will follow me pleasantly to the grave? I think the sardines are the only really good Mediterranean fish. We used to go down to the fish market, near the Mosque de la Pêcherie, very often. The table at the Régence was as fairly supplied as, I suppose, it could be. Soles we had rarely; but there they were, coarse soles, I should say; whiting, which missed their flavour; those gorgeous red mullet I pronounce to be Southern impostors. Oh *Ciel!* when I think of a Babbicombe Bay mullet! "Breathes there a man with soul so dead?" etc. Grey mullets, too, there were; but no taste—upon my word, no taste. As for the peculiar fish; if any one were to tell me he liked tunny, I should reply, "Trust no such man." The fish with queer names, which I never saw before and hope never to see again, by some twist of my imagination, always carried me back to the piratical days. They had a sub-flavour of Christian slave. I think one of these animals was, very properly, called a *loup*, a horrid, blood-thirsty Algerine tiger; but even sea-pikes were not wanting. A pair of soles—we know what we mean—is unattainable here. And thou, too, thou dainty bit of Severn salmon, with the creamy flakes; and ye, angelic whitebait, tickling the palate with your myriad delights! when shall I see ye again? I would compromise just now for a dab—a Southend dab.

NOTRE DAME D'AFRIQUE.

One of the most striking objects in the immediate neighbourhood of Algiers is the church of Notre Dame d'Afrique, which stands at some distance from the town upon a spur of the Bou-Zarea Hill. The situation is magnificent. The church looks well from a distance; the view from the plateau in front of it as beautiful as anything in Algiers, where there are so many beautiful things. It is a stiff climb, however, even for a good walker, but, happily for invalids, the spot can be reached on wheels. The church is French, therefore of modern construction, and there is not much to be said in favour of the interior. The walls are hung round with votive offerings for mercies displayed, I suppose, chiefly to seafaring men. This is a sailors' church. I had been instructed to look high up above the altar for the sword of one of the great generals who had helped to consolidate the African conquest, and there, sure enough, it was, though rather hidden from sight. We visited the church, first, as mere sightseers, to see the place, and a second time after vespers to hear the prayers for the dead who had perished at sea. There is often too much of the dramatic element in these French ceremonies. We do not all care to writhe with grace, and groan in harmony, and to pronounce *des sublimes allocutions* over the poor remains of those whom we only too dearly loved.

These things are an affair of national taste and temperament. We cannot all wear our crape in the same fashion. But even a man of the old undemonstrative Northern type must feel a certain sympathy with the ceremony which I shall attempt to describe in a few sentences. We had been careful to select a Sunday when it had been announced that the archbishop would attend, for the great man's presence helps forward even a funeral. The mourners mourn their best, the intoning priest does not slur his work, the faces of the attendants wear a more touching expression when an archbishop's eye is upon them. We drove up to Notre Dame, then, one Sunday afternoon, and were in time for vespers at 3 p.m. The archbishop was there, sitting in his chair when we arrived, and everything was done reverently and in order; but just when vespers were drawing to an end, I began to hear that shuffling of feet which denotes that people of forecasting mind are slipping out as quietly as they can to get good places. I have no right to raise any objection, for we did the same thing.

Once on the terrace outside, there was the magnificent view of the bay, and far below us the unquiet sea was breaking on the shore. The afternoon was bright and sunny, and there were some small craft in the offing sliding along under their white sails like sea-birds. "This is all very well, O sea," I thought to myself, as I looked in the direction of the Gulf of Lyons, "but there's no trusting you." A number of little boys, who looked like pupils of a naval school, in their Sunday best, had been drawn up in two rows from the door of the church to the parapet, and between them the procession was to pass. We were kept waiting for some time, but this period of preparation was not thrown away. The little boys were, I fancy, children of shipwrecked mariners; but a sound of chanting comes from within the church; the *suisse* pushes back loiterers from the steps, and a couple of acolytes, carrying crosses or something of that kind, make their appearance. The officiating priests and acolytes follow, some of the people carrying a pall, stretched out in its full length and breadth. Except this we saw much the same kind of procession as is usual on the occasion of Roman Catholic ceremonies. But what a majestic central figure is the archbishop!—I think the handsomest and most dignified ecclesiastic I have ever seen. I wish we could gain him over for some high office at home. He is every inch an archbishop, and there are a good many inches, for he is a tall and stately man, magnificently attired. He wore, if I remember right, a mauve silk cape richly trimmed with lace, and had a great gold cross, and such a lovely ring—a sapphire, I think. The costume was simply perfect.

So, quietly moaning, the pall-bearers passed between the two rows of the children of shipwrecked sailors till they were stopped by the parapet. The service for the dead went on. The nasal chants, which have so often been distasteful to me, *here* did not sound out of place. The priests, nay, I think the archbishop, sprinkled the holy water over the pall, and seawards. Was not this a requiem for all who had been drawn down beneath that larger pall below? Was the secret of one's sympathy with the ceremony that it was performed for *all* who had perished at sea? It sounded like that great and best prayer in our Litany, "*That it may please Thee to have mercy upon all men!*" I do not suppose that stately archbishop quietly excluded in a recess of his own mind all shipwrecked Protestants from the benefit of the requiem, nay, that he surreptitiously left all Dissenters who had fallen overboard to take their chance. Things can scarcely be as bad as that even in Ultramontane circles. Let us give way to our feelings for once without further Hamlet-like hesitation. I had my eye on all the assistants, and had I seen a trace of mute-like woe on any of their faces I was quite ready to expose them for a set of humbugs. If they are to pray every Sunday afternoon for all the drowned dead, I do not think they could have done it with less of regulation, stiffness, or professional *nonchalance*. The ceremony seemed to me a very affecting one in the performance, as it is certainly grand in idea, and I strongly recommend all of my friends who may visit Algiers to go up to Notre Dame for vespers one Sunday afternoon, but to be sure that the archbishop is there. Otherwise I answer for nothing.

THE ST. EUGÈNE SIDE.

Frais Vallon: Valley of Consuls: Bou-Zarea.

I have already made mention of the little excursions indicated above, but as drives or walks they are so delightful that I think they deserve further notice. If a visitor could take but one drive at Algiers, and would trust me, I should say,—Go to Bou-Zarea and to the little Arab cemetery which you will find about half a mile above the village. You will have the Metidja at your feet, the range of the Atlas Mountains over against you, the coast-line to the westward, with the cape, beyond which is Cherchell (Cape Tenez is far away). There you will see the place at which the French landed in 1830, and the country through which they wormed their way to the Fort de l'Empereur. That white spot on the mountain-side is Blidah; and what a noble view away to the eastward, and to the Djudjura range in its winter mantle of snow! Take it for all in all, the view from the Arab cemetery above Bou-Zarea is the finest in the neighbourhood of Algiers; but we are not there yet. As a walk, it is within the easy competence of a good walker. A few years ago I should have thought nothing of it, but now I might as well think of Monte Rosa or Ararat, so let us get into the carriage. I do not recommend any one not being pressed for time to unite all these little excursions in one, but as they lie together they may be united for purposes of description. Which way shall we take the round? You may go by El-Biar, and return along the shore by the Bab-el-Ouad gate, or the reverse way. As it is better to descend than to ascend the very stiff Bou-Zarea ravine, let us creep up to the Porte du Sahel, and keep for a certain distance on the Cheragas road, then turn to the right and work our way through a somewhat bleak country to Bou-Zarea. The coachman wishes to stop at the little cabaret, and turn us out, but we are bound for the Arab burying-place, and are pertinacious. So he takes us up the hill, and we alight on the right-hand side of the road, in order to penetrate into the Arab village in its labyrinth of prickly pears.

This is a very different affair from Tixeraïn, the place to which innocent strangers are generally conducted on their first landing. True, we do not find here the Arabs under their black tents, as we saw them afterwards in the wilderness between Batna and Biskra; but this is really a village of many huts—the dwelling-place of Arab householders, not the mere encampment of nomads.

As the visitor is, probably, a new comer, he will find it all very curious. Amidst these prickly pears what a site for a desirable family residence! The inhabitants must have cut down those vegetable *chevaux de frise*, so as to make alleys and paths by which they might communicate with each other. No question here of writing up, *"Passage interdit;"* "Trespassers will be prosecuted with all the rigour of the law." If you are minded to trespass—try! A man must be of iron to do so—a lunatic to think of it. You may follow up the paths which have been cut in the thicket of prickly pear, and you will come here and there upon a dirty hovel, swarming with bright-eyed children, who rush out upon you with their usual cry of "*Sordi! sordi!*" I suppose they mean *soldi*, or sous. It is just like Killarney or Switzerland. Here are women with their faces uncovered, which may mean "stick," if they are caught—but no men. As an Arab settlement, I should not have thought much of the place after we had seen Algeria; but this was the first village of the kind which we had visited, and, therefore, to us, noteworthy.

When we had had enough of juvenile Arabs and mature prickly pears, we got into the carriage again, and were driven up the hill, to a point from which we could crawl up to the Cimetière Arab. This was a work of time, but when we got to the top, to the Koubba and the dwarf palms and amidst the gravestones, what a view! The sea, and the Atlas range, the plain of the Metidja, and the coast-line, the Djudjura in the distance. Here was an African panorama indeed! You began to understand what the "Sahel" and the "Tell" really meant. The country looked wild enough. It was not then, as we saw it in spring, covered with green crops and wild flowers, but it was so unlike anything one had seen elsewhere, that it fixed attention. Very few trees—a dusky plain, with white Arab houses sparsely scattered here and there. The great features of nature are unchangeable. This is what the people saw in the days when the "Tombeau de la Chrétienne" (you see it yonder on the shoulder of the hill to the westward) was built by Berber hands. This is what the pirates saw when the unutterable Turk presided over the slave trade in all its branches—a bad business. But what were we about ourselves?

We must not, however, loiter longer, if we would look in at the Frais Vallon, and the Consul's Valley on our way home; so we go down hill again to the French cabaret, and a little further, and then descend a magnificent ravine sloping down to the sea. What can I say of this ravine, but that we sat in admiration as the two mules trotted down the slope, and the views altered as we moved on? You may visit the place again and again, but it always looks new. We drove through orange and olive trees and magnificent bushes, almost trees, of laurustinus; past a great building, where a number of old gentlemen were sitting out in the sun. It is, I believe, some kind of hospital or charitable establishment.

To get to the Frais Vallon, our next point, we have to drop down well-nigh to the sea-level, and to re-ascend the ravine on its eastern side. This we contrive to do, and at last the coachman tells us we must alight, as he can take the carriage no further.

We are bound for the house of the Arab doctor, so, taking directions for our guidance, we creep down a rugged path to a house which looked like a *café*. It was very solitary in the African glen, and we were full of the finest reflections—when, oh *Ciel!* what is this we hear? There was no mistake. The speaker was so very much in earnest. "*Chérie, chérie, ma chérie!*" Such were his expressions, which he united with certain osculatory sounds of the most alarming description. What! here in Africa, and no shame! Was it worth while to come to Algiers? But what shall we say to that young person who could countenance such effrontery in open day? He is losing all self-control, and the endearing expressions come more thickly, when something or some one seems to have disturbed him. He now begins to scream out, "*Canaille, canaille, allez-vous-en!*" I should not wonder if amongst such hot-blooded people it came to a death-struggle. Let us pursue a policy of expectancy, and await events. There is a loud guffaw, and then more of "*Canaille, canaille, allez-vous-en!*" Ah!

you've got the worst of it, have you? Some intelligent and determined *agent* of the public force has got you down, and is interposing in the name of *le repos des familles.* Clap the handcuffs on him, Monsieur le Gendarme, but let the young person escape; it may prove a warning to her. No! he won't "*allez-vous-en,*" so don't suppose it. *Canaille* yourself. If you think anything is to be gained by abusing a stern but heroic *agent* in the discharge of a most sacred public duty, you will find yourself wonderfully mistaken when you are standing before an outraged *juge de paix.* But what is that loud laughing about down there? A man is looking up at the wall from the top of which the screams of "*Canaille*" are proceeding with fresh vigour, and there I caught sight of the offender. What a weight was removed from my mind! It was not a fellow-creature, but a grey parrot with a red top-knot. The more the parrot screamed, the louder the fellow laughed, and then the parrot relapsed into a softer mood and recommenced his "*Chérie, chérie,*" with the other disagreeable sounds. Something should be done to that suggestive parrot to bring him to discreeter forms of utterance. But enough of this—let us go on.

We were in a narrow glen, and crept up a sheep-path on one side of it; on the other was the house of the Arab doctor. To get there we had to go down one side of the glen and up the other. But when we got there our labour was in vain. The great man was gone to Algiers. I had heard wonders of the cures he had effected. I wish he would try his hand on me, and as long as the prescriptions amounted to temperance and cold water, I think

I would have followed them; but I missed my chance of consulting the faculty at Algiers. A good walker would find it a pleasant stroll to the top of the glen, but this was above my powers, and so we got back to our sheep-path, to that very objectionable parrot, and to our little carriage.

The Frais Vallon is a lovely walk. Down to the seashore, or very nearly so, we drove again, and then began the ascent to Nôtre Dame d'Afrique. At this point the tourist will certainly alight to admire the prospect from the terrace before the church. Old Roman or Berber remains may mislead you, but you cannot be mistaken as to the magnificence of the sight before you. Be content for the moment to ignore the past, and admire the present. Tradition may involve you in strange vagaries; the faithful eyes content themselves with the truth. Verily, what we see before us is worth a wilderness of Roman inscriptions.

But I have spoken of Nôtre Dame elsewhere in connection with its weekly service for all who have died at sea—at any rate for all who are taking their last long rest beneath that blue restless pall which lies yonder at our feet. So let us proceed with our little expedition. It is a pleasant drive here past the Seminary, along this road overshadowed by trees. We are not very sure as to the way, nor our driver either, for it seems that not many visitors take the trouble of visiting the house where Mrs. Broughton spent some years of her childhood, and where her mother, that dear old lady, Mrs. Blanckley, lived through so many stirring events. If any one would know what Algiers was during the last days of piracy, let him read the first half of Mrs. Broughton's book, at any rate as much of it as contains old Mrs. Blanckley's diary. So, many deserving authors will be saved the trouble and vexation of recasting half-digested records of the past, and of producing a very untrue and insufficient picture.

I see it stated that the French Consulate stood on the site of the present Seminary—the one which we have just passed. The British and French Consuls were near neighbours. The path gets narrower and still narrower —there is just room for the little carriage to pass. We ask questions of any one who passes by, and arrive at last at the brickwork of a modern French fortification, and then at a point than which we can get no further. Here a Frenchman, who seems to know all about the place, points out to us Mr. Blanckley's house. It is up, above this, the furthest house on the left. You can understand how they would make their signals from that point to the British ships in the offing, so as to set the wicked old Dey's watchfulness at defiance. You can start with them in their picnic to Bou-Zarea from that house. You can, in your mind, re-enact the incidents, great and small, which Mrs. Blanckley records, and feel with her as she watched her husband going away to Algiers, on no less perilous an errand than that of bearding the Dey. In order to reach the house you must return by the same road, and take a turning to the right (that is, landward) as you return to Algiers.

Here, however, is the Valley of the Consuls at last, and to see it was well worth the trouble of the little expedition. To this Valley, to the Frais Vallon, and to Bou-

Zarea, you may go from Algiers on foot, on horseback, or mainly in carriage, according to your strength; and I will conclude with the assurance that there are very beautiful things to be seen on the "St. Eugène side" of Algiers.

The Jardin d'Essai.

One of the first drives we took in Algiers was to the Jardin d'Essai. This means a nursery ground, on a gigantic scale, for palm trees, bamboos, and every variety of useful and ornamental African trees or plants. We took the lower road, and reached a group of palm trees, called, I believe, "The Oasis of Ste. Marie," which filled us with admiration, for we had not then visited Biskra. But, whether you have been to Biskra or not, you will not fail to admire the long avenue of palms which traverses the *jardin* in its length.

We first drove round one-half of the garden, till we reached the gate opposite the Café des Platanes, a quaint little Arab *café*, which stands almost on the high road. We had not then seen much of such sights, and were pleased with the look of the Arabs lounging about, sipping their coffee, and some of them playing chess. The Oasis of Ste. Marie at one end, and at the other the Arab *café*, are very good introductions to the garden.

Here is the palm avenue from the other side. We never shall forget the impression produced upon us by the sight of a huge blue convolvulus, which had crept pretty well to the top of a tall palm tree at this end of the walk. The flowers were of enormous size, the colour as blue as the sky above our heads. They call this flower "The Morning Glory," and so it is—the glory of an African morning. Then there was an avenue of planes or sycamores; another of bamboos, which, however, looked what we used to call at school somewhat "seedy," despite their feathery tops. There were magnolias; there were plenty of india-rubber trees, really trees. Take it on the whole, it was rather a show of trees than flowers. The bigonia and the hibiscus *trees* (with the morning glory as above) chiefly furnished us with colour. Here and there you would notice plenty of roses; but they would not have been thought much of at a rose show in England. All this is soon told; but it is not easy to describe one's feelings on walking for the first time down such an avenue of palms under the Algerine sun. This was on the 25th of October. One trembles to think of what would have been found in London on the same date under the trees of the Long Walk in Kensington Gardens.

We were taken to a place where there should have been a sheet of water, with an island in the centre. There was what would have been an island, if there had been any water round it; but Algiers was suffering from drought. There was no water, so there were none of the water-flowers about which we had heard so much. Failing water-flowers, we tried for the gazelles. Alas! the den, or little paddock, was empty; the gazelles had been stolen or had come to some untimely end. There was, however, plenty to see; and I think I must invent some common form to represent the brilliancy of the air, the purity of the sky, the sun's stamp on everything around us. It is always the same, and always beautiful, so why vary the words? "The usual thing" will do as well as any other form of expression, and save much description of atmospheric effects, which one always skips, if possible. Loiter and stare about you, and be cool when everything seems so hot. Enjoy the shade when all objects outside the palms appear so bright; but I am told you must not linger here about sundown, for there are exhalations from the earth and the plants not exactly of a tonic kind. I can only repeat it is all very beautiful; and to a stranger arriving from Europe, who sees this vegetation for the first time, it is surprising also. We came back here frequently. Now it was autumn; but in winter and in spring the garden was ever a delightful lounge. Enthusiasts in such matters may make their way to a nursery of Australian trees, which is on the other side of the road, and up the hill. We contented ourselves with distant contemplations of them, for in England we had seen plenty. I should like to hear the opinion of some properly instructed man; but my own idea would be that, as a botanic collection of trees and shrubs (I leave flowers out of the question), the Jardin d'Essai at Algiers is scarcely to be compared with Kew, bar the marvel of the palm avenue. It is only fair to say that great attention is paid to utility. The gentleman who conducted us round took us to a sort of central establishment, where the packing and exporting operations were being carried on. There was no doubt as to the active industry of the place. The garden, then, should be looked upon as a "nursery ground" for practical use, not a "botanic garden" for show and scientific purposes. I can only answer for it as a lounge of a very beautiful kind. When we came to know Algiers better, it was pleasant enough on a Friday afternoon to look in first at the Arab burying-ground, with the draped women floating about like ghosts amongst the tombs, or picnicking on a gravestone, and to finish up with an hour's lounge in the Jardin d'Essai under the avenue of palms.

THE ARAB POLICE-COURT.

There is an appendage to the grand mosque, in the shape of a small court of justice, where I spent many pleasant hours during my stay in Algiers. One might have supposed that I had seen enough of such places, but this was not so. Think of Charles Lamb, and his account of his own feelings when he had been pensioned off, and could enjoy himself like a capitalist for the remainder of his days. He could now purchase that old folio over which he had been higgling for many a day. When tired of his folio he could lounge about the lanes in pleasant Islington; he could pace the quarter-deck sacred to the memory of so many old benchers; or he could look in upon his former colleagues, who were still bound to the oar, and pass "the time of day," not without a gentle self-consciousness that day and night were now equally his own. But somehow a feeling of unsatisfied habit grew upon him. He would not have disliked to be late for business again. He would have been pleased not to copy, but to be called on to copy that voluminous mass of documents bearing upon the chequered fortunes of the nutmeg trade. He might have been happier had he been back on his old stool, and had the old folio and the Islington lounges remained as stolen joys.

I feel something of the same kind whenever I come across a police-court in any part of the world. They are all wonderfully alike. My eye rests with a certain satisfaction on the unsavoury crowd outside. I can distinguish at a glance between the disorderly and the assault cases. That poor woman with the black eye is an old friend. Then you have the professional gentlemen in their infinite variety; the friends of the prisoners; the important officials; and day after day, eheu! a renewal of the same scenes.

Now at Algiers here were the old experiences translated into Arabic. I first came across a little knot of baggy women chattering fiercely, and apparently working one of their number up to vengeance point. This day a stag must die. A husband is standing in a very painful predicament. With us this would have meant "six months;" here it will probably be divorce and an allowance. Those two stout fellows in roomy slippers are eyeing each other very fiercely, but they say nothing. This, now a simple assault case, will not improbably ripen into "subsequent proceedings;" neither of those men will rest content with an adverse decision. Then there is a big, heavy-jowled man, his face is yellow, and his knickerbockers blue, who passes from one knot to another, apparently having a word for everybody; he is "touting" for business.

We slip out of the street into a court-yard, where people

are squatted about, patient as Shylocks with well-whetted knives. There is a little room facing us, open to the court; at the back of it is seated the magistrate, with crossed legs. There is a table before him, with books of practice, I firmly believe; on either side, ranged against the wall, three or four gentlemen, the ministering angels of the court. The one of them who is painting in, rather than writing, the "notes," or some other official gear, is obviously the chief clerk. He does not seem at all annoyed with the crimes, but a little put out if the evidence does not come out in a clear, handy sort of way. The magistrate, who must be a man of sense, for he says so little, lets them all go on, plays with his massive watch-chain, and looks as if his thoughts were far away, as no doubt they are. He is thinking of pleasant Blidah, and wishing himself there with a select circle of friends. Every now and then he will take up a legal document, as though he wished to gain the last assurance upon some particular point. He is simply saving appearances, and will not be drawn into the discussion. He is a man in middle life, neatly dressed, with a distinctly humoristic expression.

Now for the case before the court. A powerful-looking brute of a fellow is standing at bay before the tribunal. We, the spectators, have climbed to the best places we could find on the steps which lead to the open door. On one side of the court there is an open window, and at this window a lady is "going on" in a rare way —I should say overwhelming the strong man with a recital of his little peccadilloes. He never looks at her; seems to disdain any efforts which might induce her to soften her evidence. Nay, I think he rather gives unnecessary prominence to a big stick which has not been taken from him. The ladies are not admitted into the body of the court, but, like the present plaintiff, give their evidence through a window.

Some wretch who wished to practise on my credulity had told me that this window was connected by some cunning machinery with the magistrate's table, so that he could, by touching a spring, let it down at once when the witness indulged in irrelevant matter. I had been greatly struck with the idea, and thought of writing about it to the *Times*. Might not the custom be extended? Say that our Lord Chief Justice, by simply touching a spring on his desk, could have let down a heavy, green baize curtain between the court and Dr. Kenealy in a late celebrated case; the "interests of justice" would not have suffered much. The story was, unfortunately, not true. There is the window, but it is for the witness, not for the bar. You can scarcely imagine counsel taking objections through a window.

The case went on. The magistrate asked the witness a question, which simply elicited shriller talking. Had I been counsel for the defence, I would have encouraged the lady to proceed, for she was obviously irritating the court. Then there was an appeal to the clerk, who took down a book, and having fixed a pair of goggles firmly on his nose, read out something which seemed uncomfortable for the defendant, for he, in turn, began to growl out defiance in a deep voice. In the mean while the heavy-sterned man in blue made his way into court, pushing us all aside. It must be some matter of importance. Not a bit of it. When he had taken up position, he did not seem to be instructed in any case in particular; he simply rubbed his fat sides, and looked as if he was master of the situation. I suppose his idea was to show his importance. I wondered why my respected colleague did not cause that fat impostor to be turned out of court, but no doubt he knew best.

The plaintiff screamed; the defendant growled on; the blue man rubbed himself. The magistrate arrived at a decision which appeared to give satisfaction to the dove-cote, for the plaintiff and her backers screamed louder than ever. The defendant simply grasped his stick, and muttered something. Now, as I live, that fellow is giving notice of appeal, and so it was. He would try the French courts, and see if an Arab's inalienable right to thrash his wife was to be set aside in this summary way. Society was in danger; we were standing on the edge of a gulf. The kadi looked unutterably bored, and the court rose.

During the recess coffee was brought to the official personages; with us it would have been beer. During the whole time we were present I noticed this constant "bringing in" of coffee, and carrying out of empty cups. There is something in the atmosphere of a police-court which induces people to refresh themselves —generally, with us, by running to the public-house over the way.

I found out from one of the officials who spoke a little French that the next case was to be one for damage, and there was a contest about title. It was curious enough to watch the parties as they squatted down on the floor of the court, waiting for the kadi's return, but when it came to the discussion, each man seemed to tell his own tale, and produce his own documents or whatever they might be. I never caught sight of professional advocacy, not a trace of an Algerine solicitor, though there may be such gentlemen. Sometimes there would be a little good-humoured gossip all round, but no one seemed to get into a passion, no one shook his fist at a professional brother, no one defied the kadi. What could they all be about? There was much examination of documents in the damage case, and the matter seemed to be carefully looked into. Whether or not substantial justice was done it is not for me to say, as I could not understand the language, but certainly the kadi's court at Algiers is an orderly court, and might teach a lesson to many of our English tribunals. The only person who really puzzled me was that fat blue man, who was always turning up, and rubbing, let me say, his sides, *coram populo*. I never heard him say a word to the kadi, nor saw him do business of any kind; he might have been chamber counsel. The upshot of my impression was that plaintiff and defendant got a fair hearing, and addressed the kadi in turn, who asked a few questions, and gave a decision which generally seemed to be received with satisfaction. There was a good deal of what we should call "applications to the magistrate." The kadi was very patient, and attended to everybody. All my preconceived notions of Arab or Eastern courts of justice were completely upset. No one was bastinadoed; there were no thrilling occurrences. What I saw was a somewhat overworked and wearied man doing the best justice he could in open court. One soon got to disregard the strange dresses, and then the play of the cases seemed very much the same as at home. During our stay at Algiers I was always glad to run into this place, and got quite fond of the kadi, with whom, however, I never interchanged a word.

We had left Algiers some time, and had been to Fort Nationale, to Constantine, to Biskra, and elsewhere, when we found ourselves one day at Blidah. Well-nigh the first person we met there, neater than ever, was our old friend the kadi, who had no doubt got to know the stranger who was in the habit of hobbling into his court. We interchanged a kind of friendly grin. He was out at Richmond or Greenwich for the day, and I can only trust all things turned out to his satisfaction. What a job the kadi must have had to clear the list and catch his train!

That blue man will remain an enigma to me. Was he founding a business?

As I was totally unable to understand the words spoken before the kadi (the proceedings being conducted in Arabic), I thought it might be of advantage to give a specimen of what such discussions amount to on competent authority. Captain Richard, who was the *chef du Bureau Arabe* at Orleansville, has published a most amusing book, in which he gives the result of his experience. I suppose that these cases must be taken as a literary work, not as dry reports of cases; but the question is—Do they give a fair impression of them? Making allowance for the Boz or Pickwickian element, I fancy this is so. This is the sort of thing to which a *chef du Bureau Arabe* had to listen every day. Observe, what I saw in the kadi's court was all peaceful and orderly. The most screaming plaintiff would have known that it was not worth while to "try it on" before the kadi, who would not have paid a moment's attention to his wild pleadings. He would simply have been turned out of court. It would seem, however, that these fellows try to work on the feelings of an European judge. Here, then, is an abduction case, as tried before the Bureau Arabe. The court is open; the judge is seated. Enter plaintiff, with a face of agony, clothes filthy and in disorder, as from grief, beard grizzly, eyes sharp and restless. He drags himself to the front, his right hand raised out of his *bernouse*, with the forefinger pointing to heaven.

Plaintiff (in a shrill tone): I invoke God and His justice!

President: What have you got to complain of? Speak!

Plaintiff: I invoke God and His justice!

President: Well, explain what is amiss, and we will give you the best justice we can.

Plaintiff (with the shrillest scream human lungs can produce): I invoke God and His justice!

President: Well, see here, explain yourself, and try not to scream so loud.

Plaintiff (keeping up his yelling): I am a plaintiff.

President: Egad! I see that clearly enough; but

tell me what is your cause of complaint, so that I may do you justice.

Plaintiff: I am an unfortunate man, poor, but virtuous. I have never robbed on the highway; I have never lied, nor murdered, nor betrayed any one. My heart is pure, I say. I could produce as witnesses all my tribe, and the neighbouring tribes.

President: I have no doubt about what you say; but your private virtues are not the question. Once more, explain to me the subject of your complaint.

Plaintiff: What? What's that? What have you said to me?

President: By the Lord! what do you suppose I've said, except to tell you to explain your business? I keep on saying so over and over again.

Plaintiff (in his shrillest tone): There is but one God, and our Lord Mohammed is His prophet! There is but one God, and our Lord Mohammed is His prophet!

The usher of the court (standing at his side): Don't yell so loud. By Sidi Abd-Alla! you make the canvas of the ceiling shake!

Plaintiff: What? You don't mean it? Am I speaking a little loud?

The usher: Sidi Bou-Krasi! a little loud! Why you are screaming like a sucking-pig. Are you deaf, then?

Plaintiff: Certainly not. But I am always afraid of not being heard.

The usher: Head of the Prophet! You need not be afraid of that, I will answer for it. Lower your voice one-half; and may Sidi Lekhhol strangle me if you won't be heard from here to the market-place.

Plaintiff: Thank you for your good advice. I will speak lower, so as to meet your wishes.

President: But, at least, explain yourself. There are many other plaintiffs waiting. I cannot lose my time.

Plaintiff: Quite right, quite right. I will tell you my story at once. (Here plaintiff makes a pause, whilst he plays with his beard in the most fidgety fashion. He rolls his eyes about in every way, in a restless and uncertain manner. At length he makes up his mind to speak.) She was very quiet at our home. One day I went to the market of Sebts to buy some salt. I come back; I find my tent empty. I call Fethha. I say to him, "Fethha!" Says he, "Yes, Sidi." Says I, "How is it she is not there?" Says he, "I think she is gone for wood or water." I go to the wood and to the water;— nothing. I then began to have my doubts about the fact, for the day before he came prowling about my tent. I go to my neighbour, Kaddour Bel-Djar, a man as perfect as you could desire or wish him to be. I say to him, "O Bel-Djar!" Says he, "Sir, to you." Says I, "Such and such things have happened." Says he, "I know all about it. I saw them slip away yesterday, both of them, in the direction of the Ouled Meguerounin." So far, so good. I go to the Ouled Meguerounin. I search everywhere; I wear myself out with searching. I ask for information everywhere;—nothing. I am then obliged to go home alone. After certain days I set out again. I go to the east, to the west, in every direction.

At length, after three months of useless searches (may Sidi Bou-Krasi put out my two eyes if it wasn't three whole months!), I reach this place. One of the Ouled Taân addresses me and says, "Give me five douros, and I will show you where she is." I give him five douros, and he leads me to a tent of the Beni Krian, where I perceive him established with her, like husband and wife. I wish to enter, when I receive at once a shower of blows from a cudgel and of stones. The dogs jump upon me. See what a state my *bernouses* are in. In a word, I am forced to beat a retreat. But I came to you to make my complaint (deeply affected). O thou, the Sultan of justice! Gate of help! Support of the afflicted! Father of the orphan! will you not see right done when my complaint is so just?

President: I suppose you are speaking of your wife in this speech of yours?

Plaintiff: How? have I not said so? But I have not been speaking of anything else.

President: No matter. You are come to claim back your wife, who has been carried off from you by somebody whose name you have forgotten to mention.

Plaintiff: How? I have not named him? His name is Moustapha ben Kraïn, of the tribe of the Ouled Krian. (With a deep sigh) Ah! my poor wife!

President: If the facts are as you say, nothing will be easier than to do you justice.

Plaintiff: Holy chamber of Mecca! Nothing is more true than what I have said to you. (He drops a tear.) My poor wife, who knew so well how to make fritters and girdle-cakes. I would swear that the scoundrel took her off by force, and that she did all she could to resist him.

President: Console yourself. Here is the Kaïd of the Ouled Krian here present; he will help us to put this matter to rights.

Plaintiff (with a groan): What a wife I have lost in her! She cost me forty douros.

The Kaïd: I have, in fact, heard something of this matter; but what the plaintiff has not told you is that his wife has married again, and with her ravisher, as he calls him.

The Kadi (very gravely): The second marriage is null and void, since the first has not been annulled by a divorce. The law is precise upon this point. Sidi Malek says, in the chapter concerning the union of the two sexes——

President: That's enough. We don't want a quotation to teach us this truth, that a woman cannot lawfully marry two men at the same time.

Plaintiff (still groaning): My poor wife! It is a loss of forty douros.

The Kaïd: Come, now, could we not arrange this matter in a friendly way?

Plaintiff (with virtuous indignation): Never, never! I appeal to God and His justice. (He sobs.) My poor wife! Ah! if they had not carried her off by force I should have her still. What a dear creature she was!

President (deeply affected): Calm yourself, poor man! I promise you, you shan't go back without your wife, whom you so dearly love.

The Kaïd (sticking to his own idea): How much did she cost you?

Plaintiff: Who? What? my wife? Forty douros. Alas! the joy of my tent is departed with her. Forty douros, without counting the jewels.

The Kaïd (comes straight to the point): I am ready to give you twenty on account of the man who now holds her in possession.

Plaintiff (changing his whole manner): I beg your pardon. What's that you say? I have not understood you.

The Kaïd: I tell you I am ready to pay you twenty douros for your wife on account of Moustapha ben Kraïn, who has commissioned me to arrange this business.

Plaintiff: How twenty douros? but she cost me forty.

The Kaïd: True, you gave forty douros for her, but she was then young. She is now beginning to grow old, and she has dropped much under her first value.

Plaintiff: That's true; that's right She has gone down. She's not worth what she was. You'll give me twenty douros?

The Kaïd: At once, if you so wish it. I have got the twenty douros in my pocket-book (he makes them ring). You hear, eh?

Plaintiff (deeply affected by the ring of the coin): Twenty douros; it's a bargain. Count them out at once. My word is my bond.

(The Kaïd takes the douros out of his pocket-book, making them sound, spreads them out in a complacent way on the ground, and begins counting them to the plaintiff, who kneels before him, his eyes sparkling with greediness.)

President (completely recovered from his tenderness of feeling): But stop! Before concluding the bargain, we ought at least to consult the woman who is the object of it. The plaintiff has affirmed that she would not for all the world separate from him. Now, if this poor woman loves him——

The Kaïd: She love him! She has said, before all who cared to hear her, that she had rather be cut to pieces alive than return to him.

President: Upon my word! That's strong.

Plaintiff: There may be something in it. For some time past she has taken the bridle off her tongue more than befits a woman. I have been obliged to box her ears on many an occasion.

President: But you said just now you loved her so dearly.

Plaintiff (stowing away his money in his handkerchief, and rising from his knees): True; but she had begun to get a little the worse for wear. She limped a good bit, and her left eye was not as clear as it might have been. Twenty douros; it is a reasonable price. I am a just and virtuous man, I am; everybody will tell you so. I don't want what belongs to others, and only ask for my own.

President: You are satisfied, then?

Plaintiff: Sidi Bou-Krasi! I should be hard to please if I were not. Everywhere will I praise your wisdom and your justice.

President: Pray don't mention it.

Plaintiff: Now, I have only one more favour to ask of you.

President: What is that?

Plaintiff: It is that you should desire the kadi to give me a document which shall show that the case has been decided before you; and that the actual possessor of my wife is forbidden, under any pretext whatsoever, to bring her back to me.

President: Fair enough. They shall give you a record of the decision; and, besides, one of divorce, which will put you in a perfectly regular position. Don't be alarmed.

Plaintiff: In such a case it is better to take every precaution.

President: You couldn't speak more to the point. You have more brains than I thought at first. Go in peace!

Plaintiff: God be with you! (He goes out, perfectly satisfied.)

First Mornings at Algiers.

How beautiful they were! everything was so new and delightful. It was every day a transformation scene, for we had not had time to forget the Victoria Station, the fog, and the sloppy little boys. We woke early, opened the shutters, and were in glory; none of your sunshine and water; none of your November mornings, in which you see a little round red saucepan in the heavens, and say, "Go to! this is something like a day!" The good, stay-at-home folks who have enjoyed three score and ten years of fogs and east wind; aye, and of Julys and Augusts, cannot have a conception of that pleasant African sunlight in early morning. If the happiness of the just could depend upon atmospheric conditions, we were already blessed. There between us and Cape Matifou were the blue wavelets of the bay lolling about as though to be admired. The white town was golden in the sunlight.

Even at this early hour the bustle of the Place would begin, and noises, to which I should have objected at home, came up to us like strains of pleasant music. There was the quack doctor with his brass band under the statue of the Duke of Orleans, pulling out teeth in a way the patients must have enjoyed. Down below us, but hidden from us by the palm-tops, came the cries of the newspaper boys, which sadly puzzled me for a while, but I came at last to know them. Thus the list tripped off their tongues—"*Le Moniteur!*" "*Le Tricolore!*" "*La Vigie Algerienne!*" "*La Solidarité!*" "*L'Akhbar!*" When I got to know it, I used to fall asleep with a foreknowledge that I should hear the cry in the morning, and to look for it. I could now accentuate and emphasize the syllables as these pleasant newspaper people used to do it. Then let the door be opened but for a moment, and there would come in the noise of the public auction, which was going on so many times a week in the street behind. The highly gifted auctioneer had called in music to his aid, and had hit upon the plan of running up the biddings by the play of his trumpets. You would hear the sound of "*Cinq francs!*" "*Dix francs!*" "*Vingt francs!*" Louder and louder blew the trumpets; till, with an expiring blare, their music excited the bidders to a final offer of "*Vingt-cinq francs!*" Down would come the hammer, accompanied by a brief strain of triumphal music—a *Te Deum*, as one may say.

The sun would get higher and higher; the Place would fill with picturesque promenaders. We could scarcely tear ourselves away from the window to make ourselves tidy. Yes, there is that young rascal, Mohammed, with his red cap. Mme. Cornuz won't be down till later. And there is Beschir. Yes, Dominique, come in! Any arrivals this morning? I see the boats are in. Coffee? Yes; coffee in ten minutes. Madame is going off to the market to get some grapes and flowers; say in a little quarter of an hour we shall be ready. Accordingly Dominique would disappear, and madame trip off to the market, which was close to us.

What aisles of figs and tomatoes! what transepts of cauliflowers, carrots, peas, beans, etc.! What a nave of grapes, pomegranates, and flowers! I mean that there were long rows of tables, on which these beautiful things were set forth under the auspices of native and French salesmen; the women sold the flowers. It was easy enough to fill the basket, and in a few minutes madame would return, with a booty of roses, heliotrope, carnations, violets, and *branches* of verbena, to decorate our little breakfast-table. The grapes were, of course, not equal to the hot-house miracles of England, but they were sweet and abundant, costing, I was told, something like twopence a pound. Then a ring would bring up Dominique with the coffee and the rolls, and I assure you the breakfast-table made a very good figure. Dominique would crown the edifice with "*Et voilà, monsieur, le journal,*" producing the *Akhbar* of the day.

But the sun is getting too strong; we must close or partially close the shutters to keep the sun out. This would happen about the 5th of November, just when the good folks in London were lighting up the lamps and shutting out the fog. I don't say our glory lasted, but this was the way we began.

The Algerine Old Bailey.

Just before leaving Algiers, I had what the young men at Mr. Jay's mourning establishment would call the melancholy pleasure of assisting at a trial for murder before the Cour d'Assises. This was upon the 1st of May, 1880. But I must go back a little. A few days after we had reached Algiers, on October of last year, 1879, we were attracted by a large crowd on the quay. The object of attraction seemed to be a steamer of the Valery Company, which had just come into port. Some of the bystanders informed me that a murder had been committed on the 13th of October, by a Spanish mason, named Calderon, on the person of his wife; that he had succeeded in making his escape for the moment, but had been caught at Bougie by the police, and was on board the vessel at which we were all looking; and that he would be tried in due course before the Cour d'Assises for the crime with which he was charged.

The matter hung strangely in hand. I could scarcely conceive that any very protracted preliminary investigation was necessary. The evidence seemed to lie in a nutshell—if I may use the consecrated expression—the only question could be that of premeditation, or, in other words, could murder be reduced to manslaughter? I had long forgotten all about the matter, when, on the very day before we left Algiers, the people told me that Calderon was to be tried on that day, so we resolved to be present.

The hall in which the trial was to take place is one of the finest, if, indeed, it be not the very finest, left in Algiers, the court of an old Moorish house, with arcades and galleries, covered in at the top. We found a great crowd, and had some little difficulty in making our way in, but once there, I had but to send in my card to the president, or, as we should say, the presiding judge, and he at once, and with the greatest courtesy, directed one of the ushers to take us up to a place in the gallery, from which we could see and hear all the proceedings conveniently enough. Apart from the gravity of the crime and its fierce dramatic incidents, I was anxious, from old professional habits of thought, to see how the system of interrogating the prisoner was worked at Algiers.

The president, M. Blankaert, conducted the examination, and although there was enough in every question to make every curl of every wig of every criminal barrister in England stand upon end, I am bound to say that the examination was conducted with perfect fairness. There was no bullying, no laying of traps, the questions asked were just those to which I should have been too glad to give answers had I been unjustly charged. On the whole, my conclusion was that the system might, and probably *did*, work well for an innocent man; badly for a guilty one. Given a fair judge, it was an inestimable advantage to the prisoner to give replies to a man who only desired to arrive at the truth. Given an unfair or a violent judge, the silent jury would have put matters to rights by acquitting the prisoner in the teeth of the evidence, to show their dissatisfaction with the judge. I do not, however, say that the system would work well in England. We have been going on for ages under the belief that it would be unfair to a person charged with crime to ask him to give his own account of the matter; and that our judges would have no other thought than to procure convictions if they were allowed to question the accused. However, this is no place for a long discussion upon this point. I can but repeat that, were I innocent of a crime, with a good deal of colourable evidence against me, I would rather be tried on the French system; if guilty, I had much rather be compelled to hold my tongue, and pay a good fee to a professional athlete, who would object to every question, and browbeat every witness. But let us get back to Calderon, and the Old Bailey at Algiers.

The story, as laid before the court, was that the prisoner, Joseph Calderon, a mason by trade, had, in November, 1878, married Isabella Ramirez, then aged seventeen, a worker at the cigar trade. A fortnight after the marriage she fell seriously ill, and was attended by her mother and husband, but was finally removed to the civil hospital of Mustapha, where she remained three months. At the expiration of this time she came out, and, under the orders of the doctor, went to live in the country with her husband, as the air of the town was prejudicial to her. The young couple seem to have got on pretty well for about five months, when the young wife fled to her mother's house, and refused to return to her husband. Life with him was intolerable to her. That was her story. Calderon replied, "Mother-in-law," and persistent kindness on his part. He made every effort to induce her to return, but in vain. So at last he seems to have made up his mind to kill her, or at least to do her some grievous bodily harm. The question of intention and premeditation was the one before the court.

On the 13th of October, about 5.30 p.m., Isabella Calderon was returning from work, in company with a widow called Soucques. They were in the street Bab-el-Ouad, when the wretched woman came upon her husband, who was standing there and watching for her. He sprang on her at once, and stabbed her in the left side with a stiletto, produced in court. She was taken into the shop of a neighbouring apothecary, and died at once. The widow Soucques spoke directly to these facts, and the prisoner admitted their truth, but tried to palliate his crime by the allegation that angry words had passed between them, and that in a frenzy he struck his wife. This was denied by the witness. Calderon managed to escape under cover of the darkness, which was just setting in, but was caught at Bougie, a few days afterwards; and there he was. He said he had purposed leaving Algiers for Kabylia, and had bought the stiletto, or dagger, for his own protection. It certainly did not look like a fighting weapon, as I saw it lying on the table. I cannot, in half a dozen lines, even recapitulate the evidence which it took as many hours to lay before the court; but I will venture to say that no English jury would have retired from the box on such a case. To do them but simple justice, the Algerine jury only took something like a quarter of an hour to make up their minds. They brought in a verdict of guilty, or an affirmative to each of the three questions asked of them: (1.) Had there been voluntary homicide? (2.) Had there been premeditation? (3.) Had there been a *guet-apens?* *i.e.* a lying in wait, or, as it were, an ambush.

Guilty on all points, but with *extenuating circumstances.* What these were I was wholly unable to discover from the evidence. It seemed to me a cold-blooded, deliberate murder, if ever there had been one, so I talked with one or other of the people about me, and found the men for the most part well enough satisfied. "*Allez, monsieur.* There had been faults on both sides. If Calderon was jealous, he had very good cause for his jealousy." Female public opinion was dead against Calderon. "*Ce gredin, c'est ainsi qu'on peut tuer le pauvre monde.*" Then a world of suggestions as to the incidents of this wretched marriage, such as the fertile ingenuity of a French audience can readily supply, but which one had rather dismiss from consideration. The sentence on the prisoner was "Fifteen years of hard labour, and ten years' surveillance by the police;" and it seemed to be considered severe.

On a table near the judges was the dagger with which the murder had been committed, and an engraving which represented "The Murder of Ines de Castro," which was the one ornament of the room the married pair occupied.

This engraving was a pretext for a good deal of eloquence. "Had not Calderon threatened the unhappy Isabella with the fate of Ines?" or *vice versâ*, had Calderon not called her attention to it with the view of showing to her that, sooner or later, the wages of sin is death? What could a husband do more? Then there were the poor creature's earrings, and her marriage ring still stained with her blood, and yet another called *porte-bonheur*. The spectators seemed to me hard and unsympathizing, with the exception of a few tight-lipped women, who were all for vengeance. But I have no right to say that the Algerine audience was in any way worse behaved than would have been a similar crowd in England. There was no groaning, no applause, no marks of approbation or the reverse. It was a perfectly orderly court; and, as far as I could see, no English judge could have conducted the proceedings of a trial for murder with greater dignity or fairness than M. Blankaert, the president at Algiers.

An Algerine Library.

I wish to give the names of a few books which have afforded me much amusement and some instruction, for the benefit of those who may be meditating a sojourn at Algiers. I fear my little list will disappoint the very learned and very gushing people. To the very learned I will venture, not without fear and trembling, to say a word apart; to the very gushing I can only suggest that they will find food enough for their voracity without help from me. The first best book about Algiers, to my poor thinking, is Mrs. Broughton's, or certainly so much of it as contains the diary of her charming old mother, Mrs. Blanckley, the Consul's wife. By the help of this you can really live over again the last years of piratical Algiers. I had rather not say anything about contemporary writers from my own country, for it would seem like an impertinence in me to offer any judgment on a matter in which I may be supposed to feel a personal interest. A goodly list of names will be found at the Lending Library, Rue du Hamma, No. 5, at Algiers, from which readers can make a selection according to their fancy or taste.

Passing to the French writers, I would say that the works which have pleased me most are those of General Daumas, full of pleasant information as to the Arabs and the Kabyles. There is the work of M. Camille Housset, "La Conquête d'Alger," written from the French view of the matter. I found at Tlemçen a little volume written by M. Clamageran, which seemed to me very well done. I derived much instruction from the works of M. de Baudicour, both as regards the military government and the attempts at colonization made by the French authorities. But, leaving what is called "solid information" aside for the moment, let any one who likes a good hearty laugh by no means omit to procure "The Prodigious Adventures of Tartarin de Tarascon," by Alphonse Daudet. This is not book-making; it is almost a work of genius. He must be a dull fellow indeed who does not enjoy Algeria the more after having accompanied Tartarin in his astonishing adventures. Captain Richard's book, "Scenes de Mœurs

Arabes," is laughter-compelling, and is written by a gentleman who, as former *chef du Bureau Arabe* at Orleansville, had peculiar advantages for getting to the bottom of the Arab character amongst the humbler classes. His books are an antidote against gush, and give you the idea of sketches in Algeria by a French Boz. The tour to Constantine and Biskra by a lady who writes under the *nom de plume* of Louis Régis, is imaginative and graceful. It gives a good idea of the country, though I would not vouch for the accuracy of all the facts; but it is a very pretty book, and will give much pleasure to the reader, whether read at Algiers or in London. "Une Année dans le Sahel," by Eugène Fromentin, was in everybody's hand the winter we were in Algiers. It seemed to me very gracefully written, although I could not but envy the peculiar good fortune of the author in meeting with adventures at every turn. I am sure I poked about, and often enough, into every corner of the Ville Arabe; but I might as well have loitered about Holywell Street as far as adventure was concerned. The author would have a perfect right to say he did not wish to produce a Dutch picture. So he left a true impression; the facts were at his disposal. But he looks at nature—at African nature—with an artist's eye, and when he treats of this, one feels that he is writing the truth. I suppose everybody to have read Gerard's book about lions and lion-slaying; this has an interest out of Algiers, but there are no lions left there now. Tartarin will correct Gerard. Read "Belamare" for Abd-el-Kader, the "Insurrection du Dhara" for Bou-Maza, by Captain Richard. The French books are, of course, endless; but the reader will find himself drafted off from one to another, and requires no help beyond being set upon the right track.

As far as the learning about the old piracy is concerned, a writer will find much better information, and more books about it, at the British Museum than at Algiers. A good history of Algerine piracy is a work to be done; but it would require long study and labour to produce anything worth reading, anything beyond mere clap-trap and commonplace.

There is a good collection of books at the museum, or the library portion of the museum, where the visitor will find courteous reception and ready aid from Mr. M'Carthy, the curator, and abundant information about the Roman remains in Algeria, with which subject he is peculiarly conversant. I do not, however, think that many visitors to Algiers, who go there, presumably, for health's sake, will care to leave the sunshine, and spend their days as they would in the reading-room of the British Museum. I suppose all persons wintering at Algiers will take care to have a supply of newspapers from England; they reach you four days old. A very fair collection of English novels and light literature is to be found at Rue du Hamma, No. 5. The subscription for the winter is but ten francs.

THE TRANS-SAHARA RAILROAD.

I remember well, a few years ago, I was sitting quietly over my books, when a friend who has been lately taken from us rushed into my room, in a state of gleeful excitement, and with the cry of "I have done it; I have done it at last! Well, that's over."

I am speaking of the late Mr. W. H. Wills. The mention of his honoured name will call up many recollections of his pleasant humour to those who were happy enough to be amongst his friends. "*Quis desiderio sit pudor aut modus tam cari capitis?*" Alas! alas! yet another gone!

"Well, but what have you done, Wills? Not committed suicide, eh? If you're a ghost, I suppose you've come to give me a warning."

"No, no; not that. I have just bought twelve Eureka shirts. They are in a nice parcel down below. For many years past I have been haunted by the Eureka shirts. On the splash-boards of the hansom cabs, at the railway stations just between the Old Malabar Dog Biscuits, and Rum without Head-ache, on every hoarding in London alongside of Mrs. S. A. Allen's magnificent head of hair, I have been pursued by the question of 'Have you tried our Eureka shirts?' I have resisted the question as an impertinence. I have pooh-poohed it as a mere puff; but I am vanquished at last. I felt I must not leave the world without trying the Eureka shirt. My mind will be easier now—it was the last of my neglected duties. Take warning by me, and try the Eureka shirts."

Now, this is just the frame of mind in which I find myself with regard to the Trans-Sahara Railroad. When I first came to Algiers I thought the good people were laughing at me when they gravely proposed to run a rail across that idle desert. The sand would cover up the permanent way; the amiable Touaregs, on their swift camels, with black veils over their faces, would charge up to the working parties, and carry them away captive. Where were they to get water to keep their boilers a-going? Besides, suppose the rail to be laid down—water to be laid on in the heart of Africa in a way which would satisfy a London turncock—who the deuce wants to take a return ticket for Timbuctoo? If ever I take a ticket for that delightful place, I won't throw away money upon a "return." Besides, what do the Timbuctoo people want from us Northerners, or we from them? How about the goods traffic? The natives do not require the hair restorer, for, as a rule, their hair is copious and curly. As far as I know, tea at two shillings a pound would not be caught up in Central Africa. On the other side, we might, perhaps, take a few ostrich feathers, but even for these the demand is not lively at home.

To all this my French friends would reply, "France, mistress of the Niger, as she already is of Algeria and Senegal, will become the sovereign of Northern Africa. The regeneration of Africa is the great work of our epoch."

I ventured, not in reply, but as one desirous of information, to ask if the hopeful project for converting the desert into an inland sea had been postponed, for I could scarce think the two projects would work concurrently. A snarl at English greediness would be the answer. The Trans-Sahara line was the subject of conversation wherever I went. It was discussed every morning in the newspapers. The only doubt was whether it would be the wiser course to lay it down handy to Tunis — Biskra way; or to Morocco — Tlemçen way (this was the Oran idea); or to take the central way by El-Aghouat.

Like my dear friend with his Eureka shirts, I resisted all these polemics for a while. I was willing to admit, for argument's sake, that British cupidity embraced the universe, and that our people at home were occupied day and night in meditation as to how they could best tear down the glorious flag of France in Algeria, and make it a receptacle for Manchester piece-goods, Low-Church missionaries, rum, and young ladies with elephantine feet and a prodigious profusion of fair ringlets. Not convinced—very far from it—but wearied out, I resolved at last to buy my dozen of Eureka shirts. This I did by purchasing the great work of M. A. Duponchel, "Ingenieur en Chef des Ponts et Chaussées," Paris: Hachette. 1879.

In this book the subject will be found practically and scientifically considered. This gentleman has arrived at the conclusion, in a way to satisfy himself, that there is nothing simpler or easier than to lay down a line between the Mediterranean North Coast, and the Valley of the Niger. French enterprise would soon open out the basin of the Niger, and the end would be a vast colonial empire, embracing all sorts of rich and profitable territories—emphatically the Soudan.

It would be difficult to make Frenchmen understand that, if such a scheme were feasible, they would have behind them the hearty good wishes of the English people. Our own experience in British India is not very encouraging, but if we do not derive much wealth from this magnificent Dream-land, at least we manage to keep peace in a way amongst hundreds of millions of human beings, who, if we were not there, would devote all their spare time to the sacred duty of cutting each other's throats.

Conceive what a result: the "regeneration of Africa," whatever that may mean—and the energy of the French people devoted to keeping peace in Africa, in place of breaking it in Europe! I wish I could believe in the project, but I am sorry to say the work of M. Duponchel would have filled me with sadness if I could have brought myself to think that these railway schemes would, for the time being, be carried out beyond the limits of the French possessions, for up to this point they are of obvious and undoubted utility. No more satisfactory sight to all who wish well to Algeria and France than to see the iron line from Oran to Algiers; from Algiers, through Setif, to Constantine; from Setif to Bougie; from Oran or Nemours to Tlemçen, and other branch-work of the like kind. We English would be infinitely obliged to our French friends if they would drive the iron horse even to Biskra and El-Aghouat. First, let them do the work which is to be done in their own provinces, which will stimulate their productive powers, and make the military occupation cheap and easy, and when this is accomplished, it will be time enough to talk about the Niger and Timbuctoo.

This is not the first time we have heard of Mississippi schemes and El-Dorados, the invariable result seeming to be that a few financing scoundrels fill their pockets for a time, at the expense of the ruin and misery of countless dupes. To be sure, there is the instance of Australia, or again of North America; but was the success gained in these places the result of *coups de tonnerre?* Slowly, very slowly and surely, the ground was won. Vast communities have grown up, and are extending themselves in harmony with the laws of human nature and of economic science. The French may find their way down to Timbuctoo and the Niger, and remain there; but this will not be done by an express train. When I see before my eyes every day in Algeria how imperfectly the system of colonization is developed; that the State has not yet hit upon a rational plan for disposing of public lands to real colonists, but that it is still a matter of *concessions,* official delays, and jobbery;— how can I bring myself to believe that this wild project of tapping Central Africa by a single line can ever be made profitable or useful? No doubt the good folks who built the Tower of Babel thought their neighbours who confined themselves to the erection of cottages and workshops very slow people. I have yet to learn that the Tower of Babel ever paid a reasonable dividend to the shareholders.

After all, this Trans-Sahara question is rather one for those who may choose to risk their money upon it. I can perfectly understand that such a project should be lifted to notoriety by a financing ring at Paris or in the colonies; be puffed up in the Parisian and colonial newspapers; and that even for six days or so shares might be quoted at a premium. Who can predict what an insane patient may do in a paroxysm? We have had much and bitter experience at home, and no doubt the people are ready to begin again at the first convenient opportunity. I can only say that I have read M. Duponchel's book with great interest, and recommend it to others. They will here find the case for the Trans-Sahara stated by a clever and able man; but I would not take shares in the enterprise at a gift. To overcome engineering difficulties is merely a question of money. Others may think differently; but I have tried the Eureka shirts, and they don't fit.

Roman Remains in Algeria.

I trust that no expression I may use may be construed as a sneer, or even a joke, at the expense of really learned men, who may have turned their attention to the solution of the antiquarian riddles of North Africa. Here is to be found plenty of food for their curiosity, and I am sure the world will be much obliged to any competent persons who may devote time and trouble to the deciphering of these old inscriptions—to the explanation of these old monuments.

We all know pretty well the meaning of Roman dominion in North Africa. Carthage had lasted for a little more than seven centuries. The Romans came in at the conclusion of what are known as the Punic Wars, for the first and third of which they seem to have had but little justification, unless the policy of getting rid of a dangerous rival at any price be accounted as one. The taking of Carthage, which closed the third Punic War, is dated at 145 B.C.

Genseric, with his **Vandals**, came into Africa in the first part of the fifth century of our era. Here, then, for between five and six centuries, the Romans were masters of the country, either directly or behind the screen of tributary puppets. Africa was one of the four great divisions of the Empire.

On casting about to see if I could discover any mention of the Roman establishments in North Africa, I find it set down that in Vespasian's time, the Cherchel province alone contained thirteen Roman colonies, three free municipalities, two colonies with Latin and one with Italic rights. In Pliny's days, Numidia alone had twelve Roman or Italic colonies, five municipalities, and thirty free towns. Judge, then, if, even after the lapse of thirteen or fourteen centuries, Roman remains are not to be found in Algeria! My hasty notion would be that you would follow in the steps of learned men, and first look for your Roman remains on the seashore, even beginning with Oran, and passing westwards through Cherchel, Icosium, Rusicada or Stora, and the rest of it. I should then take a line more in shore, running through Medeah, so as to touch the inland establishments, including, in a way, Tlemcen, Constantine, and Setif; and finally, I would look for the posts nearer the desert. Were I very determined, I would even make my way to Tebessa, as we did, in point of fact, to Lambessa in the course of our hazardous expedition. There is, no doubt, plenty of work to be done; but we were roaming about rather in pursuit of health than antiquities. When we got to Lambessa, it was under the stress of a fierce sirocco, and I confess we looked over the tumble of arches and ruins in an altogether languid and discreditable way. At Cherchel it was all pure delight, and I recommend all my weak-kneed brethren to give themselves up to Cherchel and its neighbourhood, its forum, its aqueducts, its port, its baths, etc., and they will have in hand a very respectable stock-in-trade should anybody dare to twit them with defective attention to Roman remains. I did not see a thing at *Algiers* or Icosium which would have made it worth one's while to cross the street, on Roman grounds. There is a Roman road running up Mustapha, along which you are sure to pass during your stay at Algiers.

I met during our stay on Mustapha with a few bores (where is the place free from them?), but not one of such intensity that he ventured to button-hole me on the subject of Rusicada. We never went near the place. The curious in such matters may content themselves with the learned pages of dear old Dr. Shaw, and the scholar-like journals of travel by Dean Blakesley. Surely neither Dr. Shaw nor the Dean would have vexed their hearers with tiresome cram about these old-world matters. Gentlemen such as those not only read, mark, and learn, but they inwardly digest their knowledge. To such one would listen with respect as long as they were good enough to speak, but beware of a pretentious and illiterate humbug, if you are looking out for Roman remains in Algiers.

"Hunc, tu, Romane, caveto!"

Our Fire.

I am going to write a few, a very few lines upon the great event of our stay in Algiers—I mean the fire which consumed what we call the famous theatre of La Perle, and certain houses. I think our fire, the disappearance of our banker, and the squabble over the Church Fund were the three events of the season. I speak only of the fire. Who would dare to wake up the wrath which would be aroused by any description of the ecclesiastical question? I can hear the fierce hissing, "Do you mean to tell me, sir?" and then in these clerico-colonial disputes you have always the Bishop of Gibraltar rumbling away in the distance.

Now I have, unfortunately for myself, knocked about long enough in such places to entertain a fear that, on sufficient grounds, such as a tiff with the lady directress of our faith, or a squabble with the influential people of the place, the bishop might go so far as to excommunicate me or do some other dreadful thing. So I will remember the Latin word for "candle," and confine myself to the fire.

We were living up on Mustapha, and did not hear of the fire till the day after the occurrence. We went down to the town next day, and one could have told something had happened by the all-pervading odour of burnt wood. It was too true, the gay little theatre had been burnt down, and we were all grieved to hear that there had been loss of life as well. For a while there was a fear that the houses in the Place du Gouvernement, and even our dear old quarters at the Régence, might have been set on fire by the sparks. Some of our friends, who were stopping at the hotel, told us that the flames had been very considerable, and that, on the whole, it had been what is called "a fine sight." There was little to be seen now but a few charred rafters and shattered walls, when *bang—bang!* off go the great guns. The fire has broken out elsewhere; it is on the Place Bresson; it is at the Custom-house; it is here; it is everywhere. The Arabs have done it. "*C'est évident*"—this is the work of the *indigènes*. How I hated the sight of the malignant creatures, in their dirty *bernouses!* How I could have "let off" a revolver at them from the car, but for the wholesome fear that they might have turned, and beaten me to death with their odious sticks!

Bang—bang! more houses on fire; and the shrill call of a trumpet, and the rapid advance of some heroic dwarfs at the *pas gymnastique*. Let us get back to the Colonne Voirol; from that vantage-point we shall get a better view. Might it not be as well to secure a cabin by the *Saïd* for the next departure? The alarm really got very high, but luckily never attained to the dimensions of a panic, yet it was unpleasant to see the knots of baggy little Frenchmen grouped together, and scowling at the Arabs. The nonsense subsided as it rose. There was a fire; there had been loss of life; but there was no native conspiracy to burn down the town and get rid of the French. Enough had been done to gratify the hotel-keepers on the Riviera, but we could not go further.

As most things, even a calamity such as this, have their ridiculous side, we were told by our friends at the hotels that when the fire was at its height, and there was real cause for apprehension, it was at least remarkable to see how our fair countrywomen issued from their respective bowers in the hotels, carrying one brass tray or more, with which upon their knees, they sat calmly down upon the stairs to await 'events. *Chiffons*, even jewellery brought from home, were forgotten; but, "Oh, spare our brass trays! We will die with these upon our laps."

The passion for brass trays at Algiers becomes a very absorbing one. Two ladies, however, preferred parasols and umbrellas even to trays. They made their way from the threatened hotel, bearing with them three parasols and two umbrellas, stepped into a close cab, and remained there, with the proud consciousness that, frizzle who might, they had done all that could be reasonably expected from them.

THE MOSQUES.

I think the curiosity of most visitors to Algiers will be satisfied with a visit to the Grand Mosque which stands just off the Place du Gouvernement, and the Mosque de la Pêcherie which is actually on one side of the Place. There are, or were, others in the town; for example, the ugly cathedral stands on the site of a Mohammedan mosque, the little church of Nôtre Dame des Victoires was a mosque; but these are not what we came in search of. In the heart of the Arab quarter there is really a little old mosque, which deserves a moment's visit if you happen to be passing that way. I believe there are two of them; we saw only one. The Grand Mosque there, in the Rue de la Marine, is easily distinguishable by the row of pillars in front of it, which are out of character with the mosque itself. I scarcely think there is much in the interior which will detain the visitor long. The best that can be said for it is that it is not disfigured by the trumpery pictures and images which are found in the Roman Catholic churches, and is not so ugly in its nakedness as our own well-pewed places of worship before we took to church decoration. The quiet, the stillness, the quaint figures of the worshippers who drop in to say their prayers and knock their heads against the floor, give the place a certain solemnity; beyond this there is not much to be said.

You have succeeded in getting inside a mosque at last, and, now you are there, what do you find? A large white-washed hall, with a good many pillars, and the invariable Moorish arches. There is the *mihrab*, or hole in the wall; there is the pulpit. As this was the first mosque I had seen, I was compelled to admit a feeling of great disappointment. Was it to get into such a place as this that people used to run the risk of being murdered by infuriated Mussulmen? *C'est le secret de Polichinelle.* It was scarcely worth the trouble of taking your shoes off to see this. Nor do I think that the Pêcherie Mosque makes you much amends. It is like the other, with a difference—not so many columns, and a good deal more painted wood.

We often dropped into these places, for they were

close to the hotel, and there was always a feeling of freshness about the bare walls, and of repose. It was interesting to watch, from behind a pillar, the worshippers, who seemed very much in earnest. Visit them on a Friday, and follow the Mohammedan Service. The quaint figure of the imam, who appears to lead the devotions, and the rows of worshippers ducking and bowing in time and measure, seem to carry you back to those delightful days when "The Arabian Nights" was to you a new book. We liked the strange, wild chanting, and what we took for the sermon had at any rate the merit of brevity. The imam had, no doubt, heard of the golden rule, so dear to the late Baron Alderson, "Twenty minutes with a leaning to mercy."

Algerine Piracy.

I am not about to inflict a "penny dreadful" tirade upon my readers about the wicked old days of Algiers. There are plenty of old historical books at the museum in French and Spanish; there is a much more complete collection at the British Museum in London at the service of the student who would write a proper work on these horrors. At the English lending library you may find a little agony novel, in a literary sense not worthy of much regard, but as full of pirates and hair-breadth escapes, wrecks, fights, and bastinadoes, as the heart can desire. Nor is a funny Irishman, nor the jovial British tar wanting, nor pictures of the Gate of Torture, with heads stuck on spikes, with a full moon and a Turkish sentry. Nor do I think it worth while to cross my arms, and pour out a few pages of lofty moral reflections on the subject of Turkish slavery. I feel what every man of well-regulated mind ought to feel on the subject; so let that pass.

Any one who visits Algiers in the year 1880–81 need not fear that he will be set to work upon the Mole, and be cheered up with a sound bastinado if his energy should flag. But for all that there are land-rats and water-rats here present; beware of their teeth. In the first place, take it as a sound beginning of caution to consider that every man against whom you may brush shoulders wishes to let you or sell you a villa. I will not waste words upon the slouching native who imparts to you, in a whisper, that he knows of a delightful Arab villa—Mohammed-ben-Typhoid—up on the hill, and that he can put you in the way of getting it as a bargain. A man who could be taken in in this way would succumb to the "confidence trick," or be led away to a back street in Whitechapel to inspect a prime lot of cigars just landed free of duty. Nor do I wish to insinuate the most distant suggestion to the prejudice of the gentlemen who make it their business at Algiers to deal in villa property in the light of day;—it is their trade. If you should give more than the thing is worth you are a simpleton, and there is an end of it. Deal with men of business through the agency of men of business. Get every matter of title, of drainage, and what not carefully looked into; and don't believe the people who tell you that all the Algerine notaries, architects, and what not are a set of scoundrels. There are, of course, certain black sheep amongst them, some who will drive a hard bargain, and so on; but so you confine yourself to dealing in the open market, you have not much to fear. But were I wanting to buy a villa in Algiers, until I came to buying through the recognized agencies, I should shroud my purpose from human view or knowledge; I should spread a false report that I disliked the place, and possibly that I was thinking of a snug little house at Chislehurst. Even then there would be danger.

Here is a man wanting a villa somewhere. "Weave the warp, and weave the woof; let us begin the mystic spell!" Why is that gentleman who knows nothing about me so particularly civil to me? Why does he take the trouble to call upon me twice at the hotel, etc.? *Villa.* Why is that second gentleman so deeply interested in the state of my health, and why does he try so hard to fix me with a tendency to bronchitis? *Villa.* Why does that other free-handed, unselfish, good fellow explain to me how it is he has bought that undeniable site on favourable terms, but that, having been fortunate himself, he wishes others to share in his good fortune? *Villa.* He would scorn to make sixpence by the bargain; it is all pure friendship; he looks to the reward of a good conscience, and nothing else. I knew an excellent old Scotch lady who was in the habit of getting testy on these occasions, and would break in with "Bother your conscience! what's your price?" In a word, if you find yourself the object of delicate attentions to which you have not the smallest claim, if your social merits are suddenly appreciated in a more than sufficient way, dash the intoxicating cup from your lips, call out "Villa!" in a sonorous voice, and take your passage to Marseilles by the next steamer.

I believe the winter we were in Algiers a bit of ground in a proper situation might have been bought, and a trustworthy architect would have built you a very sufficient villa upon it for the sum of £2000. I have no right to mention names, but if you want a villa, that is the way to set about it. I would, however, most strongly advise my friends not to buy a villa on Mustapha till they have spent at least a winter on its sunny slopes. On your first arrival you may be misled by all the brilliancy and sunshine, by this sudden deliverance from the petty worries of your usual life. Wait for a season, and then do as you like. Never even hire but for a season on your first arrival, at the end of the season you can hire for another, and so on. Do not buy an old Arab house with the idea of improving it. These Arab houses are for the most part uncomfortable and unhealthy bargains. Given a Fortunatus's purse, you can, of course, pull down, build up, change square for round, at your pleasure; but I doubt if you will at last be satisfied with the bill or the result.

I come to smaller pirates, the men of sheep-skins, and brass trays, and Kabyle jewellery. We strangers know but little about such matters; for ourselves we were well content to make our small purchases through Mr. Bucknell, the English architect established at Algiers, and were well content to pay for the advantages of his knowledge and experience. This is the only case in which I will mention a name, and as it is done simply in honour and respect, I hope that I am not guilty of indiscretion. There are, however, a few shops which strangers affect, and, no doubt, there is a pleasure in dealing with these people if you have any real knowledge of values, and can form any true judgment as to the genuineness of the articles.

Just outside our old quarters at the Régence, at the left-hand corner of the Place du Gouvernement, as you went out of the hotel, there was a very good shop for brass things, where we made a few small purchases. Then there is Dorez, near the cathedral, for jewellery and brass *curios*. In the Place of the Cathedral you will find Solal and the two Morallis, and at each of these shops we were fairly dealt with. At Ben-Ali's, in the passage between the Place du Gouvernement and the Rue de la Lyre, you can procure many beautiful embroideries, stuffs, etc. Finally, there is Abderrahman's, 7, Rue de la Lyre, which may also be tried without much hesitation. I should be doing great injustice to worthy people if I did not add, in conclusion, the name of Mme. Midy, 15, Rue Socgemah, for Arab embroideries, *bernouses*, handkerchiefs, etc. This establishment is the outcome of the experiment made by Mme. Luce to provide honest work for young Moorish girls. How far it has succeeded I cannot say; but I know we were delighted with our visit to this strange old house, and with the sight, from the gallery above, of the Moorish damsels down below, working away as demurely as if there were no Osmans or Hassans outside. My wife made many small purchases here, and expressed herself well pleased with the deftness of the workmanship and the beauty of the design and colours.

I do not think we were imposed upon at any of the places named above. There may be others which we never tried; but, at any rate, I thought it might be useful to visitors to Algiers to be furnished with the names of a few shops where they would not, at any rate, meet with the regular pirates.

The Four Pretty Houses.

The French have made ducks and drakes of old Algiers and its pretty buildings. Where was the Dey's town house, there is now a telegraphic *bureau*, or something of that kind. In place of the old Moorish streets, we now have Bab-Azzoun, or Bab-el-Ouad, with their arcades in humble imitation of the Rue Rivoli, and which may, perhaps, take rank with the arcaded streets of Innspruck or Berne. The dirty old Arab quarter remains; but of well-nigh all the old buildings which might recall the vanished greatness of the place, there has been a clean sweep.

After a tolerably long sojourn in the place, my own fancy is that there are but four principal buildings left which are worth a visit, as samples of what the great houses were in the old days. There are a few of secondary importance; but in your rambles about the town you are sure to come across them. The timely administration of a small coin will easily gain you admission, and you will find the one very like the other. The four really fine houses of which I would speak are the Museum, the Archbishop's palace, the Governor's town house, and the Cour d'Assises. One day we got into a fifth, near the Archbishop's palace; it was sacred to the *État Major*, or something of that kind; but the four will suffice.

The court-yard in which the sessions of the Cour d'Assises are held is a noble court indeed, and finer than any you will see elsewhere; but, on the whole, the Archbishop's palace pleased us most, with its galleries and arabesques and double rows of pillars. The Governor's town house has been too much Frenchified. The people who acted as *ciccrone* to us there seemed to take more delight in a modern ball-room, which had been engrafted on to the place, than in any part of the Moorish building.

Now about the museum. The court-yard is very pretty indeed; but it is filled with greenery, and a fountain, and bits of statues are piled about in a way which distracts the attention from the lines of the building itself. Nothing can be prettier than the place; but there is a "Crystal Palace" sort of feeling about it. Sweep all the contents away in your own mind, leaving just a little greenery to soothe the eye, and the fountain to amuse the ear, and no doubt you are standing in a first-class house of old Algiers. You have the long entrance or waiting hall on coming out of the street, the beautiful inner court with its graceful galleries and arches, the old staircase to the gallery, the dwelling-rooms round it—one, a beautiful room, is now the library—the second gallery,—and above all, no doubt, would be the terrace (though we did not see it) sacred to the ladies, their gossip, and their love-passages.

With these four houses for your Belgrave or Grosvenor

Square, and with the Arab town for houses of the middling and lower class, you might, I think, build up old Algiers in your mind well enough. What you have seen in the tiny little courts into which you peered as you stumbled up the dark, dirty lanes of the Arab town, is like the larger houses in miniature and of less costly material. In place of pillars of onyx, etc., you will come across plain white-washed pillars of the rudest kind. There may be no second gallery. You may push open the door, and find yourself at once in a little court in place of a ceremonial entrance hall; but it is just the difference between the house of the poor and the rich man. Nor can you fail, as you ramble about the Arab quarter, to find houses which answer to the English idea of Bloomsbury—not that there ever was such a place at Algiers. Society housed itself in a higgledy-piggledy way. Mrs. Ali of the Bab-Azzoun street might leave cards with Mrs. Osman of the Rue Kléber without social degradation. There was no such dividing lines at Algiers as Tottenham Court Road, with the "upper ten" pirates on one side, and snug, respectable, but unvisitable rogues on the other. As you wander about, I say, you will come upon not a few houses which must have been second-class houses in their day, probably now occupied as grocery stores or something of that kind. So, with my four first-class houses, with those of the second, of which I have just spoken, and with the infinite small fry of the Arab town, you should be able to build up for yourself, in the deep recesses of your mind, a kind of old Algiers, with the houses and dwelling-places that stood therein.

I have spoken of the four beautiful houses of Algiers. There is a fifth into which we were admitted as a matter of private courtesy. It is near the port. It was occupied by some kind of Chief Justice in the old piratical days, and is a perfect specimen of the past—the most typical house we saw at Algiers. The gentleman who owns it, or who at any rate lives there, received us with the greatest courtesy, and was at much pains to explain the meaning of all we saw to us. I shall call this "The Painter's House," and strongly recommend my friends to obtain a proper introduction to the courteous owner. I must not take the liberty of writing his name. There was a nice little bagnio, in the old days, just outside his door—a horrid hole—now a *café maure*. On the whole, amongst the pirates this would have corresponded to the house of Chief Justice Tindal, in Bedford Square, with Newgate handy in case of need. In my little sketch of old Algiers, I have tried to describe how the Moorish houses were built. I recommend others to do what I did myself, *i.e.* to work down to the humblest slums in the old Arab town, but to begin with the four beautiful houses!

CHAPTER XI.

THE KABYLES AND LA GRANDE KABYLIE.

ACCORDING to the last statistical work of authority—I mean the one just published by Dr. Ricoux—Algeria contains about three millions of inhabitants, not including the army. Dr. Ricoux reckons the Europeans at 353,600. Speaking in a rough way, the balance must be divided between the Arabs and the Berbers. We may afford to neglect the smaller subdivisions, which scarcely affect the grand total. You will find the Berbers, under the name of Kabyles, in the mountains; the Arabs in the plains. Should we take "Kabyle" and "Berber" as interchangeable terms? The impression one receives from the French writers is, I think, that every Kabyle is a Berber, but not that every Berber is a Kabyle. The Arabs, in the old historic times, were the conquering race, the Berbers the conquered. The conquerors drove the conquered largely to the mountains, or the conquered took refuge there of their own accord, so as to maintain their independence. These mountaineers are Kabyles.

Who, then, were the Berbers? In a moment I will answer the question from the books. Was there any one in North Africa before the Berbers? For an answer we are driven to tradition. Originally, North Africa was sparsely peopled by creatures, half-monkey half-man —by the "missing link," in plain English. Pity that some remnants of this despised stock are not still remaining; they would greatly assist Dr. Darwin. Be this as it may, the Berbers would appear to have civilized —that is to say, to have exterminated this unfortunate missing link. But who were the Berbers? The learned Ibn-Khaldoun says they were Canaanites. Other authorities, equally weighty, incline to the belief that they were the descendants of the shepherd-kings driven out of Egypt. This is very old-world story, and I doubt if there be much certainty in the matter. Saint Augustine in his day branded as many of the indigenous population as differed from him on theological points with the name of Barbari. In those far-off times, and before the Arab conquest, the Berbers seem to have lived pretty much as the Arabs do nowadays, save that they never meddled with the Sahara.

One could wish that learned men had been able to enlighten us on another point—the origin of the Berber nation—by the help of "language." This help fails us. There is not a single book left in the Berber language; the alphabet is lost. In our time the Berber is written in Arabic characters. It is said that Berber, as at present spoken, contains a good deal of Arabic; in other words, the conquered accepted the language, as they had accepted the religion, of the conquerors. Strangely enough, there seems to be no trace left of Carthaginian, Roman, or Vandal in their language, as by each of these nations they were mastered in turn.

The matter is explained in this way. The Berbers, who had accepted the dominion, and partially the language of these conquering races, had ceased to be nomads; they had fixed habitations. There came a moment when the tide turned. The conquerors disappeared, and the rough, rude Berbers, who had kept themselves apart, turned back to the old ground, and swept the weak-kneed brethren—hybrid language and all—from the face of the earth. It was not so with the Arab. The Arab conquest was far more permanent, and there was identity of religious belief; so I suppose that the Berber or Kabyle language of our day is a kind of jargon, half Arab, half old Berber.

It would, however, require a special interest and serious study to arrive at anything like a real conclusion on such a point. Had I the desire to look it up, I think I should betake myself to the Aures Mountains, which I saw from Biskra, and try what could be done amongst the Chaouïa. There, at least, the Berbers remained in their primitive state, save in so far as their language might have become tainted with Vandal words; for the Vandals fled before the Arabs to this distant and inaccessible range of mountains. It seems strange that no light has been cast upon the matter from Tlemçen, the seat of the great Berber kingdom. I find no trace of this in the books I have read, and I presume some of the authors were competent to deal with original authorities.

Such, then, were the Berbers—the original inhabitants of North Africa, mixed up with Phœnicians, Romans, and Vandals. If we arrive at the conclusion—as my friends, the popular French authors, have done—that the Kabyles are just a portion of these Berbers, we have attained an intelligible result. King Masinissa first attempted to fix the Berber peasantry to the soil, and to convert them from herdsmen into agriculturists; but many of them were dissatisfied with the arrangement. They ran off to the mountains, which were then covered with thick forests. Here we come to the real *Kabyles* at last; but, strangely enough, the descendants of these runaways from the ploughshare and regular work have developed into hard-working field labourers and handicraftsmen.

The Romans were never able in their day to make much impression on the mountaineers. Their system simply drove the people more and more into the mountains, where they could be free from the disgusting trammels of civilized life. The Romans did not think it worth their while to make attempts at reducing these poor fellows in their strongholds, but contented themselves with establishing places of strength, which commanded the passes. So the Kabyles were allowed to hammer out their own system of civil policy and municipal arrangements at their leisure. The results at which they have arrived are strange enough, but, taking them for all in all, they remind one not a little of the Middle Ages, and the independence of towns, each one sufficient to itself.

There is a good deal here of Sismondi translated into North African, but of course without the mail-clad, feudal signori, who were good enough to protect the Italian municipalities.

This view, then, if not accurately and historically true, seems very like truth. Reconstitute the peasantry of North Africa in your own way, it is clear that they were worth something; for have I not myself, as one of a thousand gaping and curious tourists, poked about the galleries and passages of the Tombeau de la Chrétienne —*their work?* Have I not seen the Medrassen, in the province of Constantine,—*also their work?* If the Pyramids prove anything for Egypt, these massive structures, which have defied so many ages, must in their degree be allowed to stand for something in favour of the forefathers of the Kabyles.

Then there are all the beautiful things at Tlemçen. They were not only ingenious, and possessed of a certain instruction, but they were strong men of their hands. We may be sure that the Roman leaders had often enough grimly considered the matter with themselves before they arrived at the conclusion—"Pooh, pooh! it is not worth while. Let us leave them alone in their mountains."

The Romans actually held the Valley of the Sebaou, and that of the Oued-Sahel; beyond their strong posts here, they availed themselves of native help, and pushed on smaller native stations, under Roman protection, and in the Roman interest, as far as they dared. The Kabyle was free *in his mountains*, as free as any Scotch Highlander who ever snorted out his indignation and contempt for the Lowland loons. When he ventured down to the plains, he was compelled to make the best terms he could with the Roman officers.

This sort of thing went on for three hundred years.

The Roman power grew weaker and weaker, and the Roman demand for tribute of grain, etc., more tyrannous; hence revolts of the Lowlanders, more or less successful; hence more and more flights into the mountains—a stronger Kabylia, and a weaker Rome. Then came the Germans, and more civilization. Genseric and his Vandals played into the hands of the native Lowland chiefs, but they did not care to meddle with the Kabyle mountaineers. It was the same with the Byzantines.

Our poor Kabyle friends seem to have had the vaguest ideas upon religious matters. Their one notion was to adopt any system which might be displeasing to the rulers of the day. So they became Donatists, Arians, etc., just as the government of the day happened to be of the other way of thinking. When the Arabs finally got possession of the country, they did not care, more than their predecessors, to stir up these Kabyle hornets' nests in the mountains.

These Berbers are in North Africa a very ubiquitous race. M. de Slane tells us that you will find them dotted about from the Mediterranean to the Niger, from the Atlantic even to the oases of Egypt. I found them at the edge of the desert by Biskra; I found them, of course, at Tlemçen, on the frontier of Morocco; Bou-Maza's field of operations, and the Dahra country, etc., are Kabyle. Again, then, I come to the precise issue with which I have been so far fencing. What makes a Berber a Kabyle? A Kabyle is a Berber who belongs to the *k'bîla*, or confederation. So says the Baron Aucapitaine; also General Daumas. The general tells us "The mountaineers of North Africa were never really called Kabyles till after the Arab invasion" (the later one in the thirteenth century). It is to the Arabic, then, we must turn for the origin of the word. We must look to one of three roots: *Kuebila*, "tribe;" *Kabel*, "he has accepted;" *Kobel*, "before." The first of these would refer to the organization of the Kabyles in confederated tribes; the second would mean that they had accepted the Koran; the third that they were the *forerunners*, the people who came before the Arabs.

Well, then, the Kabyles are the Berbers confederated into tribes; but we shall have a word to say about this confederation, which, in many respects, is loose enough. At any rate, the Berbers, or Kabyles, are not Arabs, but they are the very opposite to Arabs, though they profess, in an easy-going way, the Mohammedan religion, and speak a language full of Arabic words and expressions. General Daumas dwells very forcibly on the antagonisms. The Arab has black eyes and hair; the Kabyle, frequently, blue eyes and red hair. The Arab has an oval face and a long neck; the Kabyle a square face and a thick-set neck. The Arab never shaves; the Kabyle does so till he is between twenty and twenty-five years of age,—he is then a man. The Arab always covers his head,—when he can, his feet; the Kabyle goes summer and winter with naked head and feet, or, if he has covering for his feet, this is accidental. He greatly affects a large leathern apron when he is at work. The Arab is a dweller in tents,—the Algerian Arab is a nomad within given limits; the Kabyle is a householder. The Arab covers himself with amulets and charms; the Kabyle thinks these mere rubbish, save in so far as the evil eye is concerned. The Arab detests work; the Kabyle is a steady worker. The Arabs cultivate the earth for grain crops, but never plant trees; the Kabyle is always delving at his garden,—the olive tree and the production of oil receive his particular attention. The Arabs are great as herdsmen; not so the Kabyles,—the Kabyle is a manufacturer and artisan. The Arab—it is General Daumas who writes it—is a great liar; the Kabyle thinks that falsehood is foul shame. Finally, the position of women is very different amongst the Arabs and amongst the Kabyles. A Kabyle lady has much the best of it: it is she who goes to market, she who buys and sells. An Arab husband will do a good deal of his household work himself. Even amongst us the British *paterfamilias* will not disdain to visit the fishmonger's shop, and select the soles and John Dorees for family use. An Arab woman must not appear in society with men; she keeps her face covered; she must not even sit at table with her husband, when they are alone; *a fortiori* when male guests are present. The Kabyle woman takes her place even amongst guests, and does the honours of her table. She gossips or chats, she sings, she does what she likes, with uncovered face. The Kabyle woman tattoos herself generally with the figure of a cross between the eyes or on the nostril. These tattoo marks are proscribed by the Koran, which brands them with the opprobrious name of *ketebet el chytan*, or devil's writing. A Kabyle Romeo must buy his bride, give so much money for her to the parents; Juliet bears a price in Kabylia. A Kabyle lady makes two toilettes a day, very much like the European; there is the usual morning ablution, etc.

but she makes herself fine for dinner. One could go on for pages, but this would simply be to copy from General Daumas's book, "Mœurs et Coutumes de l'Algerie," which I strongly recommend for the perusal of any one who meditates a visit to Kabylia.

The Kabyle, then, in his customs and ways of life, is in antagonism with the Arab. *He is the descendant of Berbers, who took to the mountains and became " men of the confederation,"* and who seem to have received the name of "Kabyle" after the Arabian *conquest*, not the first *rush*. He is a Mohammedan, but not very strong in his theology. Like Mr. Gumbleberry, the undertaker, in poor Charles Dickens's story, you may excommunicate him for the term of his natural life, but so you remit costs, he is not dissatisfied. He is a manufacturer and artisan; he is great in the oil trade; he will lend or borrow money on usance; he will leave home to earn money, and, when he has earned it, return and become a householder.

The Kabyles, I say, are confederates. The Kabyles were and are essentially a democratic people. The unit of the Kabyle system was the village, which was represented by the *djema*, or assembly of all men capable of bearing arms. This assembly decided summarily all quarrels, adjudicated upon crimes, and managed all the financial concerns of the village, which, for convenience' sake, was divided into sections. All the villagers, on a day named, met in popular assembly to elect their chief (*amine*), and, when elected, he engaged himself to respect all the rights of the villagers. The term of his power was, in the main, indefinite; he might be re-elected.

There was an appeal from his decision to the *djema*, or assembly. In some tribes the *amines* met and elected an *amine-el-oumena*, an *amine* of the *amines*, who could convoke a meeting of all the smaller assemblies, and discuss with them questions of peace and war, of their relations with other tribes, and such like principal matters.

In Kabylia there are no tribes in the Arab sense of the word. When applied to Kabylia, the term means a union of several villages. But individual property is *the basis of all these arrangements*. The land is not the property of the tribe, and therein lies the distinction. The union of a certain number of *communes* forms the tribe (*arch*). The union of these tribes constitutes the confederation (*k'bîla*), whence the word "K'bailes," or, as we say, "Kabyle." A Kabyle, then, means a man, or citizen, of the confederation. The *Zaouïa*, or religious school or college, is the head-quarters of the confederation. But, even so, the Kabyle does not think he has taken precautions enough against an abuse of power. He has invented the *soff*. A *soff* is the union of a certain number of individuals, or fractions of villages, or of tribes, who choose their chiefs and determine to resist oppression in any form. Adjacent tribes—such is the custom—never enter into *soff* together. The *soffs* are like squares upon a chess-board, but the contiguous squares never join in the form of alliance.

More powerful than the *djema*, the *k'bîla*, or the *soff* —so I find it written—are the *eurf* and the *kanoun*. The *eurf* is the common law, or traditional custom; the *kanoun* is the criminal code. The authority of these is said to be even greater than the authority of religion. Although like the Scotch in many respects, the Kabyles are unlike them in this, that they could scarcely be induced to knock each other upon the head on religious grounds.

One more custom, and I have done; that custom is the *anaya*, or safeguard. A fugitive under the protection of *anaya*, which means that he is under the safeguard of some member of the confederation, may in security traverse its territory from end to end. Each man in turn may stand in need of the *anaya*, and every one respects it. To violate the *anaya* is the greatest crime known in the Kabyle Highlands. A village, or even a tribe, may be under the shadow of the *anaya*.

Slavery was unknown in Kabylia.

The Marabouts, who exercise a kind of religious authority, seem to have come from Morocco. The influence of religion is not strong amongst these Kabyles. The Marabouts, however, can act upon their warlike propensities, and preach up amongst them a crusade, with an effect which Peter the Hermit might have envied. But I should be sorry to be the Marabout who had promoted an unsuccessful war, when his congregation came to tax costs; for my Kabyle friends are a very practical people.

Some years ago the population of these Kabyle Highlands was estimated at 435,000 inhabitants; one may speak of them roughly as about half a million. It should be understood that I am only writing of La Grande Kabylie, for there are Kabyles in plenty in the provinces of Oran and Constantine, and elsewhere in

Algiers, and plenty of them in the desert. The question for the French is how to utilize them as peaceful tillers of the soil, for no doubt these are the right men in the right place, if you can only make them feel that the French rule will give them security for life and property.

We must be just to the French. It was utterly impossible for them to leave unsubdued this Highland region of Kabylia (that is, the country which lies between the Isser and the Oued-Sahel), interposed as it is between the provinces of Algiers and Constantine. Had a similar case occurred in British India, it is certain that the Indian Kabylia would very soon have passed into our hands. Whether or no unnecessary cruelty was exercised in the seizure of the territory, is quite another question, and one upon which I had rather cite the testimony of French writers.

The first real *conquest* took place under the auspices of Marshal Randon so far back as the year 1857. Since then there have been stern outbreaks, as sternly repressed. In the early days there was question of our old (and new) friend, the "bag and baggage policy." Would it not be wiser to move away the Kabyles to some of the pleasant oases in the desert, where they would find friends and palm trees and plenty of air and sunshine? Happily, humaner and wiser advice prevailed. The French contented themselves with seizing the chief strategic points in the country, and left the labourers upon the soil which they and their forefathers had tilled for so many centuries. Your Kabyle likes his home and his village. He does not shrink from hard work, either as agriculturist or workman; above all, he does not like the Arabs, who, ever since they took possession of the country, have driven those of his name back on the mountains.

The Kabyles make excellent sailors and soldiers. As I am rather fond of the Kabyles, I regret to say that I have read in my books that, in the abominable old Turkish days, they were largely employed to man the piratical cruisers. As soldiers they have fought not ingloriously under the French standard. All this being so, it is easy to understand that the French conquerors have a much firmer and more continuous hold upon such a people than they have upon the Arabs, who are ever on the move—here to-day, and gone to-morrow. An exciseman or a bailiff might hope to deal with a Kabyle village; what could he do when he reached the encampment of an Arab tribe, and found there nothing but heaps of ashes and a cloud of dust?

Then there was the terrible insurrection of 1871. I wish any one interested in the matter would read the story of Palestro, as told by MM. Erckmann-Chatrian. This was enough to rouse the angry passions of the French. Sad, when it comes to this, that revenge looks like justice. On the other hand, the Kabyles cannot forget the cruelties of which the French had been guilty in their mountains in 1846, and in the years 1850–51, in the days of Bou-Baghla. An Englishman must not say a word of his own; but I refer the reader to "La Guerre et le Gouvernement de l'Algérie," by Louis de Baudicour: Paris, 1853, for an account of the matter. Thus it is that M. de Baudicour (page 371) writes of Marshal Bugeaud's expedition in 1846: "The illustrious marshal may have caused us to be feared—scarcely to be loved. Our soldiers, when they came back from the expedition, were themselves ashamed of this 'war of Vandals,' which they had been made to carry out, and of the atrocities which had been committed. About 18,000 fruit trees had been cut down; the houses had been given up to the flames. They had killed women, children, old men. The unhappy women chiefly excited the cupidity (of the soldier) on account of their custom of wearing earrings, and silver rings on their arms and legs. These rings have no opening, as in France; they are passed round the limbs of female children, and cannot be removed when they have grown up. In order to tear them from the women, our soldiers would cut off their four limbs, and then leave them living, and thus mutilated." So, writes M. de Baudicour naively enough, " In this war the women defended themselves like lionesses, armed with gun and knife." A story is told that one of these poor women, seeing that her right arm was cut off, with the greatest coolness stretched out the other to the soldier who had done it, so as to save him trouble. This was in the years 1845-46, in Marshal Bugeaud's time.

For what happened in 1850-51 I refer to Chapter IX. of the same writer. An insurrection, headed by a miserable impostor, Bou-Baghla, was the pretext for the atrocities which followed. Some three hundred villages were burnt in this famous expedition. The French Zouaves shot down indiscriminately the unfortunate Kabyles who were doing no hostile act, and who had simply sticks in their hands. An old man, with his two sons, two daughters, and a son-in-law, had taken refuge behind a hillock. A French corporal, catching sight of them, made them come out, put the four men in a row, and gave the word to fire on them. The old man and his son-in-law fell dead; the two sons were not hit, and escaped. The soldiers brought the two daughters in, when it turned out that they belonged to a village which had always been friendly to the French (page 477). In the next page you read of the arrival of the troops in a village where only one old infirm man was left. He tottered out, holding an olive branch; he was instantly shot dead. You read, page 488, that the Zouaves were like schoolboys; give them a moment's repose, and they scattered themselves to do what they call *chaparder*. This was to kill every one they met, without distinction of sex or age; to burn and destroy whatever came in their way.

Might not the Kabyles have something to say for themselves, when the French talk of the atrocities of Palestro? They are a fierce and vindictive race, just like the Corsicans, and never forget a blood-feud. In addition to what I have quoted from M. de Baudicour, there were the general forfeitures which followed upon the insurrection of 1871. As the tourist drives through La Grande Kabylie, he must not forget the inflammable material which lies beneath the soil. An Alsace-Lorraine village may be well enough, but upon what foundation does it rest?

A final sentence or two, and I have done. Why "La Grande Kabylie"? In the different mountains and mountain chains of Algeria there are many Kabylias. The Kabylia of the Djudjura range is the most important of all, and has given the French most trouble. Each Kabylia is a separate federation of villages, etc.; but the various Kabylias have no common bond. La Grande Kabylie is the jumble of mountains included between Dellys and Bougie; Aumale and Setif. This is the country which we propose to visit.

The great book about Kabylia is Hanoteau and Letourneaux, "La Kabylie, 1872–73." Amongst the many works I have read I have derived the greatest help from those of General Daumas and the Baron Aucapitaine.

If you would understand Algeria, study the Kabylias!

CHAPTER XII.

TO FORT NATIONAL AND KABYLIA.

OUR first considerable expedition in Algeria was to Fort National, as we hoped thus to get an idea of what La Grande Kabylie really meant. Fort National is about eighty English miles distant from Algiers. The little journey presented no obstacle or difficulty of any kind. It is simply a pleasant drive along an excellent road with a stiff hill at the end. Now, as Fort National stands some 3000 feet above the sea-level, this is no great wonder. You can retain your seat in the carriage throughout, so the hill signifies but little. There is a diligence which performs the journey at night, but as our object was to see the country, we dismissed all idea of such a low conveyance from our minds. When we got to Tizi-Ouzou, I asked the people there why it was that travellers were called upon to take this ride in the dark. They answered me that it was for the convenience of certain learned gentlemen connected with the legal profession, who were thus enabled to spend "a happy day" at Algiers, and to reach Tizi-Ouzou in the morning in time to take their places in court. As the night service is only maintained during the summer months, I should have thought that the great heat of day travel afforded the more natural explanation. In Africa, as well as in Europe, people will have their little jokes at the expense of the lawyers.

Be this as it may, acting upon the advice of our friend, Mr. McWhack, a Scottish gentleman of infinite mirth and humour, whose acquaintance we had been fortunate enough to make at Algiers, we engaged a little open carriage with three horses for the journey. The driver undertook to convey us to Fort National and back in five easy days. We were to sleep at the Col des Beni Aïcha (otherwise Menerville) the first day; the distance is a little over thirty miles. The next day we were to drive to Tizi-Ouzou, about thirty miles further, and there to sleep. The third day we were to go from Tizi-Ouzou to Fort National and back, stopping two or three hours at the Fort to look about us. We were to sleep again at Tizi-Ouzou, and to return to Algiers in two days, by the same road and in the same way in which we had come. This was about thirty miles of easy travel each day. It seemed like a very simple way of making trial of our capacity for expeditions in Algeria. I may say at once that all passed off happily, as we hoped, with the exception of a slight misadventure on account of a horse, which was suffering from a "surfeit of oats." No lady, no invalid need be deterred from driving from Algiers to Fort National. When it is considered that the Kabyle Highlands are as picturesque as anything to be found in Algeria, and that the Djudjura range is about the most striking thing (save, perhaps, the Chabet Pass) in the Kabyle Highlands, all persons who may be passing a winter in Algiers should take this drive.

Besides, throughout the winter and early spring this Djudjura range had been the mark of our daily admiration, for few indeed were the days on which we could not see from our windows on Mustapha this bit of Switzerland casually mislaid in Africa. I forget the exact figure, and I have no book at hand for immediate reference, but I believe the Djudjura to be about 6000 or 7000 feet high, consequently far inferior to the giants of the Bernese Oberland, or of the Mont Blanc or Monte Rosa groups; but then it rises sheer out of the ground, and it is in Africa, with African surroundings. This clear white mass of snow, bright as Monte Rosa, seen from the little inn at Macugnaga, had been the chief mark in our landscape all the winter; so, when spring came, we resolved to get close to it, and at any rate to have a fair look at it. Active and adventurous young gentlemen can contrive to stroll up and down the mountain itself, and can unite this expedition with an excursion to the famous Portes de Fer; but, alas! for me this was out of the question. How could I hope to hobble and drag myself up a mountain 6000 feet high? We had been told, and truly told, that on the terrace of Fort National you were placed as in a stall at the opera, and that the Djudjura was before you as the stage. From this point you would probably see the mountain far better than any one who had climbed to the top of it; that is, of course, the mountain itself, not the prospect from it. With this, then, let us be content. We had given up our lodging on Mustapha, and had come down to our old quarters at the Régence, as it was infinitely more convenient to have a starting-place in the town itself—a point of arrival and departure handy to the railway station and the steamers.

On the 23rd of March, at 12.30 p.m.—a solemn moment—we got into our little carriage, and started on a visit to our Kabyle friends. Relying upon the recommendation of Mr. McWhack, I neglected to investigate the condition of our three horses before starting—an omission which I had afterwards great occasion to regret. The road as far as the Maison Carrée, about seven miles from the town, is so familiar to all residents of Algiers, that it would be almost an abuse of confidence if I were to waste words upon a thrice-told tale about the Agha, and the Champ des Manœuvres, and the Jardin d'Essai, and the Koubba of the gentleman with a very long name, known as "He of the Two Tombs." Every Algerine who has been to the Arab cemetery on a Friday afternoon knows all about this, and the legend is told in all the guide-books.

Let us at once assume that we have passed out of the immediate suburbs of Algiers, and have reached the Maison Carrée. As we were ascending the little hill on which is the prison, I noticed that our driver was using his whip in a way which met with my strong disapproval. I told him that he must leave off at once, or we would go back to Algiers, for we were not yet without resource. The man sulkily complied, but stated that his difficulty lay with the centre horse, which had so misused the good things of this life that it was at that moment suffering from "an indigestion of oats." I thought I would have a peep at this extraordinary animal, expecting to see something like an alderman on four legs, replete with venison and turtle. The reverse was the case; anything so thin and woe-begone I had never come across, though not wholly without experience of London cab-horses brought up as *pièces de conviction* on cruelty summonses. I should scarcely have credited it with strength to accomplish the distance to the nearest knacker's yard. Whilst the road was on the level, the two other horses, which were strong capable animals enough, had dragged him along between them, and the man had been careful not to attract our notice so long as we were near the town. He persisted in his theory of an indigestion of oats, and pointed to the thinness of the creature in confirmation of his statement. The greedy animal could not be induced to give up the pleasures of the manger, and chronic diarrhœa and what we saw were the result. Argument, of course, was thrown away upon the fellow, so, with a mental resolution to lay my case before Mr. McWhack on my return to Algiers, I possessed myself of the whip, and told the man to proceed to the nearest inn which might be found on the road, and there to leave the horse. It was clear enough (all questions of humanity apart) that we should get to our journey's end quicker with two horses than three, seeing that the two had to carry the third as well as to draw the carriage and ourselves.

After some little demur this was carried out, with the further condition that the driver should provide himself with a third capable horse at Menerville, where we were to stay for the night, so that we might have the full advantage of three horses for the heavy pull up from Tizi-Ouzou to Fort National. This agreement was well and truly carried out, and throughout the journey the man proved himself a good-humoured and **trustworthy** guide, and never tried a trick on us again. So I relented, and never delivered him over to the wrath of my Scottish friend; but the moral, as far as the reader is concerned, is this—in Algeria carefully review your horses and vehicle before starting on an expedition, whilst it is yet time and **you have the** police at your back. It is to impress this caution on the reader that I have dwelt on so trivial an incident, for the consequences may be anything but trivial, if the trick be not detected before you are out of reach of help.

We proceeded on our way with two **horses and the** harness of the poor glutton, through a country not very remarkable save from the abundance and beautiful greenness of the young wheat-fields, till we reached the village of Alma, which has gained a name in the colony from a great fight won **by the French troops over a force** of Arabs far exceeding them in numbers. This took place in 1839. "It was a famous **victory.**" The little village now looked peaceful enough, and the few shops just such as you see in any outlying village. A Frenchman with whom I fell into conversation whilst the driver was baiting his horses, told me that they had suffered much during the insurrection of 1871, but that now they felt the most perfect security.

The country between Algiers and Alma is flat. There was nothing much to attract the eye beyond the freshness and beauty of the vegetation; but even when it is commonplace in an Algerine sense, **the** prospect is very different from anything we see in

P

Europe. The prickly pear and aloe take the place of our English hedges; now and again we come across patches where the asphodel abounds. I had formed a somewhat contemptuous opinion of this plant with the romantic name, as I had seen it growing in the lanes about Algiers. The charm seemed to lie in the word "asphodel," as Shelley brings it into his verse. As the word "Mesopotamia" has been taken to be a comfortable word in a theological sense, so there was something in the word "asphodel" which appealed to the imagination, suggestive of Proserpine, and Enna's flowery meads, and all the rest of it. But in reality this plant, as I had seen it, was but a lanky, ungraceful thing, and the arrangement of white flowers not beautiful. On entering Kabylia, as we saw the asphodel by the roadside in masses, we found reason to alter our ideas. It grew in masses, not singly, and attained no mean height. The clusters of white flowers, with the sun shining upon them as they were waved about by the wind, were certainly pretty enough. The asphodel, at its best, is scarcely among the aristocracy of African flowers; still, the poets are not wholly in the wrong: a "field of asphodel" is pretty enough.

After Alma we began to get amongst the hills, and, especially to the right of the road, the scenery reminded me more and more of Scotland as you approach the Highland country. The sight of a Kabyle scratching away at the earth with some insufficient agricultural implement, and the groups of Kabyles making their way to Algiers (some with camels), soon recalled us from Scotland to Africa. Every inch of the ground we were driving along in this peaceful fashion had been fought over by Kabyle, Arab, Roman, Carthaginian, Vandal, Turk, and Frenchman. If you allowed your mind to float back to the past, there was enough to think about; if to the future, this well-made road, these abundant crops, and the Alsace-Lorraine villages which we began to see about this time, were suggestive enough. Was all this to last? Were these peaceful sights but the earnest of better things to come? Was Kabylia, for the first time in human history, to take rank amongst peaceful, law-abiding, fruit-producing districts of the earth?

I need scarcely say to any one who has studied the subject, that, even during the epoch of the Roman dominion, Kabylia was a mere cockpit. The legionaries far away down at Lambessa were all very well in their way, but the masters of the world never succeeded in crushing the opposition of the Kabyle mountaineers. The French rifles have done what the Romans never could accomplish. It remains to be seen whether policy can consolidate what has been won by arms. The task is, I fear, a far more difficult one. I have greater confidence in the valour of the French troops than in the wisdom of French statesmen. All opposition has been crushed ruthlessly enough, if we take the accounts given by the French themselves, who are not likely to err on the side of unfriendly criticism of their own performances. Even the tragedy of Palestro, which has been immortalized by the genius of MM. Erckmann-Chatrian, found more than its counterpart in the horrors perpetrated by the French troops when Kabylia was invaded, as I have endeavoured to show in proper time and place, by reference to the French accounts of the facts.

All this being so ; at any rate until certain generations have passed away, it would be perfectly idle to suppose that a mere drive from Algiers to Fort National enables a traveller to answer the question, "Will what I see last?" It is not what you see, but what you do *not* see, which is the important factor in the case. Is the memory of the blood-feud staunched amongst a people more vindictive than the Corsicans ? Have they acquiesced in the forfeiture of their lands ? Are they willing labourers for hire on the fertile fields of which they were lately the possessors ? Granted that they can do nothing now, what would they do if trouble came upon their conquerors from beyond the sea ? As at present, if the testimony of a chance traveller be worth anything, I am bound to say that everything wears the outward appearance of stability and peace. It is only by a mental effort that you recall the past history of the place. May bygones be bygones, and by wise measures of conciliation may the French induce the native races to acquiesce in the inevitable ! As for armed resistance to the French power—as I saw all the strategic points of the country occupied in force by the invaders, good roads branching away in every direction, and parties of soldiers, some of them with cannon, passing and repassing us every half-hour—one could not but see that the French are fixed firmly enough in the saddle.

This word brings me back to the glutton's harness,

which I see on the box by the driver's side, and to our little journey. It was just the same story of rich cultivation all along the road on both sides, of distant hills, and, up to a certain point, of wonderful back-looks on Algiers. But then the clear, transparent sky, and the brightness of the whole scene! A clouded sky in more Northern lands has beauties of its own; but here you have a canopy of blue above you and around you—not a fleck, not a stain upon it—and all pervaded by the sunlight. How should an artist render this? I have seen some desert scenes, the work of Mr. Holman Hunt, which have given me an idea of it, but as far as memory serves me, nowhere else. It is monotonous, if you will, but it is the monotony of beauty and light.

So driving on, we came to a river, which the driver told us was called the Oued Korso, and a little further on to a tomb and a village, both of them significant enough. M. Piesse, whose guide-book I had with me, gives the history of the tomb briefly as thus: "The tomb is the Koubba of Mohammed the Cut-throat" (*l'égorgeur* is the French word). "He was sent by the Pacha of Algiers to reduce the Kabyles, and founded the fort of Tizi-Ouzou, from which place he sent forth his murderous expeditions. He was killed in a fight against the Iratin, at Tala Amara." A kind of Claverhouse, I take it; a dashing cavalry officer, without more sympathy for the Kabyle peasants than his Scottish counterpart had for the psalm-singing Whigamores. So far for the tomb, which is the past; now for the village, which is the future. It is the village of Belle Fontaine, which lies a little off the road, and which has the outward appearance of being one of the most successful of the Alsace-Lorraine villages.

A good deal might be said about the way in which the experiment has been carried out, not without unnecessary suffering and cost; but as I see the village before me, I am not inclined to moralize. It is just the flourishing little place which MM. Erckmann-Chatrian love to describe, and seems to be provided with every comfort dear to the heart of the Franco-German. May the Kabyles leave them in peace, and may they find at the end of each day's work the tall glass of beer and well-stuffed china pipe, which alone can make existence tolerable!

But the sun is sinking in the westward heaven, and the shadows have grown longer. This hill which lies before us is a long one, but at the top, so says the driver, lies the Col des Beni Aïcha, the end of our first stage. I do not wish the afternoon's drive to be over, but somehow, when you are told your resting-place is near, you are always in a fidget to get there. Just as we are well committed to the hill, down comes upon us an interminable line of waggons, reducing us to a condition of temporary immobility. Like all earthly things, this too comes to an end, and we creep up the hill somewhat ignobly, with our two tired horses, to the door of the little inn.

We are taken through the kitchen to an open stair at the back of the house, and after mistaking a white spot in the distance for Algiers (it turned out to be near Cape Matifou), we were shown into the tiny room which was to be our resting-place for the night.

Considered as a large closet, there was not much to be said against it; but as a sleeping-room for two people, the accommodation was certainly deficient. There was no fireplace, consequently no ventilation, but the room itself and the beds appeared to be clean, so we considered that, by leaving the window a little open, we might be able to get through the night without too much discomfort. Neither here nor anywhere else in our subsequent rambles about Algeria were we troubled with mosquitoes. The open window was a possibility. These arrangements being completed, we went downstairs to make trial of the supper, and found all good enough— not such fare as you would meet with at a London club or Parisian *café*, but the usual *potage* which is served wherever two or three French men and women are gathered together; the bit of stringy meat, with a rich sauce, but excellent potatoes; the invariable *poulet*, with a salad of freshly plucked lettuce; finally dessert, and a cup of coffee.

Do not let the man whose soul is heavy if he does not fare sumptuously *every* day, try a ramble in Algeria, but let no one be deterred under the idea that he will not get enough to eat, and of wholesome food. As a rule, the bread is good, and there is plenty of fruit. The wine of the country, heavily dashed with St. Galmier (which you will find in most places, and of which you can always take a small supply with you), serves well enough for drink. It is absurd to raise an outcry about defective food. To most of us it is a positive advantage to be put on short commons for a while, and I think I am neither over nor under stating the case when I write that the tourist will fare rather better in Algeria than he would in travelling through the French provinces, away from the large towns. I do not mean my statements to apply to every trumpery little wayside inn, where the coachman in Algeria may call a halt at midday to bait his horses, and to give you time for lunch. Take with you some of your breakfast bread, with a supply of fruit (wine and water you have, of course, with you), and what more can you require in reason in this hot country? You can always get a cup of coffee.

Although for two months we lived in the open air, the air was pure and delicate, and we were seldom hungry, we were glad of the food when produced, but there was no great desire nor craving for it. That tocsin of the soul, the dinner-bell, had ceased to find an echo in the heart, or, more correctly speaking, in the stomach. I remember to have felt in the same way in Norway and in the Engadine, and years ago, when riding about Spain, when one seemed to live in the saddle.

My afflicted friends in England, all ye who have attained great success in life, and, as a consequence, have lost your digestions, is there not here a suggestion for you? This is a way of becoming indifferent to food; the air is your *pabulum*, and that will scarcely disagree with you.

While we were at supper, there were at the next table to us a young couple, and all doubt about their relation to each other would soon have been removed by the way in which the lady would swallow a little soup, and then throw herself into the attitude of pointing, as a pointer does who has marked game. It was a babe, however, not a partridge, which was the object of her solicitude. You would hear a howl at the end of the passage, and off the lady would scuffle. The low howling would for the moment become a loud howling as the door was opened to admit her, and presently peace would ensue, and the lady would return to her unfinished soup. She was good enough to explain to me that, in addition to the "good-for-nothing" (with a good-humoured nod to her husband), she, being without a maid, had also charge of a babe, and that, in order to comfort her *vaurien* at his evening meal, she had left the babe in question flat on its back in the middle of a large bed, having previously darkened the room and crooned over it the mother's evensong. For a time all had gone well, but baby had just awoke, and had found out the imposture.

The husband suggested that a fat spaniel who belonged to their party, and was slobbering in anticipation of the bits of bread dipped in gravy, after the manner of Frenchmen, should be locked up with babe to keep him company. The fat spaniel seemed to understand, and hate him for the horrid suggestion. But the lady, with a woman's common sense, shattered the proposition at once.

"*Comment donc, mon ami, mais ne sais tu pas que Hippolyte*" (this was the spaniel's name) "*à lui seul ferait plus de tapage que tous les bébés de ce bas monde?*" at the same time heaping up her husband's plate with *bouilli*, and rich gravy, and gherkins, and other delicacies, so as to occupy his immediate attention. The man was tamed. That able woman had arrived at the conclusion that the way to rule him was through his appetite. Let him growl on his ineffectual growls, and give him *panem et circenses*, and the direction of the general policy would remain with her.

I was so well pleased with the soundness of her view, and her dexterous way of dealing with the difficulty, that I determined to play into her hands. If I could keep him a-talking, and the servant-girl would ply him with frequent change of diet, he would be quite content until he arrived at that stage which immediately precedes lethargy, and the poor little woman would be allowed to attend to her babe in her own way. I saw by her grateful look she took the idea, but what would the gentleman like to talk about?

If you want to impress a stranger favourably in conversation, listen, and let him talk away, probably about himself, his own views, and his own concerns. I soon found out that he was interpreter at the law courts throughout the country, and his remedy for all the evils of Kabylia, nay, of Algeria, was an abundance of law courts, presided over by upright French Magistrates in whom the natives would have confidence, assisted by able interpreters. From Tlemçen to Oran, for example, he was well known, and he might say both the judges and the clients recognized the value of a good interpreter. Here the lady gave him a fresh supply of sauce and gherkins, and abruptly quitted the room, but he never noticed her departure.

"A dishonest interpreter, monsieur, has so many chances, if he were base enough to avail himself of them. Did this new jurisdiction answer? Why should it not answer? The natives were ready enough to acknowledge and to feel what a real blessing to them was a good supply of lawyers, fresh from France, and not tainted by the corruptions of the colony, impartial judges, and disinterested advocates, men who looked not to salary or fee, but to the reward of a good conscience—and quite sufficient reward too." At this point the fat spaniel managed to abstract the last piece of *bouilli* from his plate, and was rolling it over in his mouth with a look of tearful enjoyment, when my friend the interpreter caught him, as one might say, in the fact. A kick which sent him away howling, and a "*Comment donc, sacré chien!*" was the portion which fell to the lot of Hippolyte for not confining himself to the reward of a good conscience.

At this moment madame reappeared on the scene, and contrived to enter so at length into the history of Hippolyte's misdeeds, and to throw so much interest into her rebuke to him, and subsequent appeal in his favour, that she got through the time very well till the *poulet* and salad were served. The interpreter was appeased, nay, he was brought to that state of mind that he actually inquired for the last bulletin about baby, with a sort of glance towards me which implied that he only did this in discharge of his duty as an affectionate husband and father. He could see that he and I—sharp fellows!—knew all about women's little ways. They must be humoured out of compassion to the weaker vessel. Alas! my friend, my brother!

So the evening wore on, and we retired to our tea-chest, where we managed to get through the night well enough till such time as the "early cock," who plays so considerable a part in Algerine travel, roused us up much sooner than needful. In this wonderful country you seem to be able to get on without sleep and without food. So let us shake off dull sloth and see the sun rise over the Kabyle hills.

No question of mists and clouds here. It was a dim temple, faintly lit up with starlight; then the stars faded away as it became lighter; a suggestion of glow in the east, which became a full glow; a line of red, and the mountains became golden;—the usual African sunrise, but in a mountainous country where you get shadows.

After sunrise, coffee, and so into our little carriage again. We were pleased to see that an animal not so completely given up to self-indulgence had taken the place of the poor glutton, and thus we were able to proceed on our way with the full complement of three horses.

From the top of the Col, where we had passed the night, you get a fine view of the Djudjura range shining in its coverlet of snow. At no great distance we came to the river Isser, one of the noticeable rivers of Algeria; and a little further still to another river, which we were obliged to cross in the bed of the stream, now nearly empty of water; and so to the Souk-ed-Djema (or Market of Friday), to Bordj-Menaïel (our halting-place), and to Azib-Zamoun, where there was a large caravan-serai.

At a later period of our rambles, and near to Biskra in the desert, we were destined to pass a night in one of these places, and it shall be described at its proper time; but, happily, on this occasion there was no question of calling a halt, as we had already baited at Bordj-Menaïel. I have no desire nor intention of describing minutely these small hamlets and isolated farms; but if I remember right, it was near this caravanserai that the road bifurcated off to Dellys. Through Dellys, in case of obstruction between Kabylia and Algiers, supplies and reinforcements can be thrown into Kabylia with the greatest ease.

Dellys was taken by Marshal Bugeaud in 1844; but as it is away from our present route, I will say nothing more about it here. We had made our midday halt at Bordj-Menaïel, an apparently flourishing little French village, with its Hôtel du Roulage, and drink-shops, and omnibuses. With regard to our lunch, I can only say there was a great parliament of flies at the place in which we partook of that delightful banquet, a case of sardines from Nantes, and a "tin" of Peek, Frean & Co.'s biscuits being our *pièces de resistance*. Three youngsters, "men about town" at Bordj-Menaïel, strolled in for their midday absinthe, and discussed sporting matters, and the turn of their fortunes at cards. One, obviously the superior young man, went so far as to flirt with the waiting-maid —the old, old story—to the great admiration of his companions. They would have done the same if they could, but they were not equal to the occasion. The superior young man had the ear of the house; his jokes were taken when theirs fell flat; he could at once put on an air of familiarity, which seemed to mean a good deal, and probably meant nothing; so that his friends could never rise to his position of manly dignity. If I notice such nonsense at all, it is just because the thing struck me at the time.

"Dear me! here we are in Africa; but how like to Stony Stratford!" Here was a page from poor Charles Dickens in course of action in La Grande Kabylie. I doubt not, if the French could have been ousted, some swarthy Kabylian Dick Swiveller would have taken the place of the young Frenchman, who was steadily working his way down to fever and *delirium tremens;* and would have been equally envied and admired whilst his day lasted.

But enough of this. The luncheon being concluded, we got on our road again, and so on to Azib-Zamoun, where is the caravanserai already spoken of. We were now fairly engaged amongst the hills, with the mountains in the distance; abundant cultivation on either side of the road, and, to our great delight, Kabyles far more frequently, and in greater numbers.

It was, unless my memory fails me, just after passing the caravanserai and the turn-off to Dellys that our driver pointed to a tree on the left of the road, and said, "*Vous voilà, monsieur, dans La Grande Kabylie!*" One could begin to look about with some confidence. Here was the Kabyle at home—the thing which we had come out to see. To our eyes, bleared with cockneydom, it was a striking thing to watch these Scriptural-looking figures stalking through the corn-fields, sometimes driving their camels before them, just like pictures which I remember well in the Bible at home when I was a child. As they came near us, these Kabyles seemed to be stout, sturdy, yeomen-looking fellows, apparently stronger then the Arabs.

The women, whose faces were uncovered, were for the most part short and square-built, with flat broad foreheads and good eyes. I do not think a sculptor would have selected a Kabyle female nose as a model of that feature. They generally—even the poorest of them—wore jewels, that is, Kabyle jewels, not of any great value, but very pretty. They had that appearance of having undergone hard work out of doors, which you see in the female peasantry of France, and were generally in charge of a number of children. No wonder, then, that, what with work in the fields and family cares indoors, they seemed to have gone through hard times. I was told they are married at thirteen or fourteen years of age —so they begin early with life and its cares. They had not, however, an oppressed or injured look as we passed them trudging along or resting by the wayside. On the contrary, we always found on them a good-humoured smile —not to say a grin, which displayed their strong white teeth (could this have anything to do with it?), and a touch of eager curiosity to investigate the details of the stranger lady's dress. As I was afterwards told in the country itself, the ladies of Kabylia (though hardly pressed on by the laws of inheritance, and marriage) have a very good notion of holding their own. They work hard, and expect their husbands to work hard, and have more authority in their households than their Arab sisters.

Custom, or the unwritten law of a country, is of more account than the law which is written, and is nominally supreme. But it is when the powder speaks, or in the midst of warfare, that the Kabyle ladies show themselves in their full vigour. Woe to the faint-hearted sluggard who would loiter in his own hut or devote himself to the care of his own household goods whilst the fight was on! Not only would his gentle helpmate drive him to the front with a stout cudgel, but, in case of need, would give him the contents of his own gun. Once in the front, and in a good hot corner, the gentleman becomes the object of his wife's most anxious solicitude. As long as he can pull a trigger she will load for him; if he is down, she will fight for him, and bear him to a place of safety, as fighting is no longer of avail. In fact, they are a race of short, squat Helen McGregors, and had I charge in this matter, it would be my most anxious thought how to get the women on my side. The men would soon be kissed or kicked into submission.

Then the first Kabyle huts in the country itself attracted our attention. We do not look for the camel's-hair tent of the Arab; here were *gourbis*, first made of reed or wattles, afterwards with walls of mud and stone.

It was not until we actually got to Tizi-Ouzou that we investigated a Kabyle village, and looked inside the huts. For the moment the eye just rested on what we passed on the road. Ill-built, insufficient-looking huts they were, such as would scarcely have satisfied "the finest peasantry" in our own islands. But the Kabyle had the enormous advantage on his side of light, warmth, and air. If the fleas were troublesome in his own happy home, a nap out of doors was no very great affliction. Throughout the day, except as a refuge from the sun (and Kabyle skulls are thick), there was really no reason why he should go indoors at all. We passed plenty of what would be described elsewhere as *cafés Arabes*—though, of course, you must now read "**Kabyles**" for "Arabes."

There **you would** see numbers **of** them lounging over their little cups of coffee, and gossiping, I dare say very much as they do in the Pall Mall clubs in London; but they were strong, **sturdy** fellows. In case of any rising, Kabylia may require discipline, munitions of war, and weapons, but certainly men will not be found wanting.

So we have been jogging on along a good road, **with** plenty of cultivation on either side of us, occasionally Kabyle huts, more occasionally still Kabyle villages—the real Kabyle villages are up in the Highlands—with noble mountains on our right, and the glorious, fleckless African sky **overhead**. For all purposes of romance or stirring **incident, you** might as well have been driving round the inner **circle of** the Regent's Park; but this, I take it, is in itself a great **fact.** Had I seen a panther or a jackal—to say nothing of a lion—in the path, or an aggressive Kabyle, I was quite as ready as any of my predecessors to have described the incident in the most glowing colours. There was nothing of the kind, save that here and there the *cantonniers* had been repairing the roads, and we were disquieted with the rough stones. Beyond this, nothing.

Between 5 and 6 p.m. we reached **Tizi-Ouzou,** which means in French *col des genets* (*Plantagenista*, the broom plant), and were hospitably received at a very comfortable little inn, the Hôtel de la Poste, where we were to pass the night. Having secured our rooms and ordered dinner, we rambled out to take a turn in the village.

Tizi-Ouzou is not one village, but two villages ; one is French, the other Kabyle—purely so, just as though the European intruders had never visited the country. The French one puts me a good deal in mind of the villages in the Pyrenees, a broad, open street, with trees and running water. At the back, and upon somewhat higher ground, is a barrack for the troops, and in front of their quarters a pretty enough little garden, or " Place," the work of the soldiers. It is the situation of Tizi-Ouzou which gives it its importance. It commands the valleys of Kabylia, and guards the way to the Fort National, the object of our pilgrimage. Even a civilian can take in at a glance the value of the station. However, we wanted to see the Kabyles, and so strolled on till we got fairly amongst them.

Dirt, plenty of children, plenty of good-humoured women (at least, apparently so), who seemed to be much pleased with the notice we took of the small people ; dirty lanes, ill paved or not paved at all ; dirty huts, or cottages, built of rough material, but not of branches or wood ;—*that* was what we found when we ventured to peep inside. There was no one to be seen. The inhabitants were busy or lounging out of doors. There was but little of furniture even of the rudest kind, and as far as we could see, but one large room for the accommodation of men, women, children, and live stock of every kind. There might have been more rooms, or the huts might have been divided into two rooms, but we did not see them. We dared not push our investigations very far, as so many people were about, and we could not make ourselves understood in case of difficulty. As far as I saw anything of them, the interior of these Kabyle huts was dark and dirty. This was not the sort of place one would care to spend a night in; but at any rate the huts were fixed habitations. The people outside were just like those we had met on the road, but we could examine them more closely. Many of the children were really pretty, very like Spanish or Italian children, and even the youngest of these monkeys had jewellery of some kind. Some of the women were good-looking, but all bore unmistakable signs of hard work, all were tattooed (commonly with a cross), all wore jewellery. We grinned and gibbered at each other, and were upon good terms.

The word seemed to be passed through the village. Women, carrying babes, and each with her little convoy of children, came pouring in to see the strangers. It was quite clear that the works of Dr. Malthus had never been translated into the Kabyle tongue. Here, then, was a second fact: we have already noticed these fixed, and, I regret to say, dirty huts; we have now arrived at the large families. A third fact which we remarked at the time was the apparent separation of the sexes. Whilst we were doing the best we could to keep up a conversation, in Kabyle, with the women and children, no man came near us. There was nothing to be seen of that sort of shy, strong, shambling fellow one meets in Europe in such cases, who invariably wishes for a little beer to crown the edifice, and to cement friendship. The distribution of a few sous amongst the children had carried our popularity to such a point that we felt it was best to be gone, lest we should be asked in to afternoon tea, or to whatever answers to that form of banquet in Kabylia.

Strolling on, then, we came to an open space with a *café Kabyle;* and here we found a reason for the separation of the sexes. The truth was the Kabyles were all at the club—that is, at the *café*—squatted on the ground. But for their attitude and the absence of newspapers, they might have been at Boodle's. They had the true club look. Some of them, especially the old men, were extremely picturesque. Not only did we not meet with any molestation from them, but the poor fellows did not even stare rudely at the lady. I shall always think of them as a very gentlemanlike set. Then we wanted to reach a mosque which we saw at some little distance, but time was short, and we got back to the hotel to dinner.

We were shown into a small room, but on one side of it was a long table, evidently intended for a party. This was the officers' mess, for the French officers do not manage such things as we do at home. For the benefit of those who may come after us, I may say that the dinner was very fair : soup (French soup), then something in the nature of oyster-patties—possibly snail-patties—a bit of stewed meat, the *poulet* and salad, and dessert. There is a terrible uniformity in the *menu* throughout these Algerine wanderings. The difference lies between "good," "not so good," "bad." However, the poor little dinner was good enough for us, and afterwards we found the beds clean and simply excellent.

I hope no unkindly critic will challenge me for noticing such matters. It is my design to make it clear that you can travel about Algeria as you would about Brittany or Lombardy. If you want any of those picturesque adventures which I find recorded in African books of travel, you must go in search of them. Not M. Tartarin de Tarascon, whose history I afterwards read with so much profit and delight, could have been more surprised than I was at *the absolute want of adventure*. The lions were conspicuous by their absence. The danger of African travel, if any, is a tough fowl! What may be the case on the borders of pleasant Lake Nyanza, I cannot say, but travel in humdrum Algeria, as far as appliances are concerned, is very much like travel anywhere else. That is my cuckoo-song. To say this is the chief reason I am now writing out my notes, not after the experience of twenty-four hours in Kabylia, but after two months of knocking about in the three provinces. Our rambles extended beyond Biskra on the edge of the desert, and beyond Tlemçen on the Morocco frontier.

I have nothing very wise, or deep, or learned to tell my London friends, but I can assure them that they can drive about Algeria as we did, for a couple of months, very pleasantly, without let or hindrance.

That being so, let us have a cup of nice hot coffee—is it not 6 a.m.?—and be off to the Fort National. So away we went, after delighting our eyes with the pleasing domestic sight of Monsieur le Notaire, who was accompanying his amiable lady on a morning drive, and after having had our ears regaled with the rub-a-dub and trumpet blare of the chivalry of France.

In time we reached the wide bed of a river, now only watered by little streamlets, but which would, no doubt, at the proper season, be a terrible obstacle in the traveller's way. This river is not the Sebaou, but one of its affluents, which starts somewhere from between the Fort National and the Djudjura. Any way, it is a long and troublesome bit of road to get across—but tedious? No! From this point you get the very best sight of the Djudjura, which, as seen from here, seems to rise sheer out of the ground. What a sight this great mass of snow is under the blue sky, and with the bright African sun lighting it up! Go, my friends, to Tizi-Ouzou, and drive up to Fort National between coffee and lunch "*et vous m'en direz des nouvelles.*" Stare also, and with all your eyes—as the common phrase runs—at the little Kabyle villages with which the hills are thickly studded. These are the real things at last; these are the posts which it cost the French so much blood to win; these are the eagles' nests from which the forefathers of the Kabyles for so many centuries defied Roman, Phœnician, Arab, and Turk. The great river Sebaou runs in the valley at your feet, the Djudjura glows before you. On all sides are mountains and hills of the most picturesque shapes. The fig-trees are just coming into leaf, and so, as you climb the hill, the country on either side of you is as it were golden, or at any rate thickly set with trees whose leaves are of gold, just like in the old fairy-books.

But now about this road, which we are ascending

at a very dignified walking pace, notwithstanding our three horses; for it must be remembered that we have to go some 3000 or 4000 feet up in the air. The hills about us were, and possibly are, inhabited by the Beni Iratin, a race eminently warlike amidst races of warriors. In the year 1847, and on the 14th of June (as I read in the Algerine guide-book of M. Piesse), Marshal Randon placed the first stone of the Fort National, and then set to work to connect the Fort with the station of Tizi-Ouzou, where we had just spent the night. It is about seventeen English miles from Tizi-Ouzou to Fort National, and the greater portion of the road has to pass up this dreadful hill. The road is an excellent one.

Now our driver was a Frenchman, and therefore not disposed to depreciate the achievements of his fellow-countrymen. He said that we must not imagine the road made by the soldiers in seventeen days was such as we found it. They made a practicable way, but the road we were passing over was the work of time. It *was* an excellent one. The French are deserving of all praise for good road-making, not only in this particular instance but throughout the three provinces. At a later period we had an opportunity of comparing French roads and Spanish roads, from Carthagena to the Spanish frontier. There can be no doubt as to the vast superiority of the French. So we wound along amongst the golden fig-trees, now up, now down, but of course mainly up; now gaining, now losing sight of the Fort, but at length we reached our goal.

We were within a space of ground surrounded by a wall, which is no doubt strong enough for purposes of defence against a Kabyle gathering. The enclosed space trends down on one side. Our road lay along a sort of terrace—it could not be called a street, for there was only one side of houses overlooking the enclosure. We passed the diminutive Hôtel des Touristes, mentioned in the guide-books. I wish we had stopped there, for I had heard it favourably spoken of by a young gentleman, a very promising artist, whose acquaintance we had been fortunate enough to make in Algiers. He had made this place his head-quarters whilst stopping at Fort National for some months, and for purposes connected with his art. The driver was inexorable, and insisted on conveying us to another establishment of much more showy exterior further along the terrace. At this place we got a very indifferent luncheon, and my wife, who went upstairs to examine the rooms, pronounced emphatically against them. We never had any intention of passing the night there, so this mattered but little.

After lunch we scrambled up to the barracks, and a soldier was told off to show us round, especially to the terrace from which we were to get our view of the Djudjura range—the object of our drive from Algiers. Who can describe the beauty of the scene? Right in front of us lay the range, covered with snow, divided from the place where we stood by a wide valley; underneath us, in every direction, Kabylia. It is quite worth while coming from London to spend half an hour on the terrace of the barracks at Fort National.

We were in the *midst* of the Kabyle Highlands at last. Our guide, a bright little French soldier, pointed out to us the direction in which lay the chief points of interest. Monsieur was to follow with his eye as he pointed. In that direction lay Dellys. They had the route for that place, and they were to march there to-morrow, as the relief had arrived. He, for one, was right glad to do so, for Fort National was *très magnifique*, but *très triste*.

His regiment had now been quartered here too long a time. He liked Algiers best, far better than Oran, but here at Fort National there were absolutely no *distractions*. At Dellys it was better, for there was the sea, and on the other side of the sea La France. He had but a few months longer to serve, and then he was to retire into civil life, in the form of an *épicerie* kept by his aunt (his parents, unhappily, were dead), somewhere on the western French frontier. I will not mention the name of the town, as this might be a breach of confidence. Yes, he would be glad enough to get back to civil life once more, unless trouble should come up with Germany. He and his comrades were under the impression there would be war before the winter, and they were ready.

In that other direction, behind the big hills, lay Bougie; he did not know the place, for it was rather the affair of Constantine, and he had not been quartered there. Yes, Setif should be about there, but much nearer. It was manifest that monsieur could not see through the mountains, but that was the right direction. If we would but step round the corner, he would lead us to a spot from which we could look down into the Kabyle village which stood on the knoll next to Fort National. That was the *blockhaus*, which could be reached by an underground path from the Fort, and monsieur could see what a commanding position! They had had no trouble with the *indigènes*, and in his opinion were not likely to have any, for, said the little man, proudly, "What could they hope to do against us?" Only this very day they had received a fresh supply of great guns. The armament of the Fort was in course of renewal, and against weapons of war such as these the Kabyles were powerless. I hoped it might prove so, for, despite of all my romantic impressions of the last few days in favour of the Kabyles, it was impossible not to feel that one's good wishes were in favour of civilization against barbarism, no matter how picturesque in form. My sympathies were with the smart little French grocer, from whom we parted with expressions of mutual good will. How much pleasanter, and I doubt not how much worthier, a man than the swaggering, sneering *convives* at the dinner-tables of the French hotels!

Now for a ramble about the Fort until such time as the horses were rested and ready to take us back again to Tizi-Ouzou, happily all down hill. Before leaving the Fort, our guide expressed some surprise that we had not made up our minds to sleep at the Fort, and to occupy the afternoon by a ride upon mules to a Kabyle village some seven or eight miles distant, which, as it would appear, is the head-quarters, or one of the head-quarters, for the manufacture of the Kabyle jewellery of which we had seen so much in the shops at Algiers,—I regret to say, of spurious coin also. I explained that I was by no means sure of my own ability to sit upon a mule for such a distance. My disability would not, however, apply to more valid travellers. If pressed for time, there can be no reason why they should not start from Tizi-Ouzou early in the morning, stay a shorter time than we did at the Fort, visit the village, pick up a relay at Tizi-Ouzou, and sleep at Menerville.

I think I heard of an English family who accomplished the distance from the Fort to Algiers in a single day, by means of relays at Tizi-Ouzou and at Menerville. Seeing the diligence performs the journey in a single night (it is about eighty miles), there can be no reason why this should not be done with proper changes of horses. This, however, is to convert a pleasure into a toil. We were millionaires of time, and much preferred jogging along at the humble rate of some thirty miles a day; but I mention the fact for the benefit of others.

The ramble about the Fort was pleasant enough. There was a very fine view from a point a little further than the gate opposite to the one at which we had entered; a few shops, amongst others a bookseller's, at which I noticed a guide to the Kabyle language. I wished afterwards I had bought it; but when you are hot, dusty, tired, and worn out, the perceptions are duller than they should be. At length we were told the carriage was ready for us.

The drive back, with the lengthening shadows, was even more enjoyable than the morning's ascent. Of one thing I am sure, that our driver pointed on two occasions to an animal which shot across the road ahead of us, and called out, "There goes a jackal!" As we certainly did not attain the dignity of seeing any lions or panthers, at least let us put in our claim to familiarity with the smaller animal. It was enough for us. It is more convenient to examine the more majestic creatures at the Zoological Gardens in their comfortable cages.

As a set-off I may add that many times during the day we saw a great bird soaring over our heads, which the driver said was an eagle. I hope he was right; the creature looked very majestic against the blue sky. There was a certain dignity in saying, " Look up at the eagle yonder!" and as the creature is not in the habit of swooping down upon inoffensive travellers, there was no reason for objecting to his presence. " Go thy way, poor eagle! the world is large enough for us all."

When we got to the bottom of the hill, and to the edge of the river-bed, a majestic-looking Kabyle, with a business-like air, was standing there. Without any explanation (in point of fact, explanation would have been difficult), he stepped down into the dry river-bed, and whenever we came to any little water-course, joined us, with an expression upon his face which meant that in case of accident there he was. It was a fair inference that a good many tourists were in the habit of passing this way, since a living could be picked up or eked out by an imposture of this kind. Before long, Fort National will be even as Chamouni, or the Black Gang Chine.

Back to Tizi-Ouzou to the same comfort and arrangements as last night, with this exception that they had prepared our table in a large room outside, not in the mess-room, on the ground that the noise of the young officers might be disagreeable to us! I suppose the truth was that the officers liked their own privacy, and preferred our room to our company. I was not in the least affronted, for I think, had I been so fortunate as to be one of a group of gay youngsters talking merry nonsense, it would have been just my own feeling.

Next day, as we got into our little carriage, there was a row of Kabyles, with fruits and flowers, squatted opposite the hotel; and very pretty and picturesque they were.

We reached Menerville by the same road in the evening, and next day Algiers and the Hôtel de la Régence, I regret to say, *without adventure of any kind.*

I wish to add a few lines about a thing which we did not see, but which is described in General Daumas's book, "Mœurs et Coutumes de l'Algerie," as it affords a strange glimpse into the habits and ways of the Kabyles. It will be remembered that I spoke of a village near the Fort National, which every tourist ought to visit. It is about ten kilomètres distant from the Fort, and it is usual to make the little expedition with mules.

The name of this place is Aït-el-Ahsem. It is one of the head-quarters for the manufacture of Kabyle jewellery, and, it is said, for "coining." Our industrious Kabyle friends consider coining as one of the fine arts, and are great proficients in it. From time immemorial they have carried on this branch of industry, with great success, at Ayt-el-Arba, distant forty leagues from Algiers. Their workshop is at the top of a mountain. To get to it you must pass along a narrow and almost impracticable defile. Here they produce imitations of the coinage of almost every country, in copper, silver, and gold.

Their agents and correspondents bring them in the raw material, as copper, etc., but for this they pay in good money.

It is said that the Kabyle imitations are very good. The best way of detecting them is to take accurate measurement of the diameter, which is always a trifle less in the base than in the true coin. The base coins are cast in a mould made from the real coin; they shrink in cooling; hence the difference. Any one who could overcome this difficulty would meet with high reward in Kabylia. The Kabyles are particularly hard upon coinage offences committed against themselves. Knock your wife down and dance upon her in a playful way, stew your grandfather down, but leave the coinage alone, either as manufacturer or utterer. If you are caught it means certain death; extenuating circumstances are never admitted. The Turks were just as hard as the Kabyles against the poor coiner. It was nothing but "Down with him off the Bab-Azzoun gate!" "Run a pole into him, and stick him up as a warning to others!" If they could not catch the real offender, these unreasoning Turks would catch the suspected tribe, and compel them to give up the culprit under pain of instant death all round. For all this the industry was a most flourishing one. From Morocco, from Tunis, from the Sahara, leaving the Algerine provinces out of the question, base money was in constant request. Things must have been nearly as bad as we found them on the east coast of Spain on our return journey. You will do well there solemnly to ring every gold coin offered to you, even by an archbishop.

Any tourist travelling in Kabylia will do well to look up the Kabylian jewellery. We saw there many specimens of very good pottery, and brought some away. The oil trade is the great industry of the country.

Now here was a very delightful drive of five days, along an excellent road, at the rate of about thirty miles a day. The scenery was most beautiful, the climate and weather simply divine, the people and their villages and their ways most curious. The sight at the end, at Fort National, was as well worth seeing as anything in Switzerland, for if the snow-clad mountains were not so big, they were in Africa. The cost of all this was thirty-five francs a day for the carriage, with a small donation (with which he was well content) of ten francs to the driver. The charges at the little inns were ridiculously small. If this be African travel, let us be off to the desert.

CHAPTER XIII.

FROM PIMLICO TO THE PALMS.

WE may strike off the journey from Pimlico to Algiers, as already described, and address ourselves to so much of this little ramble as may be comprised between Algiers and Biskra. It is just the same story over again, of vast shadowy apprehension and very commonplace performance. There are two points at which the pilgrims of health in Algiers are in the habit of striking the desert: the one is at El-Aghouat; the other, Biskra. Between the two the choice should not be doubtful. It is much further to El-Aghouat; the journey is attended with more small discomforts and hardships; and, finally, the Oasis of Biskra, with its surroundings, is far more beautiful than El-Aghouat. So then, ho! for Biskra. But how to get there? You may direct that a carriage shall be brought to your door at the hotel, step in after breakfast, and tell the coachman to drive to Biskra, and when you have got there desire him to drive you back to your hotel. This plan sounds easy, but after due consideration was rejected. It is a terribly long drive by the Portes de Fer to Constantine, and then there is another drive—equally terrible—from Constantine, by way of Batna, to Biskra. Then there was the sea-passage. You might ship yourself on board one of the Valery steamers, and, disembarking either at Bougie, Philippeville, or Bône, so proceed to Constantine. Bône is the furthest off of the three points, but there is thus much to be said for it, that on this route between Bône and Constantine, you may pause and visit the Accursed Baths, or the Hammam Meskoutin; a very strange place it is, and well worth a visit. The sea-voyage is longer, and then it is more troublesome to get from Bône, than from Philippeville, to Constantine. A good deal must depend on the state of the sea. We ultimately determined to leave it to chance, and to go on to Bône if the sea was smooth; if not, to disembark at Philippeville, and take the rail on to Constantine.

As far as Bougie is concerned, I say but little here, beyond this, that you must take this route either on your way out or back, or you would miss the famous Chabet Pass, which is one of the two or three great glories of North Africa. We arranged our trip so as to return by this route, and were well satisfied that we had done so.

Early, very early, in our Algerine experience, being greatly exhilarated, or spurred up by the description of African travellers, I had ventured to hope that we might be able to perform part of our journey upon camels—a theory which, no doubt, will call up a smile on the faces of those who know the real facts of the case. We never, of course, contemplated the being hoisted on our camels in front of the Hôtel de la Régence, and of so departing amidst the cheers and sobs of our friends by way of the Rue Bab-Azzoun. It would have looked grand, and I could see in my mind's eye a little illustration of "our departure from Algiers for the desert," representing the partner of my toils and myself seated aloft amidst the marmalade pots, and Peek, Frean & Co.'s biscuits, waving our adieus to all the good people who had villas to let; but we never entertained the idea as a serious one. We were to start in the usual vehicle of domestic life, and throw ourselves on our camels when we got to Batna or thereabouts.

I had never seen these "ships of the desert" save twice: once, in the Zoological Gardens of London, when I regret to say (and how can I say it politely enough?) a "ship" expectorated in my face without the smallest provocation, leaving a most unpleasant impression as to the manners and customs of his class; and, upon a second occasion, at Pisa, in the pine-woods, where a string of these "ships" sailed past in a dreary and monotonous way, leaving me with the idea that they had come there for the sake of their health, and that the climate had disagreed with them. It was better to see what camels meant before we started.

We Algerines, we "sweepers of the sea," are not without our resource. Just outside the Isly gate you meet files of Kabyles bringing in grapes and oil and what not to the Algerine markets. The Kabyles then, the men of grapes and oil, come perched upon their camels; but for very sufficient reasons, the *sergens-de-ville*, the functionaries who look after our morals and comfort in a general way, do not like to see the poor things wobbling about, and looking into the upper windows of the shops in the over-crowded streets of the town. The result is that these uncomfortable-looking creatures are left in great numbers on a large flat space of ground (outside the Iṣly gate), which is called the Champ des Manœuvres; much affected by the French soldiers, where the trumpets never cease from braying, and where the drums are never at rest.

Here is the place to study the ways and fashions of these "ships of the desert." The first point for consideration was how to get on a camel; the next was how to stick on him, when, if ever, you got settled on the hump; the third (a not unimportant branch of the subject) was how to get off. A first glance convinced me that all dreams of desert life, and of a week with the ostriches at the Oasis of Zab-el-Ouad, must be given up. The "ship" kneels down (I trust that all unkind critics will read the word "camel" for the word "ship"), and if, by the help of some friendly Kabyles, you are hoisted up to the soft dignity of the hump, do not imagine that the moment of triumph has arrived, and that nothing remains but to write home to your friends, and sneer at civilized life and "four-wheelers." Yes, you are in the saddle, but you are about as safe as the arrow which has been fitted to the string of a Tartar's bow, or the cartridge which has been rammed down by a benevolent German to the bottom of a gun. There you sit, in a position which Mr. Briggs might have envied, when all of a sudden the Kabyle in charge emits a sound of a very guttural and terrible kind. The "ship" turns out to be nothing but a catapult for propelling missiles perpendicularly. *You* are the missile. Unfortunately, since the days of the great Sir Isaac there is an end of all comfort. If you go up, you must come down, or else what would become of the laws of gravitation—I may say, of the famous University of Cambridge? A terrible "come down" it is, and perhaps worst of all is the cold malignity with which the "ship" glares at you whilst you are sitting on the sand.

"Monsieur," said to me a French gentleman, whose circumference implied many dinners, "*une telle dégringolade n'est pas une chute, c'est un attentat contre la dignité personelle d'un homme.*" I thought so too, besides the chances of thumps and bumps.

On the second point, as to how you hold on when the "ship" is in full sail over its sea of sand, I could say nothing then; but the process seemed hideously uncomfortable as I watched these creatures, under the guidance of experienced Kabyles, walking—or might I say shambling?—along the dusty roads.

However, I did see the process of "getting off;" if not so dangerous to life or limb, it is quite clear that it must be as wretched as the "getting on." The camel kneels down, not by one effort, but by many, each of which must give you the sensation of being half-way between Dover and Calais, with a cross sea on, just at that moment when you are held over the mouth of the abyss, and before you are "let go." You must have a series of such sensations, without time given you to call for help between the shocks. But all this is a trifle. Wait for the final movement, when the animal, which has bent and unbent his uncouth legs in a hundred ways, and has stowed them away as in a box of mathematical instruments, makes up his mind to lower his stomach on to the sand. Imagine all the pitchings and heavings and rollings of which a small steamer, without ballast, save human misery, can be guilty; shake them all together, and you will have a faint idea of that last playful movement of the "ship of the desert." Involuntarily you call out, "Steward! quick!" No sandy joys for me! If I want an ostrich egg or so, I know of a Jew who lives handy to the cathedral, and who, as a particular favour, and out of his personal interest in me, will let me have the articles at five or six hundred per cent. above their value. I had a fancy to try the *couscousou* under the black tent of an Arab far beyond Biskra or El-Aghouat, but now I have seen the "ship of the desert," I think I will mention the subject to the cook at the Régence—an Italian gentleman, mighty in all that concerns *pasta*.

The plain English of all this is—if you want to get a glimpse of the desert, go to Biskra, not to El-Aghouat, don't take the overland route by the Portes de Fer. It is long, tiresome, costly, and not the least worth while.

With regard to the sea route. We disembarked at Philippeville, and returned by the Chabet Pass and Bougie, and I recommend future African explorers to do the same thing. From Philippeville to Constantine the journey is one of about four hours, the distance between fifty and sixty miles. Being at Constantine, you can always take the train to Guelma, sleep at the Accursed Baths, and return to your inn at Constantine. On your way back from Biskra, you take the rail from Constantine to Setif, sleep there, and, either by carriage or by diligence, reach Bougie by the Chabet Pass in one easy day, in plenty of time to catch the steamer for Algiers.

On Wednesday, the 7th of April, about twelve of the clock, we drove down from the hotel to the quay, to get on board the steamer in which we had taken our berths for Philippeville. There was a quiet oily roll upon the water, so that even the craft in the harbour swung about in a lazy sort of a way, just as if they were yawning through a storm. Alack! alack! how one's poor mouth filled with water, as the little boats by the quay now rose to the level of your foot, now disappeared slowly as you were about to make a decisive effort, just as if they did it on purpose! What a mockery it sounded when the genial people who were so fortunate as to be remaining on shore talked to you about a "glorious passage," and "just the sort of day to see the mountains in their full beauty"! See the mountains! But it is as well to go on; another day we might be favoured with an African storm or some magnificent spectacle of that description. So aboard we got somehow, and I hoped we should get it over quick; but not a bit of it. A wretched vessel got in our way, and it was a good hour before the captain of the *Malvina*, who had sent out little boats with thick ropes in every direction, and had tied himself on to ships innumerable, and then untied himself, succeeded in getting us out of the harbour, and fairly committed us to the process of rolling in oil. How any man in his senses can say he enjoys this sort of thing, is more than I can understand. Go through the misery in order to get somewhere, I suppose you must, but as to enjoyment—good Lord! I have no doubt the mountains looked very beautiful, but as to myself, I was lying on a slippery horse-hair sofa, too short for me, in our little cabin, with nothing to hold on by, and so I enjoyed myself! Months have elapsed since that period of enjoyment, and I am now writing on quiet dry land, which does not pitch or roll, but I solemnly declare that the secretions in my mouth are far more abundant than they should be, and the photographs on the wall seem to swing slowly backwards and forwards as I think of that "glorious passage," that *Malvina*, that horse-hair sofa. It seemed to me that the stewards were perpetually laying the cloth just outside our door, and I did not shower down blessings on their heads.

To sail along the coast at a moderate distance from the shore is, however, not undelightful if a man can get rid of this wretched tendency to nausea. We saw the bay well from Cape Matifou to Algiers on our way home, when I suppose we were more toughened by travel; and what with the mountains in the background, what with the views of Algiers itself, and the surrounding hills,—it is a beautiful sight. I should doubt if you would ever thoroughly understand the "lie" of the country without having seen it from this point. The Bou-Zarea Hill—the whole of the Sahel—will fall into proper place and keeping when seen thus from the sea. I cannot say that between Cape Matifou and Dellys I saw much on our return worthy of notice; on our way out I saw nothing except the back of the odious horse-hair sofa.

About 5 p.m. we came to our anchorage at Dellys,

and it became possible to go on deck, and take a glance at the place. Dellys is the port of that part of Kabylia which we had just visited. What I saw was a long hill, with a wall creeping about it, as if it would be a fortification if it could; and a group of the usual French houses, so stereotyped in appearance that it is always sufficient to record the fact of their existence. Nor will I waste time by speaking of the usual dinner upon a French steamer; you get fresh vegetables, fresh fruit, the usual light *ordinaire*, which, with St. Galmier water, makes a very tolerable drink. The entertainment, take it on the whole, is quite as much as you care to encounter, considering how the previous hours have been spent. So I can only say the people got up their anchor at last, and back we went, ignobly enough, to our little cabin, turned into our berths, fell asleep, and awoke at Bougie, as it seemed, in the middle of the night, but it was between 2 and 3 a.m. There was nothing to complain of this time, and when we got upon deck two or three hours later, we found a good deal over which we might fairly rejoice. This bay of Bougie is simply magnificent. I will venture to adopt, from Colonel Playfair's guide-book (page 115), a quotation which he, in his turn, has taken from the poet Campbell, who visited Bougie in 1834.

The Scotch poet writes: "Such is the grandeur of the surrounding mountain scenery, that I drop my pen in despair of giving you any conception of it. Scotchman as I am, and much as I love my native land, I declare to you that I felt as if I had never before seen the full glory of mountain scenery. The African highlands spring up to the sight not only with a sterner boldness than our own, but they borrow colours from the sun, unknown to our climate, and they are mantled in clouds of richer dye. The furthest off summits appeared in their snow like turbans of gigantic Moors, whilst the nearest masses glowed in crimson and gold under the light of the morning."

On our return journey from Constantine, by way of Setif, we were to drive over this district, which we now only saw from a distance; so mention will be made of it in its proper place.

We left Bougie about midday, and, cutting across the bay, and rounding a great promontory, in the afternoon came to Djidjelli. The mountain views were very fine. The old town has been destroyed by an earthquake, and a modern French town, with the same name, has been built up, but not on the same site. As seen from the ship, a sort of natural breakwater appeared to offer some protection to any ship which might come to anchor here. I cannot say what the reasons may be for not making the protection complete, but, doubtless, such exist. The peninsula on which stood the old town, and this breakwater, would seem to offer great help for making the anchorage secure as from the westward, but possibly anticipations of fresh disturbance from earthquakes may be the cause why the Frenchmen hesitate as to proceeding with what looks like a half-done work.

Our next halt was to be at Collo, about five hours distant in point of time, but of this place I can say nothing, for we reached it about midnight, when we were in our berths, and were only roused from sleep by the cessation of the screw-noise. My brief narrative of our little trip will show that the great feature of this run along the African coast is the manner in which it is done in easy stages. A run from Algiers, even to Philippeville, might be a disagreeable thing, were the weather unpropitious, but really, as it is made up of these short runs, and you have time to recover yourself at each port of call, and gradually acquire "sea legs," the hardship is not as great as it would seem. As it was pitch dark, we remained where we were, vexed only by the noise caused by discharging and receiving cargo from the lighters which came alongside. This, however, came to an end. The screw recommenced its revolutions, we fell asleep, and awoke at Philippeville at about 6 a.m. on Friday morning. We had left Algiers at noon on the preceding Wednesday, and a very large portion of the time had been spent at anchor at Dellys, Bougie, Djidjelli, Collo, so that really the run passed off easily enough, and I do not think there is anything in it which need deter the most nervous traveller from undertaking such a voyage. Would you proceed to Tunis and the site of old Carthage, you must remain on board till you reach the next port—Bône—where you change steamers, and, with one halt at La Calle, reach your destination. Leaving Algiers on Wednesday at noon, you should reach Tunis in this way on Sunday evening. As our mark was the desert, by way of Constantine, we did not attempt this. What we wanted to see was Algeria, not Tunis, so we deferred this excursion to another opportunity. Tunis is always accessible, and easily so from

Malta, and at Malta we are sure to find ourselves one day or other if we remain upon earth, and, if not, as the old Scotch lady said, it does not matter.

Here, however, we are at Philippeville, and I recommend any future traveller to do what I did not do, that is, get on deck an hour beforehand, so as to get a good look at the island and the lighthouse, and above all at Stora, which is the ancient port of Philippeville, and which we only saw from that place. The new harbour is said to be unsafe, but when we were there we found in it two or three large steamers, and a good deal of shipping of all sizes.

The coast between Philippeville and Stora looked exceedingly pretty, and again I recommend future travellers by this route to do what we did not, that is, to take a little open carriage and drive from Philippeville to Stora.

As the steamer arrives at the former place early in the morning, and the train for Constantine does not leave till the afternoon, there is plenty of time to do this. But we were lazy, we were travel-worn, we wanted to lounge over a quiet breakfast upon a steady floor ; so we contented ourselves with a ramble about the town, and were satisfied with staring at the scenery through an opera-glass. But, first, let us get on shore, and if I make mention of anything so trivial as our own personal adventures, be it clearly understood I do so simply to break the perpetual monotony of "Left such a place—reached such another, at such an hour—magnificent scenery—saw a sea-gull." Even the word "adventures" is a misnomer ; we met with no more adventures than we should have done between Paris and Marseilles or between London and Penzance.

To tell this to any one who may honour me by reading this little book is my chief motive for writing it. I want to disencumber Algerine travel from the haze of "adventure," and to assure all intending tourists that it is as simple a matter as to drive round the English lakes. With this apology for recording trifles, let me say that at last we got into a boat, with our small belongings, and made for the shore. A crowd of *indigènes* ran down to the landing-place and boarded us. For my own credit's sake let me say that I was powerless. The utmost I could hope for was to allow myself to be helped out of the boat if the wretches would leave us alone. This was not their idea; one seized the bag, another the umbrellas, and so on, and all this time a French *sergent-de-ville* stood looking on majestically, with his arms folded Napoleon-wise.

Whether or no our nationality was an objection to him; whether or no he was diverted by the spectacle, which no doubt was funny enough, I cannot say, but at any rate there he stood, immovable as destiny, and majestic as a Frenchman in a cocked hat can look. The two larger bags were hopelessly gone, and danger threatened the smaller gear. At this point my poor little wife, exasperated beyond the point of feminine endurance by an onslaught on these unconsidered trifles, dear to her soul, snatched a brass badge from a Kabyle, flung it on the shore, and, seizing up my stick, gave the Kabyles clearly to understand that they should only reach the small parcels over her prostrate body. The men were cowed, and fell back; the French *sergent*, seeing the fight was decided, moved up in support, and with a calm and dignified gesture, dismissed the tribes. So we got ashore, and collected our goods; but I am proud to be the Homer of "The Lady's Battle." Caution to the traveller: we had been warned not to go to the hotel which is near the landing-place, but rather to search for breakfast in a large *café* which is equally close at hand. This we did, and had reason to be thankful for the good advice. The people at the *café* gave us a nice French breakfast, with plenty of fruit upon the table, and plenty of freshness and bright uniforms all around us.

The story of Philippeville is interesting enough, but I have made it a rule with myself not to enter into rivalry with the guide-books. It is just another French provincial town, with a good deal of bustle on the quays and about the harbour. It would seem that Stora was the Rusicada of the Roman world, and that in the year 1838 Marshal Valée bought the site of this once famous place from a Kabyle tribe for 150 francs, or £6 English money—just the story of Dido or Penn over again. I see it mentioned that people who are curious on antiquarian matters will find many things to interest them in the old theatre, I presume, at Stora; but as we did not go near the place, I can say nothing about it. What we did was to walk up one side of a long French street, and down another, and to gaze into the shops and *cafés*. The place is French, purely French, there was less of the native element to be seen even than at Algiers.

We left Philippeville at 2.30 p.m. by the rail, and reached Constantine at 6.45 p.m. The carriages are as comfortable as any you would meet with in Europe, and the drive a most interesting one, as you wind up amongst the mountains. At first, as my recollection runs, there was a good deal of cultivation, then a good many olive-trees. We made a halt at a place called the "Col des Oliviers," from which the views are very fine. The wild flowers were beautiful and plentiful, though but a foretaste of what we were to see afterwards.

On the drive we saw for the first time the black Arab tents in great numbers, and, when we got near Constantine, the date-palms, though we were still far off the head-quarters of this beautiful tree. You do not see Constantine till you are close upon it, and the first view from the railway is disappointing enough, as the expectations of the traveller have been highly raised by all he has read about this city. Yes, the writers have written truly enough; Constantine is second to no other city as far as the magnificence of its situation is concerned, but you must wait till you see it from the proper points. Stockholm, Edinburgh, Prague, Genoa, Naples, Granada, Lisbon, I have seen (but not, I am sorry to say, Constantinople, which will probably be Germanized or Russianized before I get there), yet, compared with any of these, Constantine holds its own, and is a very eagle's nest amidst the rocks. But let us first attend to sublunary matters, get into the omnibus from the Hôtel d'Orient, to which we had been recommended, cross the famous Kantara Bridge, and drive up the Rue Nationale to the other extremity of the town, where we found the rooms, for which we had written, ready for us. On the other side of the street is the Hôtel de Paris, which has an equally fair outside, but the primary objection to it is that you have to climb higher upstairs to reach the hotel rooms, and, as we were afterwards told by persons with whom we compared notes, the accommodation and food are not better, and the charges a very great deal higher. The Hôtel d'Orient is kept by a Swiss landlord, a good-natured man, with a good-natured wife, who did their best to make us comfortable during our stay at Constantine, and perfectly succeeded.

Constantine is a wonderful place. However often I may repeat my cuckoo-song that the personal incidents of Algerine travel are of the most commonplace kind, let me not for one moment be supposed to suggest that what you see is commonplace. You would have to go far a-field in the East or in British India to see the beautiful and strange things which you find at Tlemçen, Biskra, or at Constantine, where we are just now. True, the native quarter is disappearing fast, and French streets are taking the place of the old picturesque dwellings, but enough remains. We step out of the door of the hotel, and are on the Place de la Brèche, the point at which the city was captured by the French under Marshal Valée, in 1837. On the left is the market (not the old Arab market), and a new theatre in course of construction. The *indigènes* are squatted about, selling flat cakes of bread, which they clap together to attract the notice of customers. There is a blare of trumpets; two Zouaves, in a perspiration, blowing at their instruments with all their might, advance at the head of a body of Zouaves, also more hot than can be comfortable. The natives scarcely honour this martial display with a glance.

It is worth while to pause a while at this spot. On that sloping ground opposite to us the French breaching batteries were established. Yonder is the spot at which General Damremont fell, killed, says the gossip of the place, by a cannon-ball fired from a distant French battery. There was talk of that eternal *trahison*, without which no French martial enterprise is ever complete. Be that as it may, Damremont the Unlucky has joined the majority, and the statue of Marshal Valée, the lucky one, now stands calmly in the garden close by, and asks for the applause of mankind. He succeeded where Marshal Clauzel had failed the year before, and where his immediate chief, poor Damremont, as Carlyle would write it, had got himself blown into space in an altogether unsatisfactory way.

The view from the Place to the westward is magnificent: huge hills, which might be called mountains, all trending down to the sea; above your head to the northward a mass of rock even higher than the site of Constantine. From this point we could see the country, but not the town, well. To do this you must walk, or, as we did, drive up to the Koudiat Aty in front, or to the pyramid which marks the spot where Damremont fell. From this point you can get a very fair view of the town, north, south, and east. Speaking quite roughly, Constantine stands upon a plateau, high up and unapproachable on any of three sides. The only fair access to the town is on the side where we are now standing. You may consider it as a sort of headland, jutting out, and surrounded by a ravine on three sides, and on two of these sides flows the river Rummel.

Imagine yourself walking up Beachy Head, Shakespeare's Cliff, or any place of that sort from the sloping land side. We are on such a gradual slope. Go on, and peer over the edge of the cliff; at Constantine, on two sides, you would peer into a narrow ravine, and on the third, over a steep cliff just like that at the Castle of Edinburgh. The only feasible way to drive a gig into Constantine (bar bridges) is on one side. The city has the form of what is called a trapeze, with the angles facing the four cardinal points, and slopes gradually down from north to south. The Rummel guards it on the south-east and north-west sides. On the north, or Kasbah, side the cliffs are very steep, so that there only remains the side on which the French ultimately took the city, and where we are now standing.

M. Piesse (mine is not the last edition) gives the numbers of the population as about 30,000 in the Arab quarter, 6000 Europeans, and 5000 troops, but the Europeans are gradually encroaching. We found at Constantine, what we had hoped to find at Algiers, a real native element in full vigour. The Arabs and Kabyles stalked about in a more spirited way; the Jews, and certainly the Jewesses, were far better-looking and more splendidly attired than at Algiers. Even from the spot on which we were standing, one could see at a glance the importance of the city from the political, commercial, or military point of view. It is the key of the country. Downwards lies before us the road to the sea; all merchandise must pass that way, all reinforcements and supplies must come up that way. Far away to the southward, and between the big mountains, lies the path to the desert, along which we were to drive in a few days, and which had been travelled over for ages by the wild tribes. The Romans—no bad judges in such matters —fixed their talons firmly in the soil at Constantine and Lambessa, and so they held the country for many a long year of battle and turmoil.

We are in the old *Cirta*, the Numidian capital before it became a Roman province in the days of Julius Cæsar. Now or never is the time to think of those old names which were so painfully familiar to one in boyhood. Mine has been rather a busy life, and I have had no great time to think of such things, but at Constantine it is hard to avoid rubbing up one's old recollections, and so I began to disentangle from the frayed and knotted skein of memory such names as Syphax, Masinissa, Juba, Jugurtha, and the rest of them. In thinking of Constantine, one must always remember that, if Rome was near, Carthage was still nearer, and so the history of this, "the city in the air" (as I am told in the guide-book it was called by an old Arab writer), followed the struggles of the two mighty prize-fighters.

Narva, king of the Massæsylians, ruled here about two hundred years before Christ. He married into a good military family at Carthage, inasmuch as he conducted the sister of one General Hannibal to the hymeneal altar. Syphax followed, and imitated his example by marrying Hasdrubal's daughter, so that at this point the Carthaginian connection was clearly in the ascendant. But here begins the old, old story. General politics became sadly complicated by feminine fascinations; and yet people talk of the rights of women, just as though in all ages of the world they had not caused the more thick-headed men to knock out what they call each other's "brains" at their good will and pleasure. Syphax's queen, *née* Hasdrubal, was the famous Sophonisba, and at an unlucky moment for the working men of those days, King Masinissa, king of the Massylians (not that long word written above), caught sight of her, and his heart was reduced to a cinder. How to get hold of her!—not that he was stopped by any moral considerations, but the walls of Constantine were high, Syphax was uxorious, Sophonisba knew what was due to herself and her position, and the Massæsylians were better men than the Massylians.

At the nick of time, the second Punic War broke out, so Masinissa, being resolved to get hold of Sophonisba at all hazards, felt that it was the duty of the Massylians to form an alliance with the Roman legions. There was no other course open to him in the general interest of humanity. Had not Africa groaned too long under the tyranny of Carthage? And was not the lovely Sophonisba held in thraldom on the rock of Constantine by that scoundrel Syphax? The Roman general was one Scipio Africanus—a name not altogether unknown in history, a man who did not understand joking, or, as it turned out, lover's transports. Cirta was taken, and the lady fell into the hands of her adorer. One can imagine with what seething indignation King Masinissa handled poor Syphax. True affection was rewarded, I regret to say, by Sophonisba; but just as Masinissa was beginning to think of love in a cottage, and afternoon tea with the woman of his heart, that horrid Scipio stepped in in a practical way, and claimed Sophonisba as a prize of the Roman Senate.

Scipio was, of course, above suspicion; his previous career and general character formed a sufficient guarantee that he was only actuated by the purest and most patriotic motives. This was more than a lover, a husband, a king, a Massylian, a man could stand; so Masinissa at once handed a cup of poison to Sophonisba, who daintily sipped it off, only expressing her regret (not in a complimentary way to Masinissa) that she had not taken the refreshment earlier, "for so," the beautiful queen remarked, quite in the style of a French novel, "it would have been better, far better, for my glory."

So they buried their dead on all sides, and nobody got anything except the practical Roman, who was master of Cirta. Masinissa for all that had come and gone, stuck to the Roman alliance, and put his grievances in his pocket. Any one who will take the pains, the pleasant pains, of reading Mr. Bosworth Smith's delightful little book on what may be called "The Decline and Fall of Carthage," will see it set duly forth how this shrewd old king felt it his duty to egg the Romans on to the third Punic War, furnishing them with just the pretext they required. We all know how that ended; but it left Masinissa on the throne of Cirta, so he got some compensation after all for the loss of his Sophonisba.

His son Micipsa reigned after him; then his son Adherbal; but it was an unquiet family. One Jugurtha, a near and dear relative, knocked poor Adherbal on the head, and took possession of his throne. He seems to have been a wild, guerilla sort of a young man, good at fighting, good at intrigue, but not of solid judgment. He failed, in his day, to comply with the sovereign rule of finding out the strongest side, and sticking to it. He paid the penalty of his mistake—for I myself, as other cockney tourists have done, have peered into that unpleasant hole in the Capitol at Rome, where he was thrust down to die. A man must die somewhere, but this was the worst inn's worst room with a witness. Jugurtha must have had his reasons, but looking back at the question from this distance of time, with Carthage swept off the board, it is difficult to see how he could hope to fight Rome single-handed. Metellus and Marius soon accounted for him, for our Roman friends were as ready to bribe as to fight. Then Juba was made king, but he again was mole-eyed enough not to perceive on which side strength lay; he took the side of Pompey against Cæsar, and it was not wise to be Cæsar's enemy. Juba disappeared, and Cirta became a Roman colony, and so remained for a couple of centuries. The city seems to have shared the usual vicissitudes of places in North Africa; it was overrun by the Vandals, retaken by Belisarius (a great name in African legend), fell into the hands of the Arabs, then of the Turks, finally of the French.

This is an index to the history of Constantine for more than a couple of thousand years. When the French came to Algiers, they found it ruled by a Bey, in dependence on the Dey of Algiers. He gave the French trouble, was defeated, surrendered, and died of a bad cold, complicated with symptoms which seemed like diphtheria, and now sleeps peacefully under a pleasant little stone in the garden of the Zaouia, at the top of the Jardin Marengo at Algiers. I suppose this is enough to give a general notion of the past history of this curious city. I cannot enter into, nor would the reader have patience to read, the ups and downs of its story in the days of the Auffirides and Morinides, till the pirate Kheir-ed-Din stepped in and put a stop to this historical confusion.

M. Piesse tells us the place has been besieged and taken eighty-three times, so that in it there must have been great fluctuations in the value of leasehold property. For those who care to know more upon such matters, I must refer them to the guide-books or to the general histories, for it is my business just now rather to speak of what I saw than of what I have read.

After having well exhausted the sights from the Place de la Brèche, we thought we would search for the palace of Ahmed Bey, and then take a stroll through the Arab quarter, or so much of it as lies on either side of the Rue Nationale. This we did, returning to the hotel to order an open carriage for the afternoon, that we might drive round the town, and get a leisurely view of it from the best points, and without fatigue. We had to make our way from the Place de la Brèche, or Nemours, to the Place du Palais, which is easily done, as, from the spot on which we are standing, you can enter, indifferently, the Rue Nationale in which is our hotel, or the Rue de France, which equally traverses the city and may be said to divide it into two halves. Ahmed's palace stands in a Place of the same name, which is only a few steps out of the Rue de France. It is a gay enough little French Place, but as far as externals are concerned, the officers' club-house is a much more striking object than Ahmed's palace. Never mind, we have heard of the Oriental aversion to outward display, so, no doubt, we shall be rewarded presently. "Let us ring the bell." So we did, but of course the man who should have shown us over the place was out, and would not be at home for a couple of hours. "Might we walk round the courts, as we were already standing in them?"

There was no difficulty about this. These courts turned out to be the palace, or as much of it as we were destined to see; for on a second visit, a few days later, we were informed that a general on circuit, or some one of that kind, had arrived at Constantine, and was in occupation of the State apartments; but "Monsieur," said the very gentleman-like young French officer who was compelled to deny us admission, "do not let that be a cause of disquietude to you. There is absolutely nothing to see upstairs. The courts *are* the palace."

So round the courts we walked, and they are no doubt very pretty; but the beauty of the place has been so much overpraised, that I fear we were a little disappointed with what we saw. After all, these things are very much "matters of taste," and what sends my neighbours into ecstasies of delight leaves me comparatively untouched. I suppose it is that we had seen many fine things at the Crystal Palace, that first and best great glass-house of 1851 in Hyde Park—so many world-shows, alhambras, and transformation scenes, that we were hard to please; but, dare I write it?—the palace of Ahmed Bey went off rather flat. There are three courts, with little gardens of no great account, plenty of pillars, and, as my memory serves me now, very quaint and curious frescoes in the first court only. We strolled from one court to another, under the guidance of a *spahi*, on our second visit, and the good-natured French soldiers allowed us to enter into some of the rooms, which were dark and Eastern-looking enough. The frescoes were very curious, representing various Eastern cities. The one which pleased me best gave us the old Algiers, surrounded with a wall, and suffering bombardment from various little gun-boats with very big guns, under the weight of which they must certainly have been swamped in real life.

It was, however, curious enough to get at last a real view of the old Algiers, no matter how roughly done, by a native artist who had seen the place, and who knew that his work would be criticised by those who knew it also. Probably the more realistic the sketch, the better for our purposes. Had we come upon the place unexpectedly I dare say we should have been charmed; as it was, we were disappointed. M. Piesse, who seems to have seen things as they are more accurately than his fellows, tells us that this palace was built by the last Bey, El-Hadj-Ahmed, with materials stolen and wealth extorted from the richer inhabitants of the town. El-Hadj-Ahmed occupied it twice, once as a prince, a second time as a prisoner. "This palace," writes sober-minded M. Piesse, "has been often compared to the fairy-like dwellings described in the 'Thousand and One Nights.' There would be nothing remarkable about it but for the three gardens surrounded by galleries, which convert the place into a sort of oasis in the middle of the European streets, where, if you do not find dust, you find mud." That is just my own opinion; but people will differ on what is after all but a matter of taste.

The Cathedral of Constantine is an old mosque standing near the palace. We remember to have admired in it some stone pillars, and an old Mohammedan pulpit; but beyond this, the aspect of the place has passed from our recollection, and we never entered it a second time, which we probably should have done had there been much to see or admire in it. But as to what came next, there was no room for disappointment. Certainly neither palace nor cathedral had taken our breath away; but I wonder if there be anything better worth seeing at Constantinople, Bagdad, Damascus, or any other of those romantic places than the labyrinth of quaint native shops which we visited next.

We were first in the quarters of the shoemakers, or workers in leather. Curious little shops they were, with the fronts knocked out, the master or chief man squatting in front, looking *unwisely* towards the street, and stitching away diligently after the fashion of shoemakers and cobblers; perhaps a workman or so behind him, and high up on a shelf a boy or two working, or making believe to work, but in reality skylarking or grinning at the passers-by. This was why I wrote, as above, the word "unwisely;" the master, as I think, should have faced his *employés*, or at any rate have taken up his position at the back of the shop on that sort of raised bench, so the eye of the master might have ensured the diligence of the servant.

What we could not help remarking was that every one had by him, on a little shelf, a bright nosegay, sometimes of many flowers, sometimes only a few carnations. Then in the little shop was hung a green cage, containing one bright singing bird or another, sometimes two or three cages, with two or three birds. What with the air, and sunshine, and gossip, and flowers, and songs of the birds, it struck me that the working man at Constantine had rather a good time of it. It cannot be all play with them, for they manage to provide shoes not only for the city, but the province, and export their goods largely. In very distant towns it will be said, "Ah! these shoes are the right sort of thing; they came from Constantine." Amidst these cheerful workers we loitered away a good deal of time, and really their quarter is one of the things best worth seeing in Constantine, which does not in any way shine by the splendour of its buildings or public edifices.

Work your way down to the Place des Galettes, where we found a fruit and vegetable market, and so you will pass out of the shoemakers' quarter, and come to other trades, and to a series of pictures of Eastern or Southern life. We found the gold-workers (but not many of them) a little further off, close to the Place Negrier, in which is the Mosque of Salah Bey, of which we will speak presently, for I think it is the only mosque at Constantine much worth seeing. Pass from the Place Negrier on to the Kantara market, and so home to the hotel by the Rue Perrégaux and the Rue Nationale, and you will have seen, in a morning's stroll, the best portion of the native quarter.

Up and down you go, now under an arch, now into daylight again; past the blacksmiths, the drapers, the eating-shops, the *cafés Arabes;* past little mosques with side rooms as you enter, and in which you find bright, bead-eyed little Arab boys, chanting away at the Koran, under the auspices of a bored-looking man, with a long stick, by means of which he can communicate with the most distant delinquent; past the police-court, which was, unfortunately, not sitting that day; past shops kept indifferently by Arabs or Jews, the younger members of this persuasion always giving me the idea of having been up all night,—I had no confidence in them; past mules urged blindly on by growling Arabs;—and so, having made good your way through all this light, darkness; these ups and downs; these fruits, flowers, birds; these grotesque and picturesque sights; these smells and noises, you come out at last on the Rue Nationale, and in hail of the hotel, lunch, and civilization. It was a trouble for a lame fellow with a stick to get through the place at the time; but it has left a picture on my brain, a recollection on my memory, which will not fade away whilst I can remember anything.

In due time a very well-appointed carriage, which would have done honour to any European hotel, came to the door to take us for our afternoon ramble. Our little programme was first to drive down to the Moulins Lavie; and then to make our way on foot as far as we could scramble along the bed of the Rummel, now nearly dry, so as to pass through some of the natural arches which we had seen in the photographs of the place; then to return up the hill and to drive round the town on the southern and eastern sides, so as to enjoy the views from Mansoura and Sidi Meçid. This we did, and we found it quite enough for our first ramble. On the downward drive to the Moulins, you are too near the town to see it to advantage; though you may do so very well on this side, from the garden of the powder magazine, which we visited another day.

When we got to the mills we alighted from our carriage, and first had a peep at the cascades of the Rummel, as they are called, but which were of no great account on the day we saw them. The real curiosity was the other way. The artist or scene painter for a sensation drama might certainly take a hint from the huge arch with mystery behind it and above it. The Wolf's Glen was commonplace by the side of this strange, uncanny-looking wilderness of stone. We had to shuffle as well as we could between shallow pools of water, over a natural pavement, not too uneven nor too difficult for a crippled man, and so back to the side from which we had started, but just under the first arch. Then there was a scramble up a bank, and along a narrow pathway to another arch, where there was darkness and the sound of rushing water. But what a scene in this rocky rift!—I must not call it a glen—the dim cave in front of us, the bright scene behind, seen through the gigantic arch under which we had first passed, the brilliant African sky above; and we were so far down below at the bottom of this narrow ravine. I believe there is a way in which travellers to whom a scramble and a climb are no obstacles, could make their way round to the Kantara Bridge, but I had reached the limits of my strength, and was fain to regain the carriage, being only too thankful that I had seen so much of this strange place.

We went back to the city and down a road which led us past the Bardo, between an avenue of trees, to the Rummel again, which we crossed, if I remember right, by a suspension-bridge.

Before getting there, however, I should like to say a few words about a strange sight which amused us very much at the time we saw it. Some soldiers were being drilled in a field near the road, and our driver who, as I hope, was not imposing on our credulity, said, " This is the Jews' drill. Saturday is their holiday, and advantage is taken of it to drill the young men." I thought I should like to see a battalion of Jews under arms, for they must certainly be a terribly efficient set of fellows, as they proved themselves in the days of Joshua, of the Maccabees, and some of Napoleon's marshals. It is in mercy to mankind that they have confined their attention to bills of exchange, promissory notes, and foreign loans, for were that keen and merciless Jewish intellect once seriously concentrated on the business of cutting throats, I think they would carry the matter through in a "thorough" way. Be this as it may, the youngsters of the Jewish battalion we saw at Constantine were lithe, active fellows, who seemed to give satisfaction to the French drill-sergeants.

But whatever might be thought of Jewish valour,

there could be no doubt as to Jewish splendour and Jewish good looks (I must not go quite so far as "beauty") as exemplified in the persons of the fair Jewesses who had come out to watch the process of converting their Jacobs and Isaacs into heroes. You might have imagined yourself at a fancy ball or behind the scenes of a theatre, for surely such costumes as these were never seen before by daylight. Satin, satin of all colours, was the favourite wear—red satin, yellow satin, green satin, mauve satin, of the brightest shades; bodies highly trimmed with gold, and long hanging sleeves, veils of gold and silver tissue, and I think each lady wore a white silk shawl, and, oh! such a profusion of ornaments. As they were for personal use, I presume they were real, the cruel mockeries would be reserved for customers. The ladies had good features and bright but defiant eyes, and when their lovely forms had not expanded into over-ripeness, were certainly well looking, and very different from their melancholy Algerine sisters. The men, not being actual warriors, were equally dressed in a variety of colours, with fanciful jackets and baggy trowsers, and—may I, being a man, venture to write it?—I thought they had chosen their colours in better taste, and that they were more harmoniously blended, than was the case with the ladies. Altogether it was a gorgeous sight. What plunder!

We went on our way rejoicing, I emphatically so, as I thought of what cruelties and hardships this unfortunate race had suffered for centuries in this part of the world. There is an end of all this now. Were any one to attempt insult or injury to the Jews of Constantine, the gallant Ten per Cents. would soon ask the reason why.

It was a pleasant drive round by the Pépinière, and the fragment of a Roman aqueduct, on top of which was perched an Arab, just like a bird of prey against the bright heaven. Whether he was altitudinizing on his own account, or was watching sheep, or had been paid by the municipality to stand there as a picturesque object, I cannot say, but he certainly looked well—"a withered Arab on a Roman ruin;" Jupiter and Mahommed, both rather down in the world. I fancy some fine things might be said or written upon this subject—a sonnet or something of that kind—especially as that little French corporal yonder is *sacréing* close by at a rare rate. I do not know what has put him out, but he clearly does not care a fig either for the Olympian Jove or the Arabian prophet—*enfoncés* both, as he would phrase it.

Thus interested and amused, we drove over the hills round Constantine on this side, delighted with the magnificence of the scene, with mountain, rock, and sky. The driver took us to the Mansoura, and there below us lay the Jewish burying-ground. What a mass of white blocks, not flat slabs nor upright tombstones, but large, white blocks, closely packed! Another, and a very pretty sight we saw on these heights. Here stand the barracks of the *Chasseurs d'Afrique*, and as we got near to them we could see on the hill opposite a long train of horsemen coming down towards us. These riders, on their spirited horses, with their picturesque drapery and high-uniforms—there must have been some hundreds of them

—seemed lost in the vastness of all things around. One remembered Walter Scott's description of Claverhouse's Life Guards coming down the hill just before the fatal skirmish of Drumclog—equally magnificent, and equally insignificant on the barren hill-side.

From Mansoura, where our carriage was standing, you obtain not only a fine view of the town, but of the great rocky eminence which crowns and commands it. On our way home, the driver pointed out a plantation of firs, or pines, or some such trees, in the midst of which, as he told us, were buried the French dead—those who fell at the storming of Constantine. Poor, gay little Frenchmen!—a sad ending to all their heroics; but France must pay for her glory here, as we have paid heavily for it in India. My mind is as full of heavy commonplaces as a tombstone in old St. Pancras churchyard. But I spare the reader, and pass on—to the shame of my manhood be it spoken—with a bit of a heart-pinch dissembled under a joke, "How sleep the brave!" It will be your fate and mine, brother, maybe to-morrow, certainly next day; and perhaps we shall not get out of the scrape as creditably as these poor little French soldiers. So for the moment home by the Kantara Bridge and the Rue Nationale—a rare drive indeed.

Whilst we were, as the housemaids say, cleaning ourselves for dinner, we heard a rapid, melancholy howling in the street below our window. It was an Arab funeral on its way to the Arab burying-ground, down the Rue Nationale to the Place. The poor body, which had done for ever with life's fitful fever, was lying for this its last journey on a kind of hand-bier carried by bearers, who constantly relieved each other, and was enveloped, as its last bit of earthly pomposity, in a covering of green silk. The people followed in procession, howling out, not unmusically, a wild, wailing song. Really it sounded better than the nasal lamentations of the Roman Catholic mortuary processions to which I had been accustomed on the Place du Gouvernement at Algiers. The mourners were all men.

But what is this? A halt on the Place; the funeral procession had become entangled with a string of carriages coming the reverse way. This was a French wedding-party, who were minded to come down the Rue Nationale, and so "the Arab funeral baked meats" and the French "marriage service" got intermingled. The poor little French bride put out her head, crowned with the bridal wreath, to see what was going on; and as the stoppage did not seem to discompose her, I don't know why it should affect me. The French party—to their honour be it spoken—had the good taste to call a halt, with their bride, till the Arabs had got past with their dead.

It was a strange meeting, and I hope it will not have proved of ill omen to that nuptial train. As a set-off against that unfortunate meeting, the young lady had plenty of sunshine for the day of her great transformation scene, and we all know the old proverb, "Happy the bride whom the sun shines on!" There was plenty of sun; so we dined, and went to bed; and thus ended our first day in the city of Sophonisba. Those who come after us will remark that we had contrived to get round

T

two sides of the town, and to see something even of the fourth, under the arches. We had seen the Falls of the Rummel, and scrambled under the arches; we had driven round by the Pépinière, the Aqueduct, and the Mansoura, to say nothing of the palace of Ahmed Bey within the town, of the Arab quarter, and the cathedral.

Next day we were minded to have a peep at the mosques. On the same side of the Rue Nationale as the hotel, but further down the street, is the Grand Mosque. Let no one be deceived by the name. To see it is really not worth the trouble of kicking your shoes off at the door, and pulling them on again. The guide-books tell you it stood on the ruins of an old Roman temple. Be it so. Let us pass on; our friends at Algiers, who had seen the customs and cities of many men, had told us before we started on our journey that the Mosque of Salah Bey in the Place Negrier, was the one on which we should fix attention; and we will try to make our way there lightly touching on the Arab quarter, so as to renew our pleasant impressions of yesterday, with a second peep at the bright little shops—the shoemakers, with their carnations, and the naughty little boys. We got at last to the few shops of the goldsmiths, who in vain tempted us with their bangles, and their pretty cheap jewellery as we passed in front of them. And here we are at the mosque.

But how to get in? Little Arab boys were so obliging as to offer their help, and, under their auspices, we pushed and knocked, now at one door, now at another, but all in vain. At last a majestic, but baggy-looking native came to our help. I could not but think it was not displeasing to him that he had an opportunity of displaying his proficiency in the French tongue before the admiring crowd. His French was fearfully and wonderfully contrived, but we felt that the only thing to be done was to encourage his humour, in the hope that something would ultimately turn up to our advantage. He was courteous, he was admonitory, he advised, he rebuked, every now and then he turned round and dismissed the little boys with a majestic wave of his hand, and proceeded with his discourse to us. Gracious Heavens! were we to be talked at all day in this unintelligible fashion? Imagine a protracted sermon of which you did not understand a word. Luckily for us a French cab-driver came up, and informed us in two words that we could not see the mosque until well-nigh the evening. So we disentangled ourselves from the web of oratory which had been spun around us, and proceeded to waste our morning by staring into the Arab shops, and watching the ways of the people. It would be idle to go over the ground again, so let us get into the carriage once more, and drive down the hill, past the Arab market, to the bridge near the slaughter-house, which is called, I believe, the Bridge of the Reservoir—it stands at the very southern point of the town. We had at a certain spot to get out, and passed down to the edge of the Rummel, where a number of natives were washing sheepskins, by placing them in the shallow water and dancing upon them in the maddest fashion.

I had read in the guide-books that hereabouts were some ancient inscriptions, and I felt it a duty I owed to myself to try my poor skill upon them. Alas! I was bitterly disappointed. Beyond some faint scratchings on the face of the rock, I could not make out anything, even when we had succeeded in discovering the scratches. I may here mention, parenthetically, that nothing to me proved more disappointing than this hunting for inscriptions. It may be very well for learned men by profession to "go in"—as a dreadful young English lad as Algiers called it—for inscriptions, but I am convinced that to do it with effect you must make it the business of your life.

If we could not make much of the inscriptions *en revanche*, the peep up the glen on the southern side of the town was our great reward. It will be remembered that yesterday we had contrived to get a notion of two sides of the town, and partially of the fourth, under the arches of the Rummel. This afternoon was to be mainly devoted to the third, between the Bridge of the Reservoir and the Kantara Bridge. The other side, about which we have been walking and driving all this time—that is, the landward slope of Constantine—requires no particular or further mention. I say again what a glen, what a gloom as seen from the little bridge on which we are standing! They point out a house at the edge of the precipice, up aloft there on the left hand, from which—Io the tale is told—faithless wives were hurled in the old Turkish days. It was the Tarpeian Rock of adultery. It is all very fine to make rules *nisi*, absolute in this summary sort of way; but how about the faithless husbands and the co-respondents? I wonder what Sir James Hannen or the bar of the Divorce Court—clever Mr. Inderwick and others—would say to this sort of thing. The Queen's proctor would always have been wanting to "intervene." I think we may say that such "a system, destitute of the ordinary safeguards of publicity, and uncontrolled by all usual forms for the administration of justice, would in all probability be attended with abuses of the most deplorable kind." That sentence is really fine. It is a comfort to reflect that the ladies of the period no doubt paid out these ruffians to the full measure of their deserts. The Fatimas and Ayeshas knew how to keep their clumsy lords on moral gridirons, and make them see twelve at fourteen o'clock, despite of all their precipices and brutalities. Never let it be forgotten, when you are told a story of this kind, that women are far cleverer than men, and have much more efficient methods of torture at their disposal.

So when we had gazed our fill, and joked and moralized, we set out again upon our pleasant drive (going from point to point for good views), till the sun was disposed to slant his beams a little, so that we might see the glen of the third side to full advantage with cross light and shadow. When the proper moment came, what a sight it was as our driver walked his horses on the excellent road at the edge of the abyss! This is not "tall talk;" it is an abyss and a very fearful one; the way in which I have thrown in the "excellent road" should render me above suspicion. Well, what we saw was a real abyss, narrow and deep—so deep that we could not see to the bottom of it without getting out of the carriage at favourable points. On the other side, the town side, were perched up the houses of the tanners; on the face of the rock were many caves; far down below us were circling strong-winged birds of prey—our driver said they were eagles, and I am sure no eagles could have looked nicer or more appropriate. I should hate a matter-of-fact Mentor who came forward to tell me they were only hawks or even vultures. The scene requires eagles, and eagles they shall remain—representative birds. At any rate, the deep gloom below, the tanners' houses on the other side bathed in sunshine, the eagles moving about, the outspread or rather upspread white town, the heavy masses of Sidi Meçid above—— Well, well, I can't get further in what Lord Byron called "entusymusy." Go to Constantine, and look at the place for yourself. I have seen most parts and towns of Europe, and I know nothing in Europe like this.

"But, monsieur," said the driver—the man of eagles—"will monsieur be pleased to look at that house yonder on the highest point? A young Frenchwoman, in the despair of love, flung herself from that place last Wednesday night."

"She was killed, no doubt?"

"She was taken up a lifeless and inform mass, dead enough."

Alack, poor Amanda! But I couldn't help giving coachee a shrewd look; he was always so ready with a marvel at the right place and at the right moment. The drilled Jews and the eagles were all right—had we not seen them? But the Amanda of the glen! It might be so; let us not look the gift horses of these able men of anecdote too closely in the mouth. So rise, shadows; sink away, O sun; scream away, eagles! and let us get back to Constantine, or by George, by Jove, by Mahommed—a man gets puzzled in his common forms in such a place as this—we shall be too late for Salah Bey. We will just stop a moment by the Kantara Bridge, if it be only for the sake of dear old Dr. Shaw. Yes, one can conceive that the old bridge stood there, and there, no doubt, is to be seen that picture of the disdainful lady, which always pleased me so much in his old book. A climb down there is a job for younger men, not for me; besides, I am sure, if I did get there, I should find that the picture had been carried off to some museum or another,—that is always the end of my antiquity hunts. No, on to Salah Bey. I haven't much opinion of the lady after all; she seemed to me disposed to show her scorn for the good city in a manner of which a grave man could scarcely approve.

That is right. Here is the Place Negrier again, so find us the *custode* as soon as you can. But, hey-day! what is this? Go upstairs to a mosque! who ever heard of such a thing? Yes; the hotel is on the first floor, but as far as my very limited experience of mosques goes, this is the first time I have been obliged to go up a flight of stairs before being called upon to kick off my shoes. To be sure the stairs are of black and white marble; the court-yard is very pretty, and the pomegranate tree in the centre, with its dark leaves and bright red flowers, is just the right tree in the right place.

We get rid of our shoes as usual, and find ourselves in a large room, handsomely carpeted, and this is the mosque; it is of the shape of a parallelogram. The ceiling in green and red; there is a very fine chandelier. The thin columns are of white marble, and we were particularly struck with the tiles with which the walls are encrusted. There is the usual *mihrab*, and close beside it the *mimbar*, or pulpit, as beautiful as many coloured marbles can make it; opposite these a sort of gallery. This is a kind of inventory of the contents of this chamber, but merely to mention this is to give but a faint idea of its beauty. There is a dim religious light in the place, and the colours of the painting, of the carpets, of the tiles, are so harmoniously blended, that you pronounce the place to be the temple of good taste, whatever may be your opinion of the doctrines enforced from the pulpit upon the minds of the faithful. If South Kensington could take you part of the road on your way to heaven, the Mosque of Salah Bey would help you a good deal further.

This place is not like the sandy, solemn relic of antiquity which we afterwards found in the desert under the name of Sidi Okba; as a religious monument, it is not to be compared with the great Mosque of Bou-Meddin, near Tlemçen, which we frequently visited at a later period of our African travel; but if there were such a body as the "upper ten thousand" amongst Mussulmans, this would be their favourite shrine. It is the sort of place you would choose to be married in by special licence, even in preference to your own drawing-room. You would go there to say your prayers in a brougham. It is the very ideal of Mohammedanism adapted to the West End. It is only saved by perfect good taste from being "genteel." By the side of the mosque is the Medresa, or college, only remarkable for containing the tombs of Salah Bey and his family. The Mosque of Salah Bey is well worthy of a visit.

As we have half an hour to spare before dinner, let us drive round by the Place du Palais, and hear the military band, for this is one of their days. So to the Place we went, but soon got a hint, and a very proper one too, that we must dismiss the carriage, and walk about on our own feet, if we desired to hear the music. The Place is small, and the presence of a dozen or twenty carriages would seriously incommode the promenaders. So we got out, and soon found seats. It was a strange thing, and I thought so at the time, to be listening to the overture of "The Barber," and to a *pot-pourri* from the "Traviata," under the very nose, as one may say, of Masinissa and Scipio. Sallust, who was viceroy here, and who plundered Constantine at a great rate, would have enjoyed the music. There were plenty of French officers and soldiers too in their brilliant uniforms, and many ladies pacing up and down, painted and repaired in the latest Parisian fashion. Cato the censor, had he been here, would certainly have gone home in a huff. The music was good, the sky beautiful as it can be in Africa, so we sat the performance out, and only retired when we saw the general and his party of ladies disappear from the gallery of the club-house. This was, no doubt, the general whose presence had interfered with our visit to the State apartments of Ahmed Bey's palace the other day; but, dear good gentleman, I doubt not he knew nothing about the matter; and who were we that we should intrude upon his privacy, and poke about in rooms devoted to the use of his family? At any rate, when he was gone there was an end of the sport, and so home to the hotel, to dinner and to bed.

Next morning was wet. My wife said she would go and have a look at the Arab market outside the town, on the way down to the Bridge of the Reservoir. It was beyond my powers, for I could not manage an umbrella and a crutch-stick at one and the same time. By her account the place was dreary enough—a few miserable sheds, with dried vegetables, pieces of old leather, nails, and dilapidated hardware past service. The *indigènes* looked as far gone as their wares; they were poorly clad from the Arab point of view. But then, it was raining, and when you go out to see an Arab function, and find yourself in a village on the west coast of Ireland on a wet market-day, the spectacle is not exhilarating. She said, however, and I record it in honour of these poor sloppy Arabs, that no one gave her the smallest annoyance, not even the little boys. Who would answer for the comfort of a Chinese lady in Rag Fair in our own hospitable and enlightened land?

The rain got lighter, and the sky began to clear up, so we went for another ramble, and in the afternoon drove out to the Djebel-Ouache, where are the reservoirs for supplying Constantine with water. The advantage of the drive consists in the views of Constantine and the neighbourhood. There are two large sheets of water here amongst the hills, and some very fine trees of which botanists seem to make much account. For people who have, as we had, plenty of time to spare, it is a good drive, for you cannot see Constantine and its surroundings too often, or from too many points; but for folks in a hurry, if they are to omit any article from our little programme, I should recommend them to omit the Ouache drive. In all our excursions we have been seeing Constantine from the high ground; the point is to get down below, which we intend to do tomorrow if the skies be propitious, by visiting the Oasis of Salah Bey, down somewhat in the plain.

On our way back we drove round the interior of the town, and past the Kasbah, the walls of which were thickly studded with Roman inscriptions. Some of them I could see were topsy-turvy; we contented ourselves with peeping in at the gate, and did not go over the place, for we were tired, and it just looked inside like an ugly, huge barrack; but it might have been worth while to get out for a peep over the wall down the precipice which we had seen from the other side. Again home to dinner and bed.

One of the weak points of this African travel we find to be that after dinner there is nothing to be done—there is no evening. I can fancy that to youngsters, or to people in robust health, it must be agreeable enough to walk about these old towns in the evening with a proper guide; but in my own case this was out of the question. There was nothing for it but to go to bed soon after dinner, and to get up at some incredible hour.

The next morning was wet, and here I will take leave to remark, as concerning some of my predecessors in this part of the world, how fortunate they seem to have been in making the acquaintance of one remarkable native or another who forms the staple of the work! There is M. Florentin, for example, with his graceful little book, "Une Année dans le Sahel." He casually sees a lady in the old town of Algiers, hits upon her again at Blidah, and is a witness to her untimely end under the Tombeau de la Chrétienne.

Another author, a lady, who, under the *nom de plume* of Louis Régis, has written a most delightful story of her visit to Constantine and the desert, is, to say the least of it, most fortunate in her Arab friends, for they supply matter for a good many chapters. I have stared into *cafés Arabes* without number, chaffered with Arab stall-keepers and so on, but nothing came of it. It would be easy to invent an old Arab friend, and to make him responsible for, or the cause of, as many adventures as Sinbad the sailor—in point of fact, to concoct a little work of fiction under the name of journal of travel. But this would be to defeat my own object, as well as to lead my readers astray. I want simply to inform my friends how easy a thing it is to drive about North Africa, and to see very many beautiful things, without too much inconvenience or fatigue, and to do this by the simple process of recording what we saw, and how we saw it. To import fictitious elements, and romantic personages having no existence but in my own brain, into such a journal as this, would simply be to lead others into error; for I doubt if they would come across the picturesque old phantoms whom I could readily invent, and they would have a right to say, "We have been misled." Now, to speak truth, we were afflicted with a nasty, dull, wet day, and very tiresome it was. We did nothing, and saw nothing; and our day—take it as we enjoyed it—was very much like Washington Irving's in his inn at Stratford-upon-Avon. Constantine can be as dreary and sloppy as Dorset Square upon a wet day. The natives, with their wet clothes, look quite out of character with the season, and "boredom" reigns supreme.

This would be the time to throw in a tale of love and vengeance, or, at any rate, the narrative of an old *chasseur* who had been present at the siege of Constantine, and whose acquaintance you had made over a glass of absinthe. "Monsieur, I never saw *her* again," would be the conclusion of the broken-hearted sergeant. And what an opportunity! for you might hit upon the lady again, at one oasis or another, and find her the beloved wife of a Sheikh rich in palm trees; and the mother of a promising family. What a chance for communicating with the old sergeant as "*mon bon Pierre*," and, in a slightly sarcastic tone, insinuating that he was not the *homme fatal* whom he had taken himself to be. Or, again, a wet day would give you the opportunity of describing an Arab feast—whether you had assisted or not at such a one would not much matter; exaggerate or invent, as the case might be; or why not throw in a lion if the rain should be much protracted?

We got through the day somehow or another, but strictly without adventure, other than such as is inseparable from staying in a second-class French hotel; and the next morning was deliciously fine.

The afternoon we devoted to a drive down to the gardens of the powder magazine, and the palace of Salah Bey; and although the latter name be somewhat of a misnomer, the expedition was a most successful one. If you had time but for two drives at Constantine, take one to Mansoura and Sidi Meçid way—the other to the Oasis of Salah Bey. The drive to the gardens of the Poudrière is pretty much the same as the one we took on the first day. But you are obliged to alight from your carriage at a gate, and it is a long, a very long way to the bottom—to the very bottom we never got, for the lady was much fatigued, and we had to get back to the carriage somehow. The view upwards is, however, beautiful, and the Poudrière Gardens should certainly be visited.

We got to our vehicle again, reascended the hill, and then took another and a downward route to the Oasis of Salah Bey. What views! What wild flowers! I suppose the refreshing showers of last night have promoted the bright floral radiance of to-day. Was there ever such a flower show? Up and down the hills, the gladiolas are waving their bunches of magenta flowers. The poppies are "defying all competition," both in size and colour. By the roadside are tufts of pimpernel—no longer the little modest blue flower of domestic life in England, but each of the size of a shilling. I wish I knew the name of that abundant grey flower, like a convolvulus in shape, which I see about me everywhere; but it is idle to go on repeating names—I cannot hope by mere words to give an idea of the universal splendour. The earth is spread with a carpet worthy of the spotless blue sky overhead. I think it was when we were going up the hill to the Fort National that we first became aware of the magnificence of the African wild flowers. In Algiers itself we had been somewhat disappointed, but this might have arisen from the fact that when we were there the spring was a few weeks younger; and, in point of fact, I may venture to anticipate so far as to say that two or three weeks later we found the Metidja, from Blidah far away to Cherchel, a perfect prairie of wild flowers, which, in point of size and colour, leave anything we have in the North of Europe far behind. I do not forget the beautiful crop of primroses and violets and harebells, and, later on, of foxgloves, which one sees in Devonshire and Cornwall at the proper season; but this display of wild flowers in Africa simply puts rivalry out of the question.

It is not merely a spectacle for young ladies, it is not a mere pretext for airing your familiarity with long Latin names; the whole country is splendid with colour. You may miss what is around me just now as I am jotting down my recollections of Algeria—the sober green tints of Sussex, the lordly oaks, the glossy beeches, the graceful Spanish chestnuts, the fragrant limes, towering above the fern, in the midst of which the dappled deer are pretending to be frightened, but are in reality displaying their grace like young ladies tripping round a ball-room. These things have their charm, but they make up at best a sort of twilight banquet for the eyes; just now I speak of "Africa and golden joys." I can only conclude, as I have often done before, with "Go and see it for yourself."

So, driving up and down the hills, with very splendid views of Constantine and the neighbourhood around us we finally reach the Oasis of Salah Bey, with what Horace Walpole calls its "greenth," its Bath, its Koubba, and its remains.

Salah Bey, who is reported to have been a very respectable sort of man, and a good governor, seems to have fared with respect to this, his country palace, pretty much like poor Baron Grant with his Kensington Oasis. He could build up for others, but he could not contrive to sit and enjoy himself under his own vine and his own fig tree. Public opinion—and fancy the public opinion of a parcel of wild Arabs—turned against Salah Bey whilst he was constructing his beautiful mosque and Medresa and his pretty summer palace down here. All the envious and dissatisfied people began to cabal against him, and denounced him to the Dey of Algiers.

Not only was he charged with "battening and fattening" on the sweat of the labouring man—a charge to which his Highness the Dey would have listened with great composure, not to say cheerfulness, but it was suggested that he was aiming at independence, and trying to win the hearts of the people by "excessive texpenditure," by Allah! a very different sort of thing and which must be looked to; so Salah went the way of all Beys.

A queer little place is the Koubba, very like other koubbas, with a painted tomb inside, and the usual decorations required by African taste. But the story is as queer as the place.

It seems Sidi Mohammed was a powerful saint in his day, and Salah had forgotten to conciliate him with bribes, so he found himself in opposition to the dignified clergy of the place and the time. Salah, who had a spice of the old desert-pirate about him, cut the knot of the difficulty by cutting off the saint's head. You would have supposed there was an end of the matter; but not so. Here was just the saint's opportunity; Salah had made a wrong move.

The headless saint changed himself into a ragged old crow, and flew about, croaking and cursing the Bey in a way calculated to irritate the religious susceptibilities of the Constantine people. Finally, he flew off to the Bey's new palace—the place where we are standing—croaked a final croak, cursed a final curse, and disappeared. This was hard. As long as you could get a real crow to shoot at, something might have been done; but how are you to handle a crow which has disappeared?

The move was with Salah again; he built a Koubba in honour of his dear and lamented friend, Sidi Mohammed. Nobody could regret more bitterly than he did the late unhappy differences, but Sidi, in his abode of bliss, should know that his heart was in its right place. True, Salah had cut Sidi's head off; but what a tomb! In proof that his expiation had been accepted, the crafty old Bey caused a large crow to be put into a cage, and offered him to the devotion of the multitude, who accepted him as Sidi Mohammed el-Ghorab, "my Lord Mohammed the Crow." It must be true, for there hangs the cage over the door of the Koubba; I saw it— as good a proof of an historic legend as many another which has been accepted by grave and learned men. So ends the tale of Salah Bey and the Thomas-à-Becket of Constantine. I take the facts from Colonel Playfair's guide-book, who, in his turn, takes them from M. Cherbonneau.

When we had gazed our fill at the Koubba and the cage, we went to see the Bath. A pleasant place it was; there was a little piece of water into which an Arab had ridden his horse, or mule, I forget which. There was a large willow, weeping away over the water, and a number of little Arab children skylarking about. Underneath the white roof on which we were sitting were the little bathing chambers. It was a pretty picture, and we were well inclined to rest there for a while, so we ordered some small cups of coffee from the guardian of the Bath, to account for our loitering here, and amused ourselves by playing on the greediness of the pretty little Arab children, who seemed to be as fond of the sugar as ever I was of toffy and Bonaparte's-ribs. There are some fine trees in the garden; but it is a waste now. Alas, for the splendour of Salah Bey!

The drive home was by another road, but it was just a repetition of the beautiful things, so we made our way slowly back to Constantine, and partly by a different route.

With this drive we had terminated all that we intended to do in and about Constantine, where we remained some eight days on our way to and from Biskra; but I have thought it more convenient to throw the two achievements together. I think a week will be quite sufficient for the ordinary traveller at Constantine; not for one who wishes to follow the guide-books, and make his way into every trumpery little mosque and corner; not for one who desires to muse amongst the ruins, and meditate upon the vicissitudes of nations; certainly not for one who is suffering from the inscription mania; but I think quite enough for any one who wants simply to take in the great general features of the place, and who is there for enjoyment's sake. I really don't know what we should have done with a second week. Constantine is not like Tlemçen, a place in which one would care to live; it is a city to visit, and there are few cities, I should fancy, on the earth's surface better worthy of a visit.

The next question was, having done with Constantine, how were we to get on to Biskra and the desert? We made inquiries as to what the cost of a private carriage would be, for there is an *entrepreneur* at Constantine who undertakes the business. The price he asked for conveying us to Biskra and back to Constantine was 600 francs (or £24 English). He would allow us, for this, to stop two days at Biskra; if we desired to remain longer, we were to be charged at the rate of 35 francs a day. He would have been five days each way, if I remember right, on the road. As against this system there was the plan of engaging the *coupé* of the diligence to Batna, and arranging at that place for the *coupé* on to Biskra. The price of the places was: from Constantine to Batna, 20 francs a place, 60 francs whole *coupé*; from Batna to Biskra, 25 francs each place, 75 francs whole *coupé*; in all 135 francs. From Constantine to Biskra and return, 270 francs. Thus there is a notable difference in price, even when we found at Biskra that it was the right thing, on the return journey, to drive over-night from Biskra to El-Outaia, and there to be picked up by the diligence at about 6 a.m. The diligence leaves Biskra at 2 a.m.—

a fearful fixture for the departure, as you can't contrive to get much sleep before two in the morning, or rather 1 a.m. This is what we did, and I think the charge for the little open carriage from Biskra to El-Outaia was 30 francs. Thus, between 600 francs for the private carriage, and 270 plus 30 for the diligence, there was a difference of half. We decided upon other grounds in favour of the diligence.

I was warned before leaving Algiers, by a lady who had been an unwearied traveller, and who was a person remarkable for sound judgment and common sense, that this was the more advisable course. She had done the journey with an invalid daughter, and, as she said, with the diligence it was certainty; with the private carriage, a chapter of uncertainties. You were at the mercy of your driver in the carriage; and in such a strange, wild country. Then accidents might, and probably would, happen—a wheel come off, a horse break down. What were you to do with a delicate and sickly young lady; or, as in my case, with a hobbling invalid, who required help to get about even under favourable conditions? The diligence was bound to deliver you safe, like a parcel.

We took the *coupé*, then, and I very earnestly recommend this plan as the right one to all who may come after me, for the long distances where you can't get the rail. From Constantine to Batna, from Batna to Biskra (and the return), from Setif to Bougie, from Oran to Tlemçen (and the return), we had the *coupé*, and found it the pleasantest and most irresponsible way of covering the long distances. From Setif to Bougie another time I should take an open carriage for the sake of seeing the Chabet Pass to full perfection. For the short drives about the Metidja, as from Blidah to Cherchel and back, to Hammam R'Irha, to the Tombeau, and in fact all about that flowery plain, the private carriage is the best. But take the *coupé* for two people. With three there is inconvenience, and the unfortunate person in the middle must suffer no little discomfort; it is a thing to be avoided. But I repeat it—with the steamers on the coast, with the railways already in existence, with the *coupés* of the diligences, you should have no trouble in getting over the long distances. We never found any difficulty in hiring very fair open carriages, with active little horses, whenever we wanted to get from one place to another, or for mere excursions. Perhaps a family of four persons would find it best to take a private carriage, and to submit to the chances of the road, from Constantine to Biskra. But, having seen the country between Batna and Biskra, as an invalid, I should not care to do it.

So, then, having settled over-night our very moderate bill at the Hotel d'Europe, and having bid a cordial farewell to our good-humoured Swiss landlord and his wife, we got up early the next day, and walked round to the omnibus office; here we were to find the omnibus which was to take us to the railway station at the Kantara Bridge. We were to go the first thirty miles or so by rail, and to find our diligence at a station called El-Guerrah. This we did, and please imagine us comfortably seated in our *coupé* at this place, and off to the desert. The drive to-day was to Batna. We had left Constantine by the 6 a.m. train; we reached Batna at 5.30 p.m.

We must not waste too much time on the way, or we shall never get to Biskra. The road is a wild and a weird one, winding upwards, steadily upwards, between the arid mountains; few, or rather no trees, save in the immediate neighbourhood of the new settlements. It is a fitting approach to the desert, and even more so between Batna and Biskra. On this, the first day, there were plenty of wild flowers about, but not of the same splendid kind which we had seen yesterday between Constantine and Salah Bey's country house. They were rather dwarfed, scrubby, yellow things, but, such as they were, they somewhat lighted up the grim road. We halted for lunch at a queer place, close to a couple of large salt lakes. The inn is called "L'Auberge de Bottinelli;" the lakes are known as "Les Chotts." The place would have exactly suited such of my English friends as delight in punts, and heavy gunnery, and the slaughter of wild fowl. It was the paradise of wild ducks.

As we, the pilgrims of the diligence, gathered round the table in the inner room of the Bottinelli for breakfast, it was quite like a scene from Smollett or Fielding, in the old slow coach days of a century ago. People made friends, and had time to discuss their private affairs—who they were; where they were going; what was their business. At last an old gentleman, with a grey beard, remained master of the situation by sheer weight of metal. He talked everybody down, was familiar with all the gossip of Les Chotts, chaffed the landlady (who was a widow) on the prospect of her second nuptials; put us all right as to French policy in Algeria. He declaimed against the extensive culture of the vine as the remedy for all evils with which the colony was afflicted; he ought to know something about the matter, for was he not travelling for a Bordeaux house? He was so obliging as to furnish me with his card and price-list, and though I clothed myself with silence as with a garment, I shall ever consider it a fortunate circumstance that I did not find, on my return to England, that several pipes and hogsheads of undeniable wine had been consigned to me by my charming old friend of the Salt Lakes, and were only awaiting my signature for delivery. After lunch or breakfast we got clear of these not unpleasant swamps, and soon reached the point where, as the *conducteur* told us, travellers who wished to visit the Medrassen were in the habit of alighting.

Now, as the Medrassen is only our old friend Le Tombeau de la Chrétienne over again, and as the Tombeau stands handy to Algiers, and as we had made up our minds to visit it when we went the home circuit, we left the Medrassen unvisited. I really can't say I care much whether it was the family vault of Masinissa or of Syphax. Doctors will differ; but as you can get a distant peep at it from the road, it was enough. So the afternoon wore on, but the really striking things were the groups of black Arab tents on the hill-side, and the caravans which passed us on the road.

I shall have a word or two to say about them presently, as we saw them in greater numbers, and in more picturesque fashion, between Batna and Biskra. So trot, trot, trot between the wild hills, or mountains, until at length we seemed to get sight of trees again—a few trees, then more trees, then trees on both sides, as the horses were walked up the hill; and finally Batna, a model French town, with a few straight streets, cutting each other at right angles; a lot of *cafés*, a public Place, a bran-new church; barracks, good store; two or three inns, amongst them the Hôtel des Étrangers, where we were to pass the night and the next day. And a very fair inn it was, as far as sleeping and eating accommodation went; but in the matter of carriages for excursions, even to distant Biskra, beware of the landlord, if he be the same we found there. He sets out with the theory that it is his duty to foster and cherish the unprotected traveller; he will send for an *entrepreneur*, or man of carriages and horses, and treat him worse than roughly—I may say like a dog—in your presence, and then leave you to do the best you can. It is needless to add that, on your return from Lambessa, or wherever it may be, the price asked is extortionate. The landlord intervenes, gives the case against you, and, as we were informed by those who knew the place, pockets the difference himself. His fixed idea was to make us hire a carriage from Batna to Biskra, which carriage he would, no doubt, have supplied himself by means of the man of hay or straw, mentioned above.

Our idea of the *coupé* of the diligence stank in his nostrils, and he did all he could to defeat us; but in vain. One can only wonder that the proprietor of an establishment, otherwise so respectably conducted, could condescend to such trickery. Batna is the sentry-box of the African desert, but the tricks are the tricks of Europe. You might be enjoying an interchange of ideas with the landlord at the top of the Righi or at the Kalt-Bad, as far as the fashion of the thing goes.

From Batna it is usual to visit the Cedar Forest on a mountain near the town, and the Roman ruins of Lambessa; but as we were to see later the cedars of Teniet, we confined ourselves to Lambessa, which is some six or seven miles distant from Batna. The day was oppressively hot, a sirocco was blowing, the carriage was an uneasy one, and the driver kept us in a state of high irritation by stopping at every small public-house to drink, besides having committed the original sin of taking with him on the driving-box a very broad and very stout brother-in-law, who wished to see Lambessa. So did we, but we could not see through the fat man. We were scarcely in a calm antiquarian frame of mind when we got to Lambessa.

The first thing that strikes you, and with a very unpleasant sensation, is the modern prison. It is now used for criminals, and that is all right; but when one considers that, during the Second Empire, this is the place in which political offenders were immured for years, it gives one a heart-pinch. Look at those calcined hills all round; beyond them lies the desert. In the other direction, we know the trouble it has cost us to get here from the sea-coast, with railways and diligences to help us, and no *gendarmes* raging on our track. I doubt, if the doors had been left open, if the poor people could have escaped. The Arabs would have brought them in, if they had contrived to sustain life and escape death. But what a fate to be confined in such a place! It would be misery in a well-appointed hotel—what, then, in a prison! and for weeks, months, years you were to remain in such a place, that it might go well with the little knot of conspirators who had taken possession of France. Alack! alack! to be shut up in Lambessa, and to be thinking of the gay boulevards, the Champs Elysées, the Palais Royal!

However, let us go and see the ruins. We entered by a garden in front of the prison, and our soldier-guide led us first to a little shed, where he lifted a covering of boards, and displayed to us a fine Roman mosaic—a woman's head—just like what you see in the British Museum, as brought from Carthage, only not nearly so fine. Then we went to the Prætorium, an oblong building, now used as a museum, and filled with fragments of the past—broken statues, portions of tombs with inscriptions, and the like. The weather was frightfully hot, so we got back to the carriage, and drove about wherever the carriage could go. No doubt the place is full of interest on a cooler day, for here was the important military settlement of the Romans in this part of the world; and from here there must have run a road to Constantine, another to Setif, another to Carthage—to say nothing of the desert route. There are arches and broken arches all about you, and Roman remains of all kinds. I should think the place must look very weirdlike under the full moon, for here indeed the sun gilds but to flout the grey ruins, and shows them for what they are only too well.

We left Batna at 8.30 a.m. next morning, and again found ourselves in the *coupé* of the diligence. Wilder and wilder grew the scene, the trees scarcer, the flowers fewer. The diligence stopped for breakfast or lunch at a village with the romantic name of the Well of the Mulberry Tree (or, as we Arabs say, Aïn-Tonta). But all ye who come after me, do not be deluded by the name. Take with you from Batna a nice little basket, with cold chicken, fruit, and a bottle of wine, and avoid eating the fruits of that mulberry tree. There were some black-puddings in particular; I feel quite sick when I think upon them, even now that I am in the region of wholesome food.

On we go, and if this is not the desert, it is not a bad imitation of one. The soil is cracked sand. Imagine a long range, just like the Solway Sands with the tide out, dry and cracked by the sun's heat into fissures. Rarely indeed did we see any water, even in the deepest of them, yet these were affluents of what would be strong streams in the rainy season.

Here come the processions, or caravans, of natives from the desert, to assist at the gathering in of the harvest, having with them their tents, women, and children. There would be about fifty or sixty camels, and as many mules. The men were light and active, with grand patriarchs amongst them; the women small, ugly, but picturesque. Their gowns are always of some bright colour, and their arms and throats laden with barbaric jewellery. Their faces were bare and tattooed; down each side of the cheek would hang a plait like a horse-tail, it was so thick and black. My wife would have it that they were side or lateral chignons, as hair of that thickness and texture as the growth of a human head was out of the question. A horse's *tail* would explain everything. The children were queer-looking creatures; the little boys had shaven heads, save at the crown, where there would be a tuft as with a young Red Indian. I should be afraid to make a guess at the numbers; but where there were so many camels and mules, the human beings must be numbered by hundreds. I suppose what we were seeing is just what Abraham saw in his day. Look up there, on the top of that mound of sand at the head of the Oued-Fedala, or Col des Juifs. Mark that grand old Sheikh in conversation with a stouter and shorter man. He is pointing round him, as though to attract the other's attention. Are not these Abraham and Lot? and is not Abraham saying even now, "Let there be no strife, I pray thee, between me and thee, and between my herdmen and thy herdmen; for we be brethren. Is not the whole land before thee? separate thyself, I pray thee, from me: if thou wilt take the left hand, then I will go to the right; or if thou depart to the right hand, then I will go to the left"?

Surely all this might be said even now as the old Sheikh above there is pointing to the camels and mules and people below. I verily believe, if his dust could arise again from the cave at Machpelah and put on flesh, and could the so-resuscitated Abraham stand on the top of the Oued-Fedala to-day, he would find that he had nothing to learn and nothing to forget. All this day we have been passing through the Old Testament in action—the people, the animals, the hills, the vast solitude. The only incongruous feature in the scene is the diligence, with its contents, and we cannot see ourselves.

At any rate, at 3 p.m. we reached El-Kantara, where the rain began to fall. It is a very pretty place, possibly over-praised, for I cannot help thinking a good deal of its beauty depends upon the barrenness by which it is surrounded. We saw it well on our return journey; and no doubt the short gorge with the view of the desert Biskra-wards is a fine and a striking thing. Speaking for myself, I should not be disposed to waste a day at El-Kantara, and I say this after having seen it under every favourable circumstance of light and weather on our return. But upon this occasion I am bound to record it as fact that our introduction to the great African desert put me forcibly in mind of dear old Scotland—of Benavie or Glenmoriston, for example—as visited on a "soft day." There was the same mist over everything, and the mist very soon was converted into downright rain, the same brawling streams, the same mysterious "sough" around you.

The road was of the roughest kind, and soon ceased to be a road. The diligence now began to find its way by a kind of mysterious instinct across a plain of sand well covered with boulders and intersected by streamlets. How if these streamlets should become streams? The weather looked very bad—the rain became torrential, and we could not see far ahead. But, hey! what is this? We grind down a little slope, and then swish, slush! it is the same kind of noise I used to hear at Broadstairs, when I was a little boy, and the unkind guardians of my childhood would force me into a bathing-machine, and I was dragged out to sea far from human help, and left to the mercy of a stout bathing-woman, who did not know the meaning of the word. We are crossing a river; the water is up to the axles. I can see through the window that the horses are going in deeper and deeper, and the water is coming down in a very lively way. Bump, swish! bump again. Water, water everywhere; by George the leaders will have to swim for it! Can one hope to get out through the window, if the diligence should fall on the right side? That was a very nasty story we read the other day about a diligence which was carried away whilst crossing an African river somewhere in these parts, and every soul was drowned. Confound Africa, and our own folly for coming here! Swish! bump again. The horses are noble animals, and seem quite up to the work. About this time people are having afternoon tea and pleasant gossip in London; it can't be darker than here, so swish, swish! I begin to see the bellies of the leaders again.

Oh, joyous sight, we are through it, and the driver gives his team a spurt up the bank, and over the pleasant boulders. However, the sun is still up, though you would not think so. We left El-Kantara at 3 p.m., and the promise was that we should be delivered at Biskra at 8.30 p.m. There is yet time, for it would be a fearful thing to be benighted amidst this wilderness of stones and brawling streams, which will, no doubt, soon be torrents. So it went on as we ground our way slowly over this howling wilderness, the only difference being that sometimes we were in a stream, sometimes not, and thus about sunset we reached El-Outaia; but this place was still twenty miles or better from Biskra. A tall, melancholy-looking man, in a fur cap, who stood looking on whilst we were changing horses, kept on "chaffing" our driver and *conducteur*. "Did they expect to reach Biskra to-night? The river was out. There could be no thought of going by the usual way; we must take the higher and upper road. The people here could take the party in, and to-morrow at daylight we might pursue our journey."

But this advice, which I have given as continuous discourse, was administered in a nasty, sneering way, intermixed with profane swearing, after the fashion of the lower orders of the French nation. We afterwards heard that the man, or rather the monster, in the fur cap, owed our *conducteur* a grudge, for he had coveted his place for himself, and wished to delay the diligence on its journey, whereby the letters (for we carried the mails) would not have been delivered at Biskra, and so there would have resulted a scrape, and possibly the installation of the man in the fur cap in the post of *conducteur*. But the bright, brave young Frenchman who had charge of us knew better. The fur-cap man could only goad him on to greater speed with his straps and buckles. *En route, en r-r-route!* and away we went with our fresh team of eight horses. By the way, as it required two teams of eight horses to drag us from El-Kantara to Biskra, how should we have fared in a private carriage? Halted at El-Kantara, I suppose; but for two or three days afterwards, whilst we were enjoying ourselves at

Biskra, the waters were still out, so that would have been a nice business. Away we went at a foot pace, without a track to help us, and the light fading away to total darkness, the streams swishing about us, and a hollow deep roll, which we knew to be the roar of the river, not far off.

It came to be about 9 p.m. Hurrah! Those must be the lights of Biskra. Not so bad, after all. Alas! they turned out to be the lights of a French encampment (the soldiers were under canvas); the diligence stopped, and there was a parley. We could only catch mysterious conversation about that awful river. Once more bad language up aloft, clacking of whip, renewed progress, darkness, roar of water, and finally a standstill. There we remained, I should say, for half an hour, whilst the *conducteur* readvised himself, and we were allowed to get out, and stand upon solid ground, up to our ankles in mud, possibly for the last time. "No, monsieur. There was no danger; we were not under the necessity of crossing the river. We should soon be at Biskra."

It was clear that the man would not tell us of the danger, if any existed. You might as well have expected a London doctor to enlighten you as to the real state of his patient, who is always "going on nicely" till all is over. What was to be done? Write to the *Times*? But where was a pillar post, to which we could entrust our last literary will and testament? Mud, boulders, darkness, rushing streams, a deep river, or the roar of one. When I talked of the commonplace nature of African travel, here was certainly an exception.

At last the *conducteur* made up his mind to go on, and we were glad of it, whatever the event might be, for the awful pause in the darkness was like waiting to be shot or hung, with the night-cap over one's eyes. The diligence scrunched and splashed away. At times we thought we were fairly in the river, but, fortunately, we were only passing through pools of water. It was 10. 11 p.m., it was midnight (we should have been at Biskra at 8.30 p.m.), but at length it seemed to us as though the ground was harder. There was pleasanter *sacréing* up above, and away we went. The thoughtful *conducteur* was good enough to climb down from his perch with words of comfort, " *Madame, c'est fini ; dans une petite demi-heure nous sommes à Biskra.*"

So it was ; we were soon passing along a street. There were lights, human habitations, comfort ; an hotel with hot soup, not a river with a shroud of cold water. Such was our introduction to desert life. At 12.30 we reached Biskra, and at 1 a.m. we got to the hotel from the diligence office. The hot soup of our dreams became a pleasant reality. We were shown into a little room, with two beds ; everything clean, but of the simplest kind, whitewashed walls, tiled floor, but the beds were excellent, and, I repeat it, everything clean, and with shutters to the windows to exclude the early light. How shall I ever express my gratitude to the Hôtel du Sahara ?

When we awoke next morning, and let the sun in, what a blaze of light! and how pretty was the illuminated pomegranate, which was glorifying the window with its bright red flowers ! The room opened upon a kind of garden, with a long *tonnelle*, or arbour, and a great palm tree, with Arabs flitting about. I came to know them afterwards; the light-footed Abdallah, who waited on us; Ali, gentleman-like, but depressed; Mohammed, stouter, and just a shade below the others in position, according to Western ideas, for he not only waited, but washed the dishes; in fact, and not to put too fine a point on it, he was half-waiter, half-scullion. Then there was a pale French gentleman, smoking a cigarette and sipping his coffee under the *tonnelle;* he was humming " *Le sabre de mon père,*" and his thoughts were far away, no doubt, on the boulevards; he was the *chef.* When I came to know him better, he said to me, " *Monsieur, la nature à Biskra est grandiose; les palmiers le soleil d'Afrique; que voulez vous? Mais j'ai mes habitudes à Paris."* Poor fellow! he had a light hand for pastry.

After coffee under the *tonnelle,* we began to consider how we should employ our time in the desert, and sent for and secured the services during our stay at Biskra, of Abd-el-Kader, and I can, with a good conscience, advise all who come after me to employ him. Clean and neat in his person and dress; civil, attentive, always at hand when wanted, and not boring you when you had rather be alone; familiar with everybody and everything at Biskra; not only your guide during excursions, but your confidential servant and interpreter all the day through. You could scarcely be better served, and all this for five francs a day, with which Abd-el-Kader was quite happy, and never attitudinized for an addition, but, of course, was happier, as a matter of sentiment, if it came. It was a proof that he had given satisfaction. He was dark, even for an Arab, and came from some place in the desert beyond Tuggurt. He had been saving up money in order to get married, and his bride was waiting for him at some hot place in the sand. The wedding must needs be a hurried one, for he would have to get back quick to Biskra to resume his work. I suppose the usual Arab idea of a honeymoon would be to spend a few happy, happy days with the bride, give her a good beating with a stick, lock her up, and hand the key to a female relative advanced in years, who would redeliver the young lady to you in fair condition on your return. All happiness to Abd-el-Kader, single or married, and the next point was to hire a carriage which should be at our orders during our stay at Biskra. This too was done, and in due course we set out for our first excursion, with Abd-el-Kader on the box to "lionize" us.

What a sight this Biskra is, with its thousands upon thousands of palm trees, waving their crowns so high up in the bright air! It was a perfect day, even for Biskra; for the heavy rain of the previous afternoon and night had washed up the place as if for company. Palm trees everywhere, tall, graceful stems, waving about with the true Grecian bend. A young lady at Algiers, before we started, had imparted to me in confidence that, to her apprehension, the palm tree was the gazelle of the vegetable world. "Rather big," said I. "You are absolutely devoid of sentiment," was the reply. "I hope I am." So the conversation dropped.

Our first point was the garden of M. Landon, a

French gentleman, who has made this pretty place—and pretty it is, as palms, cocoa-nut trees, and every variety of African tree and flower can make it—in fact, if anything, a thought too pretty. The desert had been tidied by the gardener's skill and hand. But I am half ashamed to indulge in this hyper-criticism, for surely M. Landon's garden is a lovely spot, and one would be too happy to spend a month or two here every year, whilst one's friends were enjoying their colds and sore throats in the damp, dark, chilly North. From this garden we drove on to what is called the Officers' Garden, to the ruins of old Biskra, and to the native Biskra. Our hotel was in the French quarter.

I liked the look of the palms better in this half-wild state, though in truth here, as everywhere, they were the objects of the most anxious culture and attention. I believe there are supposed to be some 150,000 of them in and about Biskra. M. Piesse gives 140,000, Colonel Playfair 100,000, Abd-el-Kader 150,000. Each tree, according to M. Piesse, produces about eight or ten *regimes*, or bunches of dates, annually, each of the weight of from six to ten kilogrammes, which would be about seventy-two kilogrammes of dates for each tree. The bulk is, of course, for the ordinary consumption of the people, but certain choice samples are considered *dattes de luxe*, and are tended, sorted, and prepared with unusual care. They are most delicious. The date, purchased even from the stores of Messrs. Fortnum and Mason, is one thing; the choice date of Biskra, quite another. Leaves, trunks, even the kernels, which are softened in water and given to the cattle: every part of the palm is utilized. It even furnishes a kind of wine, of which Abd-el-Kader procured us a bottle, but I am bound to say I found it rather nasty, something like a sweet liqueur, when the cork had been left out of the bottle, and which tasted flat. It is worth while to hear upon the spot all about the system of irrigation, and about the precautions taken so that each tree and each proprietor shall receive just his and its right proportion of the precious fluid. The palm tree must have water, but cares nothing what sort of water it is. Like the rose, it is a foul feeder; but the one thing indispensable to it for growth and fruitfulness is the sun; its feet must be in water, its head in fire. Without the sun of Africa and the desert, you can have no good palms, and no real dates. About the end of March the tree begins to flower; about the end of October, if I remember right, the fruit is gathered. M. Hardy, who seems to be the Sir Joseph Hooker of Algiers, tells us that the spots where the dates ripen best are characterized by an almost total absence of rain.

Certainly the date palms are flourishing around us on all sides, but I could not help thinking of last night, when we certainly met with a few drops. This, however, joking apart, was exceptional, and there is no doubt that the palm tree, to reach its full perfection, must inhale the dry air of the desert as its ordinary diet. There are usually a hundred trees on each hectare of ground— be the same more or less, as the lawyers say—so that each hectare should yield about 7200 kilogrammes of fruit. M. Hardy's Report on the *Phœnix Dactylifera* will be found in M. Piesse's guide-book, and to this I must refer the reader who is desirous of more ample information upon the subject. All I could do would be to copy in his information at second hand—but I have done enough for my purposes.

We only skirted the ruins of old Biskra—a Pompeii of sand—worn out now, but I dare say a place of strength in the desert in its day; but at the native quarter we got out of the carriage, and loitered through the place. How the scene comes before me now, with its sandy walls, just as though you were entering a fortified town, palm trees waving against the blue sky from every available corner! the Arabs, in their white toga-like costume, leaning lazily against the walls! What a life! Do nothing, and your palm tree will support you.

If one could only get rid of Northern fussiness, and leave things alone, which would probably settle themselves a good deal better if you did so! I suppose one's mind has thoroughly deteriorated under forty years of enforced industry. With Mr. Toole, one would say, "I am not happy yet." Even with a good estate in palms, if one settled at Biskra, no more newspapers, no more political economy, no more elections, no more afternoon teas, no more crushes, no more seasons from the opening of the opera to Goodwood and Cowes!—not to be thought of. The genius of boredom smiles on you from the graceful crown of a palm tree. Back to your treadmill and your triangles. To live here a man must be to the manner born.

The native Biskra was just a collection of mud houses in narrow streets, beautified here and there by a palm tree. There was what they called a market going on, that is, a few stands or stalls, with dried fruit, pimentoes, beans, and seeds, but I cannot say business seemed very lively. As I watched the native tradesmen, I could not help thinking of the indignation of that learned gentleman on the Northern circuit, to whom an attorney once brought a brief: "What is the meaning of this, sir? If you do this sort of thing again, you will drive me from the circuit." I think a Biskra bean merchant would have spoken somewhat in the same way to a customer who had trifled with his habits. Then there was a mosque, which visit by all means; but the Mosque of Sidi Okba, which we have come all this way to see, is the only one which I will describe in this part of the world.

From the native Biskra to the Negro Biskra was our next movement. There is nothing much to say about the place, but a good deal about its inhabitants. Many of them were very gaudily dressed, and the funny little children, so stolid and yet so frolicsome, would have kept us there half the day if we had not already used up our time elsewhere. Whence this eternal good humour, and perpetual broad grin of the negro race, as we see them? Is it that they take the world as they find it, and are not troubled with forecasting and back-casting minds, neither with hopes nor disappointments? Let them have their bellies full, abundance of sunshine (from toothache I am sure they are free), and nothing to do, or just as much or as little as they please, and they are merry. Unless this suggestion, that they live by the minute, is the secret of their eternal merriment, I cannot give a better. One might conceive a negro Othello, scarcely a negro Hamlet. At any rate, they seem to pass through life as we do in our more cheerful moments. It is all banjo and broad grins. I never saw a negro in a passion, and then he may be a very terrible fellow, because totally devoid of self-restraint. To pass from this, I would say that Biskra is not one town, but is composed of several villages or townlets, the French Biskra being the chief one.

There are many villages, but one oasis, and scattered around on the desert other oases, some of which we intend to visit. Just now they look like dark spots at a distance. Abd-el-Kader points out that long black line far away as the Oasis of Sidi Okba, which will probably be the term of our pilgrimage. To-morrow we intend driving to Chetma, distant some six miles; yonder mountain is the famous Aures, or rather a portion of the famous Aures range or group of mountains so renowned in African story. We go home to the hotel by the marketplace, partly held under cover, partly in the open air. What wild-looking people! But they get through their petty hucksterings with the most perfect good humour, and the "rowdy" element, which we should certainly meet with in such a place in Europe, is conspicuous by its absence. It would be merely idle to repeat descriptions of picturesque natives, though one could keep on watching them hour after hour. I wish we could have brought away some of the baskets, which were most graceful in shape, and cheap as a song, when songs are cheap. The difficulty was transport. My wife bought some trifles for home presents from a magnificent old Arab (Abd-el-Kader interpreted), such as knives or daggers, with embroidered leather sheaths;

quaint little embroidered bags, in which the Arab women carry their paints and cosmetics; then leather cases fitted with little scraps of looking-glass, which enable them to judge of the effect. The Arab women wear these leather bags suspended by straps from the waist like *chatelaines*. They would be admirably adapted for the use of "frisky matrons" and "girls of the period" at home. The bags might hold the white, pink, and yellow powder, or paste, so well known in the fashionable world. The little looking-glass would always be handy to see that they had not botched the work. With a stroll in the pretty public garden in front of the hotel but across the street, we had got through as much of Biskra as we could accomplish in one day.

Dinner at the Hôtel du Sahara is served in a lofty, dark room of tolerable size, opening out on the garden, and our friend the *chef* gave us a very fair French dinner, quite as good as any you would find in France out of the large towns. When this was over, the real luxury of the day began, the luxury of idleness, in the garden, with coffee under the *tonnelle*, and a cigar, with Abd-el-Kader telling us yarns about the desert and desert life. A coolness seemed to have fallen over everything, the sky above our heads grew of a deeper and deeper blue. Darkness would have followed, but for the big moon overhead. The palms looked mysterious in this half-light, and there was a red glow from the kitchen furnace—of course the kitchen opened on the garden also; and Mohammed in his *sanctum*—also opening on the garden—worked and clattered away at the plates, and made piles of them; and Abdallah and Ali flitted about from the kitchen to the dining-room, like stewards on the *Flying Dutchman;* and a group of French officers, in their gay uniforms, would take up position at the next table, and it grew darker and darker, and the night-breeze of the desert would set in.

I devote a few lines to this evening, for as one was, so were all; and not the least enjoyable portion of our stay at Biskra was this period of evening repose, after the hot delights and strange spectacle of the day. I cannot but think that people who simply wish to play hide-and-seek with bronchitis, and avoid gloom and snow and fog, might do worse than spend a month or two, or even more of the winter at Biskra. Of course, you would be largely dependent on your own resources, and must take plenty of books and so forth with you; but you would have every delight which nature could afford you—an absolutely perfect climate, and freedom from all the pretensions and pettinesses which seem inherent in small colonial settlements.

I fancy there is a steamer which goes from Marseilles, by way of Ajaccio, to Bône, where you could take the rail to Constantine; then, with two days of diligence, you would find yourself in your winter quarters in the desert for two or three months. It is a long journey, but it is a long rest, and a long escape from physical suffering and social irritations. It would not suit many people, but it would suit some admirably. Next day we drove to Chetma, where as Abd-el-Kader, the buoyant one, said, the palms were even bigger and finer than at Biskra. We went across the well-nigh dry bed of a river which I believe was the Oued-Biskra, or

Biskra river. One river flows from El-Kantara (our old enemy of the night of adventure), another from the Aures Mountain; the two join, and these two Oueds form the Oued-Biskra. It was very hot jolting over the sand and stones, and I advise any one who may come after me to provide himself with blue glasses, or some protection for the eye, for the glare from the soil is intolerable.

At last we reach and skirt the sandy outer wall of Chetma. There is a sad-looking Arab burying-ground. There is a long pool of stagnant water (but water here of any kind or quality is not to be trifled with), in which some hideous old hags were washing garments. I suppose the better-looking young ladies are not allowed out, but these unfrisky matrons were certainly safe. Finally we reach a point where Abd-el-Kader told us we must get out of the carriage, as the streets of the village were very narrow, and a carriage could not pass along them. Here we were in full Africa; no civilization to trouble us. Here courteous, dusky men, draped in *bernouses*, stalked about, and swarms of children. With such an escort, we made our way to the Sheikh's house, and to our entertainment there I will confine myself, for the mud-built houses of Chetma were very like those of native Biskra. So were the little heaps of dried vegetables, beans, and pimentoes offered for sale. The palm trees were certainly magnificent, and if they were not bigger than the Biskra palms, the whole scene was so much wilder that we fancied they were. There was no French contingent here. We might have been in the heart of the great Sahara. At the door of his house, mud-built like the rest, the Sheikh came out to meet us. He was the chief man, or, as the Indians would say, the Burra Sahib of the place, and he was most courteous and dignified in his brief intercourse with us.

I had forgotten to say that we had been joined by a party of French gentlemen, with two ladies, in another carriage, so we were formidable in numbers. In the outer room we men were soon placed before a somewhat rickety table, and the Sheikh's people set before us a basket of Chetma dates of the finest kind, and a jug of fresh milk. We *habitués* of the desert—the old hands, as one may say—always wash down our dates with fresh milk when we can get it. The Sheikh did the honours of his table with as much unassuming dignity as I think it is possible for man to do, and although he only spoke Arabic, and we French, by the help of Abd-el-Kader we managed to pull through, and I can only hope we impressed the Sheikh as favourably as he did us.

I should have said that, before he took charge of us below, the Sheikh conducted the ladies of our party upstairs, and for what follows I rely on my wife's report. They first went up some steep, narrow stairs, and were ushered into a room so low that they were obliged to maintain a stooping attitude. The room was divided in two by a bright calico curtain which was afterwards drawn. In it was a bed, on which the company sat, and a long table in front of it. Here they were received by the three young wives of the Sheikh; one of them, despite her tattoo marks, was excessively pretty. She was the last married, and obviously the favourite.

Later came up three older ladies, who, in Masonic phrase, may be described as the "passed wives." They had had their day, but the most perfect harmony seemed to prevail amongst the six ladies.

After a certain amount of intercourse by signs, the prettiest and youngest of the wives drew the curtain, behind which were their garments hanging up, their kitchen utensils, and crockery. The young lady brought out some very bright china cups, and laid them on the table. Then there were set forth a basket of fresh dates, and fresh milk, just as for us downstairs. Dry dates were produced as a relay, but were not so highly approved of. This just provoked a smile. My wife told me that, in answer to their signs, she made them understand that we were monogamous in our habits in England, which seemed to surprise them; and that if any hussy dared to interfere with a wife's domestic arrangements, she would soon know the reason why. A shade seemed to pass over the countenances of five out of the six wives; the pretty one smiled in languid indifference. Before they could get any depth into the great toilette question, the Sheikh made his appearance, obviously to the great disappointment of the six ladies, and conveyed the strangers downstairs. Here, however, obedience is the word; it is not love and a cottage, but love and a stick.

It was time to start; the Sheikh, with courteous gestures, conducted us through the village, and back to our carriage, and here, with the gift of a few brilliant flowers from an Arab to my wife, ended our day at Chetma. In due course we got back, by the way we came, to the hotel, to dinner, and to our cool evening under the *tonnelle*.

The next day we were to pay a visit to the Kaïd, the Arab chief of the place. On reaching his house, near the market, we sent in our letter of introduction by Abd-el-Kader, and presently he came out to greet us—a stout, majestic-looking man, apparently about fifty years of age. One could gather a notion of the kind of patriarchal authority he exercised by the deep reverence paid him by the Arabs who were hanging about; some kissed his hand, some his garments, and seemed content so they could attract his notice in any way. He walked slowly towards us, with a kind of dignified unconsciousness of these movements of reverence and loyalty. It all appeared to be genuine enough, though the hasty opinion of a mere passer-by cannot count for much in such a matter. He received us most cordially, and, seeing I was lame, would not permit me to alight from the carriage. "Was there anything he could do for us?" Nothing; we simply wished to pay our respects to him. "Would not the lady like to see his family and house?" Of course, we were too much honoured, and although, in point of fact, the interview only took place on a second visit, I will throw the two visits into one to avoid repetition. The lady was entrusted to the care of his son, a young Arab about eighteen years of age, who spoke French fluently. I accompanied the Kaïd to a room, which was a kind of justice hall, where he sat cross-legged upon a dais or raised platform, and here he transacted business. He placed me by his side, coffee was brought, and he went on with his work.

I could not understand what was said, but it was amusing enough to watch the bearing of the suitors or applicants. The speeches were short, the Kaïd asked a question or two, and appeared to give a decision, and the parties retired. Then a horseman, the bearer of a message, would ride up to the door. The letter, or whatever it might be, was opened by a secretary, who read its contents to the great man, who, in a few words, dictated what I supposed was the answer, for the secretary wrote something and brought it to his chief, who took out a seal from an inner pocket. This seal was moistened, and applied to the bottom of the letter, which was then handed to the messenger, who galloped off with it. One rider, however, did not bring any letter, but a handful of green grain, which was handed up to the chief, and carefully examined. I suppose this was a sample of produce from some portion of the district, but it seemed to give great satisfaction. Then a gravelooking man came in, who squatted down at the Kaïd's feet, took his hand, and felt his pulse, evidently a doctor.

By the help of the secretary, who spoke French fairly enough, I found this was so, and was allowed the privilege of grasping the patient's hand. They obviously looked to me for an opinion, as I might have done in my own case to Sir William Gull. Alas! the great physician's skill was wanting. I could see that the eyes of my stout and illustrious friend looked rather yellow, and his hand was dry and feverish. What on earth was an irregular practitioner to do? I should have liked to ask him a question or two about his diet, and if he had been dining out much of late, but I feared to give offence. One must suggest something; so with the best bedside manner I could put on, I recommended him to try a cup of tea. I would send him a small supply from our little travelling stock, of which he would do well to take two or three cups as hot as he could conveniently swallow them, and cover himself up so as to arrive at a good perspiration. The tea suggestion seemed to give satisfaction, and, at any rate, I did not think it could do any harm. There was sense in my last question, "Why didn't he send for the French doctor who was there with the troops?" Before I left Biskra I heard the stout chief was all right again, for which I was thankful.

It was, however, absurd enough to watch the Kaïd whilst the consultation was going on. He squatted there patiently, letting the beads pass through his fingers, and emitting little plaintive sounds. He seemed to feel perfect confidence that we meant him well; but I was a little nervous about the swarthy, keen-looking Arabs who crowded in and about the open door. I ventured, as much for my own sake as for my patient's, to impress upon him the absolute necessity of keeping but few people in the room, and of a free circulation of air. The Kaïd emitted a kind of grunting sound, and they all disappeared.

Presently my wife came back, guided by the Kaïd's son. She told me afterwards that she had been conducted into the usual court, and upstairs into a gallery, from which there opened a long room with cushions scattered about; on five of these cushions were reclining the Kaïd's five daughters—the eldest, a young lady of about twenty-four years of age, strikingly beautiful, with the complexion of a European brunette.

One or two others of the young ladies were very pretty. The eldest was a widow. The Kaïd's wife—there was but one—was a stout, handsome, well-preserved-looking woman, apparently about forty years of age. All had their eyebrows and eyelids blackened. They wore the usual Eastern dress, baggy trousers and jackets. A negress brought in two decanters, one of *orgeat*, one with pure water; the *orgeat* was too sweet. The form of conversation on these occasions seems to be invariable: "Are you married? How many children have you? Where are you going to?" then the chapter of dress and ornaments. All this is not very exciting, but it has the merit of being truth. We took our leave of the Kaïd, and I shall always think of him as of a stately, courteous gentleman.

Afterwards we spent the morning amongst the palms, lounging about in the delicate air, and drinking in beauty and pleasure, and so back to the hotel. Whilst sipping our coffee under the *tonnelle* we heard a strange, drum-like sound at the door. We ran to see what it all was about. There stood the strangest figure, with a masque, and grotesque conical head-dress encrusted with shells. His attire was of many colours—all bright, all patchwork. He had a drum, with an animal's tail hanging to it, and a stick which he brought to the present, as a soldier does his musket, when we appeared. He must have been an old man, for I could see the sinewy hands and fingers of great age. I was told he was the "Davie Gellatley" of the place—an African "innocent"—and he gained his living by beating his drum, and by voluntary contributions. Every visitor to

Biskra is sure to come across him, for he is one of the curiosities of the place.

After lunch we drove out to the Hammam Salahin, a bath of natural water; the temperature is given as about 112° Fahrenheit. It seems to be used by the French as well as the natives. The place is worth a visit, but I dare say most travellers will think, as we did, that the best part of this little excursion is the drive there and back. What views of the desert, and of the mountains on one side! It was intensely hot as we were driving there, and for the first time we saw the "mirage" very distinctly. No doubt, at first, the desert in the distance looks like the sea, but when you come to gaze at it for any length of time the perfect immobility disabuses you of the idea. There is the vast expanse of water, there are the headlands and cliffs, but where is the perpetual agitation of the real sea?

The drive homewards was the real bouquet of this little excursion. The sun was declining in the heavens. What a glory in the westward! what lovely tints of purple and golden all around us! You seemed to see every speck on the mountains in the warm glow, every particularity of their fantastic shapes, but nothing misty, not a suspicion of vapour. Go to Biskra and see the sun setting on the desert, and on the Aures range; but for the dark specks of the oases scattered around, and but for the purple appearance of the mountains on one side, it was all gold and blue. In due time we returned to dinner, and kept time, for in the evening we were to go, under the auspices of Abd-el-Kader, to a *café Arabe*, where there was to be a great dancing "function."

About 9 p.m. he found us under our *tonnelle*, somewhat reluctant to stir—just the old London feeling, when one would rather stop at home than go out to a crush and a hot assembly. He conducted us to a house near the market, where there was a long, low room hung with rugs against the wall, and pieces of bright calico were stretched overhead for the ceiling. On each side of the room Arabs in considerable numbers were seated in two rows, above and below. There was a long open space in the middle for the dancers, and the musicians were ready. Presently a woman, one of the professional dancers, neither young nor well looking, made her appearance, and wriggled herself up the open space very slowly; she would pause every now and then, and appear to be taking aim at some one as with a gun, with a stick which she held in her hand. I suppose her wriggles and twistings of the head seemed to imply general fascination; they did not fascinate me. It seemed, however, to satisfy the Arabs, who I dare say saw more in the wriggling than I did. The women were most fantastically dressed, with abundance of what was, no doubt, sham jewellery, with a head-dress which looked like a large stool with silver ornaments hanging from it. They had many chains of silver, with a silver kind of breast-plate, and a silver belt. There was only one that had the smallest pretension to decent looks, and even in her case one had to "make believe" a good deal. We paid the proprietor of the *café* one franc a head as the charge for our entertainment, and he seemed perfectly satisfied. Any one going to Biskra would do well to give a glance, only one, at this exhibition; I do not think visitors would be inclined to stay there. Perhaps the less said the better about the dancing women, who are, if I remember right, called "oulad naïl." They inhabit a street apart at Biskra, and come from some distant part of the desert. I can only say they seemed to me very unattractive, not to say hideous.

Only one more excursion remained to be taken from Biskra, and this was to the Oasis of Sidi Okba—distant some twenty kilomètres. This is the furthest point for the ordinary tourist, although I can well conceive that the young, the strong, the adventurous, might be tempted to proceed to Tuggurt, which is about one hundred and fifty English miles off, and, possibly, further still. Abd-el-Kader said it would be easy enough, but we were not to be tempted. I had already accomplished what would have seemed to me an impossibility as I was crawling about the garden on Mustapha some two or three months before; but presumed dangers and impossibilities fade away in a wonderful manner when one faces them with a good resolution. Any ordinary invalid, any lady, may travel as we did, from Algiers to Biskra, without serious inconvenience, and see very many strange and beautiful things, just as easily as they might travel in Norway or the Salzkammergut. I do not undertake for excursions to out-of-the-way places, for camping out under tents, or adventure of any kind. The good people who aim at distinguishing themselves in this way may find trouble for aught I know, but I should fancy, from what I did see, that the books of travel are full of exaggeration.

Now, with regard to this famous excursion to Sidi Okba. A sufficient account of this great Arab warrior will be found in either the French or English guide-book. He was made Emir or Chief of Ifrikia in A.D. 670, and, says M. Piesse, founded the important city of Kaïrouan. The power of the Vandals was then on the decline; they had shut themselves up in their strong places, but the Berbers, the North African peasantry, still cultivated the plains. A man named Koçeila was one of their chiefs, Chief of the Beranes. The Arabs swept over Africa, under the command of Sidi Okba; even, some say, till he came to the Atlantic, and then returned because he could not get further. Koçeila had become a pervert, and, for the sake of a quiet life, called himself a Mussulman. Sidi Okba had retired from his command, so Koçeila returned to his original belief, and a general cutting of throats was set up. The end was that the Arabs gave the insurgents a very sufficient beating near Tlemçen, and, amongst other things, made Koçeila prisoner. He relapsed into Mohammedanism. Now, it was not probable that the fierce fanatic, Sidi Okba, the reappointed governor, and this Berber Vicar of Bray should live together on comfortable terms. They could not hit upon a *modus vivendi*, and Sidi Okba never threw away a chance of showing his contempt for Koçeila. One day he ordered him to flay a sheep in his presence, which, as it seems, was the highest indignity he could offer him. Koçeila was obliged to eat his leek nevertheless, but he swore a good deal, and as he passed his bloody fingers over his beard, was heard to say, "Never mind; it promotes the growth of the beard." Sidi Okba smiled scornfully; he did not foresee what a price he would have to pay for anticipating the famous discovery of Mrs. S. A. Allen. When he had concluded his nasty job, Koçeila went home and cleansed himself, but, like Catherine of Medicis, he hated and waited. Sidi Okba, thinking all was safe, sent back most of his troops to Kaïrouan. Koçeila had his eye upon him; he gave information to the Northern people, and to his old friends amongst the Berbers, and one day, when Sidi Okba was proceeding with a small force to Tahoud, near the place to which we were going to-day, Koçeila fell upon him and killed him. Sidi Okba had cut his way from Egypt to the Atlantic, but he succumbed to the slaughtered sheep. Such, in brief, seems to be the outline of Sidi Okba's story. The place where he lies is the religious capital of the district. I have taken the story from M. Piesse.

The drive was across the bed of the Oued-Biskra, and over the desert, with pretty views of the mountains and the oases; but the heat was intense (it was the 18th of April), and very thankful I was when we reached the famous oasis. Biskra may be sandy, Chetma sandier, but Sidi Okba is sandiest. It is the Algerine Perranzabuloe (wasn't that the name of the church buried in the sand in Cornwall?). The palm trees were sandy, the walls and houses were sandy, you walked on hot sand through the streets, and the eyes of the man who guided you were full of sand.

The village or town was very like the native Biskra, or Chetma; in fact, I suppose these Arab towns are everywhere the same collection of mud-built houses, of groups of natives squatting at corners, and of small hucksterings in beans, grain, pimentoes, and such like.

The only difference was of degree. My thought would be that you would scarce find anything wilder, or more unalloyed by civilization, between here and Timbuctoo. See Sidi Okba and return to Algiers. You have done enough.

We deposited our baskets of provisions on the first floor of a house which was nice and dark, cool, but sandy, pervaded with a powerful odour of stable, or dung-heap, and crawled out again to see the famous mosque. A very dilapidated sort of place it looked, but really it was the right mosque in the right place. The graceful neatness of Salah Bey's Mosque at Constantine would have been quite out of place here. It was a fitting grave for the wild Arab warrior. "Where he fell, there he lay," or nearly so (for he must have been brought into camp for a few miles); but to say that he fell in the desert, and he lies in the desert, would be strictly true. It was as appropriate as would have been the grave of Nelson on some high granite cliff near the Land's End, overlooking the stormy sea on which he had won his fame. What on earth would Sidi Okba have done with a grave at Westminster Abbey or St. Denis, at Kensal Green or Père-la-Chaise, with a lot of *immortels* scattered over his tomb, and with a figure of Arabia in tears, and a pompous inscription? You find yourself in a rude, square room, with rough pillars and a flat roof. The matting is sandy and gritty. The mosque is dark, but the intolerable sun forces his way in at every cranny. At one side there is a hole in the wall, and through this you climb into the *sanctum sanctorum*, the very grave-chamber in which Sidi Okba has found rest at last. There it is in this sandy corner, and beyond it there is little in the room save a few spear-heads (right again), and, happily, a *very few* articles of vertu, such as ostriches' eggs, but at these I would scarcely glance. This dark lonely chamber, with the green silk thrown over his tomb, and the spear-heads on the wall—nothing else— is the right resting-place of such a chief. As nearly as may be twelve hundred years have passed away since he fought his last fight at Tahoud.

Grope a little about the mosque, and you will come to an inscription which, according to M. Piesse, reads thus—

"Hada Kobr Okba ibn Nafè. Rhamat Allah!"

which, being interpreted, means—

"This is the grave of Okba, son of Nafè. May God have pity on him!"

I did not care to go fumbling about the place like a broker's man making an inventory, so we worked our way to the famous minaret, up which I managed to climb; and what a view of the desert we gained by doing so! How clear, how hot everything looked! The joke of the place is that there is an Arab legend, to the effect that the minaret will tremble when the name of Sidi Okba is invoked according to a prescribed form of words. We did not know the formula, or we would have tried the experiment. I heartily wish Sidi Okba would do some grievous mischief to the blockheads who have defamed his solitary resting-place by cutting their silly names upon his minaret. What have we to do here with the illustrious Jones, or the sublime Dupont? It is difficult to say who are the greater blockheads—the French or English.

We spent half an hour at the top of the minaret;— with the round cupola, which covered the grave, just at our feet; and the sandy town and the desert of sand all around; with a glare of light upon every object. Tired out at length in body, if not in mind, we got down, and staggered back to the cool, ill-smelling place where luncheon was ready for us. As this had been prepared under the vigilant eye of the *chef* at Biskra, there was no objection to be made to it. Our lunch was cheered up by the pleasant gaiety of a French fellow-traveller who had made the little excursion with us—a gentleman of infinite fun and humour, who had procured for himself an Arabian conversation-book, and submitted Abd-el-Kader to a short examination in his native tongue. When the interpreter was puzzled with the pronunciation, the way in which his French tormentor would turn round with "*Il n'est pas fort,*" was worthy of Hippolyte and the Palais Royal. I don't know that the fun was very good, but it amused us all very much, and put us in spirits for a ramble round the town. We went to the market, and to the houses where they were making carpets; to a crowded Arab school, presided over by a gentleman with a bored look, and a long stick. On a shelf was seated a hobbledehoy—an adult pupil, I was told; but the Arab children were very pretty, and, as I should think, sad *gamins*. So to the carriages, and over our twenty kilomètres of sand and stones back to the hotel.

At length the time had come for us to leave Biskra,

which we did with infinite regret. The people of the hotel were most kind and civil; the accommodation and food quite sufficient and suited to the country; the lounges under the palm trees and in the garden simply delightful; the sky and brightness such as I shall never see again till I get back to Biskra. I should like to shake hands with my host and hostess once more, and Abdallah, and Ali, and Mohammed, and our friend Abd-el-Kader; and I should like to look in on the majestic Kaïd, and find him pretty well, and sealing his despatches in an impressive way; and I should much like to smoke my evening cigar and sip my coffee again under the *tonnelle*. "Good-bye, one; good-bye, all. We shall soon come back." I hope we may.

We returned to Constantine by the same route, and in the same way, and this time without adventure of any kind. The only difference was that in the afternoon we drove over to El-Outaia, some twenty-five kilomètres off, where we were to be picked up by the diligence at 6 a.m. next day. That caravanserai was rough quarters, and would scarcely do for ladies nourished in the traditions of Mivarts or the Hôtel Bristol. We managed, however, to get a tolerable night's sleep, despite of the plague of flies and barking of the dogs.

In the evening you walk into the Arab village, stare at the Mountain of Salt from a respectful distance, and, above all, watch the sun going down over the desert. But our hearts were heavy. We sighed for Biskra and our friends there.

Very few lines should bring us back to Constantine and our old quarters. We reached the place last named in two days, as we only halted a night at Batna on our return journey. The single fact worth recording is that between Batna and Biskra we had a cloudy, cold day; in point of fact, the cold was disagreeable. This was on the 21st of April. From Constantine we took the railroad to Setif, leaving Constantine at 2.30 p.m., and arriving at Setif at 9.15 p.m. This time, as a set-off, the weather was exceedingly hot; and, with a slight change, I may repeat my phrase—the heat was disagreeable. We put up at the Hôtel du Louvre, an old-fashioned house, where the people made us very comfortable.

Next day we were timed to leave at 5.30 a.m., but the diligence did not really start till 6 a.m. We had taken the *coupé*, as before; but this was the only occasion during our Algerian experience when we had doubts about the sound policy of the *coupé* system. During one part of the journey between Setif and Bougie, you go through the Chabet Pass, and I am fully persuaded that in an open carriage you could see around you, before, and above you better. Were I to do this little journey over again, I should hire an open carriage. The price of the *coupé* from Setif to Bougie was fifty-four francs. I never asked any questions about the cost of a carriage, so I cannot give any comparison of prices. Colonel Playfair marks the price of a carriage from Setif to Bougie 300 francs.

Of the town of Setif I can say but little, as in point of fact we were in bed and asleep during the eight or nine hours we spent within its walls. On driving from the diligence office to the Porte de Bougie, the place seemed to me to be a Batna, that is, a model French town, upon a somewhat larger scale. Setif, however, has a future before it. It is a grand junction point for railways in this part of the provinces, and if ever the French engineers succeed in getting down from Setif to Bougie, it would be difficult to exaggerate its importance. From Constantine to Setif the line is complete; from Algiers to Setif it will, presumably, soon be terminated; and when once communication is established between Setif and the nearest seaport, which is Bougie, I should suppose that it will soon run up to a position of great importance in the colony.

We are out of the town, and as the horses are trotting along, at every step they bring us nearer to our old friends, the mountains of Kabylia. The Arabs and the Kabyles stand face to face in this region; the Kabyles are in the mountains, the Arabs on the high plains. Except for the views of the mountains in the distance, I do not remember anything very remarkable at this part of the journey. Interesting the country must always be, the ground being so decorated with wild flowers, the sky so bright and brilliant, the shapes of the mountains in the distance so picturesque; but, I repeat it, I cannot call to mind any particular feature during this stage of the drive worthy of record, except that we saw a good deal of cultivation on either side of the road. The books tell us that hereabouts lay the original *concession* to the Geneva Company, but that the ground is now mainly let out to Arabs, as the affairs of the company did not prosper for want of outlet for their produce. Be this as it may, if what we saw was Arab work, I should suppose that the Arabs are not such very bad agriculturists after all, if a fair chance be given them. They will not make the chance for themselves, but they will avail themselves of it if given. The chance here is the railway from Setif to Bougie, but, if left to themselves, the children of the Prophet would require some time to lay it down.

It is in such a case as this that the French occupation is a blessing to the native races of Africa. Right and left you were shown points where detached and isolated groups of French soldiers and colonists had manfully held their own during the terrible insurrection of 1871. As in all cases, whether in British India or in the United States, no matter where it may be, where civilization— that is to say, scientific gunnery—is brought to bear upon savagery—that is, upon an imperfectly shooting race—the early chronicles of the country should be written in very deep red. The French have just been compelled to do what others in the like case have done before them. This work they have done with terrible energy and precision, and if the result be that this fertile portion of the earth is made useful to mankind, all this blood will not have been shed in vain.

I remember, about thirty kilomètres or so out of Setif, we were allowed to get out of the diligence on the top of a *col*, from which there was a very magnificent view; but all the names of the places will be found duly registered in the guide-books.

The real interest of the day's journey for idle tourists in search of the picturesque commences at Kharata, at the entrance of the Chabet Pass, even though you have seen the great mountain, Babor, for some time before you reach that place.

We halted at the little inn for lunch, for, even in the presence of the sublime and beautiful, man must eat. The food was dirty and bad, and I should have great doubts as to the policy of stopping even for a day at Kharata. This is what we found; others may have found it better; but another time, if I had to halt at Kharata, I should certainly provide myself with a little basket containing the usual cold fowl, bread, and a bottle of wine from the last halting-place. Of the sleeping accommodation we cannot speak; but the place looked dirty.

A very little distance after leaving the inn we entered the famous pass, or gorge, and I mentally tried to compare it with some of the great Swiss passes. But here you must get rid of all ideas of comparison with anything you meet with on the Stelvio, or Simplon, or anything of that kind. The Via Mala is of the same class as the Chabet, but far inferior. You are in a very narrow gorge, about three quarters of a mile in length, with a stream brawling, not to say roaring, far below. Save when the sun is shining right down the turn of the road along which you may be passing, the gorge is sensibly darkened by the great height of the mountain-wall on either side. The heights are given as from 5000 to 6000 feet. I must leave it to the imagination of the reader to elaborate these hints for himself. Length, three quarters of a mile; height of sides, 5000 or 6000 feet; breadth, not worth speaking about. Each bend of the road seemed to open out something new and more fantastic in the shape of rocks and precipices than the last. Given the height of the falls, and lay on plenty of water, imagine Niagara; so I say, with the data given above, imagine the Chabet Pass. Salvator Rosa, however, could scarcely have realized the magnificence of these toppling crags; or our own Turner the atmospheric effects up aloft. It is idle to write about the place; go and see it. The gorge at last began to grow wider, and there were trees again, oaks and corks, through which we passed down to the sea-shore.

I hope I have paid my proper tribute to the Chabet Pass, which is indeed one of the wonders of North Africa; but I should wish to dwell a little upon the scenery between the mouth of the pass and Bougie, which was, I think, the most beautiful we saw in Algeria, a worthy *adagio* after the more terrible division of the sonata, to which, I suppose I should say, we had just been listening. The day was one of short, drifting showers and bright sunshine; the very weather for such a scene. On the right of our road lay the Mediterranean, emphatically *here* the blue sea; on our left were the hills clothed in verdure—oak, ash, cork, and so forth. Such was the setting of the most beautiful flower show we had ever seen in our lives, or were likely to see again till we returned to Algeria. This time it was not Messrs. Veitch or Paull who had provided the exhibition; it was the work of nature, without help of any kind—it was a world's exhibition of wild flowers. There were miles of gladioli, and of the yellow and blue iris, and the same of single and double white and pink oleanders; the convolvulus of all colours (but particularly magenta) overran everything; and I could wish that my convivial friends, who simply associate the name with the idea of cup and Greenwich dinners, could have seen what borage can do when fairly tried. Then there were "huge" pimpernels and bugloss and mallows which looked like azaleas, and heather which grew into bushes just as it does in Corsica, and the scarlet magnificence of the poppies. Let any one endeavour to realize to his own mind what this must have been on the scale on which this exhibition was laid out. The diligence was trotting rapidly, and it required from two to three hours to get through the show. It was not only the beauty of the work, but the scale on which it was done, that took your breath away. Let it not be supposed that there was a tuft of white lilies here, a group of poppies there; but the place was carpeted with wild flowers. If we had seen nothing else, it was worth while coming to Africa to see this.

At about 5 p.m. we reached Bougie, and there was lying the *Malvina*, the very steamer which had conveyed us from Algiers to Philippeville, so we got on board at once (for really the mind and senses could not take in anything more), and re-entered into possession of our original cabin. Yes, there it was, that wretched old horse-hair sofa—too short for me—on which I had rolled about when outward bound. All was quiet enough now, and the people of the steamer contrived to furnish us with a very sufficient little dinner.

We had time to make our preparations, and even to "turn in," as we nautical people say, for the steamer only started at about 10 p.m. Land folk said the sea was a little rough; but what do the "old salts" care for a tumble? We fell asleep and awoke at 5 a.m. at Dellys, which place we left at 9 a.m., and at 3 p.m. arrived at Algiers. The weather was somewhat rainy; but this time we had become so hardened that we remained on deck and admired the scenery, especially that of the bay from Cape Matifou to Algiers. This was on the 27th of April. We had left Algiers on the 7th of April, so it does not take very long to get a peep at the desert.

CHAPTER XIV.

THE HOME CIRCUIT.

THE little excursion I am about to describe may content many visitors to Algiers, who would not care to undertake a trip either to the desert or to the frontier of Morocco. This is a somewhat pompous description of a trip to Biskra, and another to Tlemçen. There is nothing in what I am about to relate which involves the smallest hardship, and the little excursion, containing as it does so many points of interest, might readily be made in an open carriage, easily procurable at Algiers. I trust it is unnecessary for me to reiterate that we do not pretend to have gone to out-of-the-way places, or to have tempted danger of any kind. Our most anxious desire was to avoid adventure in any form, and simply to see as much of the three provinces as we could in a quiet, humdrum way. We did contrive to see a very great deal, and I really believe the most interesting things in Algeria; nor did we, save on two occasions, meet with any drawback that we might not as readily have encountered on the Cumberland lakes or in the Scottish Highlands; nay, from our experience I should say that the balance of comfort was decidedly in favour of Algerine travel.

Of these two exceptions, one was when we were caught by the rains between El-Kantara and Biskra; the other I shall speak of presently, when we were overtaken by a brief but sharp storm on the top of the mountain in the Cedar Forest of Teniet. But travellers are occasionally benighted in the Cumberland fells; in this morning's *Times*, I read of a poor fellow who fell off a steamer and was drowned in Loch Lomond. Stir from home in any direction, and there is danger; you may be crushed at Clapham Junction, or well-nigh lose your life in a hansom cab opposite St. George's Hospital. A horse may turn restive in Algeria as elsewhere, or a wheel come off your carriage; but the horses, as a rule, are both strong and quiet, the carriages comfortable, the roads excellent, and the inns, for the most part, quite as satisfactory as any you will meet with in provincial France or Germany. I wish they had been as good in Italy when I travelled there as a youth—more years ago than I care to think of—*vetturino*-wise.

But let us get back to our story. This is what I call the home circuit from Algiers—Boufarik, Blidah, Gorge de la Chiffa, Cherchel, Marengo, Tombeau de la Chrétienne, Hammam R'Irha, Milianah, Teniet (Cedar Forest), Affreville, back to Algiers.

We did not visit Koleah or Tipasa, as our arrangements did not take us back to Algiers, but we might readily have done so, for we took the train from Affreville to Oran, proceeding thence by diligence to Tlemçen; but I have preferred, for the convenience of excursionists, to treat of this little expedition by itself.

If you would take in everything, some such scheme as this would answer the purpose. It was furnished me by a gentleman, long resident in Algiers, who knew the country well, and, from what we saw, it seems to me quite feasible :—

Hire your carriage at Algiers.
Koleah : sleep. (Castiglione ?)
Tombeau de la Chrétienne : take lunch with you.
Tipasa : if tired, sleep.
Marengo : lunch.
Cherchel : sleep (order rooms).
Marengo : lunch.
El-Affraun : discharge carriage, rail to
Bou-Medfa : carriage from station to
Hammam R'Irha : rail to
Affreville : from Bou-Medfa station carriage from Bath to station.
Milianah.
Teniet : and back to
Affreville : rail to
Blidah : rail to Algiers.

All the advantage you derive from this second plan is that you see Koleah and Tipasa, which you might at any time readily do from Algiers (including the Tombeau), and you avoid sleeping at Marengo, which is a dirty hole. Bar this, I prefer the plan we actually adopted, but at any rate there is an alternative.

Now for our own small proceedings. Monday, the 3rd of May, it was a wet morning at Algiers, but cleared up just as we left by the 12.40 p.m. train. We took our final farewell of M. Moutton and of the Hôtel de la Régence, where we had been made very comfortable, not only on our arrival at Algiers in October of last year, but on all the occasions on which we had used the hotel as our head-quarters during our various excursions. We were in the hotel, first and last, quite for six weeks, and although it would be absurd to speak of it as you would of the Beaurivage at Ouchy, of the Schweizer-Hof at Lucerne, or the Vierjahreszeiten at Munich, I can conscientiously recommend the hotel to all who may come after me. The Orient is of larger pretensions, but we never stopped there, and, from the account of many of my friends who did so, I should judge it to be much dearer and less comfortable than the Régence. I would hint to people who travel in a large way, there are but a very few suites of apartments on the first floor, so, if minded to try the hotel, the traveller would do well to write from London, or at any rate from Marseilles, and engage his apartments beforehand. We were on the second floor, where we had a good view over the palm trees, and dined daily at the *table d'hôte*. Our bill, exclusive of wine (other than the *ordinaire* always supplied), was thirty-five francs a day for my wife and myself. Nothing could exceed the cordiality and kindness of M. and Mme. Moutton, and we liked all the people, especially our old soldier, who had routed the Arabian forces for us on our first landing. Were we to go back to Algiers, we should certainly go to the Régence.

But for the time, as at Biskra, it is "Good-bye, host and hostess; good-bye, Dominique and Jean; good-bye, Mme. Cornuz, with your flowers; Beschir, with your chairs; Mohammed, with your blacking-box; good-bye, Oasis of Palms. Very pleasant times have we had with you all; so, heartily, farewell."

We left the station at L'Agha, at 12.40 p.m., as I have remarked above; we reached Blidah, where we intended to pass some days, at 3 p.m. This time we made no halt at Boufarik, though it was market day, for it would be absurd to include such a place in an excursion of this kind. Boufarik is but thirty-seven kilomètres by rail from Algiers, and is easily to be visited in a day. I just remark, in passing, that it is a place with a terrible story; it was the home of fever, and there thousands of French soldiers and French colonists have perished. It is now healthy enough, and is very commonly the object of an excursion from Algiers. At the modern Boufarik you will not now find the humours of an Arab fair, so pleasantly described by M. le Capitaine Richard; but a very matter-of-fact cattle market, with plenty of Arabs about, to light up the place with their queer dresses and queer ways. The village, or townlet (the cattle market apart), is now wonderfully like any place of the same proportions in Normandy, perhaps fresher and cleaner, and there is nothing about it to recall the past story of "The Dismal Swamp." At Blidah we went to the Hôtel Geronde, where we were made very comfortable during our stay.

Blidah is the home of oranges, and a lovely place it is. For miles before we reached the station we breathed air fragrant with the odour of the orange blossom, and passed through endless plantations of the dark-green, glossy-leaved tree. There is abundance of water bubbling and gurgling about in every direction. Behind the town you have the Atlas Mountains,—it is built just at the foot of them; in front, the Metidja, as we saw it, green with the abundant crops; and in the distance the Sahel, on whose slopes we had spent so many months. Blidah is now a French town, with broad streets, but low houses, for the inhabitants are very properly mindful of the catastrophe of 1825, when the town was destroyed by earthquake. You find large Places, and very tolerable shops. For our first stroll, after we had taken possession of our new quarters, we sauntered out to the Jardin Bizot, and were delighted to sit there quietly and inhale the fragrance of the air, amidst the syringas and pomegranates, though the odour of the orange blossom overpowered all rivalry. At length it was time to get back for dinner, and a very tolerable dinner they gave us at the hotel, and our little banquet was brightened by the presence of some English grumblers.

"Are you going to stay long in this confounded hole?" said one of these gentlemen to me. "Better be off by the first train to-morrow. We have been here a fortnight, and it has rained every day. But for the supplement to the *Times*, which we receive every day, I don't know what we should have done with ourselves. The place may well be green. But let any one who comes here be provided with mackintoshes and umbrellas. Why, sir, Keswick is a trifle to it, or Tarbet either. What's that you say, sir?—it has been raining at Algiers? Of course it has. There is another of your humbugs. We have spent a couple of months there, and of all the beastly holes! Typhoid and stench, sir. There is a short description of Algiers for you. I don't pretend to like the French, but I am glad they have got hold of Algiers. Serve them right, I say; it will polish them off by thousands. Climate indeed! of all the confounded climates! Why, sir, to be safe, a man must walk about with a fur cap in one hand and a straw hat in the other. On one side of the street, it is fur; on the other, straw. We are leaving Blidah to-morrow by the earliest train, and Algiers on Tuesday, and we hope never to see the confounded hole again. Give me Brighton; that is the place for real comfort."

All this was said in a jerking way, not continuously, but such was the substance of the gentleman's opinions. It was not my place to contradict him. If he liked the King's Road best—why, well; if we preferred Algeria for the nonce—equally well. We should not stand in each other's way. So my friend grumbled through his dinner, and when this was over, I had a chat with an Italian waiter, an oldish man, which interested me much. I like to make friends with people on my way through the world; one learns a great lesson of humility at times from the simplest, and one gets plenty of fun from the pompous and pretentious people. This poor man's story was sad, and I think it was true, for he knew that I had a slight acquaintance with a lady at Algiers, to whom he had acted as courier. But, after all, his manner was the best guarantee of the truth of his words.

He came, if I remember right, from Como, or somewhere near Milan. He had been married, but his wife was dead, leaving him with two children, a boy and a girl. The girl was now at Tizi-Ouzou, he or his friends having procured for her some small situation in the telegraph office. The boy had reached the age of eighteen or nineteen years, and had been the pride of his heart. When quite a youth, he had shown remarkable aptitude for drawing, and the father's hope was that one day he would turn out a great artist. That this might come to pass, the father had not spared himself; he had run about Europe as a courier, he had engaged himself as a waiter at off-seasons, he had worked early and late, that his boy might have means of prosecuting his studies. His great reward was to see how prizes and honourable "mentions" showered in upon the young student, and how all competent judges agreed that he had a great future before him.

"I didn't care for the work, sir," he said; "the more the better; the harder it was, the more I was pleased, for it meant so many more scudi or francs. I was working for my son's sake, and, sir, such a son! He had goodness as well as genius. At last I placed him in the school at Algiers. Everything went well for a time, and my reward was to read the letters which I received from him, or to run over to Algiers, and embrace him, if it were but for a few minutes. At last—woe is me!—I got one letter to say he was ailing; but it was nothing; I was not to disquiet myself. By the next I heard that he had been taken to the hospital. He died there—died of that fatal typhoid, that fever, which carries off people at Algiers, young and old, old and young; and I am a lost man! Why was I not taken, and he left? Of what good am I in the world now my son is gone?

Why should I work more, since my work can do him no more good? He was not a common boy; he would have been a great artist; he would have made his name famous! I only wished to live to see him great, and then I was ready to go and tell his mother what great things he was doing. Alas! alas! sir, I am a lost man!"

Poor fellow! what could one say? This was not a case for talking platitudes or making attempts at philosophic consolation. It *was* a hard case, and it touched me the more that the sorrowing father could only see or think of his son's genius; he never gave a thought to his own, nor did he see anything praiseworthy in the devotion of his life. I shall not readily forget the poor Italian waiter at Blidah. It came to our recollection afterwards that we had heard at Algiers that a young art student had died of typhoid in the hospital.

We summoned Mme. Geronde to counsel, that we might inform ourselves of the things best worth seeing at Blidah, and of the best way of seeing them. According to her landladyship's account there were—

The Gorge de la Chiffa, with lunch at the Ruisseau des Singes, where a few monkeys are always kept on hand at the little inn, to prevent disappointment.

The Bois Sacré, with its old olive trees.

The ravine of the Oued-el-Kebir, where there were some remarkable Arab tombs, or Koubbas; but we were recommended to let a day or so go by before trying this excursion, as much rain had fallen, and the roads were very bad.

Then there was the stud establishment, where some fine Arab horses were to be seen. This we did not visit.

Finally, it would be worth while to drive about for two or three hours amongst the orange gardens in every direction, and we should have seen Blidah.

First for the Gorge de la Chiffa, but as this was some way off, we had to engage a carriage. Before leaving Algiers, a friend had given us the name of an Arab *vetturino*, whom he described as a pearl amongst Arabs, and so he turned out to be when we found him, which was not without difficulty. My wife went out in search of the "pearl" to the Place d'Armes, near to which stand the carriages for hire. "Was there one Ali there?" "Did madame want a carriage? All were Alis." The lady wanted an Ali who had driven an English party about last autumn. All the Alis had driven English parties about last autumn. "Would each Ali describe his party?" So they did, but not one description would tally with facts. Our Algerine friend was not a venerable man with a white beard, nor a stout matron with two most lovely children, nor did he wear spectacles. A suggestion was made to help their memories, which seemed a little at fault. A gloom fell upon the assembled Alis. Yes, they remembered the party, but alas! the Ali who had driven them was no more. It had pleased Allah in His infinite mercy to relieve him from the trials and temptations of this transitory world. But poor Ali had enjoyed a good reputation in his time, and his memory was still green with his afflicted brethren of the whip.

At this moment a stout, good-tempered-looking lad, on the broad grin, with a set of very white teeth, drove up, and informed himself of the cause of the general sadness. They were wailing for Ali, who had been cut off in the flower of his youth, and, as one might say, at the outset of his useful and honourable career.

"But, *comment, madame*," said the lad. "I too am Ali, and last autumn I drove an English party about for days. The monsieur was always laughing at all things; *he laughed at me;* and the lady was the most beautiful European lady whom we have ever seen at Blidah."

This was the right description, and a few more questions and answers brought certainty. The defunct Ali was engaged to take us to the gorge, and from the moment he was engaged the other coachmen seemed to acquiesce in the inevitable, and banished from their faces the expression of mourning. They must be a very affectionate set of people. So the dead coachman came to the door in due time, and drove us out of Blidah and on the plain alongside of the railway. We were now fairly on the Metidja, on which we were to spend so many pleasant days. It was plentifully dappled with wild flowers. I do not say that it was like that wonderful scene between the end of the Chabet Pass and Bougie; but it was a prairie covered with the green crops. If wild flowers also had been a crop, the hopes of the husbandman would not have been disappointed. I trust that, in raving about the wild flowers of Algeria, I may not be leading my readers astray. A good deal must depend on times and seasons. Now we had everything in our favour.

The early part of May was the best time for our ramble. There had been two or three years of drought, but the season of 1879–80 had been very wet, so there had been abundance of water; but the weather had now settled down to "Fair" and "Set fair," and the African sun was playing its part. The wilderness of wild flowers we saw was the result. I would not say that at another date, or under other conditions of rain and sun, the Metidja would be as beautiful as during the ten days or so we were driving about it. It is easy to learn all about these things at Algiers before starting. Just putting in this word of caution, I would say that we drove for some time by the side of the railway and amongst the flowers; the white houses of Blidah, set in the dark green of the orange groves, looking more and more beautiful as the distance increased. Then—let me see—we came to a river and crossed a bridge, and turned to our left and entered the Chiffa Gorge. A passing traveller has made what in my humble opinion is a very sensible observation about this famous gorge. Do not look here for a Swiss pass—the snow is wanting, but rather take your thoughts back to Scotland. To my fancy, the Chiffa is not as fine as Glencoe, but it is the same kind of thing.

As we drove past the little inn at the Ruisseau des Singes, we stopped to direct that lunch and monkeys might be ready for us on our return journey, and drove on up the pass to the extreme point to which tourists usually go, and even a little beyond it. Were I to do this journey again I should certainly push on to Medeah, which is some twenty-five or thirty kilomètres further, but, being strangers in the land, we had not realized the fact before starting, and had made no preparations for camping out; so we turned, and went back to the Ruisseau, where we found lunch ready for us in a pleasant little dark room, where the walls were covered with (pictured) monkeys—old monkeys, babe monkeys, middle-aged monkeys, fat and thin, dressed and undressed monkeys, monkeys walking about, and monkeys hanging by their tails.

After lunch we went to the back of the inn, to see if the bright sunshine had tempted any of these interesting creatures to show themselves. I am bound to say we did not see any, so we had to content ourselves with the three quasi-tame monkeys, which are kept for the delectation of visitors. The people at the inn can thus turn on monkeys for their guests at any moment, just as the miller at the Traun Falls, in the Salzkammergut, can turn on a waterfall for you, and prevent disappointment.

Never did I see such wideawake brutes. I wonder if Darwin is right after all. Has man developed into monkey, or monkey into man? Do the monkeys say to each other, as they look at us, "What! we descended from those dull, stolid brutes? They have no sense; they are slow in their movements; they cannot run up trees, nor hang on by their tails. There is just a hideous resemblance to monkeys in their faces, but a very disagreeable likeness, my dear. Their Dr. Darwin is little better than—— Well, least said, soonest mended. Pass me a nut."

As I was standing a little behind, I watched one of the creatures picking the lady's pocket. He looked round him, with a glance conscious of larceny from the person. With one little old hand he deftly opened the pocket, and with the other abstracted something or another, with which he ran up his tree, chattering with delight. The case was complete against him; your only contention in his favour must have been that it was but a practical joke. The thievish mind was wanting. Yes, I would have gone on the idea of the practical joke, and called witnesses to character. Surely his friends would have sworn freely.

At length we had done with our monkeys, and drove home, and down the pass at a great rate, the lengthening shadows adding greatly to the beauty of the scene. The cost of the carriage was fifteen francs, with a small tip to the dead coachman. How we did wear that joke of Ali as a dead man to tatters! If forgotten for a while, the lad would turn round and gaze at us in a stony way, suggestive of hearses and weepers and other cheerful things; sometimes the provocation would come from us. It was a good travelling joke, and wore well. Such was our little trip to the Chiffa Gorge, in which we were not disappointed, as we had not looked for too much.

Our next drive was to the Bois Sacré, and I will make but a short story of it, though the place was strange and beautiful enough. When you say that at a little distance from the town there stands a Koubba, surrounded by olive trees, which I suppose are amongst the oldest in Africa, you pretty well mention the facts. But what olive trees! I remembered some very old olives between Cannes and Nice, and in Corsica I had seen some of no inconsiderable size; but they were mere bantlings by the side of these old folks at Blidah. Strange, weird, gnarled old trees, assuming fantastic forms. Like Adam's in the play, their old age was "frosty, but kindly;" they could still put forth a sufficiency of grey-green foliage to show that there was sap left in them. We said we would come back when the moon was up to have another look at the place. I should think it is worth doing, but I am ashamed to say the little project passed out of our heads, and we never went back. The Bois Sacré is one of the lions of Blidah—a very old lion, perhaps, but there is life in him still. Let no one forget to visit the place.

The Bois Sacré was not enough to fill up the day, o, despite the warnings of Mme. Geronde as to the state of the road, which were treated with perfect contempt by the dead Arab (whom by this time we had taken into our service), away we started for the Oued-el-Kebir, and the Koubbas in the ravine. The drive alone well repays the trouble of the little expedition; first through the orange gardens, and then along a road by the side of the stream, with a great mountain in front. Mme. Geronde was right, however; the abundant rain had softened the ground, and when it was in this state the heavy waggons loaded with timber had cut into the soil ruts so deep and so vast that they might be considered as models of their class. The burning sun had finished the work by hardening the ruts, just as porcelain can be hardened in a furnace. So away we bumped, to the manifest danger of springs and wheels, as well as to our own great personal inconvenience; but at length we reached a spot where Ali told us we must turn out, and do the rest of the distance on foot. It was a stiff climb, at any rate for a lame man; but at length we reached a building, where a learned Taleb, with a long stick, was goading a number of little boys through the Koran.

This we passed, and higher up still came to a wild-looking Arab burying-ground, a solitary place full of white stones. We were high up, and had a view over the great plain of the Metidja, with the mountain rising behind us. It was all on so vast a scale, but all so silent. There was no sound, except the humming from the school below, and even this reached us faintly enough.

There were plenty of old olive trees about; but we had become particular in olive trees since the morning, and amidst these olives were the Koubbas; and quaint specimens of tombs they were—at one end a square erection ending in a dome; another at the other end, but with a roof terminating in a point. Between these was a sort of long framework of gaily painted wood, the kind of art employed being much the same as that used in England or Germany, for the decoration of Noah's arks and children's playthings. In the top part of the framework, upon the top shelf rather, the saint was taking his last rest, with a green covering thrown over him. What is true of one is true of all.

I fairly despair when I try to give an idea of these strange burying-places by the help of mere words. A painter, with his colours, might succeed, where a writer who has only an ink-stand at his disposal must fail. They were rather gigantic, gaily painted toys than anything else, but they were surrounded by the sacred olives, and stood in the midst of such magnificent scenery. I think that one got at last to like them, and to feel that the bright colours were not, after all, out of harmony with the dark, wild place, and the bright sunshine around us. So peace to the ashes of Sidi Ahmed-el-Kebir and his two sons. The spot is held in great reverence by the Arabs. We were told that when Abd-el-Kader was in this part of the country, he used to pay his devotions with great fervour at these shrines. I know not how this may be; our authority was Ali the coachman.

The rest of our time was spent in wandering about the town and the gardens. In a week's time or so there was to be a great public function, and artisans were busily employed doing carpenter's work about the Place. Great surprise was expressed that we did not wait for this; why had we come to Blidah? Certainly not to see races or a country fair, was our thought, which we were far too polite to express in words, so bowed ourselves out of the situation as well as we could.

On the evening, however, before we left Blidah we drove slowly round the orange gardens; and this, after all, is the sight of the place. The oranges are as entirely the masters of the situation at Blidah, as are roses at Tlemçen, herrings at Wick, pilchards at Penzance, or coals at Newcastle.

Orange gardens to the right and to the left, and when you have come to the end of one you begin another. Dark, glossy leaves, white flowers, and the air impregnated with an odour of orange blossoms, in a way which would have driven a perfumer crazy. I could well understand how, in the wicked old days,

Blidah was something more than the Capua of this part of the world. Guy Livingstone would have said, "Let us make love, and suck oranges. Beyond that there is nothing certain." Let those who like live at Aberdeen. Give me Armida and her gardens. I resist a somewhat strong temptation to bring in a few choice recollections of Lemprière and the nymphs. I would rather state at once, in plain English, that what Sorrento is to a cabbage garden, that is Blidah to Sorrento. Everybody now, thanks to Mr. Cook, has been to Sorrento; so there is your standard of comparison.

Drive on, Ali, but slowly—"who goes slow, goes sure." A little more of the sloping sun on the dark leaves and white flowers; a little more of the bubbling streams; a little more perfume; a little more folding of the hands! But go slowly, Ali; we care not how slow. Alas! alas! it was over at last. So let us get a bit of dinner, and make arrangements for the morrow, for here in the Armida gardens we may tarry no more.

The arrangements were soon made; for these simply consisted of hiring an open carriage and pair of horses for as many days as we might require them, at the rate of thirty francs a day, with a *buona-mano* to the driver, and a reasonable back-fare to Blidah from the point at which we might discharge him. Ali was our driver, of course; but he was the man, not the master. The owner was an Italian, one Gaetano Governi, whose name I strongly recommend to all future tourists in this part of the world. He supplied us with an excellent little carriage, a pair of capital horses, and the jocular, good-humoured Ali as a driver. The only bargaining was,

"What is your price?" "So much." "Good; we agree;" and we never heard a word more about the matter. All was good humour and civility.

From Blidah, then, we started, and our objective for the first day's drive was Cherchel, by way of Marengo, where we were to lunch. As we drove along amongst the wild flowers in the fragrant morning air, we soon came in sight of the famous Tombeau on the hill, which we were resolved to visit, but not to-day.

Marengo was soon reached, but there was a fair on, or it was market-day, for the place was crowded with Arabs and sturdy-looking Frenchmen, who, I suppose, were samples of the *colons*. If they are, things can't be going on so badly after all. The men I see might turn up at a farmer's ordinary in one of our own country towns, and nobody would be surprised.

The hotel was very noisy and dirty, but the food was good enough. Our hearts misgave us somewhat, for we could not but stop one night at Marengo on our return, if we wished to see the Tombeau, which we certainly did.

We left Marengo at 1.30 p.m., and arrived at Cherchel about 4 p.m. There was vine-growing about Marengo, and I was rather on the look out for vines, for the cuckoo-song which was never out of my ears at Algiers was, "We will grow vines, make wines, and become rich." The *phylloxera*, which had ruined so many poor people in the vine districts in the South of France, was to be the making of the colony. So said the Algerines. They are certainly paying attention to the vine in the neighbourhood of Marengo.

We trotted away amidst the corn-fields, richly decorated with mallows and poppies and a thousand brilliant things ; on the side of the road, growing close to the ground, were masses of the blue convolvulus, with yellow centres, looking just as if they were made of china by some skilful hand at Worcester. So on through the village of Zurich, with its avenue of trees, which gave it the aspect of a village in the Pyrenees.

It soon became evident, by the lie of the hills, that we were approaching the sea. Some seven or eight miles before reaching Cherchel, we saw on our left a fine, a very fine fragment of a Roman aqueduct, which, no doubt, had been used in those old days of much fighting and pure water, for the supply of Julia Cæsarea, otherwise Cherchel. Ah ! there is the sea at last, and all along the road a row of tall aloes about to bloom, just like candelabra. It looked as though you could have lighted them, had you held a match to the wick. We never saw them in such quantity, at this point of growth, elsewhere. But what a gay, bright little place Cherchel is, with its white houses, and the old Roman remains, and the little harbour, and those big mountains at the back !

To the Hôtel du Commerce we got at last, but just too late. That French *commis-voyageur*-looking man who had started after us from Marengo, but who had passed us deftly at Zurich, knew what he was about. He had engaged the last vacant apartment, but the people would get us a comfortable sleeping-room just round the corner, and we could take our meals at the hotel. This we did whilst we remained at Cherchel, and we are ready to endorse the praises given in the guide-books to this excellent hotel.

People who rather dislike the brick-making business of "society," might spend a very pleasant month or two of winter in this place. I can fancy that, with a good supply of books to fill up odd moments, time would fly only too quickly in this bright little hotel, and you might undertake the chase of Roman remains and inscriptions with some little chance of success, as you would not be bound to struggle with a few half-effaced letters when your poor back was broken, your eye-sight gone, and your temples throbbing. The shooting is said to be very good in the neighbourhood.

Half a dozen sentences as to the place in which we find ourselves. I annex my information from M. Piesse, the author of the French guide-book, and in his work any one curious in such matters will find more ample details. Cherchel was originally, writes this gentleman, the Phœnician colony of *Jol*. Later on, King Juba II. enlarged it, and it became Cæsarea, the capital of Cæsarean Mauritania. His son was murdered, and his kingdom was annexed (just as I am annexing M. Piesse's story of those old days) to the Roman Empire. The fair town was ruined by Firmus; Theodosius put it to rights again. The Vandals destroyed it afresh; and, after them, the Byzantine people restored it again to somewhat of its former splendour. About A.D. 1300, the Arabs appear upon the scene, and subdued Cherchel and other places hereabouts. At the end of the fifteenth century, the Andalusians, driven from Spain, found refuge here, and, as a penultimate incident in this eventful history, Kheir-ed-Din, the Algerine corsair, took the place in A.D. 1520. The Genoese Doria, here burnt a good portion of the Algerine fleet, but was soon afterwards defeated and driven away. For three centuries Cherchel fell asleep, and when it awoke from its long slumber in 1839, it committed an act of pure idiotcy. A French merchant-ship was becalmed off the port, whereupon the Cherchelites, thinking that now was their chance for taking time by the forelock, seized the ship, and rifled her of her cargo. The French answer to this little act of provocation was not long in coming. On the 15th March, 1840, one Lieutenant-Colonel Cavaignac took the town; and French it has remained ever since, to the manifest advantage of all persons concerned. Such is M. Piesse's tale, and as he has devoted much time and labour to Algerine history and legend, it is probably correct. From the days of *Jol* and the Phœnicians, to those of the Hôtel du Commerce and its obliging landlady, you have the annals of Cherchel.

Now for our own humble proceedings. As we had reached Cherchel betimes in the afternoon, we had only to turn dinner into supper, and we had the best hours of the day before us, for the evening promised to be lovely, and kept its promise. Under the guidance of the local *cicerone*, we set out to explore the place. Our guide led us first to what had been the Grand Mosque—actually a French military hospital. In the old days it was a Roman temple. We peeped in at two large dormitories —cool, dark, and fresh—supported by a great number of ancient pillars from the Roman days, and which, as M. Piesse reminds me (for I had forgotten the fact), were of green granite. I had a good deal of chat with the poor French invalids, who were all cheerful enough, but with sad longings to get back to France. I could only hope that we might all recover our health; at any rate, moaning and long faces won't mend matters.

From the hospital we went to what they called the museum, which really looked like a stonemason's yard behind a grating. An aged man, who was the *custode*, after a time let us in. I inquired if he had any *antiquités* there? "*Monsieur, me voici!*" replied the old gentleman solemnly, raising his cap. He appeared to labour under the idea that we had come from Europe to see his photograph. He had been taken between two masks, the tragic and comic respectively, and seemed to think it incumbent on him to look at times stern and solemn, at others gay and cheerful. Just for a moment the nonsense was amusing enough, but one soon got tired of this French version of Mrs. Siddons between tragedy and comedy. On looking round the place, we saw half a dozen relics, very much like the figure-heads of ships. There was a Venus Anadyomene, who had lost her head; there was a mutilated dancing fawn, with pointed ears, but it had lost its hands; there was a boy without a head, taking a thorn out of his foot; there were a good many Roman busts, without noses; there were several draped Roman female figures, one, possibly, Diana. But lying about on the pavement, there were some really fine fragments of cornices. There were a good many masks, and such like things, probably found amidst the ruins of the theatre. All these remains of the Roman days are now lying about pell-mell in an open court, with three sheds around it. Such was the museum of Cherchel, and such an idea of its contents.

We strolled away down to the port, and peeped over the wall to see the Roman cisterns, but I am bound to say the most striking and picturesque object was a long modern French trough, at which an Arab horseman was giving his horse to drink.

Then we went to some Roman caves, which were, I suppose, store-houses in the old days, when business was brisk at Cherchel. But the relic of antiquity which pleased us most of all was a huge Roman bath, so perfect that it only wants water, and it might be used by bathers in our own time. My classical friends must get rid of all notions of Caracalla-Baths, and sudoria, and strigils, and all that sort of thing. Our place was a Roman "peerless pool," a place for "headers" and a cold bath. It was a very large oblong, with steps at two of the angles, down which timid bathers might descend gradually into the water, and a resting-place or oasis in the middle, to which they might swim, and rest. The water must have been supplied from yonder cleft. There was a great deal of Roman masonry about, plenty of wall, and, at one spot, an oval, with openings, in which the grass was growing. Our guide said this was a Roman farm, and the openings were windows;—this is what he said. I think, however, I can scarcely be mistaken when I write that we saw many foundations and walls of houses.

The Place d'Armes, however, is the spot from which to see bright little Cherchel, and to reconstitute in your mind the glories of its past history. Here probably was the forum. The guide tells you that up aloft yonder (just under the French *caserne*) was the theatre—the learned people had told him so. The amphitheatre was without the walls, but might have been seen from where we are sitting upon the shaft of an old Roman pillar. Capitals and bases are lying about, and great fragments of cornice. The guide said these were now freely used as materials for the Roman Catholic church which the French were building up there; more's the pity. Here again was one of those African sights which will scarcely fade from one's memory. The sun was going down behind Cape Tenez as we lingered on in the Forum of Cæsarea, with the port—there was but one ship in it from Algiers, a *balancelle*—at our feet, and manifest indications of the past around us on every side. At any rate, the sea, the sky, the sun, the mountains, were unchanged. You must be devoid of imagination indeed if you could not build up the old Roman town with such helps at hand. I feel a great desire to say something appropriate, after the fashion of "Childe Harold," but nothing occurs to me in particular, save a story which I have heard of a famous, of a very famous Englishman, still living. "I feel," said the immortal—"I feel that I could write quite as well as Shakespeare, but I have nothing to say." I think we may as well get back to supper.

I cannot but repeat that visitors coming to Algeria for the winter would do well to consider if it might not be pleasant to stop a month or so at Cherchel instead of passing all the long months on that weary Mustapha, with its endless card-leavings and social obligations. Capital quarters are to be found at the hotel, and plenty of inscriptions and Roman fragments about with which you can dignify your idleness, and confound all your ill-wishers by announcing the proximate publication of your great work upon the archæology of Algeria, with an especial unravelling of certain tangled knots connected with Julia Cæsarea. We were told of splendid ruins in the neighbourhood, but could not afford time for lingering here, for at Tlemçen we were resolved to spend some time before leaving Africa. Now, Tlemçen was a good way off, and we had much to get through before reaching that harbour of refuge.

So we went back by our flowery road to Marengo on another day, with the tall candelabra-like aloes to glorify our path, and the cistuses, and the mallows which Mr. Waterer would have admitted amongst his azaleas, and large white flowers with six petals and black centres, to which I cannot put a name. We drove through fields of wheat, oats, and barley, plentiful, and refreshing to the eye, amidst this great splendour of the air.

At Marengo we arrived at noon, and we were to give up the afternoon to a visit to the famous Tombeau de la Chrétienne. Our hearts sank within us as we looked at the dirty room in which we were destined to pass the night. The only clean things there were the sheets upon the beds. The food below was good enough. When you have said this you have said all you can in favour of the hotel. It is a dirty hole, and if the landlord would attract European tourists to his house, he must mend his ways. It has all the inconveniences and disagreeables of a small French provincial inn.

In the afternoon we got away to the Tombeau. It was about an hour's drive to the little house at the bottom of the hill on which the monument stands. An excited Frenchman rushed out of the house to tell us we could go no further in the carriage, for a bridge on the path had broken down. What was to be done? Even if an animal could have been procured, I had not, since I was stricken down by illness, attempted to cross the back of any quadruped, and had great doubts as to my powers. The excited Frenchman was of cheerful aspect, as my soul loves that a man should be, so we enlisted him at once—his name was Antoine. It appeared on inquiry that the carriage could take us up a certain distance, and Ali, who never troubled his head about contingencies, was equal to the occasion. So up we went, and reached the point beyond which we could get no further upon wheels. "Why, zounds, it seems as though a fellow could chuck a biscuit up yonder to the Tombeau," said I, affecting a nautical demeanour, and greater confidence than I felt. "I'll get there, if I have to crawl for it. *Allons, M. Antoine. Hardi!*"

So up we went at a funeral sort of pace, when it became clear to me that the Tombeau was a good deal further off than I had thought, and that the spirit might be very willing, but the flesh was uncommonly weak. We had made about a third of the distance from the carriage to the big round tower. So I called a halt, for I could really go no further, and consulted M. Antoine as to the policy of yelling for any stray Arabs who might be in the neighbourhood, for they could join hands, as we used to do at school some time ago, and carry an invalid up. Antoine yelled; somebody yelled in reply. The yells continued, and at last got more confidential, and an Arab appeared. He and Antoine considered themselves, and together arrived at the conclusion that *Le Bourricot* offered a way out of the difficulty. The *bourricot* is a small donkey, but I had got far beyond the point at which a man cares for the look of things. To the Tombeau I must get somehow.

The Arab brought up the small creature, which, small as it was, proved strong enough to carry me up to the Tombeau, and I believe he could have carried up another as well. The Arab proposed to sit on the creature's stern, and, putting me in front, to hold me so in position, but I would not hear of it; the *bourricot* looked so small. So we compromised matters. The Arab walked on one side, putting his arm round me; M. Antoine on the other, and I took his arm in a friendly way, and so we accomplished the ascent, which really, to a person having the use of his legs, is not worth talking about. It was to me, however, a proud moment when I reached the top, as this was my first equestrian performance.

"The Tombeau is of circular form. It stands upon a hill 756 feet above the sea." (I take the figures from Colonel Playfair's "Guide.") "The actual height of the building is 100 feet 8 inches, of which the cylindrical portion is 36 feet 6 inches, the pyramid 64 feet 2 inches. The base is 198 feet in diameter, presenting an encircling wall, vertical, and ornamented with sixty engaged Ionic columns surmounted by a frieze, or cornice. The colonnade has four false doors at the cardinal points. Above the cornice rise, in series, thirty-three steps, which gradually decrease in circular area, giving the building the appearance of a truncated cone." I doubt not the measurements have been carefully taken.

Down below is a sort of lake, or swamp, which they call the Lake Alloula. We saw not much water in it, but plenty of reeds, etc. It looked a very paradise for waterfowl. At the top of the hill we found an old man sitting at the door of a little hut, or cottage, and he was the guide who was to conduct us through the interior of the Tombeau. He was a queer old fellow of the class of people who live in lighthouses, and who do not disquiet themselves about second editions and the news of the day. He passed his nights in the village down below, but every morning with early light he got upon his *bourricot*, and ascended to the Tombeau, where he spent his days. One should have thought this daily pilgrimage would have been a kind of relief to the old gentleman, but this was not his view. The one thought of his life was to induce the authorities to build him a cottage up at the top of the hill, under the shadow of his dear Tombeau, where he might pass his days without disquieting himself about men and women, and their frivolous concerns. He had good hopes that the financial part of the scheme had been already arranged, and that in a short time the hovel in which he kept the visitors' guide-book would be enlarged into a desirable residence, in which he might wear out the remainder of his days.

Let us, however, before passing into the interior, listen to what is told us about this strange monument. M. Piesse gives the story in a very few words, which have the merit of brevity and, I hope, of truth. Some ill-informed persons used to maintain that the tomb was the place where La Cava, daughter of Count Julian, so famous in history, had found her last resting-place. Learned people nowadays regard this theory with the full scorn of which archæologists and antiquarians are capable. The sound belief is that it was the burying-place of the old Mauritanian kings. I am tempted to cite Pomponius Mela as a witness, for it looks well, and gives a kind of classical or learned smack to this poor account of the Tombeau; but, to speak the truth, it is M. Piesse who calls Pomponius Mela into court.

It would seem that a gentleman named Dr. Judas, by the help of medals, has found out the true meaning of Kbour-er-Roumia, the name by which the monument is known. He got hold of some medals on one side of which you read "Rex Juba" in good sound Latin; on the other, in Punic (a much more ticklish language), there stood "Juba Roum Melcal," which he interpreted as "Juba, Hauteur du Royaume." I suppose this would amount to Juba *crème de la crème*, or something of that kind. Dr. Judas concludes that "Kbour-Roumim," would mean "Tomb of the Kings," or of the "Upper Ten Thousand." Then, observe, a parcel of ignorant Arabs, who did not know as much Punic as every school-boy should know, substituted the Arabian termination *ia* for the Punic termination *im*, and so arrived at the phrase "Kbour-er-Roumia, or, Tomb of the Christian Woman." This let in La Cava. Cleopatra Selene, daughter of Cleopatra and Marc Antony, and wife of Juba II., would now seem to have the preference. I love this account of the matter, and the way the terminations are dealt with. It may not be forgotten that when we were in the neighbourhood of Batna we got a distant peep at a monument called the Medrassen, very like the one before us. The people down there would have it that the Medrassen was the tomb of Syphax; the one now before us is said to be the tomb of Juba and his consort. I suppose both one and the other were tombs of the Mauritanian kings, and that is all we need care for.

But now let us follow the old gentleman who leads us in a solemn sort of way to a hole at the base of the building, which looked like a fox's earth. Here he told us a long story about Marshal McMahon and Mme. la Maréchale; they had something to do with the making of this hole. Just as I was afraid he would desire us to fall upon our stomachs and wriggle our way in, like so many caterpillars, he told us to follow him round to the other side of the building, where was the true entrance.

At this side the entrance was easy enough, and we found ourselves in a dark, narrow gallery. If I remember right, we were obliged to stoop as we passed along. The guide lit a bundle of dried reeds, and, carrying with him others as a supply, he led us round the place in a triumphant sort of way.

It required a good deal of looking back at Juba and his moon-faced consort, a good deal of thought about the Numidians and Mauritanians, to make one feel the progress as other than tiresome, especially as the guide kept flicking his burning reeds against the wall, and the sparks would fly off into one's face, and the smoke was very unpleasant and made the eyes smart. Still, we were accomplishing a great historic feat, and were, I suppose, enjoying ourselves as much as tourists usually do in a pyramid. Then we came to a room of tolerable size, and then, by creeping down a small passage and through a hole in the wall, into another and somewhat smaller room, which was the holy of holies. Here, presumably, the royal pair slept their last long sleep.

The whole Tombeau may be considered as one vast trick to throw investigators who would reach this room off the true scent. There are false doors and false passages; but at length, in 1866—so the old guide told us—by means of an artesian sound modern science triumphed over ancient humbug; the true door and the true passage were found, and it turned out that there was no secret, only an empty room, nor, as far as I can make out, had anything ever been found there. Of course, the Arabs for centuries have been persuaded that vast treasures were buried in this place, and this belief gave rise to the following legend, which I have as good a right to use as anybody else, seeing that it is given in both guide-books, French and English, and I think I have found it in every work of travel through Algeria.

The story about the Queen of the Mosquitoes, and that other one of the Marabout with two tombs near the Jardin d'Essai, are the common property of authors We all try them in a condescending sort of way upon new-comers, just as though we were full of anecdotes of the like kind. But now for the story of the Queen of the Mosquitoes. I will fall back for details on my friend M. Piesse, as he cuts the story down well. Observe, no dates, no names of places are given, so that you could look out the facts, save this, that some old chronicler, not named, lays it down that Salah Rais, who reigned somewhere, and between the years 960–963 of the Hegira, was the Sultan who gave way to temptation. Beyond this all is vague.

Here is the story. An Arab who lived on the Metidja, Ben-Kassem by name, was one day made prisoner by the Christians, and carried to Spain, where he was very miserable, as he was a family man. He was sold as slave to an old *savant*, who said to him one day, "Ben-Kassem, I can restore you to your country and your people, and this I will do if you will swear to do what I ask of you; and this shall not mean anything contrary to your religion." Who so pleased as Ben-Kassem, when he felt that his soul ran no danger? "You shall embark presently," said the *savant*, "for happy Algiers. When you get there I allow you three days for domestic enjoyment; these over, mount to the Tombeau with a small furnace. When you have set the fire a-going, turn yourself to the east, and throw into the fire the paper which I now hand to you. I ask for nothing more. Don't be astonished at what you see, but return in peace to your tent."

Ben-Kassem did all this faithfully as directed, but he *was* astonished when he saw the wall of the Tombeau open, and a stream of gold and silver pieces flow out, but up in the air, towards the sea in the direction of Spain. His surprise, however, gave way to other feelings, and being sorry to see so much specie go out of the country, he chucked up his *bernouse*, and brought down some of the coin. The stream ceased to flow, the wall of the Tombeau closed up again, and Ben-Kassem was left standing there with his mouth open.

The Pacha came to hear of the matter, and being as impecunious as Pachas always have been, he thought that here was a chance of filling up his treasury. So his Highness organized a large body of workmen, and desired them to hammer and knock away at the Tombeau without stint. No sooner had they struck the first blow than an awful female figure—probably the Christian woman—appeared at the top of the Tombeau. She seemed to throw up her arms, but she certainly cried out, "Halloula! halloula!" "Help! help!" The words of power were spoken, and myriads of mosquitoes swarmed up from the lake below, and soon drove the workmen away; and as my author naïvely remarks, "they did not think it prudent to resume the work."

From this legend we may derive the great lesson that no one should tamper with the terminations of nouns substantive, for, in point of fact, the Christian woman is a mere myth—the child, as one may say, of that unlucky alteration of the word "Roumim" into the word "Roumia." Other people seem to have battered away at the tomb, but with no better success.

We were very glad to find ourselves again in the open air. Whatever doubt there may be as to the history of the Tombeau, there could be none as to the magnificence of the view from the top of the hill, as we watched the going down of the sun. The light without fairly beat the darkness within. But let us lose no time, or we too may be caught on the hill-side. This, however, we avoided by the help of the poor little *bourricot* and the Arab and M. Antoine, but right glad I was when they helped me into the carriage, and reconsigned me to the charge of Ali. We got back without trouble of any kind to Marengo, to a tolerable dinner and a dirty bedroom. Next morning we were to drive to Hammam R'Irha, where we were to discharge the carriage, for the rail would then take us on to Affreville, for Milianah and Teniet, and so would conclude our home circuit. In place of returning to Algiers we were to go on to Oran, for why should we do the 120 kilomètres between Algiers and Affreville twice over? Our next point was to be the Baths, or rather the Hammam R'Irha. We had heard much of this place during our stay at Algiers. The station for the Baths is Bou-Medfa, ninety kilomètres from Algiers, so that it is easily accessible. We were at Marengo, and as it is but a short drive, and through a very beautiful country from point to point, we resolved to proceed with the carriage, and discharge it at the Baths, taking the rail on to Affreville for Milianah, etc., when our curiosity was gratified.

The drive through a mountain pass was very splendid, and certainly, as far as scenery is concerned, the valley in which stands the bath-house shut in by the great Zakkar Mountain, is as fine as such a scene can be. We found, then, a large white building high up on one side of a valley, with a river flowing far below, plenty of mountains about, and the great mountain at the end. As you drive up you lose and gain sight of the buildings from time to time, for, as it turned out, there were more than one. On arrival we were shown upstairs to a small but neat room, with two very clean and well-appointed beds. There was a gallery running round the house outside on the story on which we were lodged, and the view was beautiful on all sides; behind us there was the slope of a hill carpeted with brilliant wild flowers.

The place, which was in the far past a Roman bath, after the French occupation was turned into a military hospital. In the year 1878, M. Alphonse Arles Dufour, the manager of the Crédit Lyonnais Branch at Algiers, a gentleman whose courtesy to strangers is proverbial, took the matter in hand, and built the hotel for the use of civilians who wished to make trial of the waters. The charges for bed and board are of the most moderate description. There is a large dining-room down below, where in due course was served a very sufficient and substantial dinner. There is a large gallery covered in with glass, where strangers and invalids can take their exercise in all weathers, a reading-room, etc. The fault of the place is that there are not bedrooms enough, and they are too small for persons who wish to make any stay, and who require the use of the bedroom by day for privacy and repose. We were told at the Baths that M. Dufour is under some sort of contract with the Government, under which he will shortly be bound either much to enlarge the existing hotel or to build another. If this were done, I should hope that his enterprise would be a source of profit to himself, as well as of health and pleasure to all visitors.

Certainly nothing more picturesque than the situation of Hammam R'Irha can be easily conceived. Leaving apart all question of the curative virtues of the waters,— as a mere place of refuge from the heat of Algiers and the monotony of Mustapha, as a mere station for *villégiature*,

Hammam R'Irha should be a success. If you go there, don't look for what you would find at Hamburg, or Baden, or Vichy, for the great hotels of those places are not to be found in the African health valley; but you will meet with a clean bed, very fair food, fresh air, and a beautiful country. As to the effect of the waters when used as a beverage or for bathing, my opinion would be worthless—and, in truth, I have no opinion at all about the matter—but at Algiers I heard them highly commended, and spoke with persons who professed to have derived great benefit from them. The patients I speak of had been suffering from rheumatism and gout.

I should be inclined to believe that the story of Hammam R'Irha is pretty much that of all bath places in Europe. There may be specific advantages in the waters, for persons suffering from specific disease. For the bulk of visitors who just require to be toned up, to have a total change of diet and occupation, the natural life of the Baths and the delicious mountain air they would inhale at every breath, would soon put them to rights, and restore them with renewed vigour to the gaieties of Mustapha.

When you are "bored" on Mustapha—and I have known instances of this kind—try a week on the hill-side at Hammam R'Irha; it only requires between four and five hours to get there by a very comfortable train; but you will do well to engage rooms beforehand. It would do no harm if you were to speak with M. Arles Dufour, if you have any degree of acquaintance with that gentleman. At any rate, go and try a week in the pine-woods of Hammam R'Irha in the spring-time before leaving Algiers, and you will have seen a very pretty place.

We were "onward" bound, so we could not stay as long as we had wished. We had to take a long farewell of poor Ali, and send him back to Blidah. We can only trust that he was as well contented with us as we were with him. A carriage from the hotel took us down to the station at Bou-Medfa. We left the hotel at 3.30 p.m., took train to Affreville, and reached Milianah at 7.30 p.m. It is considerably more than an hour's drive by omnibus from Affreville to Milianah, uphill all the way; but it is a very beautiful drive through gardens and fruit trees. At Milianah we found a very excellent hotel, the Hôtel du Commerce, comfort, and civility. Had it not been that the obliging host and hostess were essentially family people, and that their young folks were very noisy, I should have nothing but unqualified praise for their hotel, and in any case I recommend travellers to go there.

Milianah is a fresh, pleasant little French town, with very fine views from the ramparts, or walls, which go round the town. As a connection with its past history, a queer old clock tower has been left in the Place, which was formerly an Arab or Moorish minaret. There are plenty of trees and plenty of water about, and the whole feeling of the place is of rest and refreshment. We were so tired of being knocked about, that we tarried here a day or two, because the place was bright and comfortable—merely for rest. In itself, however, Milianah deserves a visit, for the views over the plain are magnificent, and our old friend the Zakkar, which we had seen from Hammam R'Irha, towers above the town.

How different what we saw from what poor Lieutenant de France describes at the close of his horrible captivity when the then Bey of Milianah inflicted upon him and his unfortunate companions so much torture and suffering! I really have nothing much more to say about the place than that we loitered about and enjoyed ourselves. One may almost give a twist to the old phrase and say, "Happy the tourist who finds no entries for his journal!" We were not in the midst of a storm; we were not climbing up steep hills; we were not perished with thirst, nor in terror of wild Arabs; we might have been at Lowestoft or Cromer but for the blue sky above. These were not our worst days. Had we foreseen what was about to happen to us on the top of the Teniet Mountain, a day or two afterwards, we should not have been lounging about in such an unconcerned way.

To Teniet we wanted to go, and asked what the price would be of a carriage there and back, to stop one day at Teniet. I forget the precise sum asked, but I clearly remember that we thought it excessive. We sallied out to the diligence office to see if we could secure a *coupé* on our old system. This we did. The price of the *coupé* was eight francs a place—or twenty-four francs for the whole *coupé*—sixteen francs return; for there were only two places in the *coupé*, it being a smaller vehicle. The seats were open to the air; and, to make a long story short, we got to Teniet and back very comfortably in the way described, which had this further advantage, that we could stop at Teniet as long as we pleased without having to pay thirty-five francs a day, or something of that kind, for carriage hire.

You go down to Affreville by the way you had come, and if you talk to any of the inhabitants you will find Affreville in a jubilant condition. The people are fully persuaded that the future belongs to them, and that that one-horse, worn-out old *bicoque*, Milianah, at the top of the hill, will shortly collapse save as a military station. We tourists have our little interests apart, and I strongly recommend my friends not to listen to the songs of the sirens at the bottom of the hill, but to go up in an omnibus, or as they may please, to Milianah, where they will find solid comfort—that is, good food, and bed in fresh air—some 2500 feet above the sea level. Why stop sweltering in the plain at a fourth-rate, new French inn, when you can get up to the higher ground?

From Affreville onwards I do not remember anything particular about the scenery; it was first on the level with plenty of cultivation and plenty of African scrub, but the last half of the journey was decidedly fine, very much on the ascent, as Teniet is some 4000 feet above the sea. I can call to mind some fine parcels of oak and pine woods, and striking views of distant mountains; but our motto was ever "Excelsior!" It got at last to be a Swiss climb, and the temperature had fallen so considerably that, when we reached Teniet, our first thought was for warmth and a good fire.

We asked for the Hôtel du Commerce; it was over the way from the diligence office. The good lady of the house made us very comfortable during our stay, though it was a queer little place, and very unlike European hotels, but we have stopped at far worse in Switzerland in the old days. The first thing was to get a good fire;

the next to inquire about the Cedar Forest, and how to get there. Alas! alas! the only carriage in the place had been sent to Tiaret, and was not expected back for a couple of days. That ingenious plan of the *cacolet*, which is so highly recommended in the English guide-book, was not to be thought of. A *ukase* had been sent forth by the military authorities, forbidding the practice.

Our hostess intervened, and suggested a third course. There was a young Frenchman in the village, whose father kept a *café* (he was the owner of the absent carriage), and he could provide us with three horses and serve us as a guide. Proud of my recent feats with the *bourricot* at the Tombeau, I thought I could manage to sit upon a quiet horse; so we went at a foot pace, and I had some one alongside of me to give me a hand. I saw the young Frenchman; he had that very day taken a party of English ladies and gentlemen up to the Rond Point, and had delivered them safely back at the inn, though later in the night than we cared to stay out. It was agreed that he should be forthcoming with his horses at 8 a.m., so that we might have a long day and twelve hours of light before us. So well pleased we went to bed, and at 8 a.m. next day were ready in front of the inn. No horses. Time passed on; it came to be 9 a.m., 10 a.m. No horses, no guide. Embassies to the *café* only brought us tidings that the young gentleman was at breakfast, that he had taken one of the horses to be shod, and so on. At length, about 11 a.m., the guide made his appearance with two horses: one an immense black creature, with a blood-shot eye, evidently out of temper,—this was for me; the other had no saddle at all, only a cloth thrown over its back, a thin, feeble old grey creature, with broken knees,—this was for the lady.

At this moment an English gentleman came out of the hotel, and said, "Madam, it is my solemn duty to warn you against those horses. I myself rode the grey yesterday; he was down every tenth step, and that I am alive to tell the tale is a miracle. Another of our party rode that large black horse; he is a bolter."

Pleasant all this! It was now 11 a.m.; three of the best hours of the day were gone, and here was a result. To use these horses was out of the question. I doubt if any human ingenuity could have hoisted me on to the top of the black creature; the animal, no doubt, would have managed the getting me off in a much more summary way. In sheer desperation I determined to make my way up to the citadel, and the *commandant supérieur*, in hopes that the sight of my stick and hobbling gait would soften his heart. By this gentleman we were received in the most courteous manner, and I explained how I had only come to him in last resort, for I did not wish to put him to the pain of refusing help to a stranger when this might be imperative on him by military obligation. Nothing could exceed his kindness: but a *cacolet* was out of the question; he would communicate with the Bureau Arabe, and get us a couple of quiet mules, "with a saddle for you, sir," he added with a smile, "out of which I think you would find it difficult to fall. Our own horses are too gay."

We went back, and about noon two very fine mules, conducted by two *spahis*, made their appearance at the door of the hotel. The saddle intended for me had a back board and front board so high that it would not have been easy to fall off; my wife's mule had an excellent English lady's saddle, which had been lent for the occasion by the courteous commandant. I think his idea was that a *spahi* was to sit behind me and keep me in the saddle, but when I had once got hoisted into this place of security, it seemed to be so impossible to fall off that I declined the offer, and we set off with an Arab to guide us, the ordinary guide of the hotel.

Oh that Arab! It was now about midday, and we calculated on being back at 6 p.m., and indulged in a few bad jokes with the landlady as to the dinner she was to provide for the hungry travellers. The sky was cloudless, the day lovely, all things promised fair; and yet we were on the threshold of the second of the two adventures which fell to our lot in Algeria, and without which our little expedition would have been as commonplace as a journey from London to Brighton in the old coaching days. The guide took a short cut across the hill-side, leading my mule, which seemed to shamble along easily enough. But no sooner were we well clear of the village, and committed to the enterprise, than the Arab began to review the bargain concluded with him at the hotel, which was to the effect that he should conduct us to the Rond Point and back, and guide us to the tall cedars, in return for the price fixed. "Wouldn't it be better to stop short of the Rond Point? That was quite a delusion." Of course, we were inexorable on this point, but we told the man that if he did his work well, and took care of us, we were quite willing to give him a good *buona-mano*. So on we went, and gained the regular path, which was a very good one, and so continued even to the Rond Point. A carriage might have travelled along it with perfect comfort to the occupants. I dare say it has been repaired and looked to since the days when it had but a poor reputation.

The further off we got, the more careless grew the guide, strolling on in front, and taking aim with my stick at imaginary partridges. His store of French seemed reduced to the words "*Ben*" (for bien) "*oui.*" This was the stock answer to every question, so we gave up all attempts at conversation.

The higher we mounted, the more glorious became the views of the mountains far and near. The day was brilliant and cloudless, but, although it was little more than midday, the air was exceedingly fresh. The village of Teniet is pretty well 4000 feet above the sea, and we were ascending a good 1000 feet higher. Soon we came to the region of cedars—cedars above and below—cedars around us everywhere. I am bound to speak the truth, so I say that, as far as the trees were concerned, we felt something of disappointment. The magnificence of the views could not be exaggerated, especially at one point, where we got a view over the desert; but the trees did not come up to our expectations. They did not offer that canopy of dark foliage which we had been accustomed to see at Zion House, or in villas in the neighbourhood of Clapham. We had expected too much. I wish we had had with us some one learned in trees—even a tree bore. Surely this could not be the cedar of Lebanon! Colonel Playfair calls it *Cedrus Atlantica.* At any rate, the trees were wild and fantastic enough, and the numbers of them made up for the shortcomings of individuals. I read afterwards in the guide-book:—"There are 9000 acres of forest in this part of the range alone, of which about four-fifths are cedars, and the rest oak of different species—evergreen and deciduous. . . . The largest of the existing trees, 'La Sultane,' is nearly a hundred feet high, with a diameter of nine feet; another, 'Le Sultan,' now fallen, was even larger." To see this big tree, you have to get off at a spot before reaching the Rond Point. This we refused to do, preferring to scramble up on our return.

We wanted faith in the Arab; if he had once got us off our mules, I doubt if we should even have seen the Rond Point that day. But we reached it at last, despite of his grumbling; and a lovely place the little *châlet* is, surrounded on all sides by great cedars. A rest, however, was indispensable. It was now 3 p.m., the day was still lovely, and we thought we had all our time before us. So we were to take an hour for rest, and to see the cedars, and surely a couple of hours would take us home down-hill. It is called thirteen kilomètres from Teniet to the *châlet*—I suppose a little more than eight English miles.

Well, we had our rest, and a chat with two very gentlemanlike young French officers, who had come there for their afternoon's ride; we saw all the cedars we wanted to see, and about 4 p.m., as determined, we set fairly off on our way homewards. The Arab was as careless and useless as he could well be, but the mules, most luckily for us, were quiet, careful animals, who stepped out at a great rate—though at a walk, of course—as soon as they got their noses turned towards their stable. We were on a path cut in the mountain's side, just wide enough, and no more, for a carriage to pass. It was a very abrupt descent to the left, an equally abrupt ascent to the right, and had the mules bolted over the edge to the left, I do not think any of us, mules or riders, would ever have seen Teniet again.

We had got some way on our homeward path, the sky was still blue, everything calm and quiet, when we heard a low rumble to the westward, like distant thunder. We did not think much of it, even although there came another peal, and another. There was soon a silence which might be felt. The sky—so blue a moment ago—became mere darkness. The forked lightning played about in every direction; the thunder pealed as I suppose artillery does in a general engagement; we could smell, as it were, sulphur. It was all the work of a few moments, just like a change of scene upon the stage, and presently the hail came pelting down upon us in a way to cause pain. I thought at the time of Moses, and how he stretched forth his rod, and "*The Lord sent thunder and hail, and the fire ran along upon the ground.*" This is just what it did. The simple fact was that we were in the heart of an African storm, or tourmente, and a very terrible thing it is. Engaged as we were amongst the trees, the lightning, which was playing round us on all sides, might strike us; or the mules, maddened with the pitiless pelting of the hail, might get frightened, and bolt over the edge of the path.

In front there was a little more open space. It seemed a prudent thing to call a halt there, and turn the mules with their backs to the drifting hail. We yelled to the Arab to catch hold of the lady's mule. He made a grab at it, but missed his footing, and fell at his full length across the path. The lady tried to put up an umbrella, to interpose between her back and the storm, but of course it was blown away in a moment, leaving her with the stick in her hand. This she threw away, and from that moment all the efforts of our besmirched Arab were devoted, not to our security, but to the recovery of the umbrella-stick. I really could not tell how long, by the watch, we remained in this uncomfortable position—it seemed an age, but might have been half an hour. The hailstones, I know not how, got into one's shoes, and the feet became like lumps of ice. The wind was bitterly cold. A pleasant situation for two people, who only wanted to see Algeria in a humdrum way, and who believed only in commonplaces!

At length the stress of the storm was past, and we pushed on. The sky above us was blue again, as though ignorant of storms, but the air was biting shrewdly: "it was very cold." We both agreed that we had never suffered so much from cold in our lives as during the ride back to Teniet, which place we reached at 7 p.m. I was so numbed and helpless that the *spahi* had to lift me out of the saddle by sheer force, and right thankful we were to find ourselves again in front of a blazing fire, with every prospect of dinner before us. My summing up of the advantages of a trip to the Cedar Forest would be, that, if you are an invalid, or in any way not fit for bodily exertion, do not attempt it, save in a carriage. The road is fair enough. The young and strong can do as they like; let them go and see the Rond Point and La Sultane by all means. I do not think it would be unwise to write beforehand to the landlady of the Hôtel du Commerce, and ascertain if you could have the carriage on a day named, and to wait for the answer at Milianah. Taken in this way, the expedition would be a mere joke. We were peculiarly unlucky, but I do not see how we had any right to anticipate the storm, or tourmente. The sky was very blue, the day seemed very fine, and the people at Teniet, who ought to have known all about their confounded climate, did not anticipate any change in the weather.

I wrote à letter of thanks to Monsieur le Commandant Supérieur at Teniet, to whom we felt greatly indebted for his courtesy. Next day we got back to Milianah, in the *coupé* of the diligence. The day after that we took the rail from Affreville to Oran. Had we returned by it to Algiers, we should have completed the home circuit.

CHAPTER XV.

TO TLEMÇEN, THROUGH ORAN.

I HAVE now reached what in my poor opinion is the crown, the bouquet, the chief reward for a little run through Algeria. Algiers is a very curious place, especially for new-comers before they have travelled through the three provinces: the Kabylian Highlands (including the Djudjura and the Chabet Pass) are a glorious sight indeed; the city of Constantine, both from its old historic associations and from the romantic grandeur of its situation, stands unequalled amongst cities; Biskra, with its palms, will ever retain a favourite corner in my heart. A visit to any one of these places will well repay the trouble of a journey to Algeria; taken collectively, they are almost more than a tourist deserves. My own impression, however, is that Tlemçen is the crown of Algeria; it is one of the most beautiful places in the world. Nor is this an impression hastily conceived. We did not "scamp" the place, for we remained there more than ten days, and I am writing these lines quietly in England, more than three months since we left this lovely place, and so my impressions have had time to shake themselves into shape and proportion. Again, this my conclusion is confirmed by a concurrence of opinion with several gentlemen with whom I conversed at Algiers, who knew the provinces well, and who had travelled backwards and forwards about them for years; so that if I am wrong, I am wrong in good company. Historic association, natural beauty, magnificent remains of the past,—you find them all at Tlemçen. I remember the time when I used to give myself airs on the strength of having spent a few days at Granada and in the courts of the Alhambra. My present belief is that Granada, to use a trivial phrase, is not fit "to hold a candle" to Tlemçen, beautiful as it undoubtedly is.

This being the state of the facts, I will hurry over the railway journey from Milianah (or rather Affreville) to Oran, and the easy night journey in the *coupé* of the diligence from Oran to Tlemçen, so that we may get at once to Tlemçen. When I have recorded my impressions of that delightful place, my small task is done. If I can induce others to follow our example, and they, in their turn, say they have not been misled, I shall hold myself fully rewarded for the trouble it has cost me to jot down our impressions of travel in Algeria.

We left Milianah on the 13th of May at 9 a.m., and reached Oran at 7 p.m. This included the drive from Milianah to Affreville (the station), and I do not think we left Affreville till 10.30 a.m., so it was only eight hours and a half of railway after all, though the journey was undoubtedly hot, and rather wearisome. You traverse a wild country, with very fine views of the mountains on both sides, over the plain of the Chelif; you pass spots famous in the sanguinary traditions of the colony—at one point you are not very far distant from the tragic Dahra cave; you find vast fields in high cultivation, and other parts where cultivation has as yet little hold on the soil; you are in the midst of the *barrages* and other experiments for irrigating the parched ground. But any one who wishes for precise information on these points would do well to consult the guide-book as he rolls along comfortably in the train; any one who desires to arrive at a sufficient knowledge of them must make up his mind to spend weeks, or months, in the district. To deal in information of this kind is no part of my little plan. It was hot—it was terribly hot—and we longed, if not for the flesh-pots, certainly for the cool drinks of Oran, and could only give a languid attention to the various stations at which the train paused for a few minutes.

I am very pleased my lot is not cast at Orleansville, or Relizane, or St. Denis-le-Seg, and right glad were we when we reached Karguentah, the station for Oran, and found there waiting for us a carriage from the Hôtel de la Paix, to which we had been recommended, and finally got clear of the railway. It is from Algiers to Oran a distance of 420 kilomètres; by starting from Affreville we had reduced this to 300 kilomètres; but this was quite enough. We paid 67 francs for two places in the first class, and we had the carriage all to ourselves from Affreville to Oran.

The first glance at Oran, as we drove through to the hotel, showed us a place something like Algiers in the way it rises on a slope from the sea; but the ravine, which cuts the town in two, establishes a substantial difference in the aspect of the two places. It is a very important town, the chief of the province named from it. It contains some 50,000 or 60,000 inhabitants. It can readily be reached in twelve hours of sea-passage from Carthagena in Spain, but I do not think any mere tourist will care to linger in it any time.

We found the Hôtel de la Paix, in the Place Kléber, very comfortable, and the landlord and landlady most obliging and thoughtful for the comfort of their guests. There is a pleasant spot near the hotel, well shaded with trees, and with beautiful views over the bay and the town. Here the band plays.

I think what first catches the eye in Oran is the Fort Santa Cruz, high up in the air, with a chapel below it, with a statue of the Virgin, of Notre Dame. It should not be forgotten that very nearly for three centuries Oran was essentially Spanish, from 1509 to 1792. I have neither time nor space to give more than brief mention of the historic facts, and I will only say that the Moors, when driven from Spain, came here in large numbers, and repaid the Spaniards in the form of piracy for their expulsion from Spain. It was a "holy war by sea against the infidels," just as the Spaniards considered their warlike achievements a "holy war by land against the infidel." This point should not be lost sight of by any one writing the story of Algerine piracy. The Turks came in at last, and piracy became a horrid trade, just like the slave-trade of the European nations. Cardinal Ximenes seems to have been quite alive to the danger which threatened from Oran, and saw that the seizure of the place was a natural corollary to the expulsion of the Moors from Spain. In this enterprise he succeeded, and in order to carry out his philanthropic and religious views with good effect, he established in Oran the Inquisition as a crowning blessing. For about 250 years and more (with brief intervals of adverse fortune) the place remained in the hands of the Spaniards. In 1831 the French got hold of it, and one cannot but speculate in one's mind on what turn affairs might have taken in Abd-el-Kader's day, had not the Spaniards retired from Oran in 1792.

But enough of history. We only remained one entire day at Oran on the occasion of our first visit, arriving on the evening of the 13th of May, and leaving it for Tlemçen on the afternoon of the 15th. We devoted the 14th to driving about the town in every direction. The Great Mosque scarcely deserves a visit. I suppose there is no regular Arab quarter, but we certainly found on the heights, near the building where the ex-Prefect of Tlemçen was then under trial for peculation, a place where the natives were huddled together in great force. Drive about the town by all means. "Do the lions," such as they are—the Château Neuf, the Kasbah, and so on. I was not so much struck with what I saw, as with what I foresaw would be if the people are right in carrying on their building operations as they are doing. You might rather have imagined yourself to be in the United States of North America than in the disunited states of North Africa. There are two harbours, which contained plenty of shipping when we saw them.

All these sights we went through as a matter of

duty, but what we really enjoyed was our afternoon drive to Mersa-el-Kebir, the naval port of Oran; it is marked as at eight kilomètres distant from the town. We passed through a long tunnel, and drove round the edge of the bay, past a few villages, and so to Mersa-el-Kebir. It seems a magnificent anchorage, and, as I was told by an old Italian sailor with whom I fell into a gossip, it is protected from the fury of the winds absolutely on all sides save one, and partially on that. Some French ships of war were lying at anchor, one with the yellow flag hoisted. Even to a civilian it seems a beautiful spot; a seaman would, no doubt, have more to say about the matter.

To Oran we returned, very much pleased with our afternoon drive; and when I say that my wife expressed herself as satisfied with the shops where she made purchases to repair dilapidations, and repeat that the Hôtel de la Paix is very comfortable, I think I have said all I have to say about Oran. An ordinary tourist will scarcely care to stop there.

We had secured the *coupé* of the diligence for Tlemçen the next day, and we paid forty-five francs for the three places, so as to have the *coupé* to ourselves. As a fact we reached Tlemçen at 8 a.m. the next day, so it was an affair of sixteen hours; but we had done wisely, on account of the heat, to travel at night.

It was at first an ascent; then a drive over an arid and dusty road, fringed with aloes and prickly pear. In sight you have the great marsh, lake, or Sebkha of Oran, a great sheet of inland brackish, if not salt, water, of which the dimensions are given as twenty-four miles long, by five broad. It is a striking object. So we rolled on, and I think about 10 or 11 p.m. we reached a place called Aïn Temouchent.

What is this? Are we at the Opera? or is this China, and a Feast of Lanterns? Down the street of the village came a long procession, bearing lanterns on the top of poles, and singing most lustily. It was really very pretty, but best at a distance.

We fell asleep soon after in our respective corners, but in the middle of the night were roused up suddenly, by a jerk and a stop. A leader had fallen, and some way or another a wheeler had tumbled on the top of him. As the vehicle progressed somewhat over the fallen horses, it became necessary to take the other six out (it was a team of eight horses), and to back the diligence, so as to extricate the fallen animals. All the passengers turned out to assist; and certainly it was a comical sight to see them in every variety of nightcaps, and to hear them swearing and grumbling in a very forcible way. At length they succeeded; the horses were got upon their legs, the team was hitched to again, the diligence went on its way. We fell asleep, and only woke at a little village, from which we saw Tlemçen above us, or rather two Tlemçens. We found afterwards, on better knowledge, that one of these was the real Tlemçen, and the other Bou-Medin, where stands the Great Mosque.

Just roused from sleep as we were, we could not help being struck at once with the beauty of the situation. We had been ascending all night, and were now considerably more than 2000 feet above the sea. The ground then sloped down seawards; there were great mountains round us, and just above the town a range of cliff—I should say of abrupt hill, which reminded us forcibly of the Undercliff at the Isle of Wight. We were in Devonshire or Normandy;—nothing but trees and flowers around us as the diligence slowly ascended the hill; nor was this green fertility relative— an oasis in a desert—we were really in a country of orchards and green leaves, and fruits and flowers. But for the minarets of the Great Mosque at Tlemçen, at Bou-Medin, and at Agadir, we might have been amongst our own people; though even on the banks of the Wye—say, between Ross and Monmouth—is there anything as beautiful as this? There was only a stern range of mountains behind us, which would not permit us to forget that we were in Africa. Yonder were the hills which we had traversed last night in the darkness, and on the other side of them Oran and the sea. There is the great fertile plain which, but for one mountain range in the far distance, would reach right away to Nemours. Not far off in front we should cross the frontier into Morocco, with its wild men. In another direction you would pass into the desert; that is the way the caravans go. This Tlemçen is a kind of Damascus—pure savagery beyond it. I have never been at Damascus, but it must be beautiful indeed if it beats this place. We have heard a great deal of the roses at Damascus; all I can say is that, long before we passed into Tlemçen, it was nothing but roses—roses before and behind, roses on each side of the road, blush pink, scentless, yet fair to the eye.

We pass close under the Mosque of Bou-Medin; a

little further on we skirt an Arab burying-ground. We enter the gate of the town, and drive up a long street of low French houses, and come upon a tall wall on our left. Behind it is the famous Mechouar, the palace, but now the site of the palace of the old native kings, and famous for its defence against the wild tribes in the days of Cavaignac—a feat the same in kind, if not in degree, as the defence of the Residency at Lucknow. Week after week, and month after month, did the gallant Frenchman hold these walls against the world, or as much as he could see of it. All honour and glory to the brave soldier and his companions in arms, who so long held out (it was for six months) against overwhelming numbers. There was famine within, there were foemen without; the French were isolated and cut off from all communication with the world. It would almost seem as though Captain Cavaignac had been left there to perish, but in right knightly fashion did he accomplish his task to the bitter end.

As we pass under the high wall of the Mechouar, we see the heads of a couple of turbaned Turcos peering down on us from above. We come to a Place, with an avenue of trees, reminding us again of Luchon, and other pleasant holiday places in the Pyrenees; we turn to the left, still skirting the Mechouar; another twist of the coachman's wrist, and we have arrived at the diligence and post offices.

It is eight o'clock, and the people are stirring. A number of young French girls, finely dressed for their "first Communion," just as you may see them at Boulogne-sur-Mer, pass by. We are in Africa, but we are in France.

It did not take us long to get down to the Hôtel de la Paix, which we had passed on our way up the chief street, and were pleasantly received by M. and Mme. Pascalin, the proprietors. This was no makeshift of an hotel; we could have spent some months in their house pleasantly enough. We were shown into a large sitting-room, with a bedroom of fair size off it; and there we remained while at Tlemçen, and were sorry to leave it.

After our night journey we were not much disposed for exertion, and truth compels me to say that it rained in the afternoon, and Sunday, the next day (it was May 16), was a wet day which would have done credit to Devonshire or the Lakes, and cold withal. We were 2500 feet above the sea. We did not, however, object to the enforced quiet, for really something like a couple of months of African travel had brought one to that frame of mind and body, that to lie still and simmer over a book was by no means disagreeable. We utilized this time by doing that which the wretched boys who are being prepared for Woolwich call "cramming." In our case the crammers were the two guide-books, and some others which we borrowed from the landlord. I will not affect knowledge where I possess none. This story of everchanging native dynasties was all new to me. I was not prepared for the fact that Tlemçen had been the capital of successive native kingdoms, a place more famous in its day than Seville, or Cordova, or Granada; that this French *place d'armes*—a little place as we now saw it—had once held something like 150,000 inhabitants; that there had been in it a quarter where the Genoese and other European traders had been well content to live under the authority of their own consuls and the gracious protection of the native kings; that Tlemçen had, at one period of its history, undergone a siege in duration like the siege of Troy; that the assailants, determined to take it at all cost, had turned their encampment into a town, of which many noble remains still exist;—in a word, that Romans, Vandals, Arabs, Berbers, Spaniards, French, had fought out their quarrels here; and that Tlemçen is one of the most notable, as it is one of the most beautiful, places in the world. I wonder if any European scholar, with the splendid exception of Señor Gayangos, could sit down and tell us the story off-hand from the accumulations of his own studies. For myself I acknowledge, in all honesty, I had to go to school to learn the A B C of the matter, and I was much pleased with the frank admission of M. Piesse, who has devoted a great deal of time and attention to the traditions of Algiers, that he was at first much in the same case. "It would require a volume," writes that gentleman, "and not a few pages, to sum up the history of Tlemçen in a proper way, and to describe its monuments, either existing or in ruins. I have consulted with advantage, for the few paragraphs which follow—much too short for my fancy—the 'Histoire des Berbères d'Ibn-Khaldoun,' translated by M. de Slane; the 'Histoire du Beni-Zian,' and the 'Journey to Tlemçen,' by the Abbé Bargès; and the noble work of M. C. Brosselard, upon the Inscriptions of Tlemçen, published in the *Revue Africaine*, Nos. 14 to 27." This confession inspires confidence.

The cradle of Tlemçen was at Agadir (we shall

soon visit the place to see the minaret, the Koubba, the remains of the old walls). Agadir stood on the old Roman Pomaria, and it was in the third century of our era (in the days of Gordian II.) a Roman cavalry station. Before the Romans, some tribes of the Mar'raoua (otherwise known as Massylians, or Massæsylians) occupied the place. The Romans called the lovely spot Pomaria, "the orchard." The olive, almond, apple, and pear trees (or their forefathers rather) were there when Flavius Cassianus was Prefect, just as we see them now. There are many inscriptions in support of this theory of Pomaria. I am but an indifferent sightseer, for I could not decipher the inscription, "Pomaria," on the stones which have been utilized by the Moorish architect in building up the walls of the minaret at Agadir. Tradition says the minaret was only built A.D. 789. You can also see some of these old-world relics in the museum. The inscriptions and relics, says M. Piesse, carry us down to the last half of the fifth century of our era. The Romans withdrew from Pomaria, and the historian of the Berbers takes up the tale. Agadir was founded on the ruins or site of Pomaria by the Beni-Ifren, and became the capital of the Zénatian states. Our old friend, Sidi Okba (of sandy memory, whose grave we visited near Biskra), paid Agadir a visit. We then arrive at a succession of native dynasties—Idrissides, Fatêmides, Ifrenides, Almoravides, Almohades, Abd-el-Ouadites, Merinides, Abd-el-Ouadites again.

The Spanish conquest of Oran, A.D. 1509, seems to have commenced the ruin of Tlemçen, which was completed by the Turkish adventurers, who established themselves at Algiers under Barbarossa and Kheir-ed-Din. In A.D. 1553 it fell, not to rise again, unless the French succeed in restoring the glory and prosperity of this famous place. The last of the Abd-el-Ouadites ran away from the Turkish invasion, took refuge with the Spaniards at Oran, and got himself baptized under the name of Carlos. This was in A.D. 1553. This Don Carlos crossed over to Spain, and went out like the snuff of a candle at the court of Philip II. For very nearly three centuries Tlemçen was a mere seat of Turkish misrule, and there is no profit in recapitulating or dwelling upon the series of executions and murders and acts of oppression which killed the commerce as well as the bodies of the Tlemçenites. It would, however, be supremely unjust not to record emphatically what happened in the year 1836. On January 12 of that year Marshal Clausel entered the town, but soon retired from it, leaving Captain Cavaignac with a battalion in the Mechouar. Here the brave soldier held his ground till he was relieved by General Bugeaud on the 6th of July, 1836. The heroic little garrison had then been brought to starvation point. By the Treaty of Tafna, May 20, 1837, Abd-el-Kader was put in possession of Tlemçen, and hoped to make it his own capital and the capital of the future Arab empire. Fate was against him, and on the 30th of January, 1842, the French retook possession of Tlemçen, and in their hands it has remained ever since.

Now, I think that the history of the native dynasties mentioned above has, for most of us, just the same interest as (according to the old illustration) the history of the squabbles between kites and crows. I will simply take from M. Piesse a few sentences which may throw light upon the somewhat tangled topography of the town, and add a few words about the great siege and Mansoura. What remains of that tall minaret at Mansoura is one of the monuments of the world. Assuming, on the one hand, that the Romans finally withdrew from Pomaria in the last half of the fifth century of our era, and, on the other, that Don Carlos, the last of the Abd-el-Ouadites, ran off to Oran in 1553, this would give us something more than a thousand years during which Berber sovereigns held the place. I have given above the names of the various dynasties which succeeded each other as I find them. We may pass over the story of the wild throat-cutting till we come to the Almoravides. In A.D. 1080 they took *Agadir* (or Pomaria), and built up the town of *Tagrart* on the place where they had established their camp. Agadir (Pomaria of old) and Tagrart now became one—Tlemçen. The Almohades came in, and first destroyed the town and then rebuilt it. Then succeeded a period of great prosperity and wall-building. I find that the dominion of the Almohade Emirs at Tlemçen lasted for 103 years. The town, with its dependencies, was but a small point in the great Almohade empire, which comprised Western Africa and the provinces conquered by the Mussulmen in Spain. I am simply condensing M. Piesse's account. A chief of the Berber tribe of Abd-el-Ouad, A.D. 1248, took the place, and set up an independent Berber kingdom. The Abd-el-Ouadites and Merinides were both offshoots from the great

Zénatian tribe, and seem to have been always struggling for pre-eminence.

The history of Tlemçen for the time is the history of their sanguinary squabbles. One of the Merinides, Abou-Yakoub, besieged Tlemçen for a space of more than eight years, and he it was who built the town of Mansoura on the site of his camp, with the walls and the great mosque and the huge minaret; but poor Abou-Yakoub was assassinated in his new town. His grandson made peace with Abou-Zian, the Tlemçen chief. This peace lasted but for a time. War broke out again between the Abd-el-Ouadites and the Merinides, and, finally, Abou-Hassan Ali, the Merinide, the Black Sultan, resumed the siege, and took the town on the 1st of May, A.D. 1337. The Abd-el-Ouadite chief fell in the Mechouar, fighting bravely to the last. He, too, as General Napier would have written, had much glory. This period of Merinide dominion was but a short one. It lasted twenty-three years, and then the Abd-el-Ouadites came back again, and held the place for two hundred years—from A.D. 1359 to A.D. 1553 as above. These two centuries are the magnificent period of Tlemçen, during which the sovereignty of the kings or chiefs who ruled at Tlemçen was extended over the two present provinces of Oran and Algiers. The town of Tlemçen contained 125,000 inhabitants. There was here a brilliant court, a numerous and well-disciplined army. Tlemçen was then what M. Victor Hugo says Paris is now, a "*foyer de lumières.*" In the neighbouring Bou-Medin you would have found the clergy and the men of science and literature. Take it for all in all,

Tlemçen was much ahead of anything to be found in continental Europe (save, perhaps, Italy) at this time. The Spaniards, and after them, the Turks, got rid of this *"foyer de lumières;"* but magnificent ruins of this great magnificence remain.

I know not if I have succeeded in making this little account clear. It is not very easy to disentangle the necessary series of facts from the story of everlasting fighting and court intrigue, which means generally that one gentleman strangled another and took his place. It is, however, a singular story. To recapitulate it. We first have the Roman Pomaria, which (barring a few bits of masonry) disappears, and we get Agadir on the site of it. Tagrart is built up by the side of Agadir, and the two become one, Tlemçen. Then the people retire gradually from the Agadir quarter into the Tagrart quarter, and Agadir becomes a thing of the past. Then the Merinides turn their camp, Mansoura, into a town, full of noble buildings, and fortified by a wall, built with the best engineering knowledge of the time. Mansoura is now a desert, but much of the encircling wall remains, and the ruins are there, better worth seeing than most towns. I have dwelt a little at length upon this matter, because it may serve to explain in some measure the labyrinth of ruined walls which the visitor will find around him on every side, and which are a sore puzzle to the new-comer. Mansoura (with its wall) stands alone, and is intelligible enough to any one who will take up his position on the hill above, and obtain a good bird's-eye view of the place. Another good point for tracing the Tlemçen walls is near the Agadir minaret; generally look for the ruins on the south side as you walk and drive about. The French engineers have not made matters more easy, but their workmanship is soon recognized. If any one has been at the pains of mastering the facts as above given, I think he will be better prepared to take a walk with us through Tlemçen, the city of two centuries of Berber dominion, with very fine legends of the past—of the Romans, of the Black Sultan, of the ten years' siege, etc.

Sunday, May 16, as I have said, was wet, and so I had time to swallow and digest as well as I could M. Piesse's bead-roll of Moslem worthies with their hard names. I was as glad as no doubt my readers will be when the task was done, and we were free to saunter about again, and just record our impressions of what we saw.

Monday was as gloriously fine as Sunday had been wet, and having secured the services of a Turkish lad, Mohammed by name, we went out for our first walk in Tlemçen. Our object could be no other than the Great Mosque. Our guide conducted us to a large Place, the Place d'Alger, I believe, and there was a low wall on one side, with a parcel of native cooking-shops, braziers, and so on, and a great minaret. We dived through a hole in this wall into a narrow court—or I suppose they would call it "street"—picturesque with its effects of light and shade, picturesque with the trees trained on trellises above our heads, and the natives lying about. We come to a little oratory shaded by an old vine, as M. Piesse has truly described it, and at this point every native who passed stopped and kissed the grating. We stood watching them for a while, for it was a pretty sight. It seems that a holy man lies buried here—one Ahmed-ben-Hassan-el-R'omari. During life he inhabited the little hole we see, and one morning was found dead in the Great Mosque hard by. The people brought him in and buried him here. Now, as he was a just man, and had led a life of strict idleness, he was canonized after death. It is supposed that by a visit to his tomb you can obtain deliverance from all moral or physical infirmities. Above the door is an inscription, which has been translated by M. C. Brosselard—

> "The virtues of this sanctuary spread themselves abroad,
> Like to the light of the morning, or the brilliancy of the stars.
> O ye who are afflicted with great evils, he who will cure them for you
> Is this son of nobility and science, AHMED."

How one wishes there was anything in it! After all, this foolery is not worse than the little black image in St. Peter's, or the absurdities of Loretto. All we can answer for here is this African alley, with the tall minaret above our heads, and the poor picturesque creatures kissing away at the painted grating.

We enter the mosque by a large court, with arcades. This court is paved with onyx, and in the centre is a fountain, also of onyx, all of which sounds very grand, but I am bound to say the onyx looks very like rough stone, with a tendency to transparency, as far as the basin is concerned. There were a few lazy devotees loitering about under the arcades, only one or two preparing themselves by ablution for their devotions.

The mosque is large, cool, and dark. The first impression was, I think, very much what one receives on entering any of the large churches or cathedrals of Roman Catholic Europe at odd times, when no service in particular is in course of celebration. The kneeling female figure in the little chapel is wanting, but the men frequent these places, and are (as far as externals prove anything) devout enough. They would, not improbably, be aggressively so if they dared, but we never received any annoyance from them throughout Algeria, beyond a side glance expressive of contempt for our supposed theological opinions. As the eye got accustomed to the darkness, you saw the roof was supported by an infinite number of columns. We did not count them, but M. Piesse seems to have done so, and he says they are seventy-two in number.

The *mihrab* is magnificent; it looks to the south. We both remember it well, and have now before us a very excellent photograph of its rich ornamentation; but it is difficult to convey one's impression to others by mere words. You have before you a recess lighted from above. You look upon a large horse-shoe arch, set, as it were, in a Persian carpet of elaborate tracery —I mean for design, not colour. Above these are three windows, also highly decorated. This is not the most beautiful specimen of Arab decoration at Tlemçen, for there is something much finer in the Arab school, and at Bou-Medin. I suppose this work is Arab, but I much wished for the presence of some skilled person, who could have informed me how far Berber workmen could be credited with the merit of these fine things.

The date of foundation of the mosque is given as A.D. 1136, when one of the Almoravide kings reigned at Tlemçen. It is explained that Almoravides and Marabouts mean the same thing. These were the people who took Agadir, built Tagrart on the site of their own camp, and made a Tlemçen of the two united towns. The workmanship, to an ignorant layman, seemed very much like what one sees at the Alhambra, only finer; so, until better informed, I shall consider it all as Arab work. This horse-shoe *mihrab* in the Djama Kebir of Tlemçen is a thing of great beauty, and just as worthy of record as the finest bits of our cathedrals.

The main things here are the general aspect and feeling of the place; the silence broken only by the trickling of the fountain in the court; the half-darkness; the vast room, with its pillars and its lovely bit of decoration; the bright colours which you get from the dresses of a few of the faithful outside, who are loitering under the arcades, or in the strong sunshine in the middle of the court. I do not think one cares to examine these places as if one was making an inventory, so I will only add that there is a huge rusty-looking chandelier hanging from the roof, which we scarcely honoured with a second glance.

We must not, however, leave the mosque without saying a word or two about the minaret, which is such a notable object from above or below, no matter from which side you approach Tlemçen. It is said to be 112 feet high. It is made of brick, square, decorated with little pillars, and gay as pieces of bright glazed tile can make it.

I can only write a few lines about the old mosque. We returned to it time after time, and loitered much about the place; for it was a harbour of refuge from the glare and heat outside, and was so "racy of the soil" on which we were standing.

I like the story (given by M. Piesse) of "Yar'-moracen," the Abd-el-Ouadite conqueror, who built the minaret, and was solicited by his courtiers to have his name recorded on it in a very emphatic way. "No," said the tranquil chief, "*Houhou issent Reubbi*"—"God knows it." A good lesson to some of our friends at home, who are not displeased to see prominent mention of their good deeds in the newspaper, with proper illustrations. "*Houhou issent Reubbi*"—"God knows it." One must not forget the lesson.

From the Great Mosque we sauntered away to the Arab school, which is situated at another end of the same Place. The English guide calls it the Mosque of "Sidi Ahmed Bel Hassan el-Ghomari;" M. Piesse more briefly calls it the Mosque of "Abou Hassan." From external signs you would scarcely suppose it to be a mosque at all, were it not for its minaret, with the usual little pillars and mosaic work. As we stepped inside, fortunately for us the pupils were away, and we only found there an intelligent teacher, with whom we communicated, by the help of Mohammed the guide. There is no use in saying you look around you in the place; you look at once at the *mihrab*, and your breath is taken away. I wonder if this be not the finest specimen of arabesque, or Arab work, in the world. It is presumptuous, perhaps, in one who has not seen the work done by the Moslems at Cairo or in India, to speak, but I cannot think the hand of man has ever surpassed what we see here. Just now I was in a kind of half ecstasy over the *mihrab* at the old mosque. By the side of this one it looks almost hard and machine-made. The patterns are the same, but look at the delicacy and the intricate beauty of the design—so minute you would like to examine it with a microscope; so grand as a whole, that you step back to take in the general effect. Cairo and India I have not seen; but the Alhambra and Alcazar (Granada and Seville) I know well enough, but I can very confidently assert that there is nothing in either of them which approaches this exquisite work.

Now look around you. The interior of the building is divided into three by horse-shoe arcades. A portion of the walls is highly decorated, and, were it not for the *mihrab*, would rivet your attention at once. The roof is of carved cedar, with precious remains of painting upon it. There is an inscription on the wall, the meaning of which was conveyed to us from the teacher, through Mohammed, but the knowledge so conveyed was thick and slab. I turn to my guide-book, and find that the mosque was founded A.D. 1296–97, in honour of the Emir Abou-Ibrahim ben-Yahïa, but that the name was really given to perpetuate the memory of the many virtues and great knowledge of an eminent lawyer, one Aboul-Hassen-Ibn-Yakhlef-et-Tenessi. All I can say is, that if this be so, there has never been a lawyer in the world who has had such a splendid monument to his memory. I will go back from London to Tlemçen to have another look at the *mihrab*.

We often visited the place, and one afternoon found it in full possession of the little Arab pupils, who were browsing over the pastures of sound learning (I suppose they were studying the Koran), under the auspices of our friend the Taleb, no longer supple and courteous, but stern and terrible as a head master should be, with the usual long stick to encourage the pupils. He certainly used it freely enough. Is it necessary to beat little boys all over the world? There is no public opinion, no press, to keep the schoolmaster in order. Even country gentlemen nowadays cannot work their will comfortably on poachers. The schoolmaster is the only despot left. I wonder how it would answer to birch them soundly all round—say three times a half—just to show them that it does hurt, and that they had better not be quite so free with their weapons? Imagine birching Dr. Keate! The little Arabs were astonished that day at some of the events which befell them; they were at any rate learning their first lesson of resignation to the will of Allah. What pretty children they were! not darker than the children you see in Spain or Italy, but more delicate of feature and brighter of eye.

We went into two or three mosques *in* the town, but these are the only two of which I will make mention. Any one so inclined can see the others for himself by the help of the guide-books, but I do not think he will find much to repay him for the trouble. Outside the town there are some remarkable mosques and Koubbas.

I cannot help recording here a little story, a sad one indeed, which made a great impression on us at the time, and which I can scarcely speak of now without emotion.

We had been instructed at the hotel to go to a street near the Place—it was, if I remember right, called "Rue Ben Sidoun"—to get photographs of Tlemçen and its buildings. We knocked at a door where there were some photographs in a glass case against the wall. An old woman opened the door. "*Ah, mon cher monsieur, ce pauvre Pedra est mort; je suis sa veuve.*"

We were of course grieved to hear it, and were for retiring; but the old lady entreated us to come in, saying that the presence of travellers was *une bénédiction* for her, and it was a charity to buy her photographs. There was no more to be said about it; we selected some, and on asking for others she said she would prepare them from the negatives. She could do it—not that she was handy at it like her son. "*Ah! mon fils, mon pauvre fils!*" said she, and burst into tears. We tried what few words of soothing and sympathy we could find, and thinking to ease her grief if she was allowed to tell her story out, asked what was the matter. "*Ah! madame, l'autre jour*" (mentioning the day) "*mon pauvre fils s'est fusillé, il est tombé roide-mort la, madame, tenez sur cette dalle*"—pointing to a flagstone in the little court—"*fi-donc c'est encore entachée de son sang.*"

The poor soul went on to tell her piteous tale. The boy had Spanish blood in his veins; the father was a Spaniard, though she was French. He married early, much too early, a girl too young, much too young— a girl "without conduct," of whom the mother never approved. She was brainless; she was fond of pleasure; she did not care for her husband; she had only married the poor boy that he might support her: but he loved her only too well. He became madly jealous, and the unhappy girl only gave him too much cause—she was seldom to be found at home. He met her in the street, and overwhelmed her with reproaches. She told him that she execrated him; that she would return to him no more; that she loved another, and was resolved to leave Tlemçen with him—at any rate, he should see her face no more. He returned home, but when his passion had a little cooled down, he began to look upon the words as words spoken in anger. Alas! it was only too true; in the course of that afternoon he heard that they had fled. "I did my best to console him, for he sat there, where monsieur is sitting now, silent and motionless. I thought I would go out for a moment, and get him something for supper. Why did I ever leave him? I had gone but a few paces from the house, when I heard the report of a gun. I hurried back, and found my poor boy lying in the yard; he had blown his brains out, and his head, or what was left of it, rested upon that miserable stone, from which I shall never be able to wash out the stains—no, never. That, madame, is the story of my poor boy, and that is the reason why I have not copies of all our photographs on hand—he always kept the portfolios full; but I am becoming cleverer at the work, I know where to put my hand on the negatives, and to-morrow I shall have the honour of bringing the photographs required to the hotel."

Such, or nearly such, was poor Mme. Pedra's story. What could we say to console or comfort her? It must have been a terrible thing to live on in that wretched yard, with the trumpery little shed, in which were the instruments of the photographer's trade, surrounded by objects which reminded her at every turn of the great disaster. We took such things as we could, and gave her commission for others, which we told her we would fetch ourselves—she need be in no hurry about them—and so returned to our hotel.

The people here were on the stir. There was to be this afternoon a sort of "function" or *festa* at the Falls of the Saf-Saf, and all Tlemçen was to be there. Why should not we go too? To us it was a matter of indifference how we disposed of our afternoon, so Mansoura to-morrow, the waterfalls to-day. We got a carriage from an *entrepreneur* in our own street, a short distance from the hotel; and I can assure those who may come after me that they will find no difficulty at Tlemçen in procuring a comfortable light open carriage with a pair of small active horses, which are more serviceable in this part of the country than animals of a far more stately and pretentious appearance, and the prices charged are ridiculously small. It was sometimes a little more or a little less; but I think I am about right in saying that ten francs a day (including *buonamano*) settled our carriage-bill at Tlemçen, and we went everywhere—so completely so that the coachman told us at last he knew of no other drives; we must begin again.

This afternoon, however, it was to be the Saf-Saf. We drove out of the gate and down the hill which we had ascended in the diligence a few days before. There was plenty of movement on the road—carriages going down full and "empties" returning for fresh loads. At about the distance of three or four miles from the town we began to hear the "bang-bang!" without which French festivals are scarcely complete; then the blare of military music; then we came to a glen with waterfalls. Waterfalls are generally a disappointment, and I do not know that those we saw at Tlemçen are an exception to the rule. There is no great single fall of water, like at the Staubbach or the Handek. These are rather a series of falls, as at Giessbach, no single fall being of great importance. It was, however, a pretty enough scene, though we should have done just as well without the merry-makers, the gentlemen shooting at a mark, the petty conjurors, the people with fruit and drinks for sale. I would make but one exception in favour of the dancers. Our French friends dearly love a *sauterie*, and the young men and women were jumping about to their hearts' content, and appeared to be quite as amused as we were at a fat, middle-aged *bourgeois*, with a thick watch-chain and a profusion of charms and *breloques*, who evidently considered himself the Vestris of the occasion. He leered sentimentally at the young ladies, or jumped defiantly in face of the men, according to the mood of the music. He never wanted partners; I dare say he was a *parti*, and owned a thriving *charcuterie* shop, or something of that kind; and mammas—French mammas, who stand no nonsense —were there to see fair play.

However, we came there for the glen, and I managed to scramble some half-way up; it is marked as 1500 feet high. I don't know how this may be, but it was very pleasant when we got away from the noise and bustle of the kind of fair below, and found quiet and leisure to look about us. I forget the precise number of the falls, but they were many. The sides of the glen were stern and African enough, of a reddish colour, the rocks assuming every fantastic shape; and on one side there were openings of caverns—one of them, of course, the Cave of Abd-el-Kader. Poor man! what a time he must have had of it, if ever he occupied half the caves which I have seen assigned to him as dwelling-places! The glen, save at the sides, was well filled with small trees and vegetation (the water would account for this); the sky above, blue and spotless as always in this part of the world. The picture, then, was of an African glen; that is, of falling water, of picturesque vegetation at the water's edge, of walls of rock, and of the blue canopy above. The glen was in comparative darkness; the plain below in a blaze of light and sunshine. There were some, but not very many, of the *indigènes* about. It was St. Cloud rather, or Versailles and the "Grandes Eaux," in Africa. We were in no hurry, and so loitered about in our cool glen by the side of the cascades, till evening was coming on and it was time to return. I saw no drunkenness, nor squabbling, nor disturbance of any kind amongst the crowd, and I am pleased to record the fact. So this afternoon ended, as did all others, with a cool drive home amidst the magnificent scenery to the hotel and to dinner.

Now, this question of dinner is everywhere an important one. The cook at M. Pascalin's, at the Hôtel de la Paix, was a very fair performer, although he could not do much with the meat, which here, as indeed throughout Algeria, is poor and tasteless. His *potage* and *entrées* did him credit; the bread and butter were very good, and the wine reasonably so. You found at Tlemçen a better dinner than you would at a place like Narbonne or Perpignan, or other towns in the south of France. There was no fish. We dined in a long low room on the first floor, and the hotel was much frequented by the French officers in garrison at Tlemçen. Save that every now and then one of these would become warm in argument, and maintain his views somewhat loudly, I never saw a better-behaved set of young gentlemen. It was really a pleasure to see their bright uniforms and brighter faces. They had a habit, however, which sorely disquieted poor M. Pascalin's soul, but which much amused me. It was in vain that he had stuck up all about his house the warning words, "*Entrée interdite aux chiens.*" Each little group or mess of officers brought its own relay of dogs, and such dogs—dogs with idiosyncrasies of character.

There was a large, yellow, setter-looking sort of creature, who had a way of laying his head upon your knee, and looking up at you with eyes languishing with kindness, when anything peculiarly savoury was on the table. He belonged to a young army doctor. There was a long rough-haired terrier whose system was different. He would recall you to a sense of duty by a short snappish bark, as much as to say "*C'est moi.*" He had been overlooked—as yet he was unwilling to give a harder name to this manifest inattention. He could bear a great deal, but he could not bear bread. With a soul equal to *entrées* or gravies of the most elaborate kind, was he to be put off with "common fixings"? So a sure way to get rid of him was to give him a piece of bread. He would not snap at you, he would not bark at you, but turn away with a sort of reproachful " Have-I-deserved-this-from-you" sort of glance, and for that day you would see him no more. He would take refuge under a chair, and glare at the dishes from between the rails, as they were carried past him, with an injured look. For his part, he had given up the world and its hollow mockeries. "Bread indeed! and to me." One more dog, and I have done. A large, wheezing corpulent, half-shaved impostor, so fat that he could scarcely sit upon his chair at table when his master had propped him up. His only claim to attention was that he digested victuals, and displayed the results in corpulence. I doubt if he had ever done a turn of work in his life—caught one poor rat or even barked at a passing carriage in a proper way. Now, this fat humbug of a dog got more bits than all the other dogs put together. He was pampered, and "poor-fellowed," and plied with savoury morsels, whilst the other dogs had nothing to do but to look on and hate him. He patronized you, not you him. If he accepted your bit of pigeon nicely besmeared with sauce, understand it was a favour. All rivers run to the sea, for there is much water in it; all fattening things fell to this dog, because he was fat. We have seen instances of this elsewhere.

So far of dogs. When I have spoken of the running

waiter, I shall have done with my little interlude, which I have only introduced as a sort of pause, or rest for any poor soul who may get weary of this monotone of enthusiasm about blue skies and mosques, etc.

The running waiter, then, was a small, active young Frenchman, who had his lair at one end of the long room. There might be nobody there but yourself, you might have the whole afternoon before you, there was no hurry of any kind; but it was enough to say, "Charles," and Charles arrived like a whirlwind, with a "*Voilà, monsieur;*" one second's glance to read your inmost soul, and then, catching up a cruet-stand, he would flash back to his own den. But it was when dinner was at its highest that Charles was swiftest. How he would dart past you with a pile of plates or a couple of soup tureens, just as though he was flogging in for the Derby winning-post! The man became a positive nuisance, but you would as soon have prevailed upon a blue-bottle to cease from buzzing, or upon a wasp to be at rest, as you could have persuaded Charles to move about the banqueting hall at anything under twenty miles an hour. How I longed for an accident! M. Pascalin himself looked after us occasionally, and then all was peace—peace and strawberries.

Our next day was to be dedicated to Mansoura, one of the greater lions of Tlemçen. We have already seen that it was an outcome of the great feud between the Abd-el-Ouadites and Merinides, and of Merinide creation. Between five and six hundred years ago these events took place. The date assigned to the first erection of Mansoura is A.D. 1302, just about the time when our Edward II. came to the throne. Abou-Yakoub, the Merinide, was then besieging Tlemçen. This was the second siege, for there had been one before, A.D. 1298, which had lasted for seven months. Then followed the long siege, the one with which we are concerned, which began in A.D. 1299, and which lasted eight years and three months. Abou-Yakoub was assassinated in his own palace in Mansoura. A kind of peace was patched up between the Merinides outside Tlemçen and the Abd-el-Ouadites who held the town. This peace lasted only for a time. In the year 1329 (A.D.) hostilities broke out afresh. Abou-Saïd, the Merinide, again attacked Tlemçen, but he died in his turn. The capture was affected by Abou-Hassan Ali, the Black Sultan, on the 1st of May, A.D. 1337. He had reoccupied Mansoura. This third investment lasted two years. Leave out, then, all questions of the first siege of seven months, and so much of the third period of hostilities as was not actual investment, and Tlemçen was attacked in this way for a longer period than Troy, reckoning eight years and seven months for the second and two years for the third siege.

What follows is from Ibn-Khaldoun, the chronicler of the Berbers. I translate from the French translation of M. de Slane. Thus writes Ibn-Khaldoun, describing the foundation of the town by the Sultan Abou-Yakoub: "In the very spot where the army had pitched its tents, a palace was erected for the residence of the sovereign." Alas! for men and their triumphs! Abou-Yakoub, a few years afterwards, was murdered in this very palace, without having taken Tlemçen. "This vast site," says

Ibn-Khaldoun, "was surrounded by a wall, and was filled with great houses, immense edifices, magnificent palaces, and gardens traversed by streamlets. It was in the year 702 of the Hegira (A.D. 1302) that the Sultan caused the circuit of the walls to be built, and that he thus established a town admirable not only for its extent and its numerous population, but also for the activity of its commerce and the strength of its fortifications. It contained baths, caravanserais, and an hospital, as well as a mosque where service was performed on Fridays; its minaret was of extraordinary height. This town received from its founder the name of El-Mansoura, or The Victorious. From day to day its prosperity augmented, its markets overflowed with provisions, and merchants flocked to it from all countries. It soon took the first place amongst the towns of the Mar'eb." But when the younger branch of the Abd-el-Ouadites recovered final possession of Tlemçen, there ceased to be a *raison d'être* for Mansoura. If anything, it was a badge of suffering and humiliation. So from this period (A.D. 1359) Mansoura was allowed to fall to pieces, the hand of man assisting in the destruction.

Five centuries have done their work. These are the ruins which we are minded to see this afternoon, and we found them to be ruins in a remarkable state of preservation. You drive out of the town by the western gate, the Porte de Fez (the opposite gate to the one by which we had entered from Oran); you pass a Koubba or two; you drive down a triumphant alley of roses; you begin to get sight of the tall minaret, and see patches of reddish wall. You come upon a very fine arch on the left of the road, which looks for all the world like a triumphal arch in Roman days. It is nothing of the sort. This is the beginning of Mansoura. This is the Bab el-Khremis, the "Gate of the Army," and was part of the wall of circumvallation. You have about three furlongs further to go before you would fairly call yourself within the circuit of wall. I defy you, however, to think of the wall from the moment you have caught sight of the minaret. The height is given as forty mètres, and it might be forty-five before ruin had set in. This would be about 130 feet English, more or less, I suppose. It stands upon a kind of hillock, which gives it additional height. At the bottom of the minaret you would enter the mosque under a large Moorish arch, highly decorated. The front side of the minaret is, practically, perfect; not so the three other sides. It is divided into three stages or stories, the upper one beautifully decorated with little pillars of onyx. The panels, as you may call them, between the stories were decorated with bright-glazed tiles, or mosaic work. The interior of the minaret was lighted by the windows which you see before you. Through the door of the minaret you pass into what remains of the mosque, that is, into a space surrounded by the old ruined walls, and open to the heavens. The dimensions of the mosque are given as 100 mètres in length against 60 in breadth, of rectangular form. Take the yard of three English feet as 0·914383 mètre, and you will have the dimensions in English feet in a comfortable, domestic sort of way. But try to imagine the tall ruins of a minaret standing in this ruin of a mosque, amidst these red ruins of walls on this African hill-side; the mountain above you, and the plain below sinking down seawards as far as the eye can reach, or until it is stopped by other mountains, and (I must revert to it) the canopy of unclouded blue above your head; the silence, the solitude of the place,—and you will have some idea of Mansoura. You are fairly enclosed in the circuit of red wall cut into sections by towers about forty mètres (say 130 feet) apart.

It is wonderful to see how perfect is this surrounding wall after five centuries have done their work of destruction. These walls, or ramparts, of Mansoura must have been very much like an irregular square in shape, as you look down upon them from the hill above. There is very little wanting to complete them, for where there is a break in the wall, you have the towers to guide your eye. M. Piesse says the space contained within these walls would be superficially 100 hectares. This would be rather 250 than 200 English acres. You must ascend the hill behind the ruins—there is a very good road—and get up some height before you take in the ramparts in their entirety, and then the idea of Mansoura is as completely before you as though you had capered about within its walls in the suite of the Black Sultan. The ramparts were twelve mètres high—and there were four gates at the four cardinal points.

Here, then, is my summing-up: an irregular square—a rectangular figure, if you will—of red ruined wall, cut by towers at every 130 feet; at the western end the tall minaret and the ruins of the mosque. For the most part all is bare within, save on one side a few sparse trees and white French houses, but not enough to affect the feeling that within the circuit you have nothing but the site of a city. That is Mansoura as we saw it.

We strolled into the mosque, and at the opposite side there was pacing slowly a stoutish gentleman who looked very like a French priest going over his breviary. There he walked as on his quarter-deck—up and down, backwards and forwards, encouraging an appetite for dinner, but evidently master of the situation. If our old friend the Black Sultan could have got hold of him! Just where he was complacently taking his "constitutional," so many times these fiery dark men must have prayed, and raised their wild wailings to Allah. Oh for an artist's hand! I should like to sketch that demure gentleman in the ruined mosque. He seemed so dignified a person, and so completely given up to meditation, that I did not care to disturb him, but fell back upon two lowlier creatures equally draped in black, who answered my salutations in that lowly, "Uriah-Heep" sort of way, which they seem to think represents humility. They were what are called "Petits Frères," and had come from an establishment of their order, hard by the El-Biar Road at Algiers—a place I knew very well, for it lay close to the villa in which we had spent three months of winter. Here was something to talk about. I did not know much about the "Little Brothers," but I knew a good deal of the Sisters, who lived in the next house, over against the Brothers. The Sisters, in point of fact, made the best butter in Algiers, and had been gracious enough to supply our wants throughout the winter; so I began in my own mind to work up through the butter to the Sisters, through the Sisters to the Brothers, and through the Brothers to the demure gentleman now on his quarter-deck—for he, it seems, was a mighty man amongst them. We continued our talk, but I could not get anything out of the neophytes about the ruins. I think they had an impression they were Roman remains, and it was scarcely worth while to disturb it.

Mansoura is a place to loiter about; so we got ourselves driven from point to point to look at a bit of wall here, a tower there, in order that afterwards, with the help of a good photograph, we might be able to recall the image to the mind's eye.

This afternoon at Mansoura shows what a tourist may do in Algeria. With the exception of Rome and its neighbourhood, and of Venice—places which we all know by heart—I really am not aware of anything in Europe more interesting, or more beautiful, than this African sight. This pleasure you can enjoy with a good hotel for your head-quarters, and without hardship or annoyance of any kind. You are just one night's drive from the sea-coast, and the sea-port from which you start on the expedition is but twelve hours distant from Carthagena in Spain, which is connected with Boulogne by the railway. This is repetition, if you please, but I wish to hammer in my nail by repeated taps. "The new playground" is very easy of access, and it contains many wonderful things which you might seek for in vain elsewhere, save in India, Central America, or in other such outlying places.

The drives about Tlemçen are all beautiful. We

jogged about the mountain above the town, so as to see it from above; we next resolved to try it from below. As the result of a conversation with our coachman, we drove down the hill to Negrier and Brera, the objective points not being of great importance. Our wish was to look *up* at the town, the minaret at Mansoura, Bou-Medin, and the other landmarks. It is only thus, I think, you will gain a fair appreciation of the situation of Tlemçen, and the real meaning of the old walls. One is astonished to find such vegetation in Africa. As you roll along you think of Orvieto, Perugia, and other beautiful spots between Florence and Rome. It is not, as elsewhere in Algeria, all aloe and prickly pears and green crops. One incident, however, reminded us of where we were. The driver pointed to a farmhouse near the road, and told us that some years back it had been the scene of a terrible crime. The *indigènes* had broken in here at night and murdered every human being whom they found there. This is a tale of the past, but it was well we should be reminded that we were on a disturbed frontier. Some of the greatest ruffians in North Africa haunt the frontier between the French province of Oran and the empire of Morocco. With our own eyes we saw prisoners brought in by mounted *gendarmes*. The features of the men were not prepossessing, to say the least of it; I should certainly not have cared to make their acquaintance at any distance from the help of our friends in the green coats. The fact is we are on the border. We are driving about in the immediate neighbourhood of Tlemçen, and are as safe as we should be on Barnes Common; but adventurous young gentlemen who might be tempted to make a plunge into the interior would do well to consult the French authorities beforehand.

The great sweep of hill is magnificent. It is all on so large a scale, nor is there wanting on either side a profusion of wild flowers such as would have gladdened the heart of Robert Herrick, and such masses of olive trees! We did not certainly see individual trees which could compare with those of the Bois Sacré at Blidah, but they were in such numbers.

I wish I could pass on to others the quiet delight we used to feel in these drives through Algeria, the brilliancy of the sky, the purity of the air, the shapes of the mountains, the dark masses of the olive groves, the gay covering of the fields, the distant minarets, the quaint dress and appearance of the natives; and all these so near home. Verily, north and south, east and west, *barbarism and civilization have kissed each other, and the result is Algeria.*

We had just shaken off the horrors of the lone farm-house, when we drove into the little French village of Negrier. Lo—what is this? A procession of young people coming arm in arm up the street. The young lady in front wears a bridal wreath; the youth on whose arm she leans **is in a full suit** of shining black, and looks as sheepish **and** shamefaced as you could wish. No doubt this is a wedding; **and** as I raised my hat as we passed, the young **madame** acknowledged the courtesy with a bright smile which said, "This is for me; this is my day." I suppose the young man was happy—he only looked awkward—but we were destined **to see him later in the day, on our return drive.**

We drove on, and there was a river and a bridge, and the driver pointed to something which he said was a Roman inscription on the bridge. To examine it, however, I should have been compelled to scramble down and scramble up in a fashion far beyond my powers; so we were compelled to leave the Roman inscription undeciphered. I love to see these inscriptions on a fairly printed page, sitting at my ease in my armchair; one's mind then has fair play. Let young and enthusiastic scholars climb up into dangerous places, and hang over rushing streams; we will applaud them, and give them our poor thoughts as to the value of the results attained by their labour.

The next village we came to was Brera, another French village with a make-believe gate at either end of it, which would not have kept out a young donkey of ordinary audacity, to say nothing of a hungry and exasperated Moor, or whatever he might be, from across the frontier. The drive back is really the bouquet of this little excursion; for then you face the mountain, and Tlemçen in its green setting of orchards and trees.

I cannot, however, help recording one painful fact. As we came back we passed again through Negrier, and again met the bride and bridegroom—no longer at the head of a procession; there might have been one or two people left with them, not more. This time the bride had the bridegroom fairly in tow, and was seeing him home, just as you see poor wives in England escorting their drunken husbands *home* from the public-house. The bridegroom had evidently taken a good deal more than was good for him. I could not help wishing that the bride, who seemed quite equal to the occasion, would profit by her new lord's sleepy and comatose state, and give him a sound thrashing when she got him alone. That was what we saw of "The Bride of Negrier." Let us hope by this time her lout of a husband is properly subdued.

So home through the endless olive woods, with the crescent moon hanging over the tops of the minarets; home to the quaint dogs, the running waiter, and our pleasant little hotel.

Next day we tried a walk to the Mosque and Koubba of Sidi Haloui, a canonized confectioner. You pass out of Tlemçen by the Gate of the Abattoir, and skirt the wall of the town (with a negro village on your right) for some way; but oh, how hot it was, with the sun shining on the white wall, and the wall reflecting the accumulated heat and glare on your face! I should think it is about a mile's walk from the hotel. At length we reached the mosque, and had to fight our way through a crowd of dark little *gamins*, till we got into the cool refuge inside. There were little arcades on either side of the open court, and in these arcades the birds of the air had built their nests in no small numbers. The chief distinguishing feature of this little mosque would be the eight beautiful columns of transparent onyx, with Arab ornamentation. The roof of the arcade is of carved cedar.

The legend of the holy confectioner, as told by M. Brosselard, has, I think, a certain interest, and whilst we are resting and cooling ourselves in the mosque, I will endeavour to tell it as briefly as I can.

Abou-Abd-Allah-ech-Choudi was born at Seville, where he lived in great wealth and honour; but he heard a voice within that others could not hear, and saw a hand that others could not see, which beckoned him away. He put on pilgrim's rags, took up the pilgrim's staff, and travelled by land and by sea from Seville to Tlemçen. Here he feigned madness (A.D. 1266). The form of his madness was to sell sweetstuff, and call crowds around him by the usual artifices of a cheap Jack. When he saw that the crowd was large enough, he would throw aside his buffooneries and his sweetstuff, and speak as never teacher spake, of man and his destiny, of fate, free-will, etc. So he soon passed, in public opinion, from the status of pastry-cook to that of saint; nay, he worked miracles. Now the Sultan heard of him, and of his great acts, so he made him tutor to his two children. This more than annoyed the Vizier, who spread the report that the saint was a mere conjurer and impostor. To cut a long story short, he got him beheaded. The people were enraged, but what was to be done? The body was left unburied, a prey to birds and beasts. On the night of the execution, the *bououab*, or gate-keeper of the town, at the regular hour was calling out his usual cry of "Gate, gate!" so as to give notice to all loiterers, when, lo! he heard a voice which said, "Gate-keeper, shut thy gate and go to sleep; there is no one left outside, save Sidi el-Haloui, the oppressed one!" This cry was renewed night after night, and at last from the gate-keeper the story floated upwards to the Sultan, who said he would watch himself at the gate. The same thing happened; there was the same ghostly cry as before.

The Sultan went back to his palace, saying, "I wished to see—I have seen." It should have been, "I wished to hear—I have heard." Be this as it may, the Sultan next morning sent for the Vizier, and had him neatly deposited in a block of concrete, just like poor Geronimo at Algiers. The remains of the holy man were collected together, and the mosque in which we are now sitting was built in his honour. The Koubba is above, the mosque below, with its minaret, at the top of which were brooding two or three storks. The sides of the minaret are highly decorated with Arab ornamentation.

This is one of the smaller lions of Tlemçen, and it should not be overlooked. There is a wonderful Eastern feeling about the spot. We went to this place in the morning, returned to lunch, and, as my memory serves me, in the afternoon prowled about the town, visiting, amongst other places, the museum, which stands in the market-place, behind the *mairie*. The first agreeable surprise as you pass through the court-yard is an enormous quantity of white roses and jasmine, which pleased us as much as anything we were likely to find in the museum. As you enter the hall itself, you would imagine yourself to be in an assembly-room prepared for a *banquet patriotique* or something of that kind. All round the hall were hanging little flags, each bearing the name of one or other of the villages or communes near Tlemçen, which had its own particular and more imposing banner. It wanted but the band and the dancers, and the museum at this place would have been a very sufficient ball-room. On looking round, however, you might see some columns which had been dug up in

Mansoura, and a number of inscriptions, some dating from the old Roman days, proving the identity of Pomaria and Agadir, as far as site is concerned. Then there were some cannon-balls, or catapult-balls, in black marble, of great size. These were picked up in the town, and are supposed to be artillery relics of the Black Sultan. There is an epitaph again—M. Brosselard has made out its meaning—it records the death of Abou-Abd-Allah, King of Granada, who died in exile at the court of Tlemçen, in Chabân of the 899th year of the Hegira (June, 1494, A.D.). The last thing I shall mention is the standard cubit measure brought here from the Kissaria. The date is given as A.D. 1328. It is a slab of marble, and on it is cut the measure. The collection is very small, but in many respects important enough as affording illustrations of the past history of Tlemçen.

We went from the museum into the Mechouar, or rather to the site of that famous palace. Nothing remains of it now but a minaret with a cross on the top of it. It is only a French barracks, with the usual ugly, but probably very useful, buildings. There is a cleaner sweep here than even in the Kasbah at Constantine or at Algiers. The *genius loci* was to me rather Cavaignac, with his faithful band, who so long held this Castle Dangerous against overwhelming odds; but this feat of arms has been spoken of before. On looking over M. Piesse's guide-book to ascertain if he had seen more than we could see in this tumble of prosaic brick buildings, open spaces, and even gardens—just like in the Tower of London—I was hugely tickled with the description of a clock which adorned the Mechouar in the days of the Sultan Abou-Hammou-Moussa. The learned Abbé Bargès has translated the description from the work of Mohammed el-Tenessi: "Above the clock-case was a bush, and on this bush was perched a bird, which covered its two little ones with its wings. A serpent used to come out of its hole at the bottom of the bush, and glide gently up to the little birds, which it hoped to snap up. In the front part of the clock were ten doors. There were two higher and wider doors at the two extremities." I leave out all about a cornice and a revolving figure of the moon. "At the end of each hour, and just as the door which marked it began to shiver, two eagles flew out of the two great doors, and each dropped from its beak a copper weight into a basin of copper with a hole at the bottom. The weights passed through this hole, and into the interior of the clock. Thereupon the serpent, who by this time had got to the top of the bush, hissed sharply, and bit one of the little birds, despite all the male bird" (for it appears there was a papa present) "could do to drive him away. Just in the nick of time the door which marked the hour, and which had already quivered, opened quite wide, and a young slave of matchless beauty, with a girdle of striped silk, stepped out. She held in her right hand an open book (*cahier*), and on its page was a piece of verse, and this verse contained the number of the hour then striking. The beautiful slave held her left hand on her mouth, as you do when you have the honour of speaking with a Khaleef." Our friend tells us nothing of what the snake and the birds were doing all this time; but I have no doubt the reptile subsided into its hole, the bird flew back to his perch, and the slave withdrew into her bower, and the show was over.

These little exhibitions are, I dare say, idiotic enough; but have I not, *moi qui vous parle*, stood over and over again under the clock tower of Berne, one of a crowd of travelling English (barristers, medical men, stock-brokers, and clergy) all intent on watching a similar piece of ingenious foolery—the crowing of a cock, the marching of armed men, the bowing of a crowned figure, etc.? You won't see Abou-Hammou's clock now in the Mechouar, but it was one of the chief ornaments of the place in his day.

As there is little to be done in this place, let us drive down to Agadir. Let us raise ourselves in our own opinion by standing on the ruins of ancient Pomaria, or Rome. As you drive along through the town, you would do well to notice the quaint little shops where the natives are carrying on their various trades. Though far less picturesque than at Constantine, they are interesting enough. The houses were very small, all ground floor. There was a good deal of leather-work and woodwork going on. The usual little stores for the sale of dried grains, beans, etc.; stores with calicoes and such like, but above all *cafés* and cook-shops. The cooking seemed to be carried out in cleanly fashion enough, but it is not so much the things as the people you come to see, and you will scarcely be disappointed.

You pass out of Tlemçen by that perpetual Porte de l'Abattoir, go down a hill between flowers and trees, and you are soon standing in front of the minaret of Agadir. Here you are at last in the Roman orchard, though thirteen centuries and more have passed away since Roman lips tasted fruit here. The date of the original minaret is given as A.D. 789, but it seems to have been, like the Highlander's pistol, a good deal repaired. It is high, square in form, with a course of heavy stonework at the bottom. You see above the little engaged columns and arabesque work, common in buildings of this description. There are traces of inscriptions on the Roman stone, though truth compels me to admit that I could not make out the word "Pomaria," as the guide-books put it. The minaret is nothing like our shattered friend at Mansoura, but it is uninjured by time, and is a great landmark. In order to get a good sight of the remains of the old walls, it is better to descend still lower, to a little Koubba named after Sidi Daoudi, which we entered, but where we found nothing worthy of particular mention. Standing outside the Koubba, you get a very fair view of the walls, in which there seemed to be a good deal of old Roman masonry. We wandered about here awhile in sunny idleness. I do not think that one indulges at the time in any very profound thoughts about the ruin of empires and such like; but you certainly enjoy yourself in a way of which you need not be ashamed, and get a number of pictures into your mind, which will help you afterwards over your books.

From Sidi Daoudi's Koubba we drove up the hill, and to the entrance of what is called Le Bois de Boulogne, where we alighted, as we thought it would be less tiring to walk down than up the little valley of the Oued-Kalia. This Bois de Boulogne is a very pretty place, but as unlike the Parisian Bois as may be. On alighting from the carriage, you pass on for a while between two hedges and on a narrow path, and suddenly find yourself in an old Arab burying-ground, in a wilderness of stately trees, mainly ash trees. We stood gazing there for a time at one in particular, the like of which is not to be found in Lord Darnley's park at Cobham. This is the Bois Sacré of Blidah over again, but for *olive* trees read *ash*. From what we saw here I should much doubt if the ash, according to the old song, does flourish best in the "North country." It would seem to attain higher perfection in Africa.

There were two or three Koubbas about, from one of which proceeded a humming sound—the usual monotonous hum of professional gentlemen who make a business of religion. Numbers of draped and veiled women were flitting about like spectres under the ash trees. It came into my head that here must be the Koubba of Sidi Yakoub which I had read about. Prayers at the tomb of the saint were supposed to be exceptionally advantageous to ladies who wished that their houses might not remain childless; hence, no doubt, the presence of so many women. Halloa! am I in the midst, or on the edge, of the Mysteries? I care nothing about these wretched women and their trumpery. Let me get back to the hotel, amongst the comfortable men, back to M. Pascalin and the running waiter and the dogs. But we see actual men descending to the tomb of the holy man. They must know what they are about; were there any danger of decapitation, or impalement, or any unpleasant result of that kind, they would not run their necks into Sidi Yakoub's net. We must have a peep. So we crept along, pretending to admire the ash trees, but gradually working our way down to the Koubba; and we found there just one old fakir-looking sort of a wretch, who was sitting cross-legged by the saint's tomb, and who was making all this pother. He hummed away like a top, as though he were paid by time, not as piece-work. He eyed us rather askance we thought, at first. Was he about to raise the cry of "Help, O Mussulmen; the Christian dogs are defiling the Prophet's beard," or some wholly unfounded accusation of that kind? But we were fascinated, and, like birds, gazed upon our snake. There must, I suppose, have been something eminently ridiculous in our appearance or in our looks, for the old fakir's face relaxed into a broad grin. Allah be praised, we may be ridiculous, but we are all right. So we got off, and away from under the ash trees.

But we were not out of danger yet. As I live, a buxom Arab matron, with uncovered face, sailed up to me and addressed me in French. She was dressed in a blue and white striped silk tunic, blue jacket embroidered in silver, large white muslin bags, and a lace veil with a quantity of gold ornaments. She had with her one or two attendants, and a little girl. Merciful heavens! what can she want with me? But here is my wife to protect me. I defy creation in general, and these baggy women one and all. I am bound to say the lady very civilly expressed her regret at seeing me walking about so lamely, and was good enough to inquire as to what was amiss. As she had given this turn to the conversation, I was but too glad to follow her lead, and told her my story. She strongly recommended me to try much praying at the tomb of Sidi Yakoub, and informed me that the holy man there would, for a consideration, deliver to me certain charms, or amulets, which could not but effect a certain and speedy cure. I thanked the lady, though I could not in my own mind see the slightest affinity between my case and those for which Sidi Yakoub was habitually consulted. The lady was fat and comely, and as I came to think the matter over with myself, I could not but fancy that she wished to "air" her French, so as to excite the admiration of her attendants. She might, again, have been one of those physicking women you meet with in all countries, who are never happy till they have got a few pills down your throat, and persuaded you to put your feet in hot water. Be this as it may, we all bowed courteous adieus to each other, and we proceeded down the valley by the side of the little stream, rejoicing in the shade of the giant ash trees, till we came to a garden and a path. It was a cool and pleasant stroll.

This evening, opposite the hotel, and under the wall of the Mechouar, we heard again, for the twentieth time since we had been at Tlemçen, the shrill sound of a little flageolet or pipe. We ran to the window, and there we saw a handsome, powerful young man, with a red skull-cup, but otherwise dressed like a European, in a kind of drab knickerbocker suit, piping away, and dancing amidst a crowd of children. They were teasing and mocking him, but nothing could exceed the good humour with which he tolerated their small worritings. Every now and then he would call out "Maria," and the children were not slow to answer him with "Marias" as loud as his own. His music was just two or three long sharp notes, and then a trill; from this he never diverged, but kept on piping, calling out "Maria," and spinning round like a dancing dervish. The poor fellow was *toqué* or *timbré*, they told me, or, as we should say, he had a bee in his bonnet—a whole hive, I should fear. He was a lunatic, but a perfectly harmless one, and therefore he was left at large, to wander about the country as he liked. He was devoted to children; it was of no use to give him sous—he merely passed them on in his turn to one or other of the children who were ever teasing him. We had met him in all sorts of strange places—on the hill above Mansoura, in the street at Negrier, in the garden of the Medressa at Bou-Medin, or piping away behind one quaint little Koubba or another. We got at last to know the cry of "Maria" and the shrill monotonous whistle as a usual incident of Tlemçen and its neighbourhood. I often tried to converse with him in French, and sometimes he would answer with a few short words, not irrationally, but quickly subside into a kind of vacant laugh, appealing by his looks to the bystanders to tell his story to the strangers, and assenting with a kind of pleased grin when it was told to his satisfaction.

The tale ran somewhat thus, and I think it might be worked up into a libretto for an opera, just as well as Dinorah, or any subject of that kind. My poor mad friend would have danced a shadow dance for you to perfection amidst the ruins of Mansoura, and I doubt little but that the constant repetition of "Maria" would have given the necessary flavour to the piece. He had borne an excellent character, and was a good steady workman; he was married, with two or three children; all circumstances seemed to promise him a career of ratepaying respectability. Here was *paterfamilias* surrounded by the most admirable commonplaces. But, alas! on what a thread hangs respectability! The poor fellow caught sight one day of a very pretty French girl, called Maria. It was soon the old, old story. He came, he saw, he was conquered. Work and wife and children were soon neglected, and he took to wandering about the country in an uncomfortable sort of way. The "breath of scandal," as the usual phrase runs, never passed over the fair fame of Mademoiselle Maria, who, as I should gather from the story, was rather annoyed than pleased with the devotion of the strange admirer. By her own wish, or the wish of her friends, she slipped away quietly from Tlemçen, and went back to France, *viâ* Oran. The young workman—he was an Arab—was not cured, nor did he return to the paths of steadiness. He had been absent from home some days, but at length came back to Tlemçen in a sadly dishevelled state, calling on "Maria" in a disconsolate way. When he could be brought to tell it, what was made out of his story was that a few nights before, when the moon was at the full, he was standing on the bridge of the Saf-Saf, watching the flow of the water, and reflecting upon his unfortunate passion.

Suddenly there appeared to him a vision at the other end of the bridge, making music such as he endeavoured to repeat upon his pipe, nothing more, nothing less. She—for it was a she vision—seemed to beckon him on, and in his ecstasy he called out her name, "Maria, Maria!" and tried to follow her. Alas! he could not move from the spot, for all her beckonings! A slight shade of sarcasm passed over the beloved features. "He woke; she fled, and day brought back his night." He wandered about without food or shelter—not so terrible a thing in these parts, as though the event had occurred amongst us in Essex and in the autumn season. At last he got home, he knew not how, but from that time his wits were fairly gone. The only thing which gave him comfort was the purchase of the tin pipe, on which, by day and night, he kept on repeating the spectre's trill, and calling for the lost one.

This is what we saw, and what we were told. I will not, of course, vouch for the truth of the tale. That the poor fellow had seen a pretty young woman, that his wits got addled, and that one night he fancied he saw her figure by a running stream, is all probable enough. That he was now a harmless lunatic was quite certain. But when you came to ask for particulars, such as the young lady's family name, the names of any person or persons in the town who knew her, even the precise date of the occurrence, I am bound to say the result was not satisfactory. Unless the poor fellow should shortly die, which did not seem probable, I think it likely that future visitors to Tlemçen will hear that wild cry of "Maria" often enough, and see the poor demented creature capering about amongst the children, and petting them in return for their ill usage. He seemed happy enough; the good people gave him food freely, and he slept about on the threshold of a mosque, at the corner of a street, or under a rock on the hill-side, with a sort of semi-ecstatic smile on his face for the "Maria" who was probably present to him. Having to choose between the prose of every-day life and the poetry of his dream, on which side would he have given his own vote? I doubt much if he would have been obliged to any one who had cured him.

But now for one of the greater lions of Tlemçen. We had resolved to see the famous stalactite caves of the Beni-Aad, distant about eight miles from the town. A French gentlemen and his lady stopping in the hotel had the same desire, so we agreed to combine for the payment of Arabs to illuminate the cave. But there was a good deal to be done before we got there. You could only reach by carriage a certain point; then, without mules and *cacolets*, you could not get to the cave, which was high up in the mountains. At M. Pascalin's suggestion, I wrote to the general commanding at Tlemçen a humble request, setting forth my earnest desire to see the caves, and my absolute inability to get there otherwise than in a *cacolet*. M. Pascalin, who took the letter and a card, brought back a ready and courteous assent: two baggage-mules, the one fitted with a *cacolet*, the other for the use of the soldier who was to attend us, should be forthcoming next day at the village where we were to leave our carriage. This was done; M. Pascalin himself, as well as our usual guide, Mohammed, accompanying us.

About 2 p.m., or a little before, we started from the village of Daya, my wife sitting in her share of the *cacolet* on one side of the mule, I on the other. The *cacolet* is just a sort of chair, with a ledge for the feet, comfortable enough whilst you are going uphill, but very much the reverse in the descent. If the descent be sharp, it always seems to you as though you were about to be shot out of your *cacolet*. How if the mule should stumble? I never saw a wilder bit of country than the hill-side up which we passed; nothing but short African scrub for vegetation, and masses of rock cropping out here and there. As it was very much uphill, all went on swimmingly. Nothing could exceed the attention of the smart little French soldier in charge of us, nor his contempt for Mohammed and his shiftless ways. It was certainly a magnificent scene of mountains and great distances. We came upon a circle of black Arab tents; these tents were to furnish our torch-bearers, and out they tumbled as soon as the dogs gave notice of our approach. As the French lady and gentlemen were a little behind, we went on, so as to get a rest before entering the cave; and glad enough I was to find myself at the top, and to sit down on a bit of rock to await events. The Arabs, by their gibberings, gave us to understand that we should pass into the cave by a kind of long fissure, which did not seem a very promising entrance; but no doubt we shall get in, as others have done before us.

But what is this? a running Arab? What has happened? There has been an accident to the party behind; two of them have been thrown from their mules on passing the little brook we remember. We were unfeignedly grieved, and equally delighted, some minutes afterwards, when we saw monsieur handing madame round a corner of the rock, unscathed as when they had left the Hôtel de la Paix. On crossing the brook in question, one of the mules had splashed some of the party, and as the last part of the ascent was very rough, the lady had preferred walking. So much for Arab stories. In war-time, people who rely upon their reports must frequently be astonished.

But now was the time for numbering our followers. There were some fifty or sixty of these poor fellows, carrying bundles of dry reeds (just what we had seen used at the Tombeau), and the Sheikh pronounced an allocution, which, I suppose, meant that he had cut down their backsheesh, and would himself be good enough to use the balance in a way which would meet with the approval of every right-minded working man. The poor Arabs grunted—whatever that might mean—and in we crawled.

It certainly was a very curious place, if not quite the scene of fairy-like splendour which we had been led to expect. Here again we were suffering from the results of over-praise. The cave is of immense depth. We went on for half an hour at least, at a very fair rate, quite to the point beyond which visitors are not allowed to go. It would be impossible to exaggerate the strange weird look of the gigantic stalactites amongst which the Arabs were perched, waving their torches and looking like so many demons. The ground beneath our feet was wet and sloppy—I suppose it must be so in places of this kind—and up one step and down another we were hustled or helped, but we managed to see everything. One really could not have imagined the existence of stalactites on so vast a scale. The only scene of the kind we had ever visited was the cave in the Cheddar Valley, near Wells, which must be known to many of my English friends. The Cheddar cave is a mere miniature by the side of a great picture, when you come to compare it with the cave of the Beni-Aad, but, if infinitely smaller, it is much cleaner and more brilliant. Here columns, and pillars, and figures resembling men and beasts surround you on every side, and, considered as a mere freak of nature, the scene is probably unequalled. There were dark passages, and suggestions of dark passages, just indicated by an Arab or two with torches. Those near us kept gibbering to me somewhat which meant, according to Mohammed, that yonder group of apparently turbaned figures had been in their time sound Moslems, but they had erred on some point of faith, and we had before us the terrible result: cats, dogs, monkeys—you might have imagined anything you pleased. Here half a column growing up from the ground, there half a column growing down from the roof, ledges, cornices, systems of pillars; you had stalactites of any size or form your heart could desire.

We had been something more than half an hour in the cave, when the Sheikh pronounced it time to return. We had so filled the place with the smoke of our torches, that the going back was not quite so pleasant; but it had to be done, and we enjoyed, as well as we could, the sight of the Arabs, perched up in queer out-of-the-way corners, flaring their torches about. We got out at last, and very pleasant was the first breath of fresh air. It was a strange, weird sight, more fantastic and on a far larger scale than anything I had imagined, but, as we both agreed, not so beautiful as we had been led to anticipate. We missed the transparent beauty of the little Cheddar cave.

It was time to mount and get home, but five minutes of downward progress soon convinced me it was useless to suppose one could go downhill in that *cacolet* and live ; so I begged the soldier to lead the mules to a place below, from which the way grew more level, and, with the help of a friendly arm, I would contrive to join him there. I was glad I had done so, though heartily sorry for the sufferer, when I saw poor M. Pascalin shot out of his *cacolet* as he was going down the hill. He cut his knee a good deal, and we were very pleased when we got him into the carriage, which the driver had the good sense to bring as high up the hill as he could go upon wheels.

The drive home was the usual thing amidst this splendid scenery. We were very glad to have seen these fantastic caves, which are a world's wonder. The cost to us was a napoleon apiece for the torch-bearing Arabs—M. Pascalin told us afterwards there were about sixty of them ; a *buona-mano* of five francs to the little soldier, who seemed quite pleased and satisfied ; ten francs for the hire of the carriage—such, I think, was the bill, beyond the debt of gratitude to the courteous French general. All we could do was to express our thanks in discharge of this. Any one going to see these caves would do well (as recommended in the guidebooks) to take with him a magnesian lamp, and blue and red lights.

The last, and perhaps the most magnificent of the sights of Tlemçen, is the mosque at Bou-Medin. I have reserved it to the last as a fitting end to our very homely rambles in Algeria. There is nothing finer in Tlemçen, and there is nothing finer than Tlemçen in this beautiful country. We visited this mosque, and the Koubba, and the Medressa many times during our stay at this place, and at length one Friday we attended afternoon prayer there. In speaking of the place I throw all these visits into one to avoid repetition.

Bou-Medin, though only divided from Tlemçen by a large Arab or native burying-ground, and by a few wild fields, is a separate place, and was in reality the ecclesiastical quarter of Tlemçen in the days of its pride. You drive out of the town by the Porte d'Oran, alongside of the burying-ground above named, and you pass two or three little Koubbas, each with a legend of its own. One in particular was sacred to the memory of "The Flying Saint," who seems to have possessed the agreeable and useful power of transporting himself by a wish to any place he might choose. Be this as it may, after something less than a mile's drive over a rough path and between rough hedges, you arrive at a spot where the driver tells you you must alight—he can go no further with the carriage. Then it is a scramble up a still rougher path, amongst a tumble-down of half-ruined houses running over with bright-eyed children. But what a luxuriance of foliage—I ask pardon for the semi-French phrase—what trees, what creepers around you! Nature has glorified the decay of El-Eubbad, for that is the right name of the place, though it be sacred to the memory of the great saint, *Sidi Bou-Medin.*

He was an Andalusian by birth; born at Seville about A.D. 1126. He was sent to college at Fez, where he won golden opinions both from tutors and undergraduates, and was looked upon as a future marabout, just as happens at Cambridge with any promising youth who comes out senior wrangler. He went as pilgrim to Mecca, got affiliated into one of the religious orders, and fairly set up as a saint and worker of miracles. He and Sidi Feredj (the man of Sidi Ferruch, near Algiers) seem to have possessed identical slippers of miraculous power. He settled for a time at Bougie, where he astonished the faithful by his words and acts; but finally, on the invitation of the then Sultan, came to Tlemçen, according to the legend, where he caught sight of the green spot where now stands El-Eubbad. He said to his companions, "In such a place as that should I like to sleep my last long sleep in peace." He died as they were passing over the *Oued-Isser,* at the age of seventy-five, and was buried in the Koubba, where we find a tomb in his honour to this day. So the Sultan who had sent for the saint never saw him in life, but his successor built the mausoleum as we see it now.

At the end of a steep bit of climbing you enter a door or hole in the wall, and find yourself in a narrow alley: on the left is the Koubba of this saint; on the right the mosque, with its tall minaret; a little higher up, but connected with the mosque, is the Medressa. So here you have before you a Mohammedan religious foundation of the highest kind. Of each in its order. To visit the Koubba you go down some steep steps, and find yourself in a small court. Round it are little arcades, with pillars of the eternal onyx. Cages with birds are hanging against the walls. You see before you more than one tomb, but to find the right one you must enter a door, and you are in a not very large room lighted from above through a cupola. The light comes through stained glass. Here is a tomb very like the others which you may have seen in Algeria since your first peep at the last resting-place of Sidi Abderrahman, at the top of the Jardin Marengo at Algiers. There are the usual banners and ostrich-eggs and looking-glasses, and I am reminded by M. Piesse of what I might otherwise have forgotten, an old clock in a varnished tin case. Pieces of silk, plain and embroidered, are thrown over the tomb. It is very like other such places—a little finer, perhaps. But let us get on to the mosque; we shall return here after service for a few minutes.

The great mosque at Bou-Medin, or El-Eubbad, has a defect in common with many of our cathedrals on the continent of Europe. It is so closed in and blocked in, that you can scarcely get a fair look at the magnificent front door. I have a tolerably clear picture of it in my memory, and have an excellent photograph of the gate lying before me even whilst I write, but I find it a little difficult to convey my impressions to others by mere words. You ascend a good many steps, pass through a horse-shoe arch magnificently decorated, and find yourself under a cupola. The walls are covered with arabesques, and in front of you there is a cedar door, decorated with metal-work of a very elaborate and beautiful kind. The legend is that a Spaniard had caused the door to be made as the price of his redemption from slavery, but some evil-minded persons threw the gate into the sea. The accident was a trifle in those good old holy days. When the difficulty was stated to Sidi Bou-Medin, he simply wished the gate back in its place, and back it went, and is there still, which proves the truth of the story. How the late Mr. Barham, of the "Ingoldsby Legends," would have revelled in the sayings and doings of these old Moh'ammedan saints!

You pass through the gate into a large open yard, with a fountain in the middle, and an arcade on either side, and from the arcade you might ascend into the minaret, which towers above your head. The mosque proper is in front of you, elevated a couple of steps above the court. The roof is supported by arcades of pillars. The *mihrab* is of great beauty. I will not say it is quite equal to the one in the Arab school, but it would certainly take rank next to it. The arabesque work on the walls is of the most elaborate and delicate kind—sculptured carpets. The *mimbar*, or pulpit of painted wood by the side of the *mihrab*, was the gift of Abd-el-Kader. This is the finest mosque we entered in Algeria. There is not only the actual beauty of the place—the artistic merit of the work before you—but you are here isolated from all commonplace associations or sights. It is quiet in the mosque, and the faithful are gathering for prayer. We stand motionless behind a pillar, not desirous of attracting attention, as we are the only Europeans there. Mohammed the guide whispers to us to come outside, and tells us that we shall have plenty of time to visit the Medressa before the service begins. It is somewhat of a climb up to the Medressa, but we get there, and find ourselves in a court which in its day must have been somewhat like the court below, with the school at one end or side of it, just as the mosque is downstairs. There are bushes in the middle of the court, heavy with white roses. A learned Taleb comes out from a side door, greets us courteously, and presents a handful of the roses to my wife. The Medressa in its day must have been very splendid, but the arabesque work is sadly effaced now. The sound of wild chanting below suggests that we had better not lose time here, so we go down again, kick off our shoes, and slip in at a side door behind a pillar. The place is full now, both the body of the mosque and the two arcades. The arcade near us is appropriated to the women—it is full of them; they are all heavily veiled, so that they may not disturb the devotions of the faithful. The congregation seem, as we say, to be singing a hymn, at any rate it is a long, wailing chant, and I suppose was composed of passages from the Koran. It was, however, difficult to get information, for our guide, Mohammed—the young Turk—was, whilst service lasted, obviously divided between two feelings: he wished to show us that he was protecting us; he also wished the faithful to understand that he had no connection with the infidels. So he squatted down amidst a devout group, and turned up his eyes higher and howled louder than his friends, in order to show the purity of his faith.

The psalmody was led by an official person near the *mihrab*, but, as these wild people wailed on, they seemed to get much excited by their own noise, and the word "Allah!" was pronounced in a defiant way more frequently than I could have wished. I noticed with a shudder that, as they raised their hands in prayer, they were white, non-working hands. These were not working men. Gracious Allah! what are they?

Nobody meddled with us or seemed inclined to do so, save an ugly, one-eyed ruffian, heavily marked with the small-pox, who never kept his one eye off us; but nothing came of it. We soon lost all sense of personality, so absorbing was the interest of the scene. I have attended services of a good many kinds, but not in Spain, certainly not in Rome, not at a Free Kirk chapel in our own Highlands, have I ever seen evidence of such apparent religious fervour as amongst these people. There was a constantly recurring wail or yell of "Allah!" as I have just said, which seemed like a signal to let the cavalry go. I suppose this is the way in which Messrs. Moody and Sankey get their effects. When they had done wailing, there was a pause, and presently an old man, a very old man, supporting himself on a long staff, made his way to the *mimbar*, or pulpit, and up the steps. He gave us a long discourse, which I dare say contained much sound doctrine, but as we did not understand a word of it, I cannot attempt criticism. I could not, however, but see how wise it was, after all this excitement, to interpose a sermon. The sermon at Bou-Medin had the same tranquillizing effect upon the faithful as I observe sermons have all over the world.

By the black tent of my fathers! by the Prophet's beard! some of the fellows are gossiping, and missing the crumbs! Even Mohammed telegraphed me a friendly grin, as much as to say, "We shall soon get to our slippers again, and make an end of the lions." The women, who had sat hitherto like rows of white sacks, began to fidget with their face-gear; but I saw nothing to drive one distracted. The old gentleman arrived at last at his words of application and conclusion, and we got to our singing again; but he had evidently preached the heart out of the congregation, for they were not at all so fierce as before. On the contrary, as they stood in long rows and bobbed down their heads to the floor at the proper places, there was something almost ludicrous in the precision with which they executed the manœuvre, more especially the ladies, who had ceased to be white bundles lying on the ground, and were now bowing as though by clockwork.

This, too, came to an end, and the congregation began to disperse. The one-eyed man had not forgotten us. He stalked up to where we were standing, with a look which seemed to say, "Would you like to tread on the tail of my *bernouse* now?" We had no such wish, but we stood with a bland smile at the edge of the two steps which led from the mosque into the court, as though lost in admiration of the beauty of the place. As a last chance, the man shot a stern glance from his one eye at our feet. If we had had our shoes on we were lost; but "No! my friend, socks, palpable socks; catch me profaning a mosque; yonder lie our shoes by the door. I only hope you won't appropriate them in defiance of

Allah, and the statute made and provided in that behalf." The baffled fiend turned away, but he had not noticed that he was standing at the edge of the steps, so he missed his footing, and came down at his full length in the court. I turned sharply round to the *mihrab*, so that he should not see the glance of triumph which I could not control. There was behind us as the sound of jeering, and we saw the one-eyed man no more. So out we went with the rest of the congregation, just like coming out of church at home.

We had not quite done with Bou-Medin, for on passing the Koubba there was the sound as the sound of Ethiopian serenaders. In point of fact, on reaching the little courtyard we found two or three negroes beating away on some uncouth instruments of music—one, I think, was blowing a pipe, but the result was monotonous and depressing. The place was crowded, so we stared for a while at the queer sight, took another peep into the Koubba, and then slipped away delighted with our afternoon.

From what I witnessed I should fancy the French have a heavy task before them in dealing with this people. If ever I saw evidence of religious fanaticism, it was there at Bou-Medin, and no doubt that was a mere sample. Had the old gentleman, in place of rocking his hearers to sleep, wished to rouse them to the duty of cutting throats, I should have been sorry for any one who had fallen in the way of that congregation as they came out of church. These people may be driven mad at any moment by a crazy or designing preacher, and do infinite mischief. For the time our

French friends are safe enough. May they long continue so! If they ever get into trouble in Europe, or **lose command of** the sea, I should not recommend them to rely much on the loyalty of the natives in Algeria. It is just a powder magazine; beware the spark!

We returned to our hotel, and next day left beautiful Tlemçen with much regret. If life be spared me I will get back to this place, for **I know** of nothing like it. I **do not suppose** one would care to spend a winter at this Eden—it would be too cold; but as the object of a spring excursion, say from the middle of April to the middle of June, what is there equal to Tlemçen? As a matter of business, I recommend all who may come after me to try the Hôtel de la Paix, and our friends M. and Mme. Pascalin.

We returned to Oran as we came, stepped on board a steamer, went into our berths, fell asleep, and awoke at Carthagena. It was a pleasant journey back to France by railway, through Valencia, Tarragona, Barcelona, etc. We saw many pretty things in these places, but nothing like what we had seen in Algeria.

CHAPTER XVI.

ALGERIA UNDER THE FRENCH RULE.

ANY attempt to describe Algeria as it is, or even to offer a few suggestions upon such a matter, must necessarily be coloured by the views and wishes of the writer. It would be easy—if I may use a vulgar phrase—to write French Algeria "up" or "down." I confess at once that my hearty good wishes are with the French, not only on account of North Africa itself, where in my humble opinion their presence is of immense advantage to the world, but because I think it would be greatly for the benefit of mankind if that restless, bright, intelligent people should turn their attention from ambitious designs in Europe to the civilizing of Africa. They are doing much good in Africa. I wish I could think that their African policy occupied any considerable portion of French public attention. Save their dominion be threatened, or warlike operations are actually in progress, we must not blame them much for this. What degree of attention do Indian affairs receive at home, save there be a meeting, or an Afghan question, or something of that kind? The Indian or the African question, as it may be, does not enter into the daily life of politicians; it does not turn contested elections; it does not subserve party purposes; it does not determine the existence or fall of a ministry. Still, making every allowance, I am surprised at the apathy—dare I write ignorance?—prevailing throughout France on the subject of these splendid provinces.

You will occasionally come across a learned essay, or a batch of squibs and fireworks in a newspaper, showing that never was there such a conquest as this Algerine conquest, never was a nation actuated by such pure and philanthropic motives as have moved France to the conquest of Algeria. All other nations have been influenced by lust of conquest, by greed of gain. It is France alone which has risen to the dignity of her great mission, and has alighted with the feelings of a dove, but the majesty of an eagle, on the shores of Africa. Lord Exmouth's bombardment of Algiers, the Treaty obtained for the abolition of piracy, and the subsequent retirement from the country, are looked upon as evidence of the brutality and timidity of England—if, indeed, they be not ignored altogether. It is true there was a small, a very small, back-water or renewal of piracy after 1816. The snake had been scotched, very much scotched, but was not quite dead. It was the mission of the Great Nation to complete the work and claim the whole merit of it.

But I am a little ashamed of writing stuff of this description, as the French ought to be very much ashamed of uttering it. Who cares what took place seventy years ago in such a business? The French have got the place, and long may they keep it! But the plain truth is, Bourmont and Duperré's expedition in 1830 had as much to do with philanthropy as with the small-pox.

The ministry of Charles X. was on its last legs, and it was hoped that a thunderclap from Algiers would divert public attention from some small matters which were occurring at Paris just then to the progress of the *war* in Africa. Of course *ces Anglais* receive their due allowance of dirty water. True it is that M. de Polignac had sent a circular round to the European cabinets, in which he announced emphatically that conquest was not the French object, but that in case the regency at Algiers was shaken, he would consult with his sovereign's allies on what was best to be done in the common interest of all. The object was to gain time, for I do not suppose the wildest patriot who ever explained his views of the predominance of France over other nations of the world, would maintain it as a probability that, if the English fleet in the Mediterranean, with or without the help of the other great Powers, had been directed to intercept the French flotilla on its run between Toulon and Sidi Ferruch, there would have been much chance of its ever reaching the place last named. As time wore on, and it was seen that all the cabinets, including our own, had received the French assurance for truth, the tone gradually grew more magniloquent and defiant. Things had got pretty much to a head; in place of diplomatic rose-water, one might write a *billet sec et laconique*, and there appears to have been finally an interview between Lord Aberdeen and the French Ambassador at London, which reads more like the climax of a *vaudeville* than action in real life. "You will obtain nothing from France, M. le Ministre, by threats; perhaps a forgotten crumb from her generosity." Put that into a quatrain; let the distinguished diplomat make his bow, and retire slowly back—centre. Confusion of English Premier, and curtain falls.

Over and over again I wonder as I read such things, aye, even in the book of M. Camille Rousset, just published, which is obviously the work of a highly cultivated and able man. If Frenchmen are absolutely devoid of a sense of the ludicrous, why should he take the trouble to defend the expedition to Algiers? It suited the French to go and conquer this country, and to keep it. There is an end of the matter, and beyond this all is vanity and idle pretension. The conquest gave them no great trouble; it would have been scarcely an episode in our Indian story. A French regiment could walk over the regency. This, however, was not known at the time. Bourmont had his head full of the Egyptian matters in the days of the first Bonaparte. Ready and ungrudging praise will be given by all to the valour of the French troops, if not to the ability of all of the superior officers. Even on M. Rousset's showing, a French division lost its way between Staoueli and Algiers, and, had the Turkish opposition been worth a pinch of snuff, must have perished. All honour, however—where honour is due—to the French soldiers!

This is just an Englishman's growl in answer to the eternal sneers and abuse of the French journals and writers. It was a rare event to take up a newspaper at Algiers without finding some taunt or some attack upon the English. Now, I would appeal to the common sense of any English man, woman, or child in these islands, is there anybody here who **wants** to meddle **with** the French in Algiers? They are developing—on paper at least—vast projects for annexing the Soudan, laying a rail across the desert, seizing Morocco, seizing Tunis, seizing the Lord knows what. They can know but little **of the** course of public affairs in England if they imagine they would meet with trouble from us. I would not say the same of all the European Powers. Italy **has** her eye on Tunis; Spain would not see Morocco absorbed without a word. Behind them both stands **the** dread spectre of Germany, if peace should be broken. The plain fact is that we are the only people in Europe from whom they have nothing to dread, but the dirty water is all for us. Finally, and before coming to **the** more agreeable part of **my poor remarks on what I saw** with my own eyes, let me say **that the French** would do well to **remember a truth of** which **we are** profoundly convinced in our own **case.** Would India, would Canada, would Australia, remain **to us, if** our superiority at sea were lost or destroyed? We think not, although, of course, I am far from meaning that either in Australia **or** Canada we hold the place by arms. **Now, let** France apply **the** same reasoning to her hold on North Africa. As long as she can keep the sea against all **comers, her** conquest is safe. **Let her fail** upon that point, and **French** dominion **in** Algiers would topple down like a house of **cards. It would** be a source of weakness, **not of strength,** to France; it would absorb a large portion of troops wanted elsewhere, or if they were withdrawn, a native insurrection would soon account for the undefended establishments. At present a native rising would not have a chance. The bulk of the natives would listen to-morrow to the wild accents of any religious impostor who should preach up a war against the infidel, were it not for a wholesome dread of the bayonets and chassepôts. Nor do I believe that Algeria has been a good training-ground for French soldiers and French officers. They are trained to one mode of warfare,—they are called upon to practise something quite different when *la patrie* is in danger in Europe. Wild yells and dashing charges won't produce much effect upon a Pomeranian regiment; the rogues are absolutely destitute of sentiment. However, that is a question for the French themselves. I simply record my belief—and I do it as a sincere well-wisher to France—that the possession of Algeria in no way adds to the military strength of that nation. I fear the very reverse is the case.

Now, about what one sees in the three provinces. I am happy to record, as the result of our wanderings, that we were as delighted as surprised with what we saw. Plentiful cultivation, abundant crops, good roads, excellent railways; plenty of harbours and refuges (whatever they may say) along the coast from Mersa-el-Kebir to Bône; towns growing in size and population, if not in beauty; order everywhere; military posts at all the vantage-points; perhaps not as many European farms and prospering villages as I should have wished: but the French have done good work, and Europe should be much obliged to them for undertaking this troublesome job. It has certainly cost them a good deal of money. The present Dean of Lincoln, Dean Blakesley, who visited the country in 1858, after careful calculation stated it as his conclusion that the cost of Algeria to France up to that time had been £60,000,000 sterling. There have been terribly expensive times since then. Would it be wrong in a rough way to put down the cost of Algeria to the French as £100,000,000 sterling from 1830 to 1880?

What is the *per contra*—whether the result be owing to mal-administration, or to the nature of things? Colonization has not been firmly established; the colonists cling to the sea-coast or to the neighbourhood of the large towns. In the Algerine journals written by Frenchmen, you read daily the bitterest complaints as to the difficulties thrown in the way of intending colonists. The object would seem to be to deter, not to invite, colonization. At the bottom, no doubt, is the impatience of the French character—they will not give time for results; and, next, their insane tendency to reliance upon Government. Where a parcel of Americans or English would shoulder their axes and firelocks, and step out into the wilderness to make homes for themselves, the Frenchman will wait till a scheme for a village has passed through *bureaux* innumerable, till roads have been begun by the Ponts et Chaussées, public buildings have been mapped out, and what not. Patience and self-reliance,—without these qualities the colonist had better stop at home. Then the Frenchman is essentially a cockney—may I venture to write it without offence?—he is firmly convinced that France is the only country in which a civilized man can exist, and the bare mention of Paris sets him off into sentimental hysteria.

It is not very easy to get reliable statistics about Algiers when you are on the spot. At first you would suppose that you have only to stretch out your hand and take; but be a little persistent, and you will find a shade pass over the face of the gentleman so courteous a moment before. You are a spy, an adverse journalist, an *Anglais* come to look into the chances of hostile attempts. I did, however, after many futile endeavours, obtain a copy of the "État Actuel de l'Algérie," prepared by order of General Chanzy, the late governor, in 1877 (therefore only three years old), under the direction of a Conseiller d'État. I suppose it contains facts as far as they go. In this report I find that there was a census of the population taken in 1876, and that it then numbered (all told except the army) 2,816,575. The army counted for 51,051 more. I give the table, distinguishing the nationalities and the amount of increase and decrease between 1872 and 1877.

Nationalities.	1872.	1876.	Increase.	Decrease.
French	129,601	155,727	26,126	—
Naturalized Jews	34,574	33,287	—	1,287
Spaniards	71,360	92,510	21,144	—
Italians	18,351	25,759	7,408	—
Anglo-Maltese	11,512	14,220	2,708	—
Germans	4,933	5,722	789	—
Other nationalities	9,354	17,524	8,170	—
Mussulmans	2,125,052	2,462,936	337,884	—
Population (*en bloc*)	11,482	8,890	—	2,592
Total	2,416,225	2,816,575	404,229	3,879

On the whole an increase of 404,229, of which 66,345 are Europeans, and 337,884 Mussulmans. Of foreigners, more than half are Spanish, i.e. 92,510 against 155,735 total foreigners, and take last term of comparison 155,735 foreigners against 155,727 French.

Dr. Ricoux has published a statistical work on Algeria, from which I have seen an extract since my return. He gives the total number of inhabitants in Algeria as about 3,000,000, which would tally pretty well with General Chanzy's results at the end of 1876; he does not include the army. He takes the Europeans as one-eighth, or about 353,600; the French at about 150,000. He gives the birth-rate of the French in Algeria as oscillating between 35 and 41 per 1000 inhabitants, as against 26 in France. The death-rate per 1000, which was at first 46, dwindled down in 1876 to 25, as against 23, the normal mortality in France. The Spaniards he gives as 92,000; birth-rate at first very high, 47·5, now 38; mortality about the same as in Spain, i.e. 30. The same thing will hold good of Italians and Anglo-Maltese. Italians, Maltese, and Spaniards scarcely change their climate by coming to Algeria. On the other hand, from the French point of view, it would be highly desirable to pass the whole of the Germanic race by drafts through the Algerian cullender. The *death-rate* of Germans was at first 55, but has descended to 33, but *it is always superior to the birth-rate*, which is less than in Germany. Given time and patience, what might one not hope for? All races in Algeria (save the Germans) are more prolific than in the mother country. I suppose this means that there are readier means of gaining a livelihood, and that number in families is disregarded. The French notably multiply in Algeria at a far higher rate than in France; but then the French ratio is one of the smallest in Europe. Dr. Ricoux concludes in favour of the prospects of the Latin races on African soil, especially of those from the south of Europe. He looks forward with hope to the results of intermarriages between French, Spaniards, and Italians.

I should hope that between General Chanzy and Dr. Ricoux the reader will gain a true idea of the sort and number of people who live in Algeria. I have no means of verifying the increase, as recorded, of the Mussulman races. I give it as given, with my authority. It does not seem likely that even the French, whilst doing their best to arrive at and publish the truth, can be very sure of their facts. It is all easy enough in the large towns and centres of colonization, but who is to number the wild Arabs and wandering tribes? One of the great difficulties of M. Grèvy, the present governor, seemed to be some rational scheme for arriving at the *état civil* of the *indigènes*. There was a terrible decrease of population between 1866 and 1872.

In discharge of a duty, rather than in the hope that these fearful-looking figures will be read with any great zest, I give the few following lines of figures, as they are published on Government authority :—

ORDINARY BUDGET.

Receipts.	Expenditure.
1875 ... 26,080,585 fr. 38 c.	1875 ... 35,049,051 fr. 89 c.
1876 ... 27,568,840 fr. 4 c.	1876 ... 28,460,235 fr. 36 c.

BUDGET (SPECIAL RESOURCES).

Receipts.	Expenditure.
1875 ... 3,370,445 fr. 57 c.	1875 ... 1,991,731 fr. 36 c.
1876 ... 3,883,585 fr. 57 c.	1876 ... 3,385,539 fr. 49 c.

BUDGET (EXTRAORDINARY).

Receipts.	
1875 ... 7,179,818 fr. 76 c.	No return for expenditure for
1876 ... 7,517,975 fr. 11 c.	these last years.

I really have not patience to copy, nor do I think my readers would have the patience to read, endless tables of figures from this report; so I will content myself with giving formally the figures of the population and of the budget of the Colony, and will henceforward confine myself to generalities.

I saw with my own eyes, not through book-spectacles, enormous districts under cultivation, and smiling with promises of the joyful harvests. Whether Algeria will ever become a great grain-exporting country must depend on the progress of colonization, which seems at present to move very slowly, if at all, and on the opposition which the colonists may be able to offer in the markets of the world to the North American exports—for I suppose those from Russia are now low enough.

The craze when I was in Algiers turned rather on her vines than on corn. Here again I can affirm that I saw a great extent of vine-culture, and listened to endless expressions of hope upon the subject. There is nothing greater in the history of the French nation than the dignity with which the awful calamity of the vine-disease has been supported. There has been no unmanly whining, no hysterical calls for help; but let any one travel through the vine districts of France, as we did on our way home, and say if the sight does not give him a sharp heart-pinch. The expatriated vine-growers were arriving in considerable numbers at Algiers when we were there, but what the result may be time must show. The vine flourishes in Algeria—in certain localities, of course; that is a great fact. You find pretty commonly a fair "wine of the country" (at La Trappe the monks gave us a really good white wine), but I should suppose there is a great gulf between the best African and the Château Margaux, Lafitte, La Tour, of the Garonne, to say nothing of the wines of Burgundy and Champagne. How will it be if, within an appreciable time, the vine districts of France recover from this horrible plague? If they be struck with permanent sterility, that is another matter.

The Algerine tobaccos—I speak of the cigars which I smoked—like others, were of fair quality and flavour, and low in price, but I cannot think the tobacco of Algeria will much affect American produce in the markets of the world. As for cotton, I am no great authority, to be sure; but how the deuce are you to grow cotton in a country of almost permanent drought, or at least where droughts are so frequent that artificial or contrived irrigation is the first thought of the inhabitants? They seem driving a great trade in Alfa. Dates, limes, oranges, and other fruits are the usual produce of this favoured land, but scarcely big articles of commerce. Throughout the winter we had abundance of vegetables which you see on London tables in the spring, but not of the flavour to which we were accustomed. At Algiers you eat green peas on Christmas Day, but they are somewhat tasteless. You enjoy writing home about them.

There are many things in Algeria which I should like to write about were I sure of the value of my own conclusions. I have not the smallest pretension to tell the French what they ought to do, on the strength of having taken a pleasure-jaunt through the three provinces. I may venture, perhaps, to mention a few thoughts as they occurred to an Englishman's mind. Had I really wanted to arrive at weighty conclusions I would have taken care to be accompanied by a friend accustomed to Indian administration on a large scale. What problem have the French to deal with in Algeria which has not already been solved in British India—at any rate, in a way which works?

Their first great difficulty seems to be in the conflict between the civil and the military authority—which is to be civil, which military ground? Has, or has not, the time arrived for bringing the provinces under civil jurisdiction? If the object be to attract colonists from the mainland, I have no doubt this is so. Nothing easier than to let the normal rule be civil government, and in exceptional cases to call in the aid of military force, or even to hand over a district to the soldiers for a while, and until order be restored. The miseries of Algeria are attributed by the French themselves very largely to this conflict between the civilians and the army. The army have won Algeria for France, and the military spirit is so widely spread amongst Frenchmen that it is difficult for them to come down to sober prose. Shall the governor be a civilian or a soldier? I should say a civilian, beyond all doubt, though I am bound in honesty to record the fact that the present governor, a civilian, did not seem to be popular at Algiers. The soldiers would like to see a soldier in his place; the civilians think that he is out-soldiering the soldiers. To be sure, there is always a danger, when you give a body-guard to a civilian, and place a few fifes and drums at his disposal, that his head gets turned. I do not say this is so in the present case, but it is one of the probabilities of human nature. I should have thought some one like M. de Lesseps, whom I only know by name, would have been the proper governor for Algeria in the present position of the colony.

In the next place, I would venture to say that the result of an Englishman's experience is that the present system of *concessions* for the granting of land to colonists, is just another word for jobbery, favouritism, and procrastination. Let there be an upset price; sell the land, and have done with it, and chance after-difficulties. Of course there are dozens of objections to this:—are there none to the present system, which has ended in zero?

A third audacious English thought is, whenever two or three colonists are gathered together at a common dwelling-spot, give them largely and ungrudgingly the control over their own affairs. Our people in North America and Australia and elsewhere have worked to results on this system. The French idea is the perpetration of nurseries for adults, the death of all independence of character. I do not, of course, mean that it is not proper to give help to colonists in outlying places at first; but let this be done very sparingly, only for roads, purposes of military defence, and such like. Whatever is beyond this is better done at a later period by the colonists themselves, to whom facilities for borrowing may be granted in proper cases, with strict exaction of repayment; but, in the name of Allah, let the poor fellows manage their own affairs, and don't hand them over to the tender mercies of *employés* who have been trained to a routine outside of which, in their opinion, there is no safety. If I may attach any credit to the constant and bitter complaints uttered by the colonists themselves in the columns of the daily press of Algiers, they are suffering bitterly from this cause.

The close proximity to France acts in one way as a disadvantage, in another way just the reverse, inasmuch as it draws Algerine questions into the vortex of politics. We at home have had experience in such a matter. British India is now governed from London. Indian questions are discussed with increasing fervour in the press, and we know well enough how the system works. We are getting to rely more and more on English rather than on Indian statesmen—on home politicians, rather than on men who have been trained to the special work from boyhood. Whatever may be urged against these men, it is a fact that they won for us a great empire, which extends from the Himalayas to Cape Cormorin. We now govern India by electric orders and counter-orders from home. Let us only hope—since the change was inevitable—that we shall not lose under one system what we have gained under the other.

It is, however, no business of mine to speak of what is happening now in British India, otherwise than for the purposes of illustration. In Algeria you are in France. During the Empire, it was all "the Emperor," "the Arab kingdom," and such like; now it is all Republic. The candidates at elections are more eager to demonstrate the purity of their Republican principles than to offer proof of their services to the colony. It is, I think, as yet, premature to discuss anything like the question of an Algerine Chamber. Where are you to look for your constituencies but amongst the 150,000 Frenchmen and 150,000 foreigners now domiciled in Algeria? The *indigènes*, in a mass, could not be admitted to the right of voting, or they would soon vote their present masters out of Algiers. The present idea of the Conseil-Général, whose duty it should be to assist, not to thwart, the Government, and of an extension of its powers by the absorption of native notables, would seem to offer reasonable prospects of success. Algeria is a conquered country, still held down by force of arms, and has just reached the point when it may be prudent to pass from military to civil government, but certainly not yet to representative institutions, if by that be meant that every adult in the provinces (without regard to race or descent) shall have an equal vote.

The records of the last few years are there, to tell us how the nation stands affected to the French *Raj*. I am now speaking of enlightened native gentlemen, who know their own country well, but who have been partly educated in France, and who can appreciate the force of European organization and resources. Why should they seek to flatter or mislead an Englishman? If anything, they would tacitly assume, whatever we might say, that we were not well disposed to the French rule in Algeria. Now, the language of the few with whom I could converse invariably was, that it was better to make the best of things as they are, than to seek relief by a change of masters. They knew well that Algeria could not stand alone, and all that was occurring at Constantinople gave them small hope of any reconstruction of the Mohammedan power. They had been shot down freely; their lands had been as freely confiscated by the French—why begin again? I believe they intended to unfold their real meaning and views; but, at the same time, it must not be forgotten that I am speaking of the very few, and of men who probably have lost weight with their countrymen in consequence of their acquiescence in the French rule.

For the bulk of the two and a half millions of *indigènes* kept down by some 50,000 French soldiers, the French *Raj* is purely a question of time, and of a short time. Captain Richard, to whose writings I have so frequently referred, tells me that the native hopes and expectations crystallize themselves round a sort of Messiah, for whose coming they look. This is the Moulé-Saâ, the Sultan, who shall exterminate the infidel and re-establish the faith. He is to come from the Mountain of Gold, and he is to be preceded by his precursors. This is convenient enough. Any fanatical gentleman, or any one who may be minded to rely upon the fanaticism of the country, comes from the Mountain of Gold, and is the Moulé-Saâ. Presently the French shoot his following down by the thousand, and he, ignobly, runs away. He was not the true Moulé-Saâ, he was only a precursor; so the good old faith in the prophecies is maintained. Abd-el-Kader was the Moulé-Saâ for a while, so was Bou-Maza in the Dahra, but they are gone. The true prophet has yet to come.

I was struggling to get at what was passing in the heads of those majestic figures in *bernouses* who passed me in town and country, like inhabitants of another world. What does the Arab or Kabyle *believe*, as the Irish peasant believes in the Pope of Rome, and some visionary Irish king of the past? I do not mean a belief which he shall be in a position to formalize, but yet one which would set him a-dancing and flourishing his cudgel at any time, and in favour of which he would cheerfully get his brains knocked out, whilst he would turn from the multiplication table with loathing and contempt. I could not, unfortunately, talk with the people; in books I came across only conventional literary theories, copied by one writer from another, and at last—credited. These were, however, not the ideas of the Arabs, but the ideas of the writers as to what the ideas of the Arabs would probably be. I had much rather have possessed the gift of Arabic for a day, and have spent my time in a *zaouia* or a *café Arabe*. It was very disappointing.

Just then I came across the account given of the matter by Captain Richard, in his "Insurrection du Dhara" (Alger, 1846). What I am about to compress into a few sentences will be found at length in page 121 of his book. The true Moulé-Saâ will drive the French away, and succeed them in the government of the country. His reign may last five, seven, nine years—wise men are not agreed about this. There will then fall upon the

Arab people greater calamities than they have ever before known. The reader must forgive me for introducing him to the "Jadjoudjaoumadjoudja." The word seems to indicate a bad joke, but it really means a countless people of savages, whom Sidi Kornin has shut up between two mountains of stone, and shut down with a cover of iron. When the iron pot-lid has been rusted by time, and shaken by the efforts of the good people with the long name, they will at last break out. Never has the world seen such desolation as will follow on their steps. They will eat up everything, from the dates to the nettles, and drink up every river, lake, and fountain of water. The earth will become a desert. At this moment Sidna-Aïssa (Jesus Christ) will descend upon the earth and exterminate these horrible people. But their carcases might produce a pestilence; so Allah, the All-wise and All-merciful, will send abundance of huge birds, who will carry off the corpses and fling them into the sea. The time which will follow will be too pleasant to last. After a short reign, Sidna-Aïssa will go and die at Mecca, and after his days the human race will cease to reproduce their kind. The end of the world will then be.

All this reads so much like a bit of the "Arabian Nights," and is so unutterably absurd, that I am inclined to think it may be true; at any rate, I give it as I find it. The attempt of Abd-el-Kader can scarcely be renewed. If it ever had a chance of success, this could only be from the profound ignorance of the conquerors as to the meaning of what they saw around them. Abd-el-Kader never represented the effort of a united country. He was never truly accepted by the Kabyles; he was surrounded by jealousies in his own house. The Emperor of Morocco bore it like a man when Abd-el-Kader was shipped off for France, and it was only by help from Morocco that he was able to hold out so long. The only chance I can see is that the French might be tempted prematurely to seize Morocco, which, of course, they could do without much trouble; but as to keeping it, that would be quite another matter. If it has taken them half a century to get fast hold of Algeria, how long would they require to reduce Morocco, a wilder country, to obedience. A protracted warfare might rouse the old Arab spirit, and if, concurrently with this, the French were hampered in Europe and on the sea, trouble might come. I see in the *Times* of this day (one of the last days of October), that there has been a congress of learned Germans, who have arrived at the conclusion that an extensive system of colonization might work well for the Fatherland. Now, professors in Germany are the stormy petrels of the race.

In conclusion, I doubt not for one moment that at the present time all native resistance is subdued in Algeria, and that any attempt at insurrection would be quickly and ruthlessly put down. It requires some generosity in an Englishman, seeing how his own country is the constant object of French sneers and abuse, not to copy from the French writers themselves a story such as that of the Dahra Cave. We are quite ready to make allowances for the stern necessities of war, but are people who have done such things in a position to fling stones at their neighbours? It matters little, however, what we think. The Arabs and the Kabyles know full well what they have suffered from the invader, and in what very red characters the chronicles of the conquest are written. I do not see how the French are to deal with the blood-feud, otherwise than by recognizing and ignoring it—the first for present security; the second, for the sake of a peaceful future. There must be a good deal of human nature about the Arab and Kabyle, after all. Make it clear to them that they can purchase and hold in security such patches of land as they may desire, keep faith with them above all, and do not administer them too much, and in a generation or two I can scarcely see why peaceful, law-abiding yeomanry and small proprietors should not grow up. When I was in the colony there was much outcry that the Arabs were most unfairly taxed in comparison with the colonists. The exemption must have maddened the Arabs, and has not attracted colonists. No more suicidal policy could be conceived. It is all well enough to attract colonists, but you must pacify the natives. In this way, too, you would arrive at a solution of the vexed problem of whether the natives are to be handled directly or through their chiefs. Interest them both in the cultivation of the soil, and they may be left to settle their reciprocal relations. I am sure that in the Metidja, and both in the provinces of Oran and Constantine, I saw land fertile enough, and plentiful enough for all.

I set down these random impressions with great diffidence; they represent the thoughts which must occur to an Englishman in travelling through the country. To my poor thinking, civil government, free municipalities (I mean that *bourgades*, or rural communities of any size, shall manage their own affairs); sale, not *concessions*, of public land; equal taxation, the review of customs and port dues, a civil governor, and a Commander-in-chief reporting to the War Office at Paris through the governor, with an extension of the Conseil-Général system, would seem to be measures of probable advantage to the colony. Above all things, let the French get rid of poetry and visions, and stick to prose. When one knows the mischief which has been done in Ireland by Tara harps, minstrel boys, and so on, a man must see of what disadvantage it has been to the French to deal with dreams in Algeria. The traditional Arab chief must take off his *bernouse*, and go to work like the rest of us.

My last sentence shall contain an earnest prayer for the happiness and prosperity of Algeria under French rule. The " pirates' home " has become an orderly as it ever was a magnificent country. The civilized world must thank the French for this. My advice to my countrymen is, " Go and travel in Algeria."

CHAPTER XVII.

CONCLUSION.

I WILL conclude as I began. "Where shall we spend the winter?" has become a common cry amongst many English people who, for one reason or another, are unable to pass the dark months at home. Failing health is, of course, the chief cause; but there are many others. It is not unnatural that people who are not bound to remain in England by business engagements, or for the sake of others, should prefer sunshine to fog—a genial, or at least a tolerable, climate to frost and damp and streets beslushed with half-melted snow. When to these disagreeable incidents of a Northern winter are super-added the physical inconveniences of colds and coughs and fits of bronchitis, there is no great cause for wonder if the shores of the Mediterranean are just now in such great request. The English are still the chief winter wanderers, because, as the intelligent foreigner is in the habit of remarking, the climate of England is so utterly detestable, that nobody who could escape from such a country would remain in it. I am sorry to be at issue with the intelligent foreigner, but the result of my own experience would be that, at any rate for the last few years, it is not only the climate of England, but that of northern Europe, which is detestable. London, bad as it may be, presents better chances of comfort than Paris, as a winter residence. Who, save under penal sentence, would spend the latter autumn, the entire winter, and early spring at Berlin? An English country house has its advantages for the young and active, if the season be an "open" one; but of late years the winters are about as open in England as in the Arctic regions. Besides, in any case, one must be strong and hearty and young to enjoy the outdoor sports of an English winter. I have spoken of all this elsewhere; so, to avoid repetitions, I think I may say that English people by the hundred and by the thousand flock every year to the shores of the Mediterranean in search of a resting-place. From Cannes to Genoa you will find the land dotted with English colonies.

But, for the last two years at any rate, it has been very cold even in this favoured spot, so we thought of something still further to the south. The choice seemed to lie between the Nile and Algiers. For reasons which would have no interest out of our own family circle, my wife and I did not wish to go so far away as the Second Cataract, and so we determined to make trial of Algiers. This we have done, having spent the winter and spring of 1879-80 in this part of Africa—all but six months in the town of Algiers and on the heights of Mustapha, and between two and three others in excursions about the three provinces of Algiers, Oran, and Constantine. The result of my observations I have now laid before those who may be asking themselves, "Where shall we spend the winter? Shall we give Algiers a trial?"

The outcome of all I have to say, as far as residence in the town of Algiers itself, and on Mustapha, is concerned, just amounts to this. For brightness and sunshine there is nothing like the climate within four days' post of London. There may be qualities in the air which render it unfit for some people, but as to the *brightness* of the place there can be no manner of doubt. The heights of Mustapha are much the same thing as Torquay, but there is the wonderful sky above and the background of mountains. Algiers is a beautiful place. As a set-off against this, the accommodation is sadly deficient. In the town the two or three hotels are but of second-rate order. On Mustapha there are a dozen or so villas fit for people with heavy purses; of a second-rate kind not many, and these not very commendable; of make-shifts not a few, but these are make-shifts indeed. The great want of the place is a good hotel on Mustapha, on the same scale as those to be found on the Riviera or the Italian lakes. Until this be forthcoming, let no one commit his family rashly to Algiers. Nor shall I have written in vain if I can but persuade the English doctors to think thrice rather than twice before packing off their patients to Algiers. An English doctor there takes in a few male boarders; beyond this, and an institute kept by a medical gentleman with a Polish name, there is literally nothing. Any advantage to be derived from a bright climate is terribly counterbalanced by indifferent accommodation, indifferent food, and doubtful drainage. Doctors, beware! Do not let patients go to Algiers till you are satisfied that a proper place of residence has been provided beforehand to receive them. Without being of the sentimental order of human beings, I may say, without exaggeration, that it filled me with sadness to see the poor creatures who were sent to Algiers in search of health, and who could not reasonably hope for anything but an aggravation of their ailments, and a last resting-place in the English cemetery. Let a good hotel be built upon Mustapha, with accommodation at reasonable rates, and of course this objection would drop. When I left Algiers in May there was some talk of this, but nothing definite had been done.

In a lesser degree, this objection of insufficient accommodation should be considered even by those who are not, strictly speaking, "invalids;" it is a very serious one.

In the next place, as a second set-off against the brilliant sky, is the long sea-voyage, and the feeling of isolation which results from it. I saw many painful instances of deep anxiety about "letters from home." I knew more than one case of sudden calls to death-beds in England which could not be answered at once; the angry Gulf of Lyons was in the way. At Algiers you are not as you would be at Cannes, or even at Naples. You can't take the next train and be off. As too many of us must have known, there is a certain feeling of relief in being actually on the move, even though you cannot hope to reach home in time.

In a lesser degree—I repeat myself—this drawback of the middle passage applies to all. Most of my homeward bound friends were twelve, sixteen, and twenty hours late between Algiers and Marseilles, and that at a fine season of the year. What I said about the hotels on Mustapha I say about the sea-voyage. There is a plan for running large and powerful steamers between Port Vendres and Algiers, and so of reducing the drawback to a minimum; but the sea-voyage will always remain an objection, and as yet it is a very serious one.

The disruption of your old habits and associations, the craving desire to see once more well-known and friendly faces, will apply to other places as well as Algiers; but in most other winter quarters frequented by the English you can shift as you will. If you are tired of one place, or the people do not suit you, try another. Not so in Algiers: once fixed for the winter, you are fixed indeed. There you are the prisoner of the sun, who may be a very bright gaoler, but you can't get out.

I am slow to speak of personal experience or personal feeling, for what can this mean but the experience and feeling of an individual? I must, therefore, ask to be credited with having done fairly and honestly what I say I have done. I took counsel with all of my friends to whom I could put the question without impropriety: "Having spent one winter in Algiers, do you intend to come back?" The answer was well-nigh universally "No," and a very emphatic "No" it was. Despite of the beauty and brightness of the place, I know not what sort of weariness, of satiety, came over one. Dare I write the result in the simplest and plainest Anglo-Saxon monosyllable?—we were all "*bored.*" At this unhappy conclusion we arrived—of course, not at once, but sooner or later all succumbed. On the first change from London to Africa it is all enchantment. How could I ever live in that dreary, foggy, murky place, whilst Algiers was open to me—beautiful Algiers, just like the transformation scene in a pantomime? Give way honestly to the feeling, and enjoy yourself as long as you can. The change will come soon enough. I can very well imagine that a visitor should spend a week or a month at Algiers, and go away with the idea that here at last was Paradise. Try five or six months, and, despite of the blue skies and Arabs, I am much mistaken if you do not find that Paradise can become very tiresome. At any rate, refer it to what cause or series of causes you will, such was the all but universal feeling of those amongst whom we spent one winter. The outcome of this—were I writing advice to a friend—would be, "Do not engage yourself rashly to spend a whole winter in Algiers," with a corollary: "If you dream of buying a villa at this place, spend a winter there first, and see how you like it."

Nothing of what I have written applies to those who may be inclined to pass a week or two at Algiers, just to see the place. Certainly nothing should deter all who may be so inclined *from driving about the three provinces* and visiting the most noteworthy places.

The idea given you by the excellent people who write gushing accounts of Algeria, for consumption at Mr. Smith's literary eating-shops, is very misleading. You may drive about Algeria as we did—and we certainly saw the best things—just as securely as you would about the lake country. The stuff about lions, and nights spent in Arab or Kabyle huts, and adventure, is just pure nonsense. The roads are better than roads in Europe. There are good bits of railroad in full work, to carry you over the long distances. The inns—well, I think they are better than the average of inns in the French provinces, in some respects, and in some instances dirty enough; but not worse than in Spain, in Italy, or the south of France.

In return for the very small amount of discomfort, what glorious scenes are opened before you! I shall always look back to our ten days' stay at Tlemçen; and at Biskra on the edge of the desert, with its thousands upon thousands of palm trees; and to the Chabet Pass, with the flowery show between it and Bougie; and to stern, romantic Constantine; and to Blidah, with its perfume of orange groves; and to Cherchel, with its ranges of aloes and remains of Rome; and to our drives about the Metidja carpeted with brilliant wild flowers, and Fort National with the snow-covered Djudjura, and the Kabyle Highlands, as bright pages in a very bright chapter of my life.

It is good to lay up a store of such recollections. Nor is there any material hindrance in the way which need deter any one from trying the little adventure. In a couple of months you can run over the three provinces, and the expense should not exceed a guinea a-head a day. I have given all particulars in their proper places. Here, then, is the moral of my long story: Don't engage yourself rashly for a winter stay in the town of Algiers, or on Mustapha; but visit it by all means, and by all means take the drives about Algeria which I have indicated. There is nothing so well worth doing within the same distance from England.

And now, one word in conclusion. Why have I thus added to the almost interminable books about Algeria? Simply because I had read as many of them as I could get hold of before I went to Algiers, and none of them told me what sort of place I should find there. Many of them, in a literary sense, seemed to me very pretty; many very nonsensical and full of "gush;" but when you land in a place, and want bed and board, this is scarcely what you require. When you desire to know about the hotels and the price of mutton, a very eloquent description of a sunrise is quite thrown away upon you. I did not care to spend a winter with the swallows. If it suited the swallows to come to Algiers, or they were ordered there by their medical advisers, well and good. I hope we shall not interfere with each other. But how I am to help a swallow to spend the winter comfortably, or the swallow me, I do not quite see. My notion is to bring down Algiers from the clouds, and to speak of it as I would about Cannes, or Pau, or Torquay. It is a very beautiful place, but I would not care to spend another winter in it, until there is a good hotel on Mustapha.

THE END.

PRINTED BY WILLIAM CLOWES AND SONS, LIMITED, LONDON AND BECCLES.

www.ingramcontent.com/pod-product-compliance
Lightning Source LLC
Chambersburg PA
CBHW021426300426
44114CB00010B/660